A HUNDRED YEARS OF
ENGLISH GOVERNMENT

A HUNDRED YEARS
OF
ENGLISH GOVERNMENT

by

K. B. SMELLIE

Lecturer in Public Administration
at the London School of Economics

NEW YORK
THE MACMILLAN COMPANY
1937

MADE AND PRINTED IN GREAT BRITAIN
AT THE CHAPEL RIVER PRESS
ANDOVER, HANTS

CONTENTS

CHAPTER I

THE STATE AND SOCIETY, 1832-70

Transformation of the Problem of Government by the Industrial Revolution—Economists and Utilitarians—The Theory of Representative Government—Socialist Critics—Political Points of View—Policies pursued: Free Trade, Combinations and Monopolies—Public Services—The Case of Ireland—Early Capitalism reviewed—The Foreign scene.

In the nineteenth century the spirit of science born in the seventeenth century had left its cradle and was abroad in the land; it had been bodied forth in a machinery of production and transport which was to change the face of the whole world. The spirit of man was incarnate in material things. The external conditions of his life, once almost as everlasting as the hills, would now be mutable as the sea. The single frankenstein of early nineteenth-century romance would breed a million robots to serve or destroy mankind. And the cradle of this race of iron and steel was in Great Britain.

The problem of government was transformed. Changes in all the conditions of life—birth, labour and of death—were beginning a new acceleration which could not be controlled and would make towards an end which could not be foreseen. But in the new dangers there lay the possibility of new knowledge and new powers. Hitherto governments and societies had flourished or decayed from causes which could only dimly be guessed. Changes of climate might subtly undermine them, unknown disease ravage them, or barbarian irruptions overwhelm them,

"determined things to destiny held unbewailed their way".

But from the end of the eighteenth century the increase in the rate of change in the conditions of men's lives made it

7

possible for something to be known about the nature of the forces by which society is controlled. As the acceleration of the film can reveal the rhythm of the growing plant so the acceleration of a series of industrial and commercial revolutions was to reveal something of the laws by which societies grow. From Adam Smith to Marx the nature of society was examined in the light of the new knowledge made possible by the quickened pace of the production and distribution of the goods and services by which men live. Just as during the war of 1914-18 and the peace which followed the spinning dance of currencies enabled the nature of money almost experimentally to be studied, so the industrial revolution of the early nineteenth century laid the foundations of economic science by revealing the hidden laws which control production and exchange.

From the first Reform Bill (1832) which is the first great adjustment made by the old governing order to adapt itself to the new social order to 1870, when the rise of modern Germany and a really United States altered our status in the world of States, there are three main currents of opinion to be considered as to the nature of our government. There is first the analytical approach developed by the economists and the utilitarians; secondly, there are the criticisms of the first provoked by the limitations of their methods; and thirdly there are the empirical devices of statesmen and administrators who had as best they could masterfully to administer the unforeseen.

(1) When population was so rapidly increasing and when trade and industry were expanding faster than they had ever done before, two problems were always to the fore: to understand the scope and nature of the changes which were taking place, and to adjust the machinery of government to a new social order. Mankind was on the march and the economists were the best scouts it had.

In his *Theory of the Moral Sentiments*, Adam Smith had

discovered a harmonious order in nature whereby, under divine guidance, the welfare of man was promoted by the operation of his individual behaviour.[1]   In the *Wealth of Nations* the element of divinity was replaced by forces statistical and natural.[2]   " Society," he wrote, " may subsist among different men, as among different merchants, from a sense of its utility without any mutual love or affection, if only they refrain from doing injury to each other." Obviously there is much virtue in that " if ".   For the new science of economics it would provide the grounds for the justifiable activity of the state.   In the *Wealth of Nations*, Adam Smith wrote that " government activity is natural enough and therefore good when it promotes the general welfare, and is an interference with nature and therefore bad when it injures the general interests of society ".   For him the functions of government were natural—by which he meant good—when they were limited to securing that those forces which were known to make for good should not be interfered with.   But what were the forces which were known to make for good?   They were the self interest of the ordinary man which had made the economic order and which were alone necessary for society if the State would prevent violence and administer justice.   But what is this justice which lurks so slyly in the text?   By justice Adam Smith meant " the duty of protecting as far as possible every member of society from the injustice and oppression of every member of it ".   This would have assigned to government the reconstruction of the whole economic order.[3]   But Adam Smith was not concerned to reconstruct the whole economic order.   He took for granted private property, class conflict, and understood by justice the legal and customary code which in his time dealt with property and contract.[4]   His real concern was to attack the specific abuses of existing governments which could be shown to hinder the co-operation for which men were in their own interests prepared.   He wished to show that with free trade in land the free choice of occupations within and between countries would add immeasurably to the wealth of nations.   Certain conditions which were necessary to wealth were prevented by the eighteenth-century State.   Adam Smith did not much consider the necessary conditions of peace and justice.   He was concerned to analyse a natural economic order; he assumed its social fabric.

After Adam Smith, Ricardo developed a fruitful method of analysis based on a technique of abstraction and applied it to the solution of many urgent practical problems.   He formidably assailed that type of sophistry which results from neglecting in an argument the full implications of any changes discussed.[5]   He exploded many bad arguments for many privileges by the right method of enforcing the necessity of tracing out the whole series of results.[6]   In an age of increasing productivity, but one still of bitter poverty, he showed that the proposition that men could not have their cake and eat it was unaffected by the size of the cake.

In Bentham, the other great formative thinker of the new age, an attempt was made to cover the whole duty of man. But with him, as with Adam Smith, the conception of nature was ambiguous.   The principle of utility had for Bentham two meanings: (1) that all men were led by their appetites for pleasure and their dislike for pain to the creation of society; (2) that the good was pleasure and that it was the duty of all men, but particularly of legislators, so to play on the appetites of all that they would be led to just those actions which would maximize their pleasures.   Mankind was under the domination of two masters, pain and pleasure, but could play them one against the other to the relief of man's estate. The Utilitarians provided the fashionable guides for the alterations in the machinery of government after 1830. "The guides of English legislation during the period of individualism . . . accepted the fundamental ideas of Benthamism . . . their immediate and practical object was the extension of individual liberty as the proper means of ensuring the greatest happiness of the greatest number."[7]   Some of them considered that the interests of individuals were harmonious and that only the interference of the State prevented the harmony showing; others who recognized disharmony considered that clumsy State action would make it worse.[8] Out of their attempt to harmonize their belief that happiness ought to be shared by each according to his capacity and their experience that such a consummation, however devoutly wished by some, was prevented by the tenacity by which those who had held on, they developed a naive democratic theory.

In both the economics of Adam Smith and the sociology of Bentham there is the same difficulty that the place which should be occupied by State action to secure the justice whose obligation they both assume is nowhere clearly defined. How came it that the invisible hand seen by Adam Smith had faltered in its cunning?   How had the natural order come to be distorted by that "insidious and crafty animal vulgarly called the statesmen or politician?"   If, as Bentham supposed, mankind were under the domination of two masters, pain and pleasure, how had they come to produce the confusion of the eighteenth-century scene?   Now that that confusion had been revealed how was it to be cleared? Would the insidious and crafty animal, vulgarly called a politician, find and keep his proper place?   Would those sinister interests which as Bentham saw preferred their pleasure to the pleasures of their neighbours be converted by philosophy to the code of one for all and all for one?

An answer to these questions was attempted by the nineteenth-century English theory of representative government.

The English theory of representative government in the nineteenth century was developed from two assumptions. The first assumption derived from the rationalist movement of the eighteenth century was that matters of opinion could be settled by discussion—that truth could get itself accepted when the last king had been duly strangled with the entrails of the last priest. The second assumption was suggested by the astonishing progress of industry and commerce and was that most of the needs of men could be satisfied without the assistance of the State. Matters of opinion could be settled by discussion and the external conditions of life could be satisfied by bargaining in a market. If men were only free to enter into whatever contracts they pleased the interests of each would be harmonized with those of all. Those few matters which experience or tradition placed outside the magic of the market could be dealt with by the democratic formula of " one man, one vote ".

Economic progress and democratic theory were closely related. The obvious vitality and seeming harmony of the economic order were a comforting demonstration of the power of reason in society. The swift advance of industry was providing a society which seemed strong enough to stand without the aid of any government. The market which the economists had analysed was providing indirectly the perfect State which philosophers had failed to plan. This strengthening of the social order by the bonds of innumerable private contracts favoured liberty of thought. For long ages liberty of thought and expression had been crushed because it was feared that a disbelief in existing religious and moral codes might destroy the basis of society. It was believed that the power of government over men's opinions and bodies was too feeble to have stood the shock of general scepticism. The real safeguards of public order were held to be the lethargy of habit and superstitious awe. The new industrial progress, by showing that the essentials of human order were rooted more firmly in men's stomachs than in their minds, prepared the way for freedom of thought. For there could be no objection to the long-run benefits of intellectual freedom when in the short run it no longer threatened the social order. The mind might change but the body remained the same.   And the bodies of men seemed now to be capable of co-operating for their mutual benefit whatever the colour of their skins or the beliefs in their heads. It was reasonable to believe that the tableau of human progress could be left to the economic loom.

Of course, as Mr. Keynes has pointed out, no economic thinker of repute really believed in a *laissez-faire* which denied the necessity for far-reaching State control.   But then no political thinker of repute really believed in the vote as an instrument for the creation of a State.   Both the market and the ballot were to be understood in their appropriate context. Freedom of contract assumed a society; freedom of discussion and the ballot a particular form of society.   But industrial progress seemed to be producing the particular form of society the successful operation of the ballot required.   For it seemed to be producing a form of society in which governments would have less to do.   But on the vital question of the necessary functions of government at each stage of the development of the economic order the economists were tantalizingly obscure.   The market required the existence of society.   Some form of private property, the enforcement of contracts and the suppression of violence were required before the subtle adjustments of human interests that the mechanism of price provides could be enjoyed.   But to admit the need for the enforcement of contracts was to abandon the philosophy of individualism which much economic thought implied.   Enforcement of contracts involves an all pervasive intervention of the organized power of the State to make men do what they do not wish to do in the interest of the general good of the community.   Why should not the State leave those who do not keep their promises or those who are poor judges of the promise-keeping nature of others to the stings of conscience or the natural consequence of vacillation, duplicity or stupidity?   In fact the economist was unwilling to consider the fundamental problem of politics which is the right use of force.   He was inclined to assume that the boundary between force and persuasion had once for all been drawn, though all history shows it to be the most wavering frontier among men.   Unless this problem of the right use of force by the community is faced the results are disastrous. For if force is not rightly controlled it will cripple and distort the mechanism of price.   Unless price is taught its place justice and violence may pass under its control.   Where the State has been enfeebled its powers have reappeared as part of the technique of competitive industry itself.   In the United States the weakness of the federal system and the social conditions of a pioneering community allowed the great industries to exercise political powers which they employed in distorting the mechanism of price for their own ends.   In the feudal age every landowner was doing the same.   Given the proper organization of the market the conflict of a million wits sharpened by self-interest may give a daring and insight to the planning of the economic order that no bureaucracy could achieve.   Given peace by enlightened legislators the Cobdens of the world may be left to garner plenty.   But who is to secure that there shall be the peace which favours all and not the sword which profits some?

No hard and fast line can perhaps be drawn between the functions that can be left to the free play of the market and those that should be left to authoritarian control.   For each pattern of price which depends upon the structure of industry there should be a social order appropriate to its needs.

Of the economists it has been said that " their individualistic doctrine of society, combined with their presupposition that respectable men and women are mainly engaged in safeguarding all details of their commercial interests led them to neglect questions of prevalent fact ".   The presuppositions of political democrats were equally vast.   In the English democratic tradition of the nineteenth century it is assumed that there will be such a balance between conflicting greeds and errors that an intelligent and disinterested minority could turn the scale.   In J. S. Mill's *Representative Government* he argues that justice and the general interest can carry their point only because the separate and selfish interests of mankind are almost always divided.

It was tacitly assumed that reason could always in an industrial society command sufficient votes to prevent its own extinction; that the change desired by a majority would never be of such a character to lead the minority to challenge the principle of majority rule itself.   Mill and others recognized that should there be such a conflict of race or religion that men could not be persuaded by discussion representative government would not work.   But for a time in Victorian England the rapid growth and the increasing mobility of economic life seemed to promise the removal of all differences save those of price.

(2) There were those who, while they might not understand what was true and useful in the economists' method of abstraction, were rightly convinced that there were vital aspects of the social order which the latter ignored.   They were concerned with the nature of that society which the economists assumed.   What were the conditions of that peace and what was the nature of the justice which Adam Smith had assumed?   But with these critics, too, the influence of the eighteenth-century idea of a natural order was powerful and confusing.   We find in them two main ideas about the relation of the State to society.   The first is, perhaps, most clearly stated by Paine: " the great part of that order which reigns among mankind is not the effect of government . . . society performs for itself almost everything which is ascribed to government . . . government is no further necessary than to supply the few cases to which society and civilization are not conveniently competent . . . all the great laws of society are laws of nature . . . but how often is the natural propensity to society disturbed or destroyed by the operations

of government."[9]   Paine, like Adam Smith, was so concerned to attack the abuses of existing government that he did not stop to remark that " the few cases to which society and civilization are not conveniently competent " might include the subordination of force to the ends of justice.   For the implication of Paine's position was far reaching.   Adam Smith had assumed that the existing laws of property and contract were the embodiment of justice.   It was only simple violence that had to be suppressed.   But to Paine the whole existing framework of society was the product of violence. In his contrast between society and government he is really contrasting an ideal society with that which actually existed. The theme was developed by the early English socialists who sensed that the enemy was not now feudal privilege but the nascent powers of coercion in the new industrial order.   They were concerned precisely with the nature of that society and the technique of its justice and peace which the economists assumed. The economic order might be natural. But were all forms of society natural? " That great man," wrote Hodgkin of Adam Smith, " carefully distinguished the natural distribution of wealth from the distribution which is derived from our artificial right of property." There was the " nature " of reason of men's interests and their power to co-operate and to persuade and there was the " nature " of men's passions and their power to coerce.   There were other forms of violence than the sword.   To the English socialists of the period 1820-30—John Grey: *Lecture on Human Happiness*, 1825; William Thompson: *Inquiry into the Principles of Distribution of Wealth*, 1824; Thomas Hodgkin: *Labour Defended*, 1825; and J. F. Bray: *Labour's Wrongs and Labours' Remedies*—it seemed that the rich were getting richer and the poor were getting poorer. Where Adam Smith had seen a natural harmony they could only see violence and theft.   To these socialists the natural harmony possible among men was prevented by the artificial rights of property.

Neither they nor the economists, their opponents, seriously considered the nature of that system of property and of laws which would secure the practical working of the market which the economists showed theoretically to be possible.   The problem which these early socialists raised as to the relation between a possible harmony of equals and the existing conflict of unequals was raised in a different way by the utilitarians. Either men were so made that they each pursued their own interest, and in so doing were led in all things by an invisible hand to pursue the interests of all; or there were some men who saw that the greatest happiness of all ought to be secured and it was their duty to arrange the system of rewards and penalties in society that it was secured.   But as the economist did not know what systems of property or of contract were necessary for the working of his ideal market so the utilitarian did not know what system of legislation was necessary to secure the happiness of all.   It was the work of the political and social theorists after Bentham and Ricardo to develop the criticism that the actual conditions of society did not satisfy the conditions which an economist might tacitly assume; and that even had they done so, there were many services vital to the relief of man's estate which the magic of a market could not command.   On the economic side there were two problems which the wide mind of J. S. Mill seized on and developed.   (1) The system of landed property in England did not satisfy the conditions that the freedom of the market required.   And this criticism of the land laws could be extended to all the monopolistic elements secreted in all communities where custom ruled and violence preyed.   (2) There was no necessary connection between a man's value in the market for his labour and the minimum costs of his maintenance as a citizen.   This, which is the vital flaw in the attempt to find a natural harmony in the economic order has been now fully admitted by the modern schools of economists who have elaborated the technique of the analysis

B

of marginal utilities.   The more subtle and complex the industrial order the less probability is there that the value of any particular worker in the market will be equal to the cost of maintaining that standard of living which the increase in the average productivity of the community makes desirable. On the political side the issues were simple.   Even had the utilitarian thesis been true that men ought to seek the greatest happiness of the greatest number the problem remained to discover the right conduct for utilitarians in a community which had not realized that those principles were true. Always as Macaulay had tried to show James Mill there was a living past with which contemporary philosophy must deal.

I suggest, then, that the economists assumed that there was a political order to provide the conditions their science assumed while the political theorists looked to the industrial order to provide the conditions necessary for theirs.   Freedom of thought and freedom of trade were mutually supporting and mutually dependent.   But their critics tried to tell them then and we can see now that they were both dependent upon certain complex conditions of tradition and knowledge which were in rapid change around them.

(3) We must now turn from those who attempted to probe the inner nature of the changing social order to those who had to meet its pressing problems as they arose.   Economists, utilitarians and socialists might sense the shape of things to come, but it was the politicians and administrators who had to meet each questioning hour.   The analysis of the thinkers had to be applied by the political administrative talent available.   " There is a limit to . . . the amount of workmanlike creative legislation or administration of which any government is capable in a given time."[10]   Before 1832 the reforming Benthamites had found their policy thwarted by the opposition or inertness of classes biased by some sinister interest.[11]   After 1832 their ideas had to be applied by the politicians which the limited franchise then allowed to power,

and in opposition to still firmly entrenched vested interests through a legislative machinery that was not adopted to the action required. Huskisson, whose speeches bring out clearly his relation to the utilitarians,[12] had to exercise the greatest caution because the West Indian interest was so firmly represented in Parliament. After the freeing of the slaves, in 1833, the moral and legal issues were so intertwined—the Whigs trying to catch votes with the cry of cheap sugar, the Tories saying that foreign sugar would encourage slave labour in Cuba and Brazil against that of the free West Indies— that the interest survived until 1874.[13] Free Trade in corn required the political suicide of Sir Robert Peel, and his success was probably due to the fact that the class which wanted cheap bread was politically stronger than the class which wanted dear bread.[14] Peel " in his hesitations, his postulates, his limits, in his honesty of purpose, his receptivity, his mastery of today's business and his often blurred view of its relation with tomorrow's needs " was the embodiment of the British State in the nineteenth century.[15] His pupil, Gladstone, in whom there was no scrap of Bentham's make-up,[16] had to undergo an " exhaustive mental rehabilitation "[17] when he was at the Board of Trade in the 'forties which transformed him from a hope of the stern and unbending Tories to the political partner of Bright. In his autobiography there is a passage which is prophetic of the problem of government in a changing world. " The gradual transfer of political power from groups and limited classes to the community, and the constant seething of the public mind in fermentation upon a vast mass of moral and social as well as merely political interests offer conditions of action that the statesman, in order to preserve the same amount of consistency as his antecessors, must be gifted with a far larger range of foresight."

If the ideas of Bentham were tried out by a Peel, a Gladstone, and a Place, the ideas of the Socialists found their

experimenters in an Owen and in the matter-of-fact bargaining of the sporadic trade unionism of the middle nineteenth
century, while Coleridge's eloquent presentation of all those
aspects of society which the utilitarians ignored found its
inarticulate champions in the prejudices of Tory squires and
its Machiavellian manipulation in the histrionic genius of
Disraeli.

In England the extension of the franchise was so gradual
that many traditions and conventions of an aristocratic system
were retained. It may be denied that the governing class
in England in the nineteenth century deserved the name of
aristocracy, but it will be admitted that as an oligarchy that
had sufficient public spirit to resist tyranny, and sufficient
common sense to adapt itself to a changing economic and
social order, it was a good teacher for the rising democratic
power. For an oligarchy which has won from royal privilege
the control of the State becomes, if it survives, a democracy in
everything but scale. For exclusive though they may be, the
members of the ruling class can only retain power by
co-operating among themselves. They have learnt how to
choose and follow a leader. They are a government of
amateurs protected by their very prejudices against the
narrowness of experts or the rigidity of bureaucratic routine.
They have been inoculated with corruption and are immune
from the worse ravages of that disease. They know something of the subtle relation between discussion and the use of
force—whether of the bayonet or the press—in the management of men. They were able to teach each section of the
people as it was admitted to the franchise that there were
other problems of government to be solved than the destruction of privilege and vested interests.

We must now briefly consider the actual policies which
were the outcome of the interplay of the various theories and
organized interests. They may be considered in four groups.
There was (1) the attack on those privileges which, indefen-

sible in theory, had lacked the political power to resist reform. Of these the most famous is the Free Trade movement which swept away the old fiscal system and the privileges of the agricultural community. There were (2) the problems implicit in a *laissez-faire* policy: What was the legal framework appropriate to the free co-operation of men assumed to know their own interests? Of these we may briefly consider the development of Company law on the one hand and of Trade Union law on the other. In the same group were the special problems presented by economic activities which seemed by their very nature to threaten monopoly. Of these the problem of the railways may be briefly noticed. There were (3) the great group of problems connected with those social and individual needs which the magic of the market in practice failed to provide. There was not sufficient effective demand for either the services of the parson or for those of the schoolmaster. And finally (4), there was the special problem of Ireland where the social conditions which economists and utilitarians had tacitly assumed were not and never had been present.

(1) The problem of Free Trade was comparatively simple. It was to the interest of this country as the first which had specialized in the new machinery of production to remove all political barriers to the development of a market for her goods and the supply of the raw materials which she needed. For acceptance of the new economic order did not require in England as it did in Ireland an actual reduction of the population. There was no conflict between economic interest and the sentiment of nationalism. The interest which was most profoundly affected—the agricultural—had to submit only to a comparative and not to an absolute reduction in importance. Moreover, as previous economic revolutions had destroyed our peasant proprietors, there was no great numerical political force wedded to a traditional way of life to oppose its transformation.

In 1820 the practical needs of the London and Edinburgh merchants impelled them to petition against " every restrictive regulation of trade not essential to revenue ".   A Commission of 1820 laid it down that " commerce must be a source of reciprocal amity between nations and an interchange of production to promote the industry, the wealth and the happiness of mankind.   At that time special interests were in full possession of vested rights to which they laid claim. There was the Corn Law of 1815; there were the differential duties in favour of the West Indian proprietors; the monopoly of the East India Company; and a rigorous application of the navigation laws against competition.   There were heavy duties on raw materials of industry and prohibitive or extravagant duties on foreign manufactures.[18]   By 1852, as a result of the work of Huskisson, Peel and Gladstone, customs policy had almost ceased to be discussed.[19] The principles of free trade had been introduced by a skilful interpretation of the mischief of protection.[20] But on the side of the free traders was the balance of political power and a multiplicity of discoveries and events—the first English railway in 1830; the telegraph in 1837; the first ocean steamer in 1838—which prepared the way for the almost unlimited economic development of 1850-73 which seemed to confirm their policy.[21]

Of (2) the problems implicit in a *laissez-faire policy*, that of the law relating to companies is one of the most interesting. For here the relation of the State to the very heart of economic individualism was most directly concerned.   What were the legal instruments without which the co-operation of each for his own and the good of all was not possible?   In 1844 Gladstone, when chairman of a committee on Companies, met lawyers, county magistrates, promoters and artisans, and learnt much about an industrial organization which seemed content to misdirect the wealth of the nation.[22] " The nation was groping blindly for a policy which would regulate the savings of the people by converting all surplus capital into instruments of production . . . and the task of the legislator was to bring home to the investor the full significance of an ordered system of financial regulation."[23] But the State was to show itself slow and uncertain to regulate and control the new economic forms.   The essential problem: What were the legal conditions under which those who wished to combine for purposes of trade and industry might do so? involved the whole theory of the relation of the State to the economic order and was a convincing demonstration of the complex legal forms an economic order requires.   In the first place the law in 1844 was so absurd and obscure that it was said that a man had either to be a knave or a fool to venture his money in partnership with a stranger.   Partnership law was so imperfect that its technicalities amounted to a denial of justice to partners and to their clients.   The Registration Act of 1844 gave to trading associations the power of sueing in a corporate capacity. After 1850 there was a demand for the relaxation of all restraints on the free action of individuals in economic activities and in the application of capital.[24] But such freedom required that there should be freedom to combine with a limited liability.   And while English law had no objection to limited liability in principle, the method of notice and agreement which it required was very inconvenient.   Only in special cases before 1850 was it possible to secure a charter which confirmed limited liability. Where the object was hazardous and deterrent to small partnerships as in mining, or required capital beyond the resources of a few individuals as in railways, or required extended responsibility as in insurance, or an unusually large membership as in the case of literary societies, such charters were available.[25]   But after 1850 it was found that " limited liability was needed for local enterprises of a useful kind, financed by numerous passive investors under the guidance of their richer neighbours ".   Investments in land or landed securities were much desired by the middle and working classes, but the uncertainty and complexity of titles and the length and expense of conveyance together with the cost of stamps placed them beyond the reach of such investors.[26] The problem of the railways secured the acceptance of the principle of limited liability.[27]   By the Joint Stock Companies Act, 1856, any seven or more persons could, by registering a " memorandum of association ", become a body corporate with a limited liability.   In 1862 a great consolidating Act was passed.   In 1867 an official enquiry was held into the operation of limited liability.   Though it was thought by some that the government ought to protect people who were ignorant and foolish, the prevailing sentiment was against any additional publicity.   Limited liability had been opposed by those who held that it would endanger the reputation of British merchants.   It had been secured by those who held to the general principle that perfect freedom should be allowed in the making of contracts between man and man, only guarding against wilful deception.   But the legal instruments were difficult to forge.   Partnership law was not made adequate until 1890.   The Companies' Acts of 1856 and 1862 only mitigated the game of beggar my neighbour for the good of all.

While Company law was concerned with the problem of defining the legal conditions for the co-operation of capital, Trade Union law was concerned with the problem of the co-operation of labour.   At the beginning of the century the Combination Acts had been passed because it was feared that unions of workmen under the guise of trade activities might engage in revolutionary propaganda.[28]   As the fear of revolutionary activity died down the unions were opposed on the ground that the individual should be free to dispose of his capital or his labour as he chose.[29]   But it could be argued that freedom to choose ought to mean freedom to combine, and in the then fluid condition of the market for labour it was rightly argued by Place that to allow combinations of workers for the purpose of bargaining about wages would facilitate the organization of industry and trade. And so in 1824 and 1825 the Combination Acts were repealed. But the real problem was then revealed. The organization of a market for labour requires more than freedom of the workers to combine. It requires that the wage of the lowest paid worker shall be such that he can secure the conditions necessary to live as a citizen—and there is nothing in economic theory to suggest that this condition will be met; it requires also that there shall be a knowledge of the wages offered and received throughout the economic system; and it requires that the parties concerned shall be willing merely to persuade and not be tempted to coerce. So the problem of the State was how to regulate the conditions of buying and selling of labour not merely where there might be fraud, but where there might be violence, open or disguised, and where the failure to the parties to agree might threaten the public order. It was dealing with a particular aspect of the central problem of politics—how to control the substance of force within the forms of persuasion.

The issue was complicated by the fact that between 1825 and 1875 the best and wisest of the judges believed " that the attempt of Trade Unions to raise the rate of wages was something like an attempt to oppose a law of nature ".[30]   While the Act of 1825 had removed the statutory prohibitions of combinations it left them liable to prosecution under the common law if they were in restraint of trade. This doctrine of the " restraint of trade " involved the judges in an attempt to solve a complex problem in economic analysis for which their training was nil, while their social and political prejudices were likely to lead them astray. They developed the doctrine that it was an obstruction of an employer to persuade a worker to leave his service unless paid a certain scale of wages. In 1859, the Molestation of Workmen Act, though it defined more precisely the freedom of combination given by the Act of 1825 and extended it in certain directions, still left it open for the courts to say that the inclusions of any object other than the determination of wages and of hours would make the Unions' action illegal.[31]   There was also a controversy as to the distinction between peaceful persuasion and intimidation and threats.   The Trade Union Act of 1871, the outcome of exhaustive investigation by a Royal Commission, declared that " the purposes of any Trade Union shall not, by reason merely that they are in restraint of trade be deemed to be unlawful so as to render any member of such Trade Union liable to criminal prosecution for conspiracy or otherwise ".   The Criminal Law Amendment Act repealed the Acts of 1825 and 1859.   But the immunity of strikes and other combinations from criminal prosecutions, either under statute or at common law, for actions which would otherwise have been lawful had they not been in furtherance of a trade dispute, was not fully secured until the passing of the Conspiracy and Protection of Property Act, 1875.[32]   But though criminal liability had been removed by statute the judges indefatigably developed the doctrine of civil conspiracy.

It was possible for some economists to argue that a proper currency might be secured by leaving banking business wholly free from legislative interference.   But other economists found cogent arguments against this development of *laissez-faire*.   McCulloch argued that under competitive conditions the expanding banks would not be controlled by the more conservative, but would on the contrary be compelled to dance to their tune.[33]   With ordinary commodities in a competitive system the public secure the best supply at the lowest price while the producers bear the losses due to their own errors and miscalculations; but " with respect to a paper currency . . . the interest of the public is of a very different kind; a steady and equitable regulation of its amount by fixed law is the end to be sought and the evil consequence of any error or miscalculation upon this point falls in a much greater proportion upon the public than upon the issuers ".[34]   How could labourers, women, minors and all the variety of those who do not worship Mammon be expected to distinguish a bad note from a good?   The case for regulation was stated by Tooke: " free trade in banking is synonymous with free trade in swindling . . . it was a matter for regulation by the State and came within the province of police ".[35]

Whatever the merits of the theoretical discussion force of circumstances had practically decided that there should be a central bank with a recognized responsibility for safeguarding the public interest in a pure and stable currency.   Since the foundation of the Bank of England in 1694, due to the casual emergency of Charles II's repudiation of his debts, there had developed out of a series of exchanges of favours between a needy government and an accommodating corporation a responsibility of the Bank of England which it found impossible to avoid.   Though at the time of the Bullion Committee (1819) the Directors of the Bank of England protested to Parliament that they should not have placed upon them the responsibility for " supporting the whole national currency ", circumstances were too strong for them.   The Bank Act, of 1844, gave to the Bank of England the ultimate monopoly of the note issue.   The crises of 1847, 1857 and 1866 were to prove that the government must support the Bank in time of stress and Bagehot was to reveal in *Lombard Street* that the Bank was the controlling element in the country's credit structure and that it was under an obligation to pay attention to the public interest in framing its policy and was not at liberty to act merely for the benefit of its shareholders.[36]

The problems of the railways and of shipping may be briefly noticed.   In the 'thirties and 'forties of last century the railways presented the threefold problem of safety of

planning and of possible monopoly.   The Acts of 1840 and
1842 introduced a system of Board of Trade inspection which
was to develop into a pervasive and meticulous control of the
conditions of safety.   But thirty years were to elapse before
the State secured the power to compel disclosures of the conditions which might have caused an accident.   As to planning,
the parliamentary procedure for railway bills was concerned
more with the adjustment of private grievances of property-
holders than with the planning of a railway system.[37]   Gladstone seems, from his experience at the Board of Trade, to
have thought that there was need for a logical system of
railway planning.[38]   In 1840 the Railway Department of the
Board of Trade was established, but its powers were those of
suggestion rather than of positive regulation.   From
1844-55 a distinct board for railway matters existed within
the Board of Trade.   After that railway business was thrown
into the ordinary business of the Department.   A Railway
Commission had a brief life from 1846-51.   Gladstone failed
in the 'forties to secure any effective control of railway
development partly because Parliament was wedded to the
system of private bills, but mainly because the threatened
monopoly did not develop.   Though each committee that
reported was concerned by the apparent diminution of competition no monopoly emerged.   By 1872 men were convinced that a private system of railways was not necessarily
a monopolistic danger.[39]

In the case of shipping the State was to assume the power
to watch over a British merchant vessel from the day when
her materials assumed the form of a ship to the day when
they finally lost that form.   The great consolidating Merchant Shipping Act of 1854 carefully regulated apprenticeship . . . contained a whole wage-paying code, but no
wage regulations, and made premature solicitation of seamen
by lodging housekeepers illegal.[40]   Only in the case of marine
insurance did the State fail.   It was found impossible to

regulate improper contracts without interfering with innocent and proper contracts. This detailed regulation of shipping did not prevent its prosperity or its growth to over 50 per cent. of the known tonnage of the world.[41] Similarly the most regulated industries of cotton and coal became the two leading export industries.[42] But though the Commission of 1867 showed abundant scope for State intervention in agriculture very little was done. " There is," wrote Jevons, " a wonderful contrast to the elaborate regulations of the factory, workshop, shipping, coal mines, metalliferous and other Acts relating to the various branches of manufacturing and commercial industry. It would lead us too far to inquire whether the absence is due to its needlessness or to the unwillingness of landowning legislators to touch the interests of their own order."[43]

(3) The importance in English politics of organized religion must never be forgotten. For most of our politicians the religion learnt at their mother's knee or acquired in adolescence has been the only philosophy they knew. If they have ever been tempted to forget the English Bible or the Reformation they have been prevented by their Scottish and Irish colleagues. Most of the philosophical reflections to be found in the letters and diaries of many a hard-boiled politician are emotional and muddled references to their adolescent creeds. Political wisdom has led them to let religious dogs lie, but, at the same time, the code of a gentleman which forbids him to disturb the mind of a friend has made the individualism of the Englishman's religion a formidable political force. As he can only discuss religion with those with whom he is agreed both toleration and the essential bigotry of minds which are closed have developed side by side.

In the 'thirties of last century Churchmen, Dissenters and Roman Catholics were reported to exist in the ratios of 120, 80 and 4. Such figures are not very precise, for the estimates were made by men who felt immortal longings in them and cannot with indifference have enumerated the saved and the damned.   At least 25 per cent. of the population—those who lived by bread alone because they could afford no other food—were without any religious views at all.   A fair proportion of the prosperous artisans were a sceptical and thinking race.   Many of the middle and upper classes were utilitarians who admitted no religion but humanity.   But more than half the population felt that the Church of England—or their particular form of Dissent—was the most important thing they needed here below.

It is, perhaps, of little importance that Disraeli should have defined the organized hierarchical church as " a sacred corporation for the promotion and maintenance in Europe of certain basic principles ".   But Gladstone is incomprehensible unless it is remembered that he began his political career with the publication of his views on Church and State, views which Macaulay found " after full and calm consideration to be false, to be in the highest degree pernicious, and to be such as, if followed out in practice to their legitimate consequences would inevitably produce the dissolution of society ".[44]   All save the atheistic poor and the philosophical Radicals felt that some form of organized religion was necessary to the existence of society.   Though Bentham had held that the Church of England was ripe for dissolution and James Mill had prepared a scheme by which lay priests should lecture weekly on utilitarian ethics and the elements of natural science, much as Moscow now broadcasts its materialistic determinism, it was the Evangelical party in the Church of England which made possible humanitarian legislation which the philosophical Radicals could not have carried alone.   The experience of the Methodists had far-reaching effects on party and trade union organization.   The High Church party was stung by the Liberal attacks on the privileges of the Established Church into the Oxford Movement which, had it not been undermined by post-Darwinian scepticism, might have transformed the political and social life of England.

The Tory felt with Coleridge " that the Christian Church and the National Church are as little to be confounded as divided ";[45] that it transplanted to every parish of the United Kingdom a germ of civilization " that in the remotest villages there is a nucleus round which the capabilities of the place may crystallize and brighten ".[46]   On the Tory view, writes Leslie Stephen, the relation of State and Church might be compared to that of man and wife in Christian countries where, though the two are one, the husband is bound to fidelity.[47]   The Whig regarded the Church as part of a government system providing him with patronage.[48]   The Radicals opposed it for the same reason that they opposed the landlords, because it was a monopoly as unjustifiable in the religious sphere as the landed system was in the economic.[49] But when the Church of England was attacked the most notable dissenters flew to the succour of the Church.   In opposition to the poor and Papist Irish the cause of the Church became the cause of the country.[50]

But after 1832 the English aristocracy clearly recognized that the abuses of the Church of England must be reformed if it was to survive the attack on economic privilege.   Its accounts, if not its creed, would have to bear inspection.   In 1835 Peel was writing: " I feel it my solemn duty as a minister and as a member of the Church to advise the Crown to administer its Church patronage . . . on a new principle. . . .   Ecclesiastical sinecures must share the fate to which all sinecures have been doomed. . . . I think it impossible to maintain the principle that an office of the Church without corresponding duties shall have large emoluments attached to it, while the cure of souls in some populous districts is wholly unprovided for ".[51]   The growth and shifting of the population made it necessary to reorganize the financial and administrative system of the Church of England.

At the time the income of Durham was more than twenty times the income of Llandaff, while in St. Margaret's and St. John's, Westminster, with a population of 50,000, there was no decent provision for even a single minister.   In 1836 Parliament created a Permanent Ecclesiastical Commission to equalize the incomes of the various bishoprics and to reorganize their territorial extent.   The Church Pluralities Act of 1838 virtually abolished pluralism.   The Church Establishment of 1850 had been adjusted to the financial, if not to the philosophical, criticism of the Radicals.   The political power of Dissent was sufficient to secure the removal of some of their most serious grievances—the compulsory levying of Church rates, the monopoly by the Church of England of the ancient universities, the legal compulsion to employ an Anglican cleric at their marriage, or burial. These would have been remedied sooner but for the opposition of the House of Lords.

But the most serious part played by organized religion was neither in the support it gave to humanitarian legislation nor in the justification it enabled some to find for the privileged station to which God had called them, but in the obstruction it caused to the development of education.   " Any attempt at educational reform had to reckon with the most intense of Victorian emotions, sectarian animosity."[52]   There were times when the sectarian rivalries of dissent and the Established Church, together with a bigoted anti-Romanism, gave to our internal politics the passions of nationalism in war.

The history of English elementary education cannot here be summarized.   It was obvious that when the factory replaced the village neither the parish priest nor the village schoolmaster could prevent barbarism.   With the growth and shifting of the population, schools, like roads and drains, required the attention of the State.   Nor could the magic of the market be expected to provide for morals any more than it could provide for health.   Most statesmen and economists must have agreed with Kaye Shuttleworth that it would be a fallacy to assume " that knowledge . . . is a natural want, certain to assert itself like the want of food or clothing or shelter, and to create a demand ".   They would have agreed that " all statesmen who have wished to civilize and instruct a nation have had to create the appetite ".[53] Nor were the shameful facts in dispute.   Graham in 1843 had " no doubt that a frightful case might be clearly established of brutal ignorance and heathenish irreligion ", and that it was the paramount duty of the Government to apply a progressive remedy to an evil of such magnitude and danger.[54]

But there was no possibility of securing the agreement of Parliament to a scheme of national education.   " The dissenters would not stand the parson in a State school.   The Established Church would not stand anyone else."[55]   So the Government's influence was limited to the giving of meagre grants to the two great voluntary organizations—the National Society of the Established Church and the British and Foreign Society of the Dissenters.   England, which led the world in drains, was far behind in schools.   Not until after the Reform Bill of 1867 and the industrial threat of a united North America and a triumphant Germany was it clearly recognized that the voluntary system had failed.   The price paid for sectarian passion was that England entered the fierce economic competition after 1870 with artisans the least trained, and a middle class the worst educated in Europe.

It was in Ireland that the limitations of the current English ideas as to the relaxation between the political and the economic order were most clearly revealed.   For, in Ireland, there was lacking that underlying unity of character and opinion which enabled the English political system to adjust itself without a civil war to the new society the industrial revolution had made.   In Ireland there was an absentee aristocracy, an alien Church, and a starving population. Their poverty was due to the fact that a population of eight

c

millions in 1841 (nearly double what it was to be in 1911) was mainly dependent upon a primitive system of tillage. The only other occupations were the linen manufactures of Ulster, the distillation of spirits, and the undeveloped fisheries. In 1841 more than 80 per cent. of all the farms were under 16 acres and only 7 per cent. were over 30 acres. To the economic causes making for a system of tillage which kept the population dangerously near the level of subsistence, there was a political system which gave to the landlord who had a large number of tenants considerable power. The English rule was little more than a provisional government in a half-conquered country. The Government had to use military force in order that the income of an alien Church should be devoted to exactly one-tenth of the population. In the 'thirties Peel had recognized that force could not provide a permanent remedy. The remedy, when it came, was to be an agrarian revolution which was to halve the population of Ireland, to create in the United States the political force of the Irish-Americans, the most dangerous enemies England has ever had, to create in the British Parliament the Irish Nationalist party, and at last to destroy the English Liberal party for a generation. Free Trade and the great famine of the 'forties compelled a transition from small to large holdings, and from tillage to the pasture. By 1851 26 per cent. of all farms were over 30 acres in size and only 51 per cent. were under 16 acres. The population had sunk to 6.5 millions. Between 1851 and 1911 the number of persons to each 1,000 acres of land would decrease by 30 per cent. while the number of cattle would increase by over 60 per cent., the number of sheep by 88 per cent., and the number of swine by 35 per cent.

It was in this context that the Government had to determine the validity of a system of freedom of contract applied to the ownership of land. In Ireland the law regarded the landowner as the sole owner of the farm, whereas in fact and in

equity the tenant was the co-owner.   For the tenant in Ireland, unlike the English tenant, provided the stock and the
improvements and had moreover, if dispossessed, either to
starve or emigrate.   The Irish ejectment code was entirely in
favour of the landlord.   As early as 1816 he could obtain an
ejectment order by a simple procedure in the County Court
which no English landlord could do until 1856.   In 1860,
by Deasy's Act, it was proposed that the relation of landlord
to tenant should be founded on the express or implied contract of the parties and not upon tenure or service.   The Act,
as Morley said, imported into Ireland the English ideas of
landed property and contract with a definiteness and a
formality that would in England have been impracticable.
The evictions which followed in the 'sixties were no doubt
in the general interest of cultivation.   Pasture and the large
farm were the only sound basis for Irish economic life.   But
the methods employed created the political force of the Irish-
American in the United States, the Irish proletariat in
English cities, and the Irish Nationalists in the British Parliament.   In 1870 Gladstone attempted to give a legal recognition to the co-ownership which in fact and in equity existed.
The Act gave compensation for disturbances and for improvements, but it failed because of the variety and complexity of
its exceptions, the timidity with which it was administered
and the fact that the landlords had still power to raise rent
at will.   When in the 'eighties the fall in agricultural prices
began the land question became amalgamated with the
national to the destruction of the English Liberal party, the
creation by State action of the most favoured peasant proprietors in Europe and in the fullness of time, the Irish Free
State.[56]

What can be said of the part played by the State in the
social and economic changes we have briefly sketched?   It
is obvious at once that there is no simple formula which will
cover the interplay between the reason impulses and custom

by which material goods are produced and distributed and the same reason impulses and custom by which the State is run. There are certain fundamental questions to which we shall never know the answer. Had there been a fully representative system would it have secured a more effective control, and would that control have been to our economic advantage? It is impossible to say how far an emancipated peasantry instead of backward agricultural labourers, or politically enfranchised unskilled labourers would have affected the main outlines of our economic development. In all these cases the exigencies of our present problems have led to barren speculation on past history. It is, for example, urged that had taxation for home services and development been more thorough, much of the wastage of capital exported abroad would have been avoided—that Birmingham might have had the treasures wasted on Brazil. The difficulty here is that for every hypothetical change there is introduced a maze of possible consequences. The most that can be done is to consider some of the special cases where we have the safeguard of a comparative check. We do not know whether universal suffrage would have produced the sobriety of Switzerland or the intoxication of the Third Empire. We do not know whether a Chartist revolution in 1848 would have produced a Trotsky or a Stalin. But we can say that we produced a political system which satisfied certain essential conditions of order and of liberty and that it was the means of inventing certain essential political tools: a technique of co-operation between local and central authorities; a method of changing governments; an ordering of opinions and powers organic enough and large enough to rule by persuasion and not by the bayonet or the bomb. But we can also say that we remained until the end of the century one of the most uneducated nations in Europe; that our manners and customs were open to the criticism that they were not unfairly pictured in the novels of Dickens. We have the evidence of sensitive contemporaries—of Matthew Arnold, of Ruskin, and of William Morris, that there was a sickness in our acquisitive society which the touch of Midas failed to cure. We think we can detect—though here it can only be a guess and not a demonstration—that many changes were possible without requiring any wisdom or knowledge that the common people did not possess. We can ask whether the failure to produce those changes was due simply to human ignorance or to a culpable brutality and greed.

Looked at in this way most of the strictures on the early English capitalists will not stand. They were neither Boundabys nor Gradgrinds. Nor can we fairly say that the economic system could have been other than it was. Whether the means of production and distribution should or should not be owned by the State might be a debatable question by the end of the century, but it was not possible at the beginning. The technique of control did not then exist. There were neither the means of communication nor the experience of industry to make that possible. It is possible that revolution in the 'forties might have produced a Napoleon of industry; but it is so improbable as not to be worth considering because the technique of industry differs vitally from the technique of war in that it is for purposes which continuously increase and change, while the problem of war is for a limited and almost definable end.

The aspects of our political behaviour which can be criticized are those which were connected with old traditions where there was only the excuse of prejudice and not the obvious reason that neither the end nor the means could be defined.

There is little value in the judgment that " it was the British capitalist who, fortified in his faith by the early political economist, first made of the pursuit of pecuniary gain what we may not unfairly call a national religion . . . it was . . . British commercialism that prepared the moral conscience of mankind for the German theory of world power. Bismarck and Treitsche were the spiritual descendants of Ricardo and Nassau Senior ".[57]   The spokesmen of British commercialism were Cobden and Bright, and it was their faith that if only those elements in the English political system which were based on privileges faintly resembling those of a German caste were removed, that universal peace would ensue.   It was the privilege and the flunkeyism of British society that they criticized.   And it was the privileges and the flunkeyism that were its greatest weaknesses.   It was privilege which destroyed Ireland, and flunkeyism which enervated politics. But the theory of pecuniary gain was a rational belief in the only method known for the amelioration of the lot of man.   There may have been intellectual error in their rejection of certain proposals: Bright for the fencing of machinery, Senior for the reduction of hours; but it was caused, not by a religion of pecuniary gain, but by a belief in an analytical argument.   It is too often forgotten that while the early socialists were right in their sensing of the problem of the relation between the economic and the political order that they had at the time no analytical or experimental approach to offer.   During the whole of Marx's residence in England no contribution of any importance to technical socialist thought was made by an Englishman.[57a] Before 1890 the English socialists were Arnold, Ruskin and Morris, who complained that culture and beauty and equality were in peril.   But beauty, truth and freedom are always imperilled in pioneering communities.   England in the nineteenth century was a frontier civilization.   Would she have been better as as armed camp?

It would be unreal to discuss the problems of English government without some reference to that international order or anarchy in the midst of which her continued survival was a necessary condition for the development of the ideas and experiments in social organization we have just discussed.

There is a complex interaction between the foreign and the home policy of any government. A despotism may make its foreign policy a mere means to its retention of power at home, or again it may organize every detail of its internal policy with a view to an external policy of power. In the case of constitutional governments the problem is more subtle. While there is the possibility that a constitutional statesman will use foreign policy for the purposes of party power, the real problem lies in the need for preserving the essential conditions of external security when the policy of governments is open to the criticism of public opinion. How is the technique of persuasion considered to be appropriate for the most fundamental principles and the most urgent crises of internal policy, to be reconciled with the necessities of that international anarchy in which the final arbitrament is war. The constitutional Foreign Secretary has to have two sides to his head; the one in which he shares with his colleagues the obligation to advance his principles only by discussion; the other in which he is responsible for the security of the State by his manipulation of power.

Between the fall of Napoleon and the supremacy of Bismarck the foreign relations of this country were determined by three classes of problems, the strategical, the constitutional, and the economic which subtly interacted. We may briefly consider them in turn.

In Europe, after 1815, there were in the East three despotic powers, Russia, Austria, and Prussia, united in a Holy League. Each of these had advanced a step into Western Europe. Russia had obtained Poland; Austria, the Dalmatian coast and Venice and Milan on the mainland of Italy; while Prussia had secured those detached territories of the old Western Germany, the Rhineland and Westphalia. In the West there was the enveloping power of the British Navy, based on Heligoland, Portsmouth, Plymouth, Gibraltar and Malta. To Syria or Africa, Austrian, French or Russian soldiers could go only by the permission of the British fleet.[58]   But the continued existence of the power of Britain required that the route to India must be secured by preventing either Russia or France dominating the Mediter-ranean; that the Low Countries should be controlled neither by Prussia, nor by France; that the Baltic should be dominated neither by Russia, nor Prussia.   English statesmen under-stood by the balance of power that no one of the great Con-tinental powers should be in a position to break British sea power by their control either of the Mediterranean, the North Sea, the Baltic or the Black Sea.   They feared the possible outbreak of revolutionary France or the advance of autocratic Russia.

But this simple strategic issue was complicated by the con-stitutional issue.   The balance of power depended partly upon the support of smaller nationalities struggling to be free against the despots, but partly, also, upon the continuance of political systems which could not claim any popular basis whatsoever.   On the one hand Greece, Belgium and Den-mark could be supported as thorns in the side of despotism; on the other the structure of Europe seemed to be dependent upon the continuance of the rambling corruption of Turkey in Europe, the ramshackle despotism of Austria-Hungary, and the continued partition of Italy.   In some cases nationalism and constitutionalism seemed to be the allies of a constitutional government against despotism, in others their claims threatened the disintegration of the Europe created when Napoleon fell.   A brief survey of some of the main incidents of diplomacy before Sedan will illustrate the problem.

To Canning it seemed that the English spirit of ordered freedom could hold the balance between despotism and democracy.   He kept Britain free of a Congress dominated by despotism and called in America to redress the balance of the old world.[59]   Palmerston, as the heir of Canning, sided with constitutionalism. He was the adversary of the Holy Alliance, the patron of nations struggling to be free, and the opponent of intervention for the suppression of liberty and upheld the balance of power.[60] He fostered the independence of Greece. When, in 1830, the revolt of the Southern Netherlands threatened the independence of the Low Countries, he secured the independence and neutrality of Belgium. In 1834 he secured the alliance of the constitutional governments of Britain, France, Spain, and Portugal, in mutual defence against the autocracies of Russia, Austria, and Prussia. But when, in 1840, there was a revolt of Mehemet Ali in Syria, against his Turkish overlord in Constantinople, Palmerston opposed him, even at the risk of war with France, because he believed that the integrity of the Turkish Empire was essential for upholding the independence of Eastern Europe.[61] In 1848 to 1850, when the democratic movement spread eastward of the Rhine and Central Europe was ablaze with ideas of freedom and nationality, because he regarded Austria as a European necessity, Palmerston could not oppose the Russian military action which crushed the Hungarians and restored Austria as a political power.[62] Finally, in 1857-60, though the British Government desired a free Italy they were not prepared for a united Italy, which would disturb the balance of power in the Mediterranean. Britain was unwilling to weaken Austria, her ally against France and Russia, by furthering the union of Italy unless driven to do so by the fear of finding France predominant in the peninsula.[63] Though they acquiesced in the annexation of Central and Southern Italy to Sardinia, they did not support the attacks on Rome and Venice because they did not realize that the cause of liberalism and the cause of national unity were in Italy now one. The opportunity Britain missed was taken by Bismarck.[64]

Finally, something should be said of the interplay between nationalism and economic organization which was beneath the surface transforming the balance of power in Europe and the world.   Palmerston was most skilful in enlisting public opinion by pushing the commercial interests of Britain.[65] While constitutional France had to be supported against Russian despotism, Syria was, in 1840, considered worth the danger of an Anglo-French war because it led to Mesopotamia and the avenues of India, and a Franco-Egyptian shore from the Levant to the Persian Gulf was thus prevented.   In 1853 the Crimean War was made the opportunity for England to check the Russian advance towards India.   " We must have," said Sidney Herbert, a member of the Cabinet, " a power at the Bosphorous to hold the keys of the Mediterranean from the East which shall not be Russia."[66]   There is some evidence that while Turkey was becoming a better customer for British manufactured goods, the Russian protectionist system was unfavourable to British trade.   Russia and England were entering upon an era of industrial competition for the control of Asiatic markets.[67]

It is the irony of history that the major forces which were most to determine the fate of the British Empire, the unification of Germany and the preservation of the Union of the United States, were hardly understood at all by those concerned with the threat of immediate seeming perils.   In 1847 Palmerston wrote to the Prince Consort " both England and Germany are threatened by the same danger and from the same quarter.   The danger is an attack from Russia, or from France separately, or from Russia and France united. Hence, England and Germany have mutually a direct interest in assisting each other ".[68]   But Palmerston could not favour a unification based on a Zollverein because English manufactures were thereby put at a disadvantage.   In 1865 England was anxious that the Prussian Zollverein should not be extended to include the free cities of the Empire, and desired to preserve a route to Leipzig over which Prussia had no control, and also that the agricultural States of North and North-West Germany should not change their customs union favourable to England.[69]   But as Clarendon told Bernstorff, Bismarck " was not an ordinary minister; he exercised supreme power; he dictated the policy of Prussia which was territorial aggrandisement, he was a man of purpose and what he announced he was likely to execute ".[70]

[1] Jacob Viner : Adam Smith & Laissez-Faire.   Chapter V of *Adam Smith* 1776–1926 (Lectures to commemorate the sesquicentennial of the publication of the *Wealth of Nations*), University of Chicago Press, p. 126.
[2] Jacob Viner, op. cit., p. 128.
[3] ibid., p. 144.
[4] ibid., p. 144–145.
[5] Leslie Stephen : *English Utilitarians*, Vol. II., p. 218.
[6] ibid., p. 219.
[7] Dicey : *Law and Opinion in England* 2nd edition, p. 306.
[8] Halevy : *Histoire du Peuple Anglais*, Vol. III., p. 79.
[9] Paine : *Rights of Man*, Part 2, Chap. 1.
[10] J. H. Clapham : *Economic History of Modern Britain*, Vol. I., p. 378.
[11] Dicey : *Law and Opinion in England*, 2nd edition, p. 306.
[12] Leslie Stephen : *English Utilitarians*, Vol. 2, p. 53.
[13] Hyde F. E. : *Gladstone at the Board of Trade*, pp. 54–8.
[14] Leslie Stephen : *English Utilitarians*, Vol. 3, p. 164.
[15] J. H. Clapham : *Economic History of Modern Britain*, Vol. I., p. 378.
[16] ibid., Vol. II., p. 389.
[17] F. E. Hyde : *Gladstone at the Board of Trade*, p. 35.
[18] Bowley : *England's Foreign Trade*, 2nd edition, p. 48.
[19] J. H. Clapham : *Economic History of Modern Britain*, Vol. 2, p. 398.
[20] F. E. Hyde : *Gladstone at the Board of Trade*, p. 51.
[21] Bowley : *England's Foreign Trade*, p. 55.
[22] F. E. Hyde : *Gladstone at the Board of Trade*, p. 186.
[23] ibid., p. 190.
[24] J. H. Clapham : *Economic History of Modern Britain*, Vol. II., p. 178.
[25] H. A. Shannon : The Coming of General Limited Liability.   *Economic History* (Supp. to *Economic Journal*), January, 1931, p. 278.
[26] ibid., p. 286.
[27] ibid., p. 287.
[28] Milne-Bailey : *Trade Unions and the State* (1934), p. 175.
[29] ibid., p. 176.
[30] Dicey : *Law and Opinion in England*, p. 199.
[31] Milne-Bailey, *Trade Unions and the State*, 181–2.
[32] ibid., p. 183.
[33] McCulloch :   Historical Sketch of the Bank of England, 1831, cited Vera C. Smith : *The Rationale of Central Banking* (1936), pp. 63–5.
[34] S. J. Loyd : Further Reflections on the State of the Currency, 1837, cited Vera C. Smith, p. 69.
[35] Tooke : *History of Prices*, Vol. III., p. 206, cited Vera C. Smith, p. 69.
[36] Vera C. Smith, op. cit., p. 125.
[37] Hyde F. E. *Gladstone at the Board of Trade*, p. 139.
[38] ibid., p. 136–7.
[39] Cleveland Stevens : *English Railways and their Relation to the State*, p. 60.
[40] J. H. Clapham : *Economic History of Modern Britain*, Vol. 2, p. 410.

[41] Farrer and Giffen : *The State in its Relation to Trade*, p. 157.
[42] Knowles : *Industrial and Commercial Revolutions*, p. 116.
[43] W. Stanley Jevons : *The State in Relation to Labour*, p. 89.
[44] Macaulay : *Gladstone on Church and State*.
[45] *Table Talk*, Feb. 22, 1832.
[46] Coleridge.
[47] Leslie Stephen : *English Utilitarians*, Vol. 2, p. 58.
[48] ibid., p. 60.
[49] Thomas ; Unpublished Thesis on House of Commons, 1832–67.
[50] Halevy : *Histoire du Peuple Anglais*, Vol. 3, p. 228.
[51] Peel : *Memoirs*, 1858 edition, pp. 72, 76, 78.
[52] G. M. Young : *Early Victorian England*, Vol. II., p. 465.
[53] Frank Smith : *History of Education*, p. 258.
[54] Parker's *Life and Letters of Sir James Graham*, 1792–1861, Vol. I., p. 346.
[55] G. M. Young : *Early Victorian England*, Vol. 2, p. 465.
[56] For details of land tenure and land acts see M. Bonn : *Modern Ireland and her Agrarian Problem* ; and W. F. Bailey : *Irish Land Acts*.
[57] Sidney and Beatrice Webb : *Decay of Capitalist Civilisation*, p. 155–6.
[57a] J. H. Clapham : *Economic History of Modern Britain*, Vol. 2, p. 482.
[58] H. Temperley : *The Crimea*, p. 61.   For the general idea of this section see H. J. Mackinder : *Democratic Ideals and Reality*, p. 157–60.
[59] Cambridge *History of Foreign Policy*, Vol. II., p. 116.
[60] ibid., Vol. II., p. 289.
[61] H. Temperley : *Crimea*, p. 90.
[62] ibid., p. 259.
[63] Cambridge *History of Foreign Policy*, Vol. II., p. 431.
[64] ibid., Vol. II., p. 451.
[65] Temperley, op. cit., p. 60.
[66] ibid., p. 358.
[67] V. J. Puryear : *England, Russia and the Straits*, p. 128.
[68] Cambridge *History of Foreign Policy*, Vol. 2, p. 325.
[69] ibid., Vol. 2, p. 465.
[70] ibid., Vol. 3, p. 5.

CHAPTER II

GOVERNMENT AND PARTIES, 1832-67

The Reform Bill of 1832—Development of Parties—Party Creeds—
Changes in the Constitution, 1832-67—Constitutional Crises—Melbourne,
1834—Bedchamber Question, 1839—Repeal of the Corn Laws, 1846—
A second Reform Bill, 1867—Parliamentary procedure—Cabinet
Government.

IN 1859 Sir James Graham, a timid Whig fearful that
Bright might change the House of Commons into a " mere
creature of numbers apart from property and intelligence ",
wrote to Lord John Russell: " In 1832 we based the representation on property and intelligence and carefully maintained the balance of power, so blending the influence of land
and numbers in the election of the representative body that
collision with the Crown and an independent House of Lords
might be avoided. It was a question of balance and proportions. Our calculations were just, our proportions were
safe, and our bloodless revolution has yielded for the last
quarter of a century better legislation, greater national prosperity, more internal peace, less civil discord than any other
period of our parliamentary history can boast ".[1] Thus does
the perspective of middle age find reason in its own past while
it sees decay of reason all around. What were the balance
and proportion of the bloodless revolution of 1832 and what
relations between property and intelligence did it plan and
what did it secure?

Had the Reform Bill of 1832 not been passed blood would
certainly have been shed. But its balance and proportion are
visible only to the eye of political faith. For it was a complicated compromise framed to meet a pressing need. " I see

45

no reformer," said Coleridge, "who asks himself the question what it is that I propose to myself to effect in the result."[2] The old constitution had lost that minimum of popular support without which a governing class must try to sit on bayonets. And such a position an English aristocrat finds compatible neither with his religion, his dignity, nor his purse. If he were to preserve anything of the constitution whose spirit Montesquieu had praised and Burke had worshipped, there had to be a drastic redistribution of political power. Continuity with the past would provoke a revolution. Changes in the distribution of population, in the value of money, and the economic interests of the governing families had thrown the machinery of government hopelessly out of gear.

There was " Old Sarum with its bare field and two members, contrasted with unrepresented Manchester's rising population of 180,000. Birmingham, Leeds, Sheffield, Wolverhampton, Huddersfield, Gateshead, were also voteless, while eight members sat for the whole of London. The 23 northern counties of England included only 74 of the 203 Parliamentary boroughs in the country, in spite of the fact that the centre of gravity had been rapidly shifting northwards since the industrial revolution. The south coast on the other hand, was dotted with boroughs, while Cornwall alone returned 44 members, one less than the whole of Scotland ".[3] In the small boroughs the new-rich were securing a monopoly. Two-thirds of the closed boroughs were held by the Tories.[4] In the Scottish counties the right of voting was attached to the small class which possessed feudal superiority over land, though not necessarily holding the land itself. In Banff 19 voted, and in Ross and Cromarty, 29.[5] Had the electoral system not been reformed a change of government by peaceful methods would soon have been impossible. The franchise was too narrow for a pendulum to swing. Nonconformists, the professional classes, merchants and manufacturers, tradesmen and artisans in towns, and the Whig aristocracy were for the bill; while against them were the Church, the Law, the Universities, the Services, many great bankers, and most farmers and country gentlemen.[6]

To understand the effect of the Reform Bill of 1832 it is necessary to consider not only the change in the qualification for the vote, but the redistribution of seats. The dis-franchisement of the rotten boroughs was the main blow to the Tories. Fifty-seven small boroughs which had returned 113 members were disfranchised. From each of 30 boroughs which had returned two members, one member was taken away and two were taken from each of two other boroughs which had returned four. The allocation of 63 seats to the in-dustrial towns of England was the main hope of the Liberals. Other changes in the distribution of the seats were the giving of 62 additional seats to the counties, the distribution of 18 seats taken from England to Scotland (8), Wales (5) and Ireland (5). Of the changes in the voting qualification the most important were: In the boroughs the enfranchise-ment of £10 householders, but also the abolition of a variety of customary voting rights which had favoured the artisans. In the counties the addition of copyholders, leaseholders for lives and tenants at will paying over £50 per annum to the previous freehold franchise. In the boroughs the artisans were worse off than before 1832 by the loss of the old quali-fications. Instead of forming more than half of the total borough electorate the artisans were, after 1832, outnumbered by more than two to one.[7] In the counties the admission of tenants at will actually strengthened the hold of the bigger landowners so long as voting was kept public in deference to " legitimate interests ".

The total effect was to increase the electorate by 217,000, or 40 per cent., but the distribution of voting-power was fantastically uneven. Although more than two-thirds of the seats withdrawn had come from the south of the Thames

and Severn, the advantage of the small boroughs and therefore of the South remained overwhelming. North of the
Wash to the Severn line the boroughs returned 86 members,
and the counties 39; south, the boroughs returned 248, and
the counties 123.[8]

One in thirty of the population of the United Kingdom had
the vote, but the distribution of voting power varied from
1 in 5 in Westmorland to 1 in 37 in Lancashire and 1 in 39
in Middlesex; in the boroughs from 1 in 4 in the small
boroughs to 1 in 45 in the manufacturing towns. Harwich
and Lyme Regis returned two members each for an electorate
of less than 200. Ireland, with one-third the population of
the United Kingdom, would return only 105 out of 658
members.

If the aristocracy accepted reform to save the constitution,
the middle and lower classes sought in reform the road to
their Utopias. For the aristocracy a limited reform might
save their order and the throne; for the middle class it
might secure in politics the honesty, which business proved
and religion taught, was often the best policy. It might
shrivel up " the monopolies, Church craft, sinecures, armorial
hocus pocus, primogeniture and pageantry " which battened
on industry and thrift.[9] For the lower class reform might
provide a defensive weapon in a competitive age.

The expectations of all three were to be disappointed. The
aristocracy thought that they had adjusted the voting power
to the new distribution of wealth the industrial revolution
had caused. They were giving political recognition to their
economic equals. But a franchise based on the rent of houses
was to prove a shifting basis for a stable political order. The
rise in wages and in rents due to the discovery of gold in Cali-
fornia in 1848, and in Australia in 1851, was to enfranchise
many which the qualifications of 1832 had been designed to
exclude. The Reform Bill added 217,000 to an existing
electorate of 500,000, but within the next generation the

qualifications prescribed added 600,000 more. So great was the rate of economic change that the compromise of 1832 could not acquire the force of custom long unchanged. As the slow changes of an agricultural order were replaced by the swift accelerations of an industrial community, there was brought home to every politician the economic basis of the State. In particular were the ruling classes to be driven to consider the economic basis of the State, but the middle class were to discover also that there was more in the art of politics than the higgling of a market or the abstractions of fashionable philosophers. While the poor were to discover that to compel attention is not to be understood or to know your own mind.

The complexity of the franchise stimulated the development of parties. The Reform Bill of 1832 provided for a registry of those qualified to vote; but it left it to those who had the right to vote to see that their names were on the register—at the cost in England of 1s., and in Scotland of 2s., and unless they were there they could not vote. " Registration became a gap through which the parties, hitherto confined to Parliament, made their way into the constituencies and gradually covered the whole country with the network of their organizations."[10] In 1835 the Radicals opened a registration office in Cleveland Row with a full-time secretary.[11] In three years they established the Reform Club, the Reform Association, and had attempted to provide the Liberal party with a financial basis. In 1832 the Carlton Club took the initiative in scrutinizing the electoral roll, though the idiosyncrasies of local Toryisms compelled a cautious policy. Between 1832 and 1841 Peel, who saw that the registration of voters was " a perfectly new element of political power . . . more powerful than either the sovereign or the House of Commons ", linked up a central party organization with a network of local associations.[12]

An increase in corruption flowed from obvious causes.

D

When the Reform Bill was drafted the King had refused to consider the ballot. The aristocracy clung to the open system of voting as a method of safeguarding the " legitimate interest " of property, and of excluding men from the House of Commons " who would be following impulses not congenial to our institutions . . . men incapable of taking large views and looking only to penny and shilling gains and losses ", a course to be disapproved by " all the intelligent and respectable classes ".[13]

And so the " perfectly hideous " system of the hustings remained. It disgraced candidates and depraved electors while the scenes which took place at almost every particular election were, as Bright said, " a frightful price to pay for parliamentary government ". With small electorates the possibility of securing a purchasable margin of votes was not to be resisted. The aristocratic system of nomination, which had been practised by the eighteenth-century owner of a rotten borough, was succeeded by the no less aristocratic system of intoxication. The Parliament of 1841 was known as the bribery parliament. Between 1832 and 1854 the 200 electors of St. Albans absorbed in one way and another over £24,000. As late as 1867 it was still common for every voter polling to cost £1 a head.[14] " May I venture," wrote Mrs. Disraeli to Sir Robert Peel, " to name my own humble but enthusiastic exertions in times gone by, for the party or rather for your own splendid self. They will tell you at Maidstone, that more than £40,000 was spent through my influence alone."[15] If those who had the vote were prepared to sell it dear, those who had no vote used what influence they could command. In 1837 " Sir William Graham at Carlisle was hunted through the streets and his son knocked down ". Scenes took place which even he found " disgraceful to the free institutions under which we live."[16]

Though the House of Commons condemned bribery, individual members continued to practise it. Disputed elections were tried by parliamentary committees, boldly partisan, but prepared to wink at the obvious collusion of rival candidates in the maintenance of loose practices. Whig committees decided for the Whig candidate; Tory committees for the Tory. But should the parties desire to split the difference, and in constituencies returning two members divide the spoils, the committee would offer no objection.[17] An Act of 1854 defined bribery but failed clearly to define undue influence. In 1868 the House of Commons imposed upon an unwilling judiciary the trial of disputed elections. The Ballot Act was not passed until 1872, when at the same time the provision that nominations should be made in writing abolished the clamour of the hustings. The indirect power of aristocracy through electoral influence was not firmly controlled until the Act of 1883.

If the confusion and corruption in the constituencies was thick, the confusion in the minds of the party leaders was thicker still. In 1828 the Duke of Wellington had complained " we hear a great deal of Whig principles and Tory principles and Liberal principles . . . but I confess that I have never seen a definition of any of them and cannot make myself a clear idea of what they mean ". The Duke's capacity for political analysis was no doubt inhibited by his fear of the " blackguard influence " in politics. But we have a similar complaint of confusion from the " blackguards " themselves. " Politics," wrote the Radical Parkes, in 1838, " are about as confused as Bottom's dream, which was past the wit of man to say what dream it was."[18]

The confusion of parties between 1832-67 is profoundly important in the development of the constitution. It had required the insight of Burke to see that " party divisions, whether on the whole operating for the good or evil, are things inseparable from free government ". But the creation of a system of parties which should embody a triple unity of ideas, interests and persons schooled in co-operation and dedicated to the service of the State was to be the work of a century. Between 1832 and 1868 we have the transformation of the conflicting cliques within a governing class into the party organization of a democratic State. After 1868 it seemed to popular tradition that Gladstone and Disraeli had given to the airy nothings of speculative thought a concrete embodiment in the interests, the organizations and the traditions of two great parties. But Gladstone and Disraeli learnt their magician's arts in the period we are now considering. It was in this period that the technique of persuasion by discussion in place of the tyranny of custom and the power of the purse or the terror of the sword was first systematically developed. The development of parties is inevitably complex. If we accept the simplification that all parties are an expression of economic interests that complexity remains. For even in the strategy of a class war there is an opportunity for a variety of tactics. The goal may be determined but the routes may be many. A class may advance its own interests in many ways—by the sword, by the purse, or by the tongue. As men do not live by bread or by privilege alone, an economic group may be defending a system of beliefs as well as a group of economic advantages. Even if we can believe that its religion, its morals and its customs have developed as so many defences to its economic privileges, those defences may be manned in many ways. The division between parties had not to be so trivial that it made politics a game for the prize of office, or so fundamental that the one desires to destroy the other. The slow extension of the franchise meant that a happy mean between the play of equals and the war of classes was maintained.

In 1832 the Whigs and Tories had been riven and battered by the storms of a changing world. They represented both a conflict of interests and a conflict of traditions. And their difference of traditions would affect their defence of their interests. " The ideal Tory and the ideal Whig . . . agreed in the necessity and benefit of an exact balance of the three estates; but the Tory was more jealous of the balance being deranged by the people, the Whig of its being deranged by the Crown " (Coleridge). The Whig party had been disorganized by forty years in opposition, and the problems of the new industrial age were to disintegrate it further. Their principles were vague and general. They believed in nothing in excess not even constitutional reform or the reduction of corrupt expenditure.[19] They believed that truth would prevail if men were free to argue out their differences, but they held that only in a balanced and complex constitution could such freedom be secured. The prerogatives of the Crown, the privileges of the two Houses of Parliament were a necessary safeguard to the rights and privileges of the people. Universal suffrage would destroy an ordered liberty and create a lawless tyranny. They believed that privilege might be the parent of freedom; that it was the duty and the privilege of property to extend the empire of reason. But they convinced themselves that political corruption was an inoculation against religious prejudice and popular violence. They played their part in providing an antidote to the religious fanaticism sporadic in a period of rapid social change and disintegrating faiths. An old Whig, like Russell, had " a noble confidence in the power of truth to prevail and a naive confidence in himself as its exponent ". But if Russell believed in government by discussion within the forum of privilege, a new Whig like Macaulay could bring his colleagues to accept sweeping constitutional changes as natural and inevitable consequences of all great changes in the distribution of property and the diffusion of political intelligence. The Whig party compelled the Tories to save property by reconstruction and saved them from provoking revolution by reaction.[20]

The Conservative party was new born in 1833. " Unlike the Whigs it had no traditions, but it had interests and it was alive. . . .   Its strength lay in the support of substantial interests alarmed at the prospect of radical change."[21]   If the Whigs represented the eighteenth-century blend of rational-ism with the constitutional traditions of 1688, the Conserva-tives represented the economic interests most severely threatened by the new industrial and commercial order. There was the corn interest, the cattle interest, the sugar interest.   But there was also the tradition of reconstruction as a method of defending their order.   The Whig would have government corrupt and the Church subordinate to the State so that the people should be safeguarded against despotism and bigotry.   The Conservative desired a strong government and was prepared to reform for strength, but he looked to the Church as a bulwark against the lower orders. Sir Robert Peel was the architect of the new party, he thought of it as " a beleaguered garrison whose right and whose duty it was to evacuate and demolish untenable positions in order that what remained might hold out the longer ".[22]   The essence of his doctrine was that if the traditional institutions were to be conserved in the midst of a changing society they must be incessantly adapted.[23]   " His mission was not so much to originate as to moderate, control and instruct . . . he was the great minister of the middle classes who, by rallying them round the reformed constitution, was able to save both his own order and their's from the revolution which seemed to menace both ".[24]

In 1832 it seemed to J. S. Mill that there was " nothing definite and determinate in politics except Radicalism ". Through their influence slavery was abolished throughout the British Empire in 1833; the Poor Law reformed; the first grants given to education; the trading privileges of the East India Company abolished.   But they failed to establish themselves as a third party.   Had they done so the House of Lords might have been reformed and the English Church in Ireland disestablished.   The limited franchise of 1832 did not allow them to develop into a permanent third party in the House.   Neither in 1832 nor in 1865 did the House of Commons have a single representative of any class except the possessing and employing classes.   Macaulay wrote in 1833 that a man of honour could not make politics a profession unless he had a competence of his own without exposing himself to privations of the severest kind.   It was impossible for any man to write enough to procure a decent subsistence and at the same time to make politics a profession. The first reformed parliament was composed for the most part of country gentlemen.   More than 400 were without any profession and nearly 200 were related to peers.   One analysis of their membership gives 508 as landowners, 73 financiers and 100 members of the Army and Navy.   In 1865 the same groups were respectively 436, 163 and 125.   Though artisans secured no direct representation, commerce and manufacturers did.   In 1832 and 1835 there was an important group of East and West Indian proprietors, and in 1847 the railways were represented by 86, and in 1860 by 160 members.[25]

In 1832 the Radical party had many influential and wealthy members; barristers, merchants, writers, military and naval officers, bankers, doctors, squires and Whig peers' sons all stood in its interests.[26]   But the worst feature of the Reform Bill it seemed to a contemporary " was the few leading minds created by it.   In Parliament many of our really honest Radicals are not fit to be even abbots in a monastery. The system is too costly to allow better men to get it ".[27] Neither Hume, nor Grote, nor Buller possessed the art of leadership, and Cobden was the first Radical capable of sitting with credit in a Cabinet.[28]   In the constituencies they were at a disadvantage because their indifference in religion and freedom in morals could not command the support of pious dissenters.[29]   The £10 householders of the working and small shopkeeper class showed a desire for candidates of unimpeachable respectability. Even in 1832 Tower Hamlets, "the vastest and dingiest urban constituency sent to the House of Commons Lushington, a Whig ecclesiastical lawyer, and Clay, a wealthy merchant.[30] For a time the Radicals established a complete electoral domination in the Metropolitan area, but the Tories, using the "Church and King cry" with one section of the electorate and "Conservative, not destructive reform" with another, and supplementing these with money for the bribable and influence for the intimidable, were able more than to hold their own.[31] The *laissez-faire* policy of their intellectuals alienated them from working-class opinion in the country, and in the towns they were destroyed as a party by the reaction of the middle-class electors against the revolutionary violence of Chartism and discredited by their alliance with the Irish leader, O'Connell, which the balance of parties imposed upon them in the House. After the Radicalism of the Dissenters had been placated by the removal of their religious and civil grievances, the Whigs and Tories held a strategical position.[32] The Radicals were not prepared to dismiss the Whigs when the alternative was a Tory Government. The Whigs were not prepared to unite with the Radicals in an attack on the House of Lords, where the Tories were securely entrenched. So as Greville wrote in 1842 only "the Tories can carry liberal measures. The Whigs' work prepares, but cannot accomplish them; the Tories directly or indirectly thwart, discourage and oppose them until public opinion compels them to submit, and then they are obliged to take them up and to do that which they can do but the Whigs cannot do ".[33]

Whether universal suffrage would have produced a better England it is impossible to say. It is unlikely that the rationalism of a Bentham would have recommended itself to the countryside or the economics of his followers to the towns of the hungry 'forties. It is possible that an extended suffrage in 1832 would have given power to many an unscrupulous demagogue. A younger Disraeli might have bewitched a younger Queen, and England have produced her Jackson, or Napoleon the Third. It is doubtful if, at this time, the essential conditions for successful representative government were developed. People were not in a condition to be persuaded by discussion. Economic hardship and religious bigotry—in the case of Ireland racial distrust based on economic fear and religious contempt—might have been fatal to the Mother of Parliaments. The Anti-Corn Law League of the 'forties showed both the power of the middle class and their limitations. It was successful because it did not meddle with religious prejudice, because it did not relate to Ireland, because it touched none of the theoretical problems of government.[34] Cobden had succeeded in educating every section of English society in a common enthusiasm for a proposition in economics. A moral and religious spirit had been infused into a topic of bread and profit. But if the League was a success the Chartist Movement was a tragic failure. Universal suffrage in the 'thirties might have meant a struggle between those who could organize, as Cobden organized the League, and those who could manipulate the discontents voiced in the Charter. But though Bright, in 1848, hoped that it would be possible to organize a party for political reform more formidable than the League, he did not succeed until 1860.[35]

But the political ideas of the upper middle class were almost exhausted by 1846. " Their Nonconformist Liberalism, the cause and symbol of their rebellion against the landlord caste that had at once starved and insulted them, was now, in the more prosperous time of Free Trade, gradually giving way to Churchmanship in religion and Conservatism in politics."[36] They were prepared for no further attack on Church or land monopolies in Great Britain and Ireland, or on the aristocratic control of place and power.[37] " Politically," wrote Graham, " power is now vested in the hands of the middle classes; transfer it again and it will pass into a divided empire between the aristocracy and the working classes which will bring town and country into hostile array . . . a war of classes and interests will commence, the end of which I cannot foresee."[38] Even the Duke of Bedford was persuaded " that if a successful attempt were made to retrace our free trade steps we should witness the commencement of a war of classes ".[39] " A government of progress was indispensable ", Aberdeen wrote to Princess Lieven; " none can be too Liberal for me provided it does not abandon its Conservative character ".[40] " Resistance to reform was not grounded on attachment to the old forms of the constitution . . . it rests mainly on fears of peril to property."[40a] In 1852 Gladstone was " on the Liberal side of the Conservative party rather than on the Conservative side of the Liberal party ".[40b] In 1856 Gladstone wrote " for all purposes for which I value Liberalism the Liberal party is dead. It is held together by two bonds: one which is called the loaves and fishes, or the patronage of government; the other, votes for the ballot and other such trash to which I am conscientiously opposed ". But there was, he said, " a policy going begging, the general policy which Peel in 1841 took office to support—the policy of peace abroad, of economy, of financial equilibrium, of steady resistance to abuses, and promotion of practical improvements at home; with a disinclination to questions of organic change gratuitously raised ". To this he could add " happily, no longer a question of party—the accomplishment of what yet remains for the liberation of commerce from the shackles that it ought not to bear ".[41]

His struggles for the liberation of commerce led Gladstone to the great Budget of 1860, and in 1861 to a tacit alliance with Bright. The latter wrote to him in 1861, " the past is well-nigh really past, and a new policy and a wiser and a higher morality are signed for by the best of our people, and there is a prevalent feeling that you are destined to guide that wiser policy and to teach that higher morality ".[42]   This alliance between Bright and Gladstone—between the popular forces which, after the collapse of Chartism, Bright had reawakened and trained in constitutional methods, and the driving force of Gladstone's parliamentary genius, developed during the stultifying ascendancy of Lord Palmerston, is a good example of the process of English political change. Gladstone, the pupil of Canning, and of Peel, the colleague of Palmerston, the representative of Oxford and of Lancashire, the vaguest of philosophers and the most meticulous accountant, was brought into alliance with all those interests the existing system of government ignored.

In this general background we can study the changes in the art of government from the Reform Bill of 1832 to that of 1867. It was the government of an oligarchy. The Reform Bill had not weakened the hold of the governing families upon the Cabinet, and their younger members were still dedicated to the service of their country and their order in the popular chamber.   In the 'sixties a landed aristocracy of about 2,250 persons owned together nearly half the enclosed land of England and Wales, or nearly 15 million acres out of 33 million; and 400 peers and peeresses owned nearly 6 million.[43] In 1848, out of a Cabinet of 14, four were united by the ties of the closest relationship.[44]   Russell's Cabinet of 1852 was called the Dukery.   In the Cabinet of 1859, which included three dukes and the brother of a fourth, Gladstone, Milner Gibson and Cardwell were the only three men without titles.   It was felt to be " of great importance to the country and highly conducive to the working of the constitution that young men in high aristocratical positions should take part in the administration of public affairs and should not leave the working of our political machine to classes whose pursuits and interests are of a different kind ".[45] This system of family alliances has its advantages.   An oligarchy which is a real power and not merely the puppet of a despot is a very subtly organized party system within a miniature State. A healthy oligarchy is the seed of a Liberal democracy. Its members know very clearly the distinction between laws and conventions, between principles and the exigencies of policy. Though balanced on the razor edge of privilege they can observe fine points of honour. A powerful oligarchy is a miniature State in which persuasion has replaced violence and broken friendships' broken heads. But this system also has its disadvantages; and these are not merely that it is not a government of the people—for the people may not yet be fit to govern—but disadvantages due to its family character. Loyalty to persons is more important than reasons of State. The curse of age is too often upon it. Palmerston, the Regency buck, survived to be the old and slippered pantaloon of 1860; Gladstone, the " young man with the black hair and the white face ", survived to be the tragic octogenarian of the Cabinet of 1892. The Russell of 1845, who precipitated the crisis of the Corn Laws, survived to lose his political reputation in the 'sixties. In the formation of Cabinet, as in the life of ancient China, the dead had more consideration than the living. Seniority was almost as fatal in the arts of peace as it was in the arts of war.

To the statesmen of 1832 the problem was whether or not the constitution could be worked at all. For a constitution in any changing social order must provide for a change of government. The succession of governments " affects the sanity and health of the whole state ". A king must choose his favourites in such a manner that he is neither made a puppet nor deposed; an aristocracy must divide its spoils so that it is not dissolved in civil war; a democracy must provide a mechanism by which the play of thought and the swing of opinion may be registered in political power. It must provide for the maintenance of order while there can be discussion and experiment to secure agreement as to change. The advantages of the mixed constitution of England had been thought to be that it did provide for both stability and change. It did allow, as far as was then possible, for the methods of government to approach the methods of thought. Governments have their roots in violence, how can they be pruned to flower into persuasion? The methods of power and the methods of reason are so different that it is only occasionally that the powers that be have been the powers that think. Before 1832 the apologists of the constitution would have said that it operated at three levels: for the ordinary adjustments of policy there were the alternations of different groups within the governing class; at longer intervals there were the elections in which the pulse of a wider social order could be felt; while in times of emergency there was the monarchy to initiate change or to resist uncritical enthusiasm. King, parliament and people were supposed to be bound, each to each, by natural piety. The hereditary king was a barrier to despotism; the " grave and thoughtful considerations " of the Lords a check to the intemperate vote of the Commons; while the middle class was the conscience of the State, " the most disinterested, the most independent, and the most unprejudiced of all ".[46] But the bonds of natural piety had been strengthened by more material cords. The King had bought his own retainers in the Commons, and the Lords were represented there by their nominees.

The Reform Bill of 1832 made it impossible for the House of Lords to control a majority in the Commons. There were now two Houses and not two departments of a single House. Nor in time of crisis could the Minister chosen by the King be certain of a majority in the Commons. " How ", asked Peel, " could the King hereafter change a Ministry? How could he make a partial change in the administration in times of public excitement with any prospect that the ministers of his choice, unpopular, perhaps, from the strict performance of necessary duties, would be returned to Parliament?"[47]   But if power no longer rested in a subtle trinity of King, Lords and Commons, where did it rest and through what channels did it flow?

In a civil government Locke had written the people must have power to cashier their rulers.   But how, after 1832, was this to be done?   If by the King he might be brought in violent conflict with the people; if by the people there were the alternative dangers of the development of party groups, or of a despotism derived from a plebiscite. In 1841 Disraeli argued that Melbourne, defeated at the election, should have resigned.   Melbourne said that it was not right " to judge what the conduct of the members may be by their declaration on the hustings ".[48]

Members, then, were to be free to support or oppose whatever government seemed in their wisdom to be best.   But who, then, was to decide when the House of Commons must be dissolved?   Suppose a confusion of parties so that no government could remain in power; suppose a crisis in which the government of day was not prepared to accept the verdict of the House; what then could be done?   It was here that the Crown was felt to be the lynch-pin of the constitution. It was the Crown which was to decide which Minister should be invited to conduct in the House of Commons the business of the State.   It was the Crown which was to decide in consultation with the Minister of its choice the most suitable occasion for the dissolution of the House of Commons.   But the position of the Crown was by the extension of the franchise made delicate indeed.   It must accept a government which could control a majority in the House of Commons.   If a government defeated in the House desired to appeal to the electorate it was not clear whether or not the Crown need grant the dissolution required.   So obscure was the position that it was believed by Melbourne that the

Minister acceptable to the Crown ought not to dissolve unless there were a certainty of success, otherwise the prestige of the Crown would have been damaged by having a majority returned slap against it. That the position of the Crown should depend upon its being able to choose before an election the party or group of parties which would therein succeed, or that the electorate would always support the Minister the Crown had deigned to choose, would have produced a constitution fantastic indeed. The actual solution by which the Crown came to accept the duty of inviting a Prime Minister to form a government from that party or parties which could control a majority in the House of Commons and to accept from that Prime Minister and his Cabinet advice as to when a dissolution was most desirable; and that a Minister defeated at an election should then resign, the Crown then sending for the leader of the party or parties which seemed to have been successful was a subtle and complex discovery of half a century of anxious experiment. The interplay of tradition and experience, the moulding of a subtle constitution by the exigencies of new conditions are shown in the crises, grave and gay, of: the Dismissal of Melbourne, 1834; the Bedchamber Question, 1839; the Repeal of the Corn Laws, 1846.

In 1834 the dismissal of Melbourne showed that neither the King nor his Ministers had had time to appreciate the effect of the Reform of 1832. The elevation of Lord Althorp, a member of the Ministry, to the House of Lords by the death of his father, gave the Prime Minister, Melbourne, a problem in Cabinet reconstruction. He proposed that Lord John Russell should be the new leader of the House of Commons. Russell was not acceptable to the King, who considered that he had now the opportunity and the right to reconstruct the Government under a Minister of his own choice. Melbourne was not actually dismissed, but his veiled offer of resignation was accepted by the King as something he had a right to ask. The significance of the crisis lies in the sequel.

Peel, who took office in a minority, failed to secure a majority when he appealed to the new electorate as the King's Minister. In his Tamworth manifesto he said that " he had a firm belief that the people of this country will so far maintain the prerogative of the King, as to give to the Ministers of his choice not an implicit confidence, but a fair trial ". Though defeated in the election he met Parliament and only resigned when, after several months, it was obvious that the House of Commons would not support him. He gave as his reason for resignation that he saw " the greatest prejudice to the cause of good government and to the prerogative of the Crown " in " exhibiting the executive government without control over the House of Commons ". The incident is significant for two reasons. Peel specifically accepted the responsibility for whatever part the King might have played in the dismissal of Melbourne. " I have been asked," he said, " whether I would impose on the King in his personal capacity the responsibility for the dismissal of the Government. . . . I claim all the responsibility which properly belongs to me as a public man; I am responsible for the assumption of the duty which I have undertaken and if you please, I am by my acceptance of office responsible for the removal of the late Government."[49] This was a somewhat Delphic utterance. The King could not in his personal capacity dismiss a Minister; but could he dismiss a Minister whenever he could find someone prepared to take office and responsibility for his predecessor's dismissal even though he were in a minority? What would be the position of the Crown when the new Minister responsible for the dismissal of the old was defeated in the House and at the polls. If there was not to be a direct participation of the Crown in party politics it was obvious that the Crown must accept the advice of its present Ministers as to whether resignation or dissolution was to take place. The Crown might be left with the freedom of whom to try as Minister, but it could not enjoy the power of deciding when to change.

The Bedchamber Comedy was produced in 1839. The Melbourne Cabinet, one of the weakest ever known, and entirely dependent upon the Radicals and O'Connell, was defeated on the Jamaica Bill. Melbourne advised the Queen to send for Wellington and if he refused for Peel. " Your Majesty appears to Lord Melbourne to have no other choice. The Radicals have neither ability, honesty nor numbers. They have no leaders of any character." When the Queen sent for Wellington, he explained " that he had no power whatever in the House of Commons, if he was to say black was black they would say it was not ". Peel, who was next applied to, would only take office in a minority if he might have the evidence of the Queen's confidence which would be given by her acceptance of his nomination of the ladies of her household. The Queen refused. " I replied that I never would consent and I never saw a man so frightened." The Melbourne Cabinet returned to office.

The central political fact was that Peel was in a minority and knew that with the existing registration he could not secure a majority. But the responsibility which the problem of a change of government throws on the Crown is shown by the fact that when the outgoing Melbourne Cabinet met and advised the Queen to refuse Peel's conditions, Greville said that it " was utterly anomalous and unprecedented and a course as dangerous as unconstitutional ". But, like every constitutional precedent in English history, the conditions were unprecedented and never to be repeated. Neither Melbourne nor Peel wished to dissolve. The Queen was advised by Melbourne to do " everything to facilitate the formation of a government . . . we must not have the position they have in France of no party being able to form a government ". She was to " urge this question of the household strongly

E

as a matter due to yourself and your own wishes " and " not to give a promise that you will dissolve, nor to say positively that you will not ". The Queen herself was triumphant, writing to Melbourne, " she must rejoice at having got out of the hands of people who would have sacrificed every personal feeling and instinct of the Queen's to their bad party purposes.".[50] She wrote to the King of the Belgians that she had acted " quite alone and shall be supported by my country who are very enthusiastic about it and loudly cheered me on going to church on Sunday ". Until the verdict of the electorate on an existing Ministry should be taken as final, the Crown could not avoid a central responsibility in the procedure of forming a Government. When two parties were neither sure of the Commons or of the electorate, the fate of governments hung on the gossip of a household.

The underlying confusion of principle was clearly revealed two years later when the Melbourne Ministry, after a series of defeats in the House of Commons, did not offer to resign. In the debate on a motion of no confidence, moved by Peel, he argued that it was " at variance with the principles and the spirit of the constitution for a Ministry to continue in office without the confidence of the House ". In reply, both Russell and Macaulay held that inability to perform the administrative duties of the State was a ground for resignation, but that it was not necessary for a government to command general support for its legislative programme. To this Peel made the significant reply that legislation and administration were " so interwoven as to render it utterly impossible to draw a line of distinction between them ", and that " the character of administration and the claims upon public confidence was infinitely stronger on account of their legislative measures than on account of their administrative acts ". But this recognition of the fact that in government administration is not enough did not lead to the acceptance of the principle that that party should govern whose legislative programme was acceptable to the electorate. For when Melbourne at last advised the Queen to dissolve, he misled her as to the significance of that act. He told her that an unsuccessful dissolution would be a bad thing as the defeat of her Ministers would be an affront to the Crown. In consequence the Queen came to think of a dissolution of Parliament, not as an appeal to the political sovereign people to select their government, but as " a valuable weapon in the hands of the Crown which should only be used with certainty of success ".[51] Disraeli had a clearer insight when he urged that Melbourne should have resigned without meeting Parliament.

The crisis of the Corn Laws in 1846 revealed not only important problems in the nature of the constitution, but in the very nature of government itself.   The Conservative party had been formed from the alliance of a group of interests—sugar, cattle, and corn.   But their leaders had begun the transmutation of " Old Corruption " into the efficient machine which was later to serve Gladstonian finance. They feared above everything the possibility of their dependence upon the blackguard influence in the House of Commons, or such an extension of the suffrage as might threaten monarchy, property or their conception of public faith.   A Conservative statesman was in a difficult position.   In the House he would not displace a Whig Government if it meant his own dependence upon the Radical vote.   In the country he feared the people even when they were on his own side. It required the genius of Disraeli to see that a Phillip drunk might be made a useful ally to a Percy sober.

The failure of the Irish potato crop presented Peel with fundamental problem in the relation between the technique of politics and the necessities of government.   Out of the crisis of 1846 was developed the nineteenth-century conception of party government.   It was a critical test of the issue whether, in a national crisis, party is enough.

The case against Peel is simple enough. The leader of a party, with a majority in the House of Commons, he used his position as Prime Minister to betray their interests that the country might be saved—his opponents add by him and not by others.

When Peel became convinced that the Corn Laws must be repealed and was not supported by his Cabinet, he resigned, advising the Queen to send for Lord John Russell. When it was obvious that neither his own colleagues nor Lord John Russell could form a government, he announced that he was prepared to stand by the Queen, that he would undertake to deal with the difficulties and that he would serve the Queen if she called upon him to do so, and that those who would not go with him he would dismiss at once.[52]   He claimed that " the real interests of the cause of constitutional government must be determined by the answer which the heart and conscience of a responsible Minister might give to the question ' What is the course which the public interest really demands?' "   " It was," he said, " no easy task to secure the united action of an ancient monarchy, a proud aristocracy and a reformed constituency."   He carried repeal and disrupted his party.   Was this as Melbourne said, " a damned dishonest act " or, as Aberdeen thought, " very noble " and of " great courage "?

It is said that he made " the higher obligation of preserving political good faith in political life subservient to the repeal of the Corn Laws ".   That, if their repeal was necessary to save the State, it was not for him to do it.   That there were other leaders with heart and conscience to secure the united action of an ancient monarchy, a proud aristocracy and a reformed constituency.

Whatever blame may be attached to Peel it is to misunderstand the constitution to regard him as false to the spirit of party.   All statesmen of the time would have been prepared on various issues to serve the country against their party. The existing parties were based on an electorate which was far narrower than the middle class. Peel was not prepared to appeal to the uncertain verdict of an election if reform could otherwise be secured. " I thought," he said, " such an appeal would ensure a bitter conflict between the different classes of society and would preclude the possibility of dispassionate consideration by Parliament, a number of whom would probably have committed themselves by explicit declarations and pledges." Peel was in a false position. He regarded himself as the natural leader of the middle classes, but he thought they could only be led from within the Conservative party. As Greville said, " he was the Liberal chief of a party in which the old anti-Liberal spirit was still rife; they regarded with jealousy and fear the middle classes . . . with whom Peel was evidently anxious to ingratiate himself and whose support he considered his best alliance . . . there was an unexpressed but complete difference in their understanding and his of the obligations by which the Government and the party were mutually connected. They considered Peel to be not only the Minister, but the creature of the Conservative party, bound above all things to support and protect their special interest according to their own views and opinions. He considered himself the Minister of the nation ". The tragedy of Peel was that he considered himself to be the Minister of a nation to which he dare not openly appeal. When, after the Corn Laws had been repealed, he was defeated by a combination of the Protectionists, with the Whigs and Irish, Peel resigned rather than dissolve on the Irish question or Free Trade. " I am decidedly against dissolution," he wrote to Wellington, " on an Irish question, above all, on such a question as the Coercion Bill. Shall we dissolve on some other ground? . . . On what ground shall we appeal to the country? We must appeal to it on some principle. The natural one seems to be Free Trade and the destruction of Protection. If we are to succeed we shall

succeed by an unnatural combination with those who agree
with us in nothing but the principles of Free Trade.   A
short time only would pass before this combination would
be dissolved and we should be at the mercy of our new
allies."[53]

The period between the fall of Peel, in 1846, and the
formation of the last government of Palmerston in 1859,
shows the perils to which constitutional government, without
the guidance of party organizations with clear programmes
and broad-based popular support, is liable.   It was in this
period that Disraeli learnt how to manipulate the Queen, and
Gladstone the need for an extended suffrage.   It was in this
period that we drifted into our most shameful war and that
Palmerston gave to the middle class the politician they really
deserved.   It is in this period, too, that our political leaders
" behaved so like children " that the Queen, advised and
assisted by the Prince Consort, had to organize our Cabinets
and direct their policies.

A brief summary of the different Cabinets and their
character will give some idea of the anæmia of the
constitution: —

The 1st Russell Cabinet, 1846-52.   Russell took office on
the resignation of Sir Robert Peel.   At the dissolution of
1847, 325 Whigs and Liberals were returned, and 226 Tories
and 105 Peelites.   In a minority Russell had to rely on the
antagonism of the Protectionists and the Peelites.   In 1851,
when he was defeated and resigned, no combination could be
found either to form a government or to dissolve.   He
finally resigned in 1852.

1st Derby Cabinet, 1852.   This was the weakest government which has ever tried to govern the country.   Derby
knew that if he taxed food he would have a rebellion, or as
good, in the towns; and that if he threw over Protectionist
principles his party would do the same by him.   The Queen
wrote to Leopold, " in the present case our acquaintance is

confined almost entirely to Lord Derby, but then he is the
Government ". Disraeli was, for the first time, Chancellor
of the Exchequer. The election of 1852 returned 300 Conservatives, 270 Whigs and Liberals, 40 Peelites, and 40
Irish. Meeting Parliament, the Government was defeated
on Disraeli's Budget by 19 votes and resigned.

The Aberdeen Coalition, 1852-55. The formation of this
Cabinet of six Whigs, six Peelites and one Radical taxed the
full resources of the Court. Would Johnny and Pam serve
together? Would Aberdeen work with Russell? Could
anyone persuade Johnny to serve under Aberdeen? To
contemporaries it was a " tessellated pavement ", " a clique of
doctrinaires existing as a government by Court favour ".[54] It
was melancholy to see " how little fitness for office is regarded
on all sides and how much the public employments are treated
as booty to be divided among the successful combatants ".[55]
Graham indeed said that " on the whole they were gentlemen
and they have a perfect gentleman at their head ". In 1855
it collapsed from inability to conduct a war it had been unable
to prevent. The parties then behaved as Albert complained,
a good deal like children. The country was without a
Cabinet, for a weak Derby refused to form a government,
though his party was 250 strong. His error, Gladstone considered, was gross.[56] Disraeli was annoyed because, as he
wrote at the time, " we had actually the Court with us, for the
two Court favourites, Aberdeen of the Queen, is extinct, and
Newcastle of the Prince, in hopeless condition; and our rivals
were Johnny, in disgrace, and Palmerston, ever detested ".
But the last was the inevitable man for the public opinion of
the Crimean War period.

Palmerston Cabinet, 1855-58. For a brief fortnight the
Peelites, Graham, Gladstone and Herbert, were in his
Government. The general election of 1857 was practically
a plebiscite for Palmerston after he had dissolved on his
China policy being censured in the Commons. But, in 1858

he was defeated by a combination of the whole of the Conservative party, the Peelites, Lord John Russell and the Radicals.

His Cabinet unanimously resolved to resign. Palmerston declined to give the Queen any advice as to his successor, but laid before her the state of parties as it regarded Russell and Derby.[57]   She sent for the latter.   Derby, after his refusal in 1851 and 1855, was compelled to accept or to break his party for ever.   With a majority of 2 to 1 against him in the Commons, might he understand that he would be allowed to dissolve?   Aberdeen, who was privately consulted, said that if a Minister advised the Queen to dissolve she should certainly do so; that while the sovereign might refuse a dissolution, whoever was sent for to succeed, must, with his appointment, assume the responsibility for that act; that a government had the right to threaten dissolution, but that they would be wrong to join the Queen's name with it. So the Queen allowed Derby to know that a dissolution would not be refused him and trusted that her honour would be safe in his hands as to the use to be made of that knowledge.   The Crown was now in the dangerous position of supporting a party in conflict with a majority in the House of Commons.[58]   Derby, after the dissolution, was defeated in the House by 13 and resigned.   The Queen sent for Granville, who opened delicate negotiations with Pam and Johnny.   But Granville could not be Prime Minister as with him, in the first place, either Johnny or Pam would have to be third instead of second.   " With Palmerston I would only have to consider who is to have the first and who the second office in the State.   With you I could only occupy the third."[59]   These fine points of honour were bleeding privilege to death.   The worst possible combination was the result. Palmerston became Prime Minister, pledged to domestic sterility and Russell, Foreign Secretary, when his powers had failed.   It was Gladstone's experience as Palmerston's Chancellor of the Exchequer in this Government which convinced him that the constitution must be revitalized by the touch of popular power.   For the real issue, as Disraeli saw in 1858, was " whether parliamentary government is compatible with our existing institutions.   The House of Commons is broken into sections which, although they have no unity of purpose or policy, can always combine to overthrow the Queen's Government however formed ".

This confusion of the Commons had reprieved the House of Lords.   In the first session of the Reform Parliament, when there was a large Liberal majority in the Commons, the lords had acquiesced in the first part of the programme of radical reconstruction.   But as the division between the Radicals and the Whigs grew and the former were forced into alliance with the Irish the courage of the peers revived. By 1835 " it presented the appearance of a dominant party faction . . . too numerous to be affected by any constitutional process . . . too obstinate to be turned from its fixed purpose of opposing all measures which have a tendency to diminish the influence of the Conservative party ".[60]   It was only through Wellington's support in the Lords that Peel carried the Repeal of the Corn Laws.

After 1846, as the Lords had no direct interest in factory organization, they passed the Factory Bills sent up to them from the Commons.   But they strenuously opposed the amelioration of the conditions of the Irish peasant, or the reduction of the privileges of the Established Church.   In 1856, when they refused to admit life peers, they " rejected the inestimable and unprecedented opportunity of being tacitly reformed " (Bagehot).   The fact that the Prince Consort was believed to be in favour of the introduction of literary and scientific peers no doubt stimulated the Lords in the defence of their privileges.   The Queen was of the opinion that an absolute duty devolved on her of requiring that peerages should not be conferred upon any person who did not, in addition to other qualifications, possess a good moral character.

But though they won the battle of privilege in 1856 they lost the struggle with Gladstone in 1861. In that year they rejected a measure which repealed the excise duty on paper, the last survivor of the taxes on knowledge. Lord Lyndhurst said: " I do not dispute . . . that we have no right whatsoever to amend what is called a Money Bill. We have no right to originate a Bill of that nature . . . but the principle does not apply to the rejection of Money Bills." The Lords had a good tactical case because their rejection of a Bill which repealed a tax, far from embarrassing the executive, presented a large sum of money to them. As the annual Budget then consisted of a number of separate Bills, the Lords, by rejecting one, ran no risk of incommoding the Chancellor of the Exchequer. But Gladstone, who then held that office, retaliated first by securing the appointment of a Select Committee which examined the precedents and confirmed that the Lords had not the right to amend a Money Bill and showed that their power of rejection had never been exercised purely on financial grounds; secondly, by persuading Palmerston to move resolutions asserting the financial privileges of the Commons and declaring that it had " in its own hands so to impose and remit taxes and to frame Bills of Supply that the right of the Commons as to manner, measure and time may be maintained inviolate "; while thirdly, in 1861, he combined in one Bill the entire financial scheme of the year so that the Lords could neither amend nor reject the measure without directly challenging the Commons.

The last scene of this eventless history was the passing of the Second Reform Bill in 1867, of which the circumstances epitomize the character of the period it was to supersede. Palmerston died in 1865 and Russell was again Premier. All the leaders were committed to reform, though the Parliament was against reform. When Gladstone introduced his Reform measure it was defeated by a revolt of the Whig cave under Lowe.   The choice for Russell lay between immediate resignation or dissolution.   " To dissolve would have been a daring act and an appeal from a shuffling Parliament to an awakened people."[61]   It was the course most comformable to the principles and spirit of the constitution.[62] But, owing to the present risk of war between Prussia and Austria, the Queen was not inclined to consent to a dissolution.   Russell resigned and the Reform Bill was carried by a Conservative Government, by a government in a minority and through a Parliament elected to support Lord Palmerston, who detested reform.   The new measure added a million voters, whereas the rejected measure of 1866 would have added only 400,000.   Whether Disraeli's dishing the Whigs was the " half-accidental result of a balance of forces and of manœuvres of attack and defence prepared in swamp of expediency ", whether they were a deep laid design or the result of unprepared opportunism, we shall never know. But the shock to men's confidence in the political morality of English statesmen was severe.   Three Conservative statesmen left Derby and Disraeli as a protest on behalf of political honour against mere party expediency.[63]

We have given a brief sketch of the conditions which determined the party and strength of the government in power.   How were they organized for the performance of their functions?   While the Cabinet was dependent upon the House of Commons, it was not yet prepared to appeal to the electorate to break a deadlock in the House.   Only slowly was the conception developed of the opposition as an alternative Cabinet prepared to take office when the one in power should fail.   In 1831 Peel had written, " there are two parties which call themselves Conservatives: one which is ready to support monarchy, property and public faith; there is another which is prepared to ally itself with Radicals if only it can turn out the Government ".   But experience taught that " it is safer and easier to displace a Ministry than to change and direct its policy by the active intervention of Parliament ".[64]

In 1859 Palmerston told the Queen that " those who unite to turn out a government ought to be prepared to unite to form a stronger government than that which is overthrown ". In 1864 Disraeli complains to Derby that " the principle now conveniently assumed by our opponents that the Opposition is a body prepared to take office and therefore bound to give official opinion on the conduct of every department, seems to me to have no sound foundation ".[65]   In spite of the broken state of parties, the changing character of government compelled the Government of the day to demand that it should be supported unless there were an alternative party prepared to take office.   For as Lord John Russell said in 1840, " there has been, in the course of the last thirty years, very great changes made in the mode of conducting business . . . when I first entered Parliament it was not usual for governments to undertake generally all subjects of legislation.   Since the Reform Bill it has been thought convenient that the Government should propose changes in the laws; there is more discussion and more motions by more members ".

This extension of the business of the State involved a modification of those ancient forms of Parliament procedure which, in 1832, were essentially no different from those of the seventeenth century.   These procedural forms had been developed to defend the representative body against the overwhelming power and influence of a powerful executive.   But as the power of government passed to the Commons it became necessary that they should organize themselves for the exercise of that power.   Instead of the rules of procedure being ramparts against corruption by an executive in the service of the Crown, they had to be made an aid to the Ministry in their task of government.

Before 1832 the functions of the government were chiefly executive. Changes in the law were proposed by independent members and carried not as party questions but by the combined action of both sides. After 1832 the business of the House was continually on the increase (Committee of 1848) and the proportion of its time required for government business steadily increased too. It was essential, if there was not to be chaos, that the rule of procedure should secure that there should be certainty, day by day, as to the business to be transacted (Committee of 1861). This could only be done by limiting the privileges of private members to move amendments at every stage of the consideration of legislation or the grant of moneys for the business of the State. While unofficial members " endeavoured by cunningly-devised arrangements to entrench themselves against the superior power of the Government " the broad problems of parliamentary procedure were treated on a non-party basis. That there must be more certainty; that the Government must have more time for essential business was recognized by all parties; but it was also almost unanimously agreed " that the old rules and orders, when carefully considered and narrowly investigated, are found to be the safeguard of freedom of debate and a sure defence against the oppression of overpowering majorities ".

The radical transformation of parliamentary procedure was not made until after the Reform Bill of 1867 and the attack of the Irish party on the whole traditions of the House. But the following changes were made in the period 1832 to 1872. In 1833 committees were given power to meet from 10 a.m. to 5 p.m. and to sit during the sitting of the House. In 1835 the first printed questions appeared on the notice paper. In 1839 so great had been the flood of petitions that all debate was forbidden on their presentation. In 1849 it was settled that the first reading and printing of a Bill should be decided without debate or amendment moved. While by the " rule of progress " the abuse was stopped of allowing the merits of a Bill to be debated each time the House went into committee for its discussion, although its principles had been debated and accepted upon its second reading.   In 1846 Mondays and Thursdays were fixed as Government days and a third day was usually conceded towards the middle of the session.   In 1852 the Committees of Supply and Ways and Means were fixed for Mondays and Thursdays and also for Wednesdays.   But this did not secure the Government certainty of control over financial business, so in 1861 it was decided that the Committee of Ways and Means and the Committee of Supply might be fixed for every day upon which the House should meet for the dispatch of public business.   Finally, in 1872, it was resolved that the " rule of progress " should be extended to the Committee of Supply; that is to say that amendments on the occasion of going into such committee should only be allowed on a day when a new division of the Estimates was being taken, and not at subsequent sittings.   In 1879 the Government was secured one day a week for supply by making it impossible to move amendments on that day.[66]

The dependence of the Cabinet upon a House of Commons which neither the Crown nor the House of Lords could now control meant that the principle of collective responsibility became a condition necessary if the Cabinet were to be able to control the Commons in the carrying out of necessary business, and necessary also if loyalty to party principles was to provide the place of loyalty to the person of the Crown as the mainspring of political action.   To the old Tory, Wellington, there was " a great difference between willingness to serve the Crown if called upon " and " volunteering in a course of measures which are to have for their object to force the administration to resign, and the sovereign to call for the services of others, myself included " (1839). On the same occasion Graham wrote that " the possession of

power in our popular government is the sole object of political warfare . . . it is not in human nature that a great party
can be kept together by the abstract hope of checking the mis-
conduct of a bad administration, in the absence of the fixed
purpose of displacing them. . . .   Let it once transpire that
you are afraid to take the government and your party is
gone ".[67]   If power were to be respectable those who shared it
must have in common principles to which they would
devote its use.   Graham, when in 1835 he declined an invitation to join Peel, said that " the sudden conversion of long
political opposition into the most intimate alliance—no
general coincidence of principle, except upon one point, being
proved to exist between us—would shock public opinion ".[68]
And the same point is made in an entirely different context
when Cobden in 1859 refused Palmerston's offer of the Board
of Trade.   He wrote to his wife that " to take office now,
without a single declaration of change of view regarding his
public conduct, would be so monstrous a course that nothing
on earth shall induce me to do it " (1859).[69]   If honour
required that there should be agreement with those you
joined, efficiency required also that there should be solidarity
among those in power.   No Cabinet could live if there were
to be openly avowed and tolerated differences of opinion upon
matters standing for immediate action.   A dissentient was
expected to resign his office before he openly voted and spoke
against the policy of the administration.   There had, of
course, to be diversity in consultation, but it must be followed
by unity in decision.   " That which of course you will skilfully avoid," wrote Palmerston to Gladstone in 1862, " will
be the appearance of proclaiming or divulging to the public
differences of opinion which may have existed in Cabinet discussions, but which have been merged in an aggregate
acquiescence." After 1846, when there were few deep
cleavages of principle between the politicians of the day, their
differences were drawn to fine threads of honour.   Loyalty

to Peel's memory kept the Peelites out of office from 1846-55. But party lines were then so indistinct that it could be seriously considered that Gladstone should be in the same Cabinet with Disraeli,[70] and Gladstone, who had considered Palmerston the worst possible Prime Minister, could serve with him as Chancellor of the Exchequer in 1859.

In the construction of his Cabinet, a Minister who had accepted the duty from the Crown had a delicate task. It was considered that there were two situations of influence in the general as distinguished from the departmental government of the country: the one that of the Prime Minister, the other that of the leader of the House. Whoever was Prime Minister with a colleague of equal political prestige would have to make him leader of the House. But this was complicated by the necessity of having powerful Ministers in the Lords and by the overshadowing importance of the Foreign Office, whose holder must manage to placate the Queen. In the 'forties it was almost indispensable that there should be a confidential friend of the Prime Minister at the Home Office then mostly concerned with the disturbances that accompanied the Chartist movement.[71]

The office of the Prime Minister received its modern stamp from the capacity of Sir Robert Peel. Whereas Melbourne's Cabinet had been a mere government of departments without any centre of unity—" our Cabinet is a complete republic and Melbourne, their ostensible head, has no overruling authority " (Greville, August 24th, 1840)—Peel's small Cabinet of twelve was a government of departments made a unity by him. The problem of Cabinet organization was already acute. " I defy the Minister of this country to perform properly the duties of his office, to read all that he ought to read, including the whole foreign correspondence; to keep up the constant communication with the Queen and the Prince; to see whom he ought to see; to superintend the grant of honours and the disposal of ecclesiastical patronage;

to write with his own hand to every person of note who chooses to write to me; to be prepared for every debate, including the most trumpery concerns; to do all these things, and also to sit in the House of Commons eight hours a day for 118 days." (Peel to Arbuthnot, 1854.) In the formation of a government " Nobody ", he told Greville, " could form an idea of what he had to go through in the disposal of places, the adjustment of conflicting claims, and in answering particular applications, everybody thinking their own case the strongest in the world and that they alone ought to be exempted from the general rule . . . everybody . . . fancying that to any office they had ever held they had a sort of vested right and title, and forgetting that younger men must be brought forward ".[72]

How far was the English Cabinet system effective for the conduct of foreign relations, for the preservation of peace, and when the need should arise, for success in war?   It is impossible to give a final answer when the factors involved are so numerous and intangible. The minutest research of modern scholarship is still unable to determine whether or not the Crimean War might have been avoided. Criticism is easy if we are permitted to suppose a change in some vital contemporary factor of the problem and to leave the rest the same: e.g., had the Cabinet in England between 1840 and 1853 been dominated by the spirit of Bright and Cobden while still served with the political skill a Palmerston could command; or had there been a sovereign as intelligent as the Prince Consort, but as much at home in its traditions as the Queen we had; or had there been a democratic franchise which was yet free from the passions of nationalism—the suppositions are endless but they can have no bearing on our criticism of the actors in the constitution as it was. And in criticizing them it is almost impossible to avoid making a judgment based upon facts which at the time they could not have known. But even a prophetic eye will not give power

F

to control the present in which the prophet lives.   Palmerston thought that Russia and France were the two main threats to Europe when he lived; could he have foreseen the future unification of Germany under Prussian control his problems would have been the same.   Some believed that Turkey might be reformed and others that her reform was impossible.   The vision of Gladstone saw that nationalisms in the Balkans might solve the problem of the future of Eastern Europe.   But even with that knowledge the root problem remained that nationalism and Liberalism and nationalism and industrial revolution could not be reconciled. The brotherhood of man is poisoned by the cousinhood of States.

Before the Reform Bill of 1832 the unity of the Cabinet in their responsibility for the main outlines of foreign policy had been secured.   When, in 1825, the King had sent a memorandum to the Cabinet requiring that individual answers should be given to the question whether Canning's policy was a departure from that of Castlereagh and Wellington, they refused to state their individual views and supported Canning in his decision to recognize South America. The King could not personally communicate with foreign Ministers or require the individual opinions of his Ministers.

But the problem remained that neither foreign governments nor the Crown itself, nor its Ministers were precisely agreed as to its proper place in foreign affairs.   For eleven years, from 1830 to 1841, Palmerston was an expert Foreign Secretary, exercising autocratic control in his department and dominating Cabinets.   But when, in 1840, the Czar Nicholas asked for the word of a gentleman that Britain would support him against France, Palmerston had to explain that it would be difficult to induce Parliament to accept an " agreement " which bound England to take up arms in a contingency which might happen at an uncertain time and under circumstances which could not as yet be foreseen.   He said that " it would be scarcely consistent with the spirit of the British constitution for the Crown to enter into a binding engagement of such a nature, without placing it formally upon record . . . if the engagement were merely verbal, though it would bind the Ministers who made it, it might be disavowed by their successors ".[73]   But it was not only that foreign governments did not understand the responsibility of the Ministers to Parliament for the exercise on their advice of the powers of the Crown, they also misunderstood the seeming personal power of the Queen.   The Crimean War might have been avoided had Czar Nicholas realized that the words and friendship of the Queen were not in the last resort important,[74] and had he realized that Aberdeen, unlike himself, could not order his Cabinet.[75]

But the position of the Queen was not only misleading to foreign governments, it was a very real source of embarrassment to governments at home.   As Cabinets were not broad based on popular power, as both wings feared the extension of popular sovereignty they were reluctant, the right firmly to use, the left firmly to oppose, the pretensions of a Court. When the Cabinet was divided it was inevitable that the Queen should exercise an influence always awkward for the Minister and sometimes dangerous to the constitution.   This is clearly shown in the case of Palmerston's difficulty with the Queen and the Prince Consort.   The Prince was a man of knowledge and sagacity particularly in foreign affairs and with him to guide her the Queen could make some attempt at statesmanship.[76]   It was reported in 1845 by Greville that while the Queen had the title, he discharged the functions. But the Conservative and Whig aristocrats were not prepared to accept the guidance of one who was hardly a gentleman and probably a highbrow.   The Prince was under grave suspicion of having an interest in what we should now call rationalization and scientific research.   His planning of the Great Exhibition was a sinister suggestion of what he might do with the machinery of government. In their hearts the Ministers believed that the only safeguard against despotisms lay in the confusions of privilege. If the sword of government were once sharpened, who might not wield it? So in 1848-51, when Palmerston was in conflict with the Court, he was in the dilemma that he had either to endure or to challenge a conflict which might prove fatal to the Crown. The objection of the Court was not really to his manners, but to his policy.[77] The Court wanted to be friendly with Louis Philippe, it favoured Prussian hegemony in Germany, took the Austrian side in Italy and was ashamed of Palmerston's support of Scandinavian rebels, peninsular Radicals, and was indignant at his support of the Danes.[78] So long as Palmerston had Radical support he was secure. But when in 1851 he approved the *coup d'état* of Napoleon III, he fell. But this temporary eclipse of Palmerston only revealed the essential weakness of the position of the Court. When in December, 1851, the Queen requested that Russell, the Prime Minister, should ask the Foreign Secretary, Granville, to submit a regular programme that would enable her as well as the Cabinet to see that policy should pursue certain agreed principles, Russell replied that " the traditional policy of this country is not to bind the Crown and country by engagements unless upon some special cause shown arising out of the circumstances of the day ".[79] The Ministers could promise no more to the Queen than to the foreign governments the course which responsible government might impose. While the Queen failed to control the course of policy to be pursued, she could exercise irritating pressure upon a divided Cabinet. In 1859 the issue of the Risorgimento opposed the people to the Court and divided the new Palmerston Government into contending camps. The Prime Minister, the Foreign Secretary and Gladstone were for the Italians, the Queen and their colleagues for the Austrians. The Queen used Granville as her mouth-piece in the Cabinet against Palmerston and Russell, till he had to protest to the Prince Consort that " Lord Palmerston and Lord John Russell are the Ministers to whom it is natural that the Queen should look for information respecting discussions in the Cabinet respecting foreign affairs . . . they would resent such information being afforded through any other channel. They would consider it a want of confidence on the part of Her Majesty and an improper interference on the part of a colleague ".[80]

In 1864 the Queen, through Granville, asks the Cabinet to be firm and support her in the Danish question,[81] and again Granville is careful to avoid appearing to trench in any way on the rights of the Prime Minister and the Foreign Secretary. In 1860 the Queen opposed intervention between France and Austria which led Russell to complain of despotism, though Sidney Herbert and others of the Cabinet said that she had come to their rescue.[82]   In 1866, when the Cabinet resigned over the Reform Bill of that year, the Queen was indignant that reform should be considered before foreign affairs.   While she considered that Austria should be supported, no British statesman had at the time any idea as to what settlement of Germany would or would not be compatible with British or European interests.[83]

Foreign policies were profoundly affected by the varying power of the parties.   From 1830-41 Palmerston exercised a dominating control; then for four years, 1841-46, Aberdeen followed a policy of healing and reconciliation, called by Palmerston an " antiquated imbecility ".[84]   Then again from 1848-51 Palmerston held power; and from 1851, when he fell, to the outbreak of war, there was complete uncertainty. Clear-sighted Palmerston could give unity to his Cabinet even if his policy were wrong.   But a far-seeing Minister and a still more far-seeing group could not.   The Cabinet of 1853 had as Foreign Secretary a trained diplomat, and there were three ex-Foreign Secretaries in a Cabinet of fourteen.

They were as united as aged gentlemen could be. But though neither ignorant nor even fundamentally divided they clung to half-measures. Some, like Palmerston, believed that the administration of Turkey could be reformed; others, like Russell, that it could not; others, like Aberdeen, felt that the Turk in Europe was a disgrace. They clung to half-measures because " in peace-time a British Cabinet rarely takes decisions involving a clear risk of war ".[85]

The Queen herself wrote that " Lord Palmerston's mode of proceeding always had the advantage that it threatens steps that it hoped would not become necessary; whilst those hitherto taken, started on the principle of not needlessly offending Russia by threats, oblige us at the same time to take the very steps which we refused to threaten ".[86]

Further Cabinet divisions occurred after the Crimean War. In 1863 Granville, on his own initiative, took a leading part in defeating the proposal made by Palmerston for a joint intervention with France in the American Civil War;[87] while as late as the summer of 1863 Gladstone affirmed that the maintenance of the Union was impossible.

[1] C. S. Parker : *Life and Letters of Sir James Graham*, 1792–1861, Vol. 2, pp. 367–8.
[2] Table Talk, Nov. 1, 1830.
[3] J. R. M. Butler : *Passing of the Great Reform Bill*, p. 236.
[4] G. T. Garratt : *Lord Brougham* (1935), p. 254.
[5] S. Maccoby : *English Radicalism*, 1832–52 (1935), p. 60.
[6] J. R. M. Butler, op. cit., 227.
[7] Charles Seymour : *Electoral Reform in England and Wales* (1832–1885), 1915, p. 88.
[8] ibid., p. 97.
[9] Morley : *Life of Cobden* (1883 edition), p. 84.
[10] M. Ostragorski : *Democracy and the Organisation of Political Parties* (1902 edition), Vol. 1, p. 142.
[11] J. K. Buckley : *Joseph Parkes of Birmingham* (1926), p. 138.
[12] C. S. Parker's *Sir Robert Peel*, Vol. 2, p. 368 (1899 edition), Nov. 8, 1838. Peel to Mr. Arbuthnot.
[13] Palmerston to Gladstone.
[14] Lord George Hamilton : *Parliamentary Reminiscences*, 1868–85, p. 3.
[15] Parker's *Peel*, Vol. 2, p. 487. Mrs. Disraeli to Sir Robert Peel. Sept. 5, 1841 (confidential).
[16] C. S. Parker's *Graham*, Vol. 1, p. 256.
[17] T. H. Ward, *Reign of Queen Victoria*, Vol. 1, p. 33.

18 Buckley : *Joseph Parkes*, p. 154.
19 H. W. Carless Davis : *Age of Grey and Peel* (1929), p. 268.
20 ibid., passim., Chap. XI.
21 Parker's *Peel*, Vol. 3, p. 618 (quotation from the summary of Peel's life by his grandson, the Hon. George Peel, pp. 561-622).
22 H. W. C. Davis : *Age of Grey and Peel*, p. 299.
23 Halevy : *Histoire du Peuple Anglais*, Vol. 3, p. 179.
24 T. E. Kebbel : *History of Toryism* (1886), p. 299.
25 H. R. G. Greaves : *Personal Origins and Inter-relations of the Houses of Parliament* (since 1832), *Economica*, June, 1929.
26 S. Maccoby : *English Radicalism*, p. 68.
27 J. K. Buckley : *Joseph Parkes*, pp. 157-8.
28 H. W. C. Davis : *Age of Grey and Peel*, p. 239.
29 Halevy : *Histoire du Peuple Anglais*, Vol. 3, p. 183.
30 Maccoby : *English Radicalism, p.* 65.
31 ibid., pp. 130-131.
32 ibid., pp. 143-144.
33 Greville : *Journal*, Feb. 5, 1842.
34 Scrope : *Life of Lord Sydenham*, p. 89.
35 Trevelyan : *John Bright*, p. 184.
36 ibid., p. 177.
37 ibid., p. 177.
38 Sir J. Graham to Mr. Lewis, April 22, 1848 : Parker's *Graham*, Vol. 2, p. 69.
39 ibid., Vol. 2, pp. 91-2.
40 *Later Correspondence of Lord John Russell*, 1840-78, Vol. 2, p. 102.
40a ibid., Vol. 2, p. 222.
40b Parker's *Graham*, Vol. 2, p. 178.
41 ibid., Vol. 2, pp. 295-6.
42 Williams : *Rise of Gladstone to Leadership of the Liberal Party*, pp. 47-8.
43 G. C. Brodrick : *English Land and English Landlords* (1881), p. 166. Cf. Clapham : *Economic History of Modern Britain*, Vol. 2, p. 253.
44 Walpole's *Russell*, p. 63.
45 Holland's *Devonshire*. Palmerston to Devonshire, Feb. 7, 1863,Vol. 1, p. 55.
46 H. W. C. Davis : *Age of Grey and Peel*, pp. 269-70.
47 C. S. Emden : *The People and the Constitution*, p. 147.
48 Hansard : 59, 3rd series, p. 71.
49 C. S. Emden : *The People and the Constitution*, p. 148.
50 *Letters of Queen Victoria*, 1837-43, Vol. 1, pp. 167-8, May 10, 1839.
51 ibid., Vol. 2, p. 91. July 16, Queen to Russell.
52 ibid., Vol. 2, pp. 62-3. Dec. 21, 1845, Peel to the Queen.
53 Parker's *Graham*, Vol. 2, p. 42.
54 Disraeli to Derby, Dec. 19, 1853.
55 Parker's *Graham*, Vol. 2, pp. 198-9.
56 Morley's *Gladstone*, Vol. 1, p. 527.
57 Fitzmaurice's *Granville*, Vol. 1, p. 293.
58 Parker's *Graham*, Vol. 2, p. 376.
59 Fitzmaurice's *Granville*, Vol. 1, pp. 340-41.
60 Greville : *Journal*, Aug. 15, 1835.
61 Morley's *Gladstone*, Vol. 1, p. 631.
62 *Later Correspondence of Lord John Russell*, Vol. 2, p. 351.
63 A. D. Elliott's *Goschen*, Vol. 1, p. 84.
64 Parker's *Graham*, Vol. 2, p. 316.
65 Buckle's *Disraeli*, Vol. 4, p. 405.
66 J. Redlich : *The Procedure of the House of Commons* (1908 edition), Vol. 1, Book 1, Part 2, for material here used.
67 Parker's *Graham*, Vol. 1, pp. 288-9.
68 ibid., Vol. 1, p. 239.
69 W. H. Dawson : *Cobden and Foreign Policy*, p. 40.
70 Buckle's *Disraeli*, Vol. 4, p. 164.

[71] Parker's *Graham*, Vol. 1, Chap. XV.
[72] Greville : *Journal*, Sept. 17, 1841.
[73] Temperley : *Crimea*, p. 253.
[74] ibid., p. 279.
[75] ibid, p. 299.
[76] *Cambridge History of British Foreign Policy*, Vol. 3, p. 571.
[77] See *Memoranda of Prince Albert*, August 5 and 8, 1850, *Queen Victoria Letters*, 1837–61, Vol. 2, pp. 260–264.
[78] *Cambridge History of Foreign Policy*, Vol. 2, pp. 328–30.
[79] ibid., p. 337.
[80] July 31, 1859.
[81] Fitzmaurice : *Granville*, Vol. 1, pp. 457–9.
[82] ibid., Vol. 2, p. 356.
[83] *Cambridge History of Foreign Policy*, Vol. 3, p. 8.
[84] ibid., Vol. 2, p. 292.
[85] Temperley : *Crimea*, p. 338.
[86] *Cambridge History of Foreign Policy*, Vol. 2, p. 357.
[87] ibid., Vol. 3, p. 28.

CHAPTER III

THE MACHINERY OF ADMINISTRATION, 1832-70

Administration and the Oligarchy—Development of Government
Departments : War Office—Admiralty—Foreign Office—Board of Trade
—Local Government Board—The Treasury—Civil Service Reform—
The character of the Civil Service—Of the Judiciary—And of Local
Government.

THE industrial revolution compelled the State to create a
machinery of administration almost as complex as the new
machinery of industry itself. The eighteenth-century conception of liberty, equality and justice had to be protected
against the inequality and violence implicit in an uncontrolled
industrial revolution. The growth of industry would have
created a new and more unequal feudalism had not the democratic State produced administrative devices for the protection of the elements of social justice against the principalities
and powers of greed.

But it was inevitable that a representative government
should suffer from the defective planning of its administrative machinery. For, when government is based upon persuasion, continuity with the past is often a political duty when
revolution is an administrative necessity. In England the
history of every government department is almost as complex
as the history of the constitution itself. In each department
there have been revolutions, restorations, in a few cases,
almost civil war between conflicting personalities and policies,
while over all has lain a thickening crust of custom.

Every department of the State has been profoundly affected
by the circumstances of its origin. Some go back to the great
offices of a feudal monarchy: the Lord High Treasurer,

89

the Lord High Admiral, the Lord Chancellor; others have derived from the peculiar development of the office of the Secretary of State in the struggle between Parliament and the King; others have had their origin in committees of the Privy Council—which has been used as a kind of potting shed for new administrative plants.   Even those which have been established by the legislation of the last hundred years bear in their powers and organization marks of the political conditions under which they were set up.   Of the older departments only the research of scholars in dusty archives can trace the process by which they emerged; of the more recent, while their legal framework may be found in statutes and official orders, their real working is only to be darkly seen in the evidence produced before committees of enquiry and in the material scattered here and there in the biographies of statesmen.

The complex law of the prerogative, the exigencies of responsible government, the political tradition of *laissez-faire* have all left their mark upon our executive machinery. What the United States has suffered from the tyranny of a written constitution we have suffered from that burden of the past which so firmly rides many of our executive departments. " The rusty curb of old father antique, the law " is in the mouth of every bureaucrat. Our system of government is haunted by the ghosts of extinct offices and confused by a terminology which might have been deliberately designed to confuse appearance and reality. Our councils are not councils, our committees are not committees; nor are our boards boards, or our commissioners, commissioners. Every Minister presides over not only a part of the machinery of government of the modern state but also over a legal museum which illustrates the continuity of our constitutional development.

There was throughout the nineteenth century " an obstinate prejudice against the organization of a competent bureaucracy ".[1]   There was little progress in reconciling the compromise which government by discussion compels with the simplicity of form that technical development requires. Responsible government may require that any detail of administration may be made the occasion of a political battle, yet it is on the development of a political sagacity that will not butcher an administration to make a party holiday that the stability of democracy depends.

The development of English administrative machinery was stunted by the continuity of her political and legal tradition. We paid too big a price in administrative immaturity for our national tradition of gradualness.   The drama of politics attracted much of the ability that should have gone to the drudgery of administration.   The Henry Irving tradition in the drama had its political counterpart in the Prime Minister actor-manager.   The allocation of political talent among the different departments was determined too much by the traditional prestige of the departments and too little by their real social and political importance.   It was almost in the first half of the century an insult to offer an able statesman the Department of Education, the Colonial Office, or the Department of Woods and Forests which controlled our drains and health.   Not until the 'nineties did our politicians begin to discover the importance of being earnest in such matters as the structure of Local Government or the provision of higher education.   In the first half of the century only the toughest eccentricity could secure serious administrative changes in the face of the tremendous complacency of the legal and political traditions.   A man had to be obsessed with one idea or be a hardened egoist to break down the obstruction of the official world—a Brougham in law, an Owen in industry, a Chadwick in health, or a Wakefield in colonial affairs.   A measure of efficiency in Local Government was only secured with the grim assistance of the cholera.   If there were many who would rather see England free than sober, there were others who would rather see Englishmen dead than governed. Education, like Peter Pan, seemed as though it would never grow up. Only the threat of German and American industrial supremacy and the fortunate accident that, in Morant, at the Board of Education, there was a civil servant whose experience of the dynastic and religious feuds of Siam equipped him to understand the Anglican and Nonconformist minds, produced at long last the Education Act of 1902.

The development of our government departments in their modern form may be taken as beginning in 1782, when the secretariat which, throughout the eighteenth century had been divided into a Northern and a Southern department, the one dealing with Northern Europe and the other with Southern Europe and a variety of miscellaneous duties was reorganized. The Northern department became the Foreign Office, and the Southern the Home Office, with Irish and Colonial business attached. From the latter have been budded off the different Secretaries of State as the pressure of war and social change compelled.

In 1794 Pitt appointed a Secretary for War, but there was no clear definition of his duties. In 1798 he was made Secretary for War and Colonies because our army was mainly concerned with the capture of scattered colonies. But his responsibilities were not clearly defined because there existed a Secretary at War with an undefined responsibility for finance, and a Commander-in-Chief who was the representative of the King as head of the Army. The War Office was, in fact, destined to suffer every ill that an administrative body can be heir to. In 1904 a committee reported that " its organization had been built up piecemeal as the result of constant changes and compromises while fundamental principles were subordinated to temporary exigencies or to personal and political considerations ". Since the seventeenth century an efficient Army had been suspect as an instrument of despotism. What Army we had had to be organized, not for the protection of a land frontier, but for the defence of scattered possessions overseas. Confusion was confounded by the constitutional principle that the sovereign was head of the Army. This effectively prevented the development of the clear responsibility of a Secretary of State to Parliament for its efficiency. Instead of a Secretary *for* War there emerged in the eighteenth century a Secretary *at* War who, once the subordinate secretary to the Commander-in-Chief in the field, had acquired an anomalous and imperfectly defined responsibility for military questions in the House of Commons. So we began the nineteenth century with a Secretary *at* War who had an undefined responsibility for finance; a Secretary *for* War who was also the Secretary for the Colonies; and a Commander-in-Chief, whose relations to both no one could define. Finally, the Home Office was responsible for the relation between the military and the civilians.

After the Reform Bill of 1832 the establishment of the clear responsibility of a Secretary for War to Parliament was opposed by Wellington as a dodge of the Whigs to destroy the Army and debase the Crown. He determined that the Whig dogs should get no military bones. Largely through his influence, the Commander-in-Chief retained control of patronage and discipline in the Army and when, in 1856, the Duke of Cambridge, cousin to the Queen, was made Commander-in-Chief so that the obstinate personality of Queen Victoria was enlisted in defence of his powers, a wisely-planned War Office became a political dream.

At the outbreak of the Crimean War the Army was managed by seven separate departments with sleepy inefficiency. For the War Office was " a very slow office, an enormously expensive office, a not very efficient office, and one in which the Ministers' intentions can be entirely negatived by all his sub-departments and those of each of the sub-departments by every other ".[2]

(1) The Secretary of State for War and Colonies was responsible for the general control of the Army. Though in time of peace responsibility for general control meant little more than responsibility for its size, in time of war it meant responsibility for major strategy. The staff of his office did not include a single soldier. (2) The Commander-in-Chief was responsible for the discipline of the Army; but he could take no action involving any cost without the Secretary for War, and had no control over the troops outside the United Kingdom. (3) The Secretary at War was responsible for the estimates and the protection of civilians from the military, but he had no control over the material of the Army. These were under (4) the Master General and the Board of Ordnance with a constitution going back to Queen Elizabeth. The Master General supplied material for the Army at the request of the Secretary for War, and for the Artillery and Engineers at the demand of the Chancellor of the Exchequer. The Board met without the Master being present and he could rescind all they did without discussion. (5) The Commissariat Department was responsible for the provisioning of the Army abroad. It had its headquarters at the Treasury and its own officials abroad. Because during the Napoleonic wars financial experts were necessary to secure there should not be undue competition for bills which officers then drew on the Treasury, they were now to be responsible for the health and feeding of the troops. " By sheer force of routine the troops abroad were fed chiefly upon salt meat."[3] (6) The Home Secretary was responsible for the use of the military in Great Britain, as before 1846 the Army was the only effective police. Finally (7), the Board of General Officers clothed the cavalry and infantry of the Army. As Albert complained to Granville, " English statesmen never look at any subject as a part of a whole ". Nobody ever asked themselves the question " Why we wanted an army?" and then " what that Army should be ".[4]

The Crimean War secured some reorganization.   In 1854 the Secretary of State for the Colonies was separated from the Secretary of State for War.   But though the Secretary of State for War was now free for new duties there was no thorough reorganization.   Against the realization of a War Office dealing with the Army as a whole, there was a tacit combination of Court, Tory and bureaucratic influence, before which Parliament was helpless.[5]   The Army Medical Board and the Board of General Officers passed under the control of the Secretary for War.   The militia and yeomanry, which had been transferred to the Secretary at War from the Home Office in 1852, were transferred in 1855 to the Secretary for War.[6]   In 1854, against the vigorous protest of Sir Charles Trevelyan, the Treasury was deprived of the Commissariat.[7]   In May, 1855, the Letters Patent of the Board of Ordnance, which dated back to the fourteenth century, were revoked and its duties divided between the Commander-in-Chief and the Secretary for War.   The Commander-in-Chief became responsible for the administration of the Artillery and the Engineers, while the Secretary of State undertook the supervision of the civil side of the Board's activities.   The Secretary of State was given the office of Secretary of State at War until that office was abolished in 1863.[8]   But no real effort was made to make the new office an organized whole and the real cause of the muddle, the dual control of the Secretary of State for War and the Commander-in-Chief remained.

When, in 1860, a Select Committee on Military Organization, presided over by Sir James Graham, examined their relation, neither of these two high officers could clearly explain their relations.   But, in fact, the Commander-in-Chief was becoming gradually and imperceptibly more and more dependent upon the Secretary for War, as the Army could not exist without certain services which were entirely supervised by the Parliamentary head of the War Office.[9]

The Northbrook Committee recommended in 1869 that the War Office should be divided into three departments: (1) The Commander-in-Chief, who was to be the sole military adviser of the Secretary of State and in charge of the regular Army and auxiliary forces; (2) the Surveyor-General of Ordnance, who was to be responsible for supply, transport, clothing and munitions of war, including the purchase, construction and charge of material; and (3) the Financial Secretary, who was to control all the financial business of the Army. The Committee also considered that it was essential that the Commander-in-Chief should be under the same roof as the Secretary of State for War.[10] At the same time Cardwell, Secretary of State for War in the Gladstone Cabinet of 1868-74, claimed full responsibility for the Secretary of State.[11] By the War Office Act of 1870 the Secretary of State became responsible for Army business as a whole, and his duties were defined in an Order in Council of June 4th of that year which placed the Commander-in-Chief in a position of complete subordination to the political head of the department.[12] The War Office was divided into three departments of the Commander-in-Chief, the Surveyor-General of Ordnance and the Financial Secretary.[13] But though the offices of the Commander-in-Chief were removed from the Horse Guards to Whitehall in loyalty to his spiritual home, he continued to write his letters under the address " Horse Guards, Pall Mall ".[14]

Compared with the War Office the Admiralty in the nineteenth century seemed a model department. The basis of its organization was laid down by Sir James Graham in 1832. He reformed a dual organization which, inherited from Elizabeth, was not working without friction. There were two departments: the Admiralty Office and the Naval Board. The Admiralty Office was the department of the Lord High Admiral which, since 1708, had been put in commission and dealt with appointments, promotions, the

movement of ships and the control of general policy.   The
Navy Board, subordinate to the Admiralty Office, dealt with
the management of ships, dockyard accounts, stores, victual-
ing and transport.   Graham transferred the duties of the
Navy Board to five principal officers, under the direct control
of the Board of Admiralty, each department being placed
under a superintending Lord, who represented it at the
Admiralty.

This concentration of power on the grounds of efficiency
and economy was open to serious criticism.   Even in the
eighteenth century the Board of Admiralty had had too much
to do.   Its administrative duties had interfered with its consideration of higher problems of policy in the preparation
and conduct of war.   Graham's centralization abolished the
Admiralty Board as an independent, superior Board, concerned primarily with the function of command, undisturbed
by details of management.   " It was apparently supposed
. . . that the work of planning and conducting war could be
performed simultaneously with the departmental duties."[15]
The Board was, in fact, to suffer severely from undue
centralization and confusion between its powers as a whole
and those of the individual members.   The Board met daily
and almost all the business of the Admiralty was brought
before it by the several Lords for decision and consideration.
By 1861 the Lords were working at least ten hours a day.[16]
As the powers of the Lord High Admiral were vested in the
Board, the First Lord had no authority to give orders alone.[17]
The exact power of the Board were by no means clear because
they were derived from a patent which referred their powers
to the Lord High Admiral and his powers had depended
largely on usage.   Graham, examined by a Committee in
1861, thought that no new " patent would carry all the
powers which by usage, prescription and former patents have
been exercised and any omission might be fatal at a moment
of extreme urgency ".[18]   The First Lord was specially

G

concerned with the efficiency and strength of the fleet. But no Lord was specially charged with responsibility for finance. The position of the Controller of the Navy was anomalous, for he conducted the work of the dockyards outside the Board acting under the First Lord, but with no civilian to control his expenditure. Absorption in administrative business not only took the Board's attention away from the problem of strategy but also from those of tactics.[19] By Order in Council, in 1869, the Board was extensively reorganized. The First Lord was made responsible for all the business of the Admiralty and the others were to be his assistants. The duties of the Board were divided into three branches: material, personnel and finance.

In the organization and work of the Foreign Office there has been a continuous, if slow, progress towards greater representation and greater efficiency.[20] The existence of constitutional government made it necessary that English statesmen should put more truths on paper that those of other countries so that as early as 1815 documents were more carefully kept and the organization of the office was in advance of that of other countries.[21] The establishment of a modernized procedure and rules of business dates from Canning (1820-27),[22] and from his time the diplomacy of the nineteenth century was carried on by what was for the times a highly-organized machine.[23] For though a powerful Foreign Secretary might master every detail of the office, yet the policy which he directed was the product of a number of different processes, carried out by an office machine increasing rapidly in size. In 1828 the Foreign Office sent out 5,000 dispatches; in 1853 the number was 35,000; in 1854, 49,000.[24] When in 1851 the Queen required that Lord Palmerston should take no action of importance before her pleasure had been consulted she was requiring an administrative impossibility. The battle which Palmerston then lost was gradually won by the growing complexity of the business of the Office.[25] In the 'sixties the hierarchy of the Foreign Office consisted of the Secretary of State, the permanent Under-Secretary and the transitory Parliamentary Secretary; an Assistant Under-Secretary had been added in 1858; then came the Chief Clerk and three others to deal with audit, estimates and accounts.   Eight Senior Clerks, each with an assistant, had charge of one of the eight divisions under which, for Foreign Office business, the countries of the world were grouped.[26]   In the 'seventies the Foreign Office was composed of four departments: the Political Department, which alone dealt with policy; the Librarian's Department; the Treaty Department; and the Chief Clerk's Department, which was purely financial.

In the staffing of the office a revolution was begun in 1856 when Clarendon introduced a qualifying entrance examination.   This was not severe, but a nomination from the Secretary of State was first required and after appointment there was a probationary period, both exacting and effective.   Granville stiffened the examination that only those who had spent at least four years swallowing languages abroad and many months being crammed with geographical minutæ could hope to succeed.   The essential principle of Foreign Office appointments was that while it was desirable to eliminate patronage, because it imposed on the Foreign Secretary the invidious task of both remembering his relations and not forgetting his friends, only gentlemen should be admitted to the competitive field.   In the diplomatic world a wide gulf was thought to yawn between the mere expert and the accomplished man of the world.   It was said that a hundred spies could not ascertain so much as an English gentleman, whom princes and ministers believed that they could safely trust.[27]   Not until 1822 was the first attempt made to create a salaried diplomatic service responsible to the State and not merely part of the Ambassadors' family circle.   But the idea of the Ambassadors' " family " remained throughout the nineteenth century and not until after the war of 1914-18 was the diplomatic service assimilated to that of the Foreign Office. In the Foreign Office itself the system of nomination, while it secured that the Secretary of State felt the same responsibility for the efficiency of his office that a colonel of a crack regiment may feel for the warlike and social qualities of his officers, had the disadvantage that gilded youth, however intelligent, was wasted on routine work that could as well have been performed by competent clerks. But the closeness of its relations with the Queen and the prestige which it derived from its responsibility for affairs of blood and State prolonged, for the Foreign Office, the period of class-conscious puerilities. It is significant that the able Secretaries of State for Foreign Affairs were often exasperated by the inefficiency of its gilded youths and dusty seniors.

The Board of Trade is an excellent example of the fortunes which shape and warp an English Department of State. In the eighteenth century there had been a Committee of the Privy Council—" the Lord Commissioners for promoting the trade of our Kingdom and for inspecting and improving our plantations in America and elsewhere ". This possessed advisory powers only, and for execution depended upon the instrumentality of a Secretary of State. With the industrial revolution its influence declined. In its offices Gibbon enjoyed his " days and weeks of repose without being called from the library to the office ". In 1784 Pitt established a Consultative Committee and in 1786 a board intended to be a permanent part of the machinery of government dealing with problems of trade. " The original idea of the Board of Trade was that it was a board composed of men whose opinions and judgment upon all commercial questions submitted to them was of a kind to carry great weight with the public and the Government . . . (its reports) became State papers and the ground work for the Imperial policy of the State upon commercial questions." But the collective authority of the Board of Trade as a deliberative committee did not survive the Napoleonic Wars. It became a mere meeting of the President and Vice-President, and two secretaries. In 1853 the minute-book was discontinued and a departmental register substituted. Moreover, its powers were entirely transformed by the development of free trade and the industrial revolution. For free trade meant that tariffs were regarded merely as a matter of revenue to be decided by the Treasury, while commercial policy became a mere appendage to the system of power and prestige controlled by the Foreign Office. In Palmerston's time negotiations for commercial treaties were referred to the Board of Trade.[28] In the 'fifties Cardwell was of the opinion that it should only advise on matters which came specially under its cognizance in connection with its executive duties.[29] In the 'sixties the Treasury did not consult it on tariff changes,[30] nor was it consulted by the India Office and but seldom by the Colonial Office.[31] But while the Board of Trade was losing its significance as a department for the determination of commercial policy, its executive functions were rapidly and confusingly growing as the State became responsible for conditions of industry and trade. From the 'forties it was entrusted with the administration of various statutes regulating railways, shipping and company organization. A report of 1854 said that fresh business had been heaped upon it without reorganization. It was divided into four distinct departments, each with a separate class of clerks and a separate class of messengers. There was no security that correspondence would not be carried on by two departments on one and the same subject, each ignorant of what the other was doing. After 1870 we shall see that it developed into a complex structure, a federation of departments, whose separate technical and executive duties over-shadowed its consultative functions as a whole.

In 1872, when the old Board of Trade was abolished, Colonial business was entrusted to the Home Secretary,

assisted, after 1786, by a Committee of the Privy Council.
In 1801 the Secretary for War and Colonies was made
responsible for both war and colonies. By him they, too,
have been shamefully neglected. " Colonial Governors
reported crises, complained of their wrongs and even died
without the Minister seeming to be aware of the fact."[32] But
in 1812, with Bathurst and Goulburn as Under-Secretaries,
the nucleus of a true Colonial Office came into being. It
had the disadvantage that its Secretaries of State rarely
remained more than three years in office; but it enjoyed the
advantage of a succession of able and long-serving permanent
secretaries. Its work was inevitably complex, for our colonial
possessions, after the disruption of the first British Empire
by the Declaration of Independence, was a thing of shreds
and patches. It must often have seemed to the permanent
secretary that his was the head upon which all " the ends of
the world are come " and to his critics he seemed a little
weary.   " One day the Colonial Secretary is in Ceylon a
financial and religious reformer promoting the interests of
the planters and casting discredit on the religion of Bhudda,
the next day he is in the West Indies teaching the economical
manufacture of sugar, or in Van Diemens striving to reform
the fiends that he has transplanted to that pandemonium; now
he is in Canada dealing with a war of races; at the Cape of
Good Hope dancing a war dance with his Kaffir subjects; or
in New Zealand an unsuccessful Lycurgus."[33]   When, in
1854, it was made a separate department it had to fight hard
to establish its claim to have the final decision in all matters
except those involving important foreign or financial policy.
The delays for which it was often blamed were due as much
to the procrastination of other departments which it had to
consult and the niggardliness of the Treasury, as to its own
shortcomings. A question about the transportation of con-
victs would involve the Treasury, the Home Office, the
Ordnance Department, the Inspector of Prisons, and the agent

of the colony!   All financial dispatches had to be referred to the Treasury; all tariff dispatches to the Treasury or the Board of Trade; all convict dispatches to the Home Office; and all the question of land and immigration to the Commissioners concerned.   The Treasury and the Board of Trade were at loggerheads about the limits of their jurisdiction and " while adjusting between themselves points of etiquette " the two boards agreed in the leaving the business undone. Correspondence was " uselessly and idly protracted by certain departmental feelings of dignity or independence indulged in on all sides at the expense of the public services ".   The transfer of Malaya from the India to the Colonial Office took seven years to effect, mainly because of the wrangles between the India and the War Office.[34]

But it is the development of the Poor Law and Public Health Departments that best illustrate the interplay of experience of theory and the pressure of casual emergencies.

The administrative machinery of the new Poor Law in 1834 was the outcome of a national emergency and a political philosophy.   The administration of the new scheme was given to three commissioners who were not members of Parliament; the policy of the new code was based on a simple faith that if the market for labour were uncorrupted by charity, private or public, the labourer would be found worthy of a hire ample to maintain a citizen and his family.   Both the policy of the new Poor Law and the administrative machinery for its application were severely modified by experience.   From the deterrent Poor Law was to develop a system of State control of public health and of the organization of the labour market and from the three commissioners the Ministry of Health of 1919.

The administrative device of conducting a public department by an authority independent of Parliament broke down. " Parliament poked at it until it made it impossible . . . the House of Commons would not let the Commissioners alone.

For a long time it was defended because the Whig Lords had made the Commission and felt bound, as a party, to protect it . . . but afterwards the Commissioners were left to their intrinsic weakness . . . the Commission had to be dissolved and a Parliamentary head was added." The three kings of Somerset House, as the Commissioners had been derisively called were superseded by a Poor Law Board—though why a Board has never been explained. But with due solemnity a collegiate authority was established—the Minister even being endowed with a casting vote in case his fictitious colleagues should prove to be equally divided in opinion. In practice the civil servants took the place of the Poor Law Commissioners (Webb). Their lucid and didactic reports gave place to the dull and colourless effusions which are a department's protective colouring against possible Parliamentary attack. They must be dull enough to be above suspicion.

In the meantime the early reports of the Commissioners had laid bare the relation between poverty and ill-health. If the Englishman's home was his castle it could not be defended by the owner against disease. Chadwick, in 1848, secured the appointment of a Board of Health for five years, with himself as one of the Commissioners. This, like the Poor Law Commission, was not responsible to Parliament, though one of its members was a Government representative. It consisted of the Head of the Office of Woods and Forests, an unpaid member, and two paid members. With cholera about Chadwick was tolerated, but without the cholera he was too much for opinion and the constitution. In 1854 the Board was reformed, Chadwick and Southwood Smith being deposed, and made to consist of a President and ex-officio members, i.e., the President and Vice-President of the Board of Trade and the Principal Secretary of State. Internal disagreements followed between the ex-officio members and the working members; antagonism was aroused in the

engineering profession, and resentment in the localities.   In
1858 the Board was abolished.   Its scientific and medical
functions went to the public health branch of the Privy
Council; its local government powers to the local government section of the Home Office; while the Admiralty and
War Office were appropriately selected for the control of
contagious diseases.   For some decades the countryside was
in the happy position that a complaint as to the condition of
privies would go to the Home Office, while the fever they
had caused might be studied by the Privy Council.

The result of this interplay of new theories, tactless
administrators and cautious politicians was revealed by
the Royal Sanitary Commission of 1871.   They reported
that a single and powerful Ministry was necessary
" not to centralize authority but to set local life in
motion ".   Economy and efficiency demanded that there
should be a single authority for two subjects so necessarily
cognate as public health and the relief of destitution.   " Sanitary laws must bear a constant ratio to Poor Law, the one
making provision for health, while Poor Laws are necessary
for the relief of destitution of which sickness is both cause and
effect; so that Local Government . . . seems most capable of
being arranged into two departments under one common
head."   A timid and unconvinced Cabinet merged three
scattered departments: the Public Health branch of the
Privy Council, the Local Authorities branch of the Home
Office, and the Poor Law Board itself into a new Ministry,
the Local Government Board of 1871.

How has the technique of co-operation between the Treasury and the other departments been secured?   Its achieve-
ment was one of the triumphs of Victorian bureaucracy.   The
foundation was laid by the Exchequer and Audit Act of 1866.
Before that the Treasury was both ignorant and despotic.   In
1853 Northcote and Trevelyan reported that " at the
Treasury neither the political nor the permanent officers . . .

possess . . . personal knowledge of any portion of that vast extent of civil and military business which they have to control . . . the internal arrangements and regulations of the different departments are very imperfectly understood at the Treasury and the general supervision with which that office is charged on behalf of the public is either entirely omitted or performed in . . . a loose, superficial and perfunctory manner". The reason for its inefficiency was that, though since the revolution of 1688 Parliament had controlled expenditure by appropriating annual grants to specific purposes, it had not provided for any clear accounts of the way in which, in fact, they might be spent. The only information available as to the way the money had been expended was that given by the Chancellor of the Exchequer in his annual Budget speech. Even the finance accounts which were begun in 1802 were ineffective because they gave only the issues from the Exchequer to the departments with no details as to how the money had actually been spent. "It somehow escaped the financial genius of Pitt and Peel that control of the Estimates was ineffective unless the House of Commons also knew how its grants had been expended— Chancellors of the Exchequer, their advisers and Parliament itself were still under the illusion that Parliamentary control over expenditure could be effectively secured by safeguards in the issue of money from the Exchequer without following the expenditure further." Although in 1831 Sir J. Graham, at the Admiralty, began the reform by securing that an annual balance sheet should be laid before the House of Commons, based on an audited account and showing the actual expenditure under each head of service, down to 1854 the cost of collecting the public revenue was defrayed out of the gross revenue and was not specially voted by the House; nor were the accounts of the Treasury itself subject to an outside audit. In 1857 a powerful committee recommended that the appropriation check applied to the Navy in 1832 should be extended to all departments and that " these audited accounts be annually submitted to the revision of a committee of the House of Commons nominated by the Speaker ". In 1861 Gladstone moved and carried the appointment of a Public Accounts Committee and in 1866 the Exchequer and Audit Act replaced the separate controller of the Exchequer and the Board of Audit by a single officer, the Controller and Auditor-General. He, though appointed by the Chancellor of the Exchequer, was to hold his office like a judge, independently of the executive. This secured the formal safeguards for the control of public expenditure. Money was voted only on a vote moved by a member of the Government; the monies granted had to be specifically accounted for to an independent official and he had to report to a special committee of the House of Commons—the Public Account Committee.

The position of the Treasury was transformed. Before 1866 " Parliament, not knowing anything about audited accounts, the Treasury was absolutely autocratic; it could allow or disallow expenditure and there was nobody to check it. The audited accounts came before the Treasury, and if the auditors objected the Treasury might pass them over. At the same time the Treasury—although it was autocratic as far as the control by Parliament went—could not exercise that control beneficially because it did not know what the other departments were doing ". After 1866 the reports of the Comptroller and Auditor-General told the Treasury what the departments were doing and subjected the Treasury itself to the same supervision as was applied to them. The Treasury was now informed, controlled and responsible. The co-operation of the Public Accounts Committee, the Comptroller and Auditor-General and the Treasury secured the development of an efficient code of financial procedure. The Public Accounts Committee never considered that the Comptroller and Auditor-General should limit his reports merely to the points he was specifically bound by the terms of his appointment to bring to the notice of Parliament. He brings to the notice of Parliament any facts which in the course of his audit he discovers may indicate improper expenditure or waste. At the close of the South African War he drew attention to the dual system of contracts by which large sales of surplus stock were made to contractors concurrently with the purchase of similar stock from the same gentlemen at an enhanced cost.[35]

After 1832 it was impossible that the old system by which the public services were the outdoor-relief department of the aristocracy should long continue. When the scale of government was small the skilled assistance required by a Pitt or a Canning could be found among their private friends, while the routine work could be left to the attentions of party patronage. But the scale of government changed. The kindness of patrons to incompetence had been partly responsible for the loss of America. Was the second British Empire to be lost for the same cause? The administration of Ireland had taught Sir Robert Peel the necessity for integrity in the public service. The revolution of 1848 gave everyone a shock and created a disposition to put their house in order. The Crimean War suggested that if Britons had never yet been slaves, their freedom was due more to geography and luck than to the efficiency of the War Office. In India it was becoming obvious that while empires might be won by adventure they could only be kept by competent administration. Organization and integrity could alone retain what genius and luck had won. At home the advance of industry and science meant that the traditional governing class had to fortify themselves with technical and professional advisers in matters strange and new, like factory legislation and sanitation. The State had to take over the elements of the new knowledge that was being won in the factory and the laboratory. The period following the industrial revolution was an age of tough and eccentric reformers. A sensitive statesman or head of a department may well have desired skilled assistance to meet the trenchant criticisms of a Wakefield or a Chadwick.

The growth of industry would have destroyed the State, created a new and more unequal feudalism had there not been developed a new science of administration to be the servant of representative government. The development of the Civil Service was contemporaneous with the reorganization of the learned professions—medicine—engineering, and even the law. The development of organized professions in all branches of knowledge compelled the professionalizing of the ancient craft of ruling men. This obviously raised new and subtle questions as to the nature of political freedom which we can even now only dimly see. But it was fortunate for our political life that the first steps to provide professional knowledge and trained ability at the service of the State should have taken place under favourable conditions.

It may be said it was the very slowness with which in England democratic government was substituted for aristocratic privilege that made possible the success of our Civil Service. It was rescued from private patronage without becoming public spoils. Had there been a revolution in England in 1848 the organization of the public service might have been determined on the basis of abstract political principles popular at the time. The Civil Service might have been made a crazy monument to a fanatical misunderstanding of the doctrine of the quality of man. Some uncultured Benthamite might have imposed an organization based on the cruder ideas of Gradgrind. A sudden introduction of universal suffrage might have caused the public service to be enrolled as one of the battalions in the battle between the Ins and the Outs of party warfare. It happened otherwise. An aristocracy was on the defensive and compelled to improve its efficiency if it were to survive. Instead of a sweeping change which might have left the new organization open to the destructive influence of all those forces in a nascent popular government which may cause despotism or corruption, the changes in the English political system and its administrative machinery were so slow as to enable them to secure the best of both worlds—the dying *noblesse oblige* and the disinterested scientific service struggling to be born. To say this is not to claim that the course of administrative change in England in the nineteenth century might not have been swifter and more thorough than it was, but merely to emphasize the blessings that, in fact, were secured and the possible dangers avoided.

It is against this background that we should set the report of a Treasury committee (the Northcote and Trevelyan report of 1853) which thoroughly examined the staffing and organization of the existing Government departments. It is one of the most important State papers ever published. " When ", they said, " we came to make our general report we had arrived at an ample induction and our premises were so large and we had gone with such detail into the state of the different establishments that the conclusions arrived at in our report were the necessary logical inference of what had preceded." They made three fundamental proposals: (1) that clerks should be selected by open competitive examination; (2) that in all public offices intellectual work should be separated from the merely routine and mechanical; (3) that the examination for the admission to the public services should be conducted by an authority independent of the particular department that was to employ them. That is to say the brilliant Trevelyan and the wise Northcote were led by their inductive study to state in their own way the necessity for the State to adhere to three important principles of a democratic, industrial and scientific age: the career open to talents; the division of labour; and the acceptance of the judgment of professional organizations on matters coming within their special competence—the professors were to decide who had potential ability for the service of the State.

Their proposals were acutely and bitterly discussed. Civil Service reform and particularly the competitive system was exceedingly unpopular in the House because it would deprive members of the advantage of putting their friends and relations into public offices.[36] But in their defence of the interests of their class, politicians and administrators and others of contemporary eminence in educational theory and practice brought forward arguments which have still an interest for some problems in administration that have not yet been solved. The report had said that government " could not be carried on without men possessing sufficient independence, character, ability and experience to be able to advise, assist and to some extent influence those who are from time to time set over them ". But they had found that Government service, far from being the prize of the strong, was the refuge of the weak. The absence of any test of capacity plus the certainty of provision in the case of sickness had furnished a strong inducement to the parents of sickly youths to obtain appointments for them. Admission to the public service was eagerly sought after by the " unambitious, the indolent or the incapable ". While no pains were taken in the first instance to secure a good man for the office nothing was done after a clerk's appointment to turn his abilities, whatever they might be, to the best account. Ability might be passed over to satisfy the whim of a patron. Thus a vicious circle had been set up. " Civil servants were habitually superseded because they were incompetent and were incompetent because they were superseded." Northcote and Trevelyan proposed to harness to the services of the State the strongest of all motives, the desire to excel. They were for the full rigour of the game of competitive examinations both as a safeguard against patronage and as an incentive to ambition. A mere qualifying examination, they said, would repudiate all ideas of excellence and make possible the return of patronage in the method of selecting from among those who were qualified. The examination they said " should be in all cases a competing literary examination ". They saw no other mode by which (in the case of inferior no less than superior offices) the double object can be attained of electing the fittest person, and of avoiding the evils of patronage. " The examination should be based on the subjects studied at the universities and not on any technical knowledge that might afterwards be required by the successful candidate in his work. Only by throwing the examination entirely open could the proper class of candidate be attracted." Proficiency in " history, jurisprudence, political economy, modern languages, political and physical geography, besides the staple of classics and mathematics, should be made directly conducive to the success of young men desirous of entering into public service ". " We believe that men who have been engaged up to two or one and twenty with studies which have no immediate connection with the business of any profession, of which the immediate effect is merely to open, to invigorate and to enrich the mind will generally be found in the business of every profession superior to men who have at eighteen or nineteen devoted themselves to the special duties of their calling." A judgment which, though it might result in the then educational organization of England in making the public service the monopoly of a privileged class, is certainly true and was particularly valuable as securing a tradition of general culture against the narrow specialism that a desire for economy and the coarser tradition of the competitive industry might have imposed.

To these proposals the men most experienced in the public service offered criticisms sometimes foolish and sometimes shrewd. As they were Englishmen defending a privilege they wrote many high-sounding phrases about character.

Sir G. C. Lewis said that men of intellectual ability were not necessarily trustworthy; James Booth, Secretary to the Board of Trade, thought that " the lower you descend in the social scale the less probability was there that the candidate would possess the moral qualities which are more important than the intellectual in the important business of life ". Nineteenth-century Christians may have believed that it was difficult for a rich man to enter the kingdom of heaven, but they found it difficult to believe that the poor could deserve to. Inspired as many of them were by the Puritan conception of a calling they could not avoid confusing it with a sense of social distinction. Unto him that had social standing had been given the virtue that deserved it. Stephen thought that competition would not secure that " strange faculty of dominance which seems to stand apart from other powers of the mind and is not increased by polished cultivation ". Others suggested that no " man of ability would submit himself to an arduous examination in order to earn a post so ill-paid, obscure, and subordinate " as that of a Government clerk. What young man crowned with the highest Oxford or Cambridge honours would enter a calling that would at the best make him a chief clerk the day that his friend became a bishop or a judge?

Hammond, of the Foreign Office, thought that all his clerks ought to come from the same social class. Addington went so far as to claim that in the Foreign Office, by every clerk entering as a copying clerk and working his way up, an office had been developed unsurpassed if not unequalled in its working power. Romilly feared the democratization of the Civil Service, while the legislature remained aristocratic. Graham, a timid constitutional purist, wrote to Gladstone, " It is clear that if this measure be adopted the reign of patronage is at an end. . . . I am not certain that

H

parliamentary government can be conducted on such principles of purity. . .   It leaves the House of Commons, . . . that mighty engine, without its accustomed regulator at the very moment when you are about to increase its powers ". He thought that " jobbing was a part, though an ugly part of the price a free people pay for constitutional liberty ". Others protested that the competitive system was too high a code for a lax world; that it was too uncharitable, leaving no shelter for the weak and helpless.   Others feared that to abolish patronage in the State would mean that it would be attacked in the Church with results that good Churchmen might boggle to consider.   The heads of the departments were, of course, in favour of electing their own recruits for their particular department whether a test were imposed or not.   In short, most of the arguments showed the naïveté and the shrewdness found in club and counting-house with here and there a touch of common-room facetiousness.[37]

J. S. Mill thought that " open competition would be one of the great public improvements, the adoption of which would form an epoch in history.   The knowledge that the Government would bestow its gifts according to merit and not according to favour would be a moral revolution in the lowest classes ".   This, the essential principle of the Northcote and Trevelyan report was not fully applied until 1870.   In 1854 the Aberdeen Government expressed its intention in the Queen's Speech to reform the Civil Service, but was replaced by the Government of Lord Palmerston which was not quite so convinced of the evils of patronage.   However, in 1855, three Civil Service Commissioners were appointed to conduct the " examination of the young men proposed to be appointed to any of the junior situations in the civil establishments ".   This secured that new appointments to the junior ranks could be made from among those pronounced qualified by an authority independent of the authority appointing them.   But such a method of appointment was not obligatory on the heads of departments, though the Superannuation Act of 1859 brought pressure to bear by providing that no one should be eligible for a pension unless they possessed the certificate of the Civil Service Commissioners. But a mere qualifying test was found to be worse than useless. It merely stereotyped mediocrity and concealed bad appointments. Nor was the device of a limited competition any better, for it enabled the Minister to retain in practice his power of nomination while relieved of any sense of responsibility. It was quite possible for an unreal competitive test to be held between the nominee it was intended to appoint and two gentlemen (sometimes known as the Treasury idiots), who could be relied upon to be beaten however weak their opponent might be. The Civil Service secured neither the advantages of competition nor those of patronage. A committee of 1860, fearful of offending vested interests, contented themselves with insisting that there should be a real, though limited, competition. For ten years the Civil Service was recruited from among nominated candidates who had passed a qualifying test of fitness. In 1870 there was a vital change. An Order in Council made a competitive test obligatory for admission to certain departmental situations. The power of the head of the department (under the Order in Council of 1855) to dispense with the certificate of the Civil Service Commissioners was withdrawn and in future the Civil Service Commissioners alone might dispense with it when moved by the head of the department and the Treasury. The power of the Treasury was extended from the region of finance into the conditions of departmental administration, for they were to approve the rules about admission that the Civil Service Commissioners and the departments might frame. Henceforward the civil servant was to be under three masters: —The Civil Service Commissioners, who held the key to the entrance to the public service and were the St. Peter of the bureaucratic heaven; the Treasury, who decided that general conditions of service to be enjoyed by those who passed the scrutiny of St. Peter; and the heads of the departments, who remained responsible for the particular careers of their staffs.

The Order in Council allowed for important exceptions to the competitive principle. A certificate of the Civil Service Commissioners was not necessary in the case of certain offices held directly from the Crown, in the case of Section IV of the Superannuation Act of 1859, in the case of promotions from officers already within the departments, nor in the case of menial and temporary posts.

The conventions which govern the relation between the civil servants and the Minister were first clearly developed after 1832 when the new administrative technique and the financial probity required by an industrial and trading community were developed by a series of great Ministers from Peel to Asquith. It was during this period that the technique of Treasury control, which was the administrative counter-part of middle-class policy and the elimination of patronage, was carried through. But it was also the time when any development of a scientifically planned bureaucracy was impossible because of the opposition of aristocratic prejudice and middle-class parsimony. We were governed mainly by brilliant amateurs with aristocratic prejudices and middle-class paymasters.

In spite of the abolition of patronage the leading civil servants were drawn from the same social class and often from the same families as the great political figures they served. " Ministers preferred to have as the permanent chiefs of their departments men of the same social standing as themselves, whom they had known at Eton or other great public schools or at Oxford or Cambridge and who, by kinship or marriage, belonged to their world." Temperament or the wealth and influence they could command led some to politics and others to the Civil Service, where power could be had without fame.   However they might differ in their views, politicians and civil servants were rarely incomprehensible to one another.   One political chief might see the world of politics as an exclusive society which it flattered his vanity to enter; another as a stage on which to show his parts; some administrators might regard their departments as a kind of club which they could run in the service of the State; others as a field for their missionary efforts.   But the relations of both were governed by a tradition as strong and uniform as that which ruled in the clubs to which they both belonged.   The effects of these old traditions has lingered on though the conditions which gave them birth has passed away.   The Civil Service still has something of the traditions of the common-room and the country house.

In the eighteenth century the permanent officials had been little more than the clerks of their political chiefs.   Chatham allowed no one but himself to take any responsibility.   It was considered a peculiarity in Mr. Pitt that he used to take a Treasury clerk into his confidence.   In 1812 the position of an Under-Secretary in the Foreign Office was little more than that of a private secretary.   Palmerston told Queen Victoria that a Minister should conduct and direct the details of his department himself.[38]   And later, Lord Salisbury was to define bureaucracy as " allowing your civil servants to think instead of doing the work yourself ".   When he was at the Foreign Office he kept the large political question in his own hands, and with his Civil Service " the asking or receiving of advice, the taking of council together did not form recognizable elements in their relations ".[39]   But this tradition of supreme subordination was peculiar to the Foreign Office, which worked often under the eye of the Queen and under several pressures of the normal Victorian atmosphere of deference.   In the Colonial Office the tradition was rather different. There the political head was often transitory and undistinguished, while the permanent secretaries were of long service—Stephen eleven years, Merivale and Rogers twelve years each, Herbert twenty-one years—and of exceptional ability. " I never ", wrote Sir J. Stephen, " served but one man (Mr. Huskisson), who extorted the concession that his was a dominant understanding; nor but one (Lord John Russell) who compelled us to feel that his was a dominant soul. The rest were throwings up of the tide of life; complacent men in high station or at best dramatists, I should say actors ". At the Treasury the prestige of station in the Minister might be mitigated by intelligence in the officials. We have the testimony of Lord Welby, who served no less than twelve Chancellors of the Exchequer, that " while Mr. Gladstone was always ready to deal with questions submitted to him . . . Lord Beaconsfield never cared for Treasury business ". " Sir Charles Wood had the reputation of taking kindly to Treasury papers " but " Sir G. Lewis preferred a classic, though ready to deal with what came before him ".[40] In new departments like the Local Government Board and the Committee of the Privy Council on Education, as also in older departments like the Home Office and the Board of Trade which had to venture into new and technical problems of administrative control, the influence of the civil servants might be far greater, especially when these departments did not secure the best Cabinet talent. Occasionally there is evidence of friction and discontent. According to Greville, " nothing ever equalled the detestation " with which Palmerston was regarded at the Foreign Office, though they did " justice to his ability and to his indefatigable industry ".[41] Despatches drafted by Hammond, the Permanent Secretary, were often redrafted by Palmerston.[42] At the Board of Trade, Gladstone considered that he had a very bad adviser in the secretary Macgregor.[43] While in the 'seventies Disraeli made sweeping and unfair judgments on the Foreign Office and our diplomatic representatives abroad.[44]

Gradually the gulf between the statesman and the civil

servant was to be widened.   In old times wrote Bagehot,
" Men like Lord Liverpool, Sir G. Rose and Mr. Huskisson
were found eminent in the public offices, and in consequence
of that eminence were brought into Parliament.   Now permanent heads never think of changing places any more than
a Hindoo thinks of becoming an Englishman ".   The abolition
of patronage did much to promote the separation.   But there
has been a steady change in the scope of the problems with
which politicians and civil servants have had to deal.   Before
1870 the life of politics was to be found in the struggle to
change the common opinions of men rather than in attempts
to mould the world in which they lived.   A great leader
could guide and educate a small electorate because he felt
and knew in himself the emotions and the thoughts which
were also theirs.

> . . . I only speak right on ;
> I tell you that which you yourselves do know.

His followers could see in him themselves writ large.   It
was not yet the function of the politician to persuade and the
bureaucracy to perform.   The ability by which the leader
got his power was often the same ability that he required to
perform what he had promised.   The politician had to apply
to politics the accepted principles of the family and business
life of an age of peace and plenty.   The problems of politics
were comfortably contained within the scope of common
morality and the common sense of business.

In the administration of justice we find in a concentrated
form all the virtues and defects of our administrative system
—insight and tenacity within an accepted tradition allied with
a readiness to produce the most fantastic theories in defence
of vested interests which are challenged by experience or
thought.   But it is not surprising that the shadow of their
glorious past should have eclipsed the reforming vigour of
our legal minds.   In English history the artificial reason

of the law has been a weapon to hack down the divinity which might have hedged a king.   Small wonder that a lawyer sometimes thinks of his profession as an art to be exercised to the glory of God rather than a technique in the service of man.   But there is another less romantic cause.   The nature of their work is such as to produce a profound belief in the value of certainty even if it is certainly wrong and a respect amounting to awe for the rights of property.   Everything in their experience tends to stress the value of certainty. They see the application of general rules in the most concrete way—to the determination of disputes that go to the heart of individual lives and fortunes.   But except for the preservation of order when they are the servants of the State, the services of lawyers have been mainly required by the rich. And in England, where the judges are selected from among the most successful advocates, there is little to modify the general tone of a profession whose highest skill must be mainly in the service of the rich.   Compare the lawyer with the doctor, and it is evident at once that except in the case of the legal members of the Civil Service there is nothing in the profession to correspond to the hospital service of the great physicians.

As judges our legal minds are trained to the most vigorous examination of the facts that are brought before them.   But to what end?   To determine whether they are such as to bring the case within a given rule.   They have no responsibility except for the determination of the facts, the application of the rule and the development of its implications.   They do not have to consider consequences except in so far as a particular decision may imply interpretation of the rule in a manner which may be illogical or confused.   But they are concerned only with the consequences to the rule and not with the consequences to those to whom the rule must apply. Their training forbids them to consider the hardship of individual cases, and if they accumulate a sense of the injustice of a given rule they have no responsibility for its reform. They see the social order only through the medium of individual cases of dispute, and there is little in their work to produce the administrators' sense of the need for continuous change.

But whatever the explanation, the facts are plain and startling. " Scarcely ever has any occupant of the bench led the way to reform. Seldom, if ever, has the bench collectively asked for or initiated reform."[45]   When in 1730 English took the place of Latin in judicial proceedings, Lord Raymond considered the innovation dangerous.   In 1810 the proposal to abolish the death penalty for stealing seemed to Lord Ellenborough a " measure pregnant with danger to the security of property ".   Drawing and quartering in 1814 was, the Attorney-General considered, a bulwark of the constitution not hastily to be removed.[46]   In 1847 some of our most eminent judges were consulted on the problem of juvenile crime, and they gave it as their opinion that reform and imprisonment were utterly irreconcilable.   The introduction of County Courts in 1846—without which the enforcement of his contracts by the small man was impossible —the legal profession strenuously opposed.   The reform of the administration of justice in 1873 was nearly wrecked by the opposition of the Inns of Court.   Neither Bentham, Brougham, Selborne nor Haldane could induce the acceptance of a Ministry of Justice.   And to this day the English legal system remains the least intelligible of any modern civilized community.

A hundred years ago the judicial system was so centralized that " it is almost true that he who had aught against his neighbour had to seek his remedy in Westminster Hall ".[47] In 1800 almost all the judicial work of the kingdom was done by fourteen men.   " If the administration of the common law was centralized the administration of the supplemental law called equity was still more centralized; it was all centre; the two Chancery judges never sat out of London ".[48]   But centralization was perhaps the least of the evils.   On the substance of the law " the dust of antique time " lay so unswept that " mountainous error " was " too highly heaped for truth to o'er peer ".   The Common Law Courts were distinct from Chancery.   Instead of a reasonable division of labour with the Court of Chancery providing the more flexible and discretionary services which the rules of Common Law did not permit, the two systems " applied different notions of right and wrong to the same matters ". " The Common Law treated as untenable claims and defence which equity allowed and one side of Westminster Hall gave judgment which the other restrained the successful party from enforcing . . . the bewildered litigant was driven backward and forward from law to equity and from equity to law.   The conflict between the two systems was one which, if it had not been popularly supposed to derive a sanction from the wisdom of our forefathers, might well have deemed by an impartial observer to be expressly devised for the purpose of producing delay, uncertainty and untold expense."[49] The three Common Law tribunals: Queen's Bench, Common Pleas and the Court of Exchequer had each different history and different functions, but were alike in having a procedure, " antiquated, technical and obscure ".[50]   While of the Chancery side it was said by Dickens that it " had its decaying houses and its blighted lands in every shire, its worn-out lunatic in every workhouse, and its dead in every churchyard"; and in 1839 by a legal expert that " no one could enter into a suit in chancery with any reasonable hope of being alive at the termination if he had a determined adversary ".   In early days the Lord Chancellor had sat alone as Judge of First Instance; alone on appeal from the Master of the Rolls and from the Vice-Chancellor; alone in the House of Lords as a Court of Appeal from himself or a writ of error from the Common Law Courts, except when assisted by a few peers.

Even when in 1840 the judicial staff of the Court of Chancery was seven, the state of business was scandalous.[51]

The substitution for this chaos of a single supreme court, each department of which should administer the same principles of equity and law and guided by a common and swift code of procedure had been the dream of Bentham and the aim of Brougham.   But not until 1873 was Lord Selborne able to bring forward and carry through Parliament the Judicature Act of 1873 which brought together in one Supreme Court divided into two branches, the one of original and the other of appellate jurisdiction, all the judicial powers of the previously existing Superior Courts of England.[52] Even then the bill was nearly shipwrecked on the question of appellate jurisdiction.[53]   Selborne wished " to put an end to the expense and delay incident to the system of double appeals; and for that purpose to concentrate in one Court of Final Appeal all the judicial power which was or could be made available for that purpose; abolishing the intermediate jurisdictions of the Exchequer Chamber and the Court of Appeal in Ordinary ".[54]   He considered that the appellate jurisdiction of the House of Lords ought not to stand in the way of the establishment of the best possible court of final appeal for England.   But such a final court of appeal raised the question as to whether or not it should hear Scotch and Irish appeals.   Uncertainty over this lasted until a new Government under Disraeli was in power, with the result that in 1876 the jurisdiction of the House of Lords, strengthened by the addition of salaried life peers, was restored.   " The system of double appeal . . . was brought back without check or restraint ".[55]   There was now a Supreme Court which was not supreme and the Court of Appeal was a mere court of appeal.

During the eighteenth century and the earlier part of the nineteenth century " the pressing demand for cheap and local justice was staved off by the occasional and sporadic creation of little courts, *courts of conscience*, or *courts of request*. About a hundred of these were erected as now this town, now that, made its voice heard. In general a body of unpaid commissioners, of local tradesmen or the like, was empowered to adjudicate without a jury upon very small debts. Not until 1846 was the serious step taken of creating a new system of courts throughout the land, though already in 1830 Brougham, inspired by Bentham, had proposed the plan which in main was at last adopted ".[56] During a seventeen years' struggle the Bar opposed the scheme. The limit of the competence of the new courts was fixed first at £20, but in 1850 it was raised to £50 and in 1903 to £100. Though every session of Parliament has witnessed an extension of their powers, in 1933 the Bar Council still felt obliged to " view with grave concern " any extension of County Court Jurisdiction.[57]

The needs of commerce imposed a reformation of the jurisdiction of the courts. For Criminal Justice and Police the problem was quite as bad. The social and political importance of the justices of the peace to the ruling classes prevented the development of a paid and trained magistracy. The English labourer was denied the justice that was given to the Indian ryot. When, in 1842, the Cabinet considered employing assistant barristers in aid of the unpaid magistrates at Quarter Sessions, Peel said that on the one hand it would conduce to a speedier and better administration of justice, civil and criminal, in several districts; but on the other " it will strike a severe blow against the useful influence of the best part of the local and provincial aristocracy of the country ". While Wellington said more bluntly that " it would destroy the influence of the landed gentry and of persons of education and good social manners and habits ". Whatever their influence on social manners and habits in 1837 " over a considerable portion of England, property was less secure than in any great European country, excepting only Italy and Spain ". Commercial travellers were loth to travel after dark—property was safe neither on the river nor on the canal, nor upon the turnpike road,[58] while rural crime went unprevented, undetected and unprosecuted. In 1839 there were upwards of 500 voluntary associations for promoting the apprehension and prosecution of felons—for performing in fact by individuals the first duty of a civilized government.[59] In 1829 the Metropolitan police had been establishment for the capital; in 1839 and 1840 Parliament enabled police forces to be established in the country. But not until 1856 was their establishment made compulsory.

In 1832 the organization of local government carried a greater burden of the past than even that of the central government. In the following century it was the local authorities who would first feel the impact of the forces released by the industrial revolutions. For it is in local administration that the outlines of any Utopia have to be filled in. It is only on the experience of local authorities that the evidence for or against a particular scheme of reorganization of the structure and policy of the central government can be collected. Only when there is life at the extremities can there be reason at the head. This, of course, is true whether or not the local administration is representative or not. If there is a completely centralized government it must act thorough local officials who are given wide discretionary powers. But if the central government is to be representative —to depend for its efficiency on the willing co-operation of its subjects some form of local representative government will be advisable. The existence of local representative and responsible councils will bring home to the people the nature of the process of government—the subtle interaction of law and convention of logic and of experience of reason and of character. They provide for experiments in policy and method and a training ground for political skill. By making possible local variations in policy and law they help to maintain a habit of obedience to the law which a centralized system might destroy.   But the maintenance or creation of a system of local government is a searching test of the political genius of a people and its leaders.   For it involves continuous compromise on and a succession of decisions in matters which are dull in detail but in bulk the very basis of the State.

It is in the problems of local government that we are dealing with the most searching test that the development of the application of science can apply to the political capacity of a people.   It is nothing less than the problem of securing a living unity when the development of technical services— in health, in education, and in transport—threaten a mechanical specialization.   To say this is not to prejudge the question whether a system of territorial decentralization will be appropriate to the conditions which the transport developments of the twentieth century may impose.   But it is to say that the vital problem of local government has been to secure a compromise between the tradition of different local areas and the revolutionary changes in areas and policy science demands. And on the success with which that is done at every stage depends the real health of the body politic whatever physical unity of its people science may hereafter provide.

In England local government has had to be adapted to great changes: the redistribution of the population caused by the revolution in industry after 1750; the changes in methods of transport, particularly the development of the bicycle and the motor at the end of the nineteenth century, which made speed a necessity and a sport; the development first of sanitary science and then of preventive medicine, which meant that a government which had performed its first duty of securing order had now the power and duty to secure health.

The method of adaptation was determined partly by the development of the franchise.   The great changes in English local government have followed closely on the Reform Bills of 1832, 1867, 1884 and 1918.   The winning of the franchise by the middle class in 1832 was followed by the Poor Law Act of 1834 and the Municipal Corporations Act of 1835; the winning of the franchise by the industrial worker, in 1867, was followed by the creation, in 1871, of an efficient central authority for the supervision of local government and by the organization of an ordered system of local sanitary administration; the grant of the franchise in 1884 to the agricultural labourer was followed in 1888 by the democratization of county government and the coming of universal suffrage since the War has produced the radical reconstruction of the Acts of 1929 and 1933. Our local government has been entirely remade by Parliament during the last hundred years. But for the most part those Parliaments were fearful of popular power. It is to be noted also that nearly fifty years separate the three great reforms 1835, 1888 and 1929 one from the other; that the principles on which our local councils are organized was laid down in the Municipal Corporations Act of 1835, and was extended to the counties in 1888; while the areas and particularly the relation between urban and rural authorities was determined in 1888 before the motor car had begun to replace the world of Dickens by the world of H. G. Wells. But the Government departments concerned with local authorities have been given wide powers to adjust the local machinery to a shifting population and changing needs.

In 1830 the English local government was in complete disorder. Two distorted and decaying systems existed side by side. For rural areas there were the county and the parish; for some urban areas, the boroughs. The names of these authorities recall the weight of tradition which lay behind them. The parishes, the smallest unit of which there were more than 14,000 in England and Wales, go back to the conversion of England to Christianity and they had been made by Queen Elizabeth the basis of English Poor Law administration. The County, the largest unit, we owe to the reorganization of our Government by the Norman lawyers;

" while the boroughs were the special areas in which trade or local industry had induced a special organization by their inhabitants for their common purposes ".   The boroughs are the English form of the great medieval cities whose democratic development had been arrested here by the successful centralization of our Norman kings.   By 1830 both systems had been transformed by the social and political influences of many centuries.   In the Counties, the Justices of the Peace, once the nominees of the Crown, had come to be the more important local gentry, appointed practically by a system of co-option by the existing bench.   The Justices were the landed aristocracy exercising locally the powers which they had given themselves in Parliament.   In the boroughs there had been a process of selection by which some 179 out of 246 had been incorporated by the Crown and given a constitution and certain political privileges.   But charters of incorporation had been given by the Crown not with an eye to administrative efficiency but as a weapon in the strife of parties.   The most important functions of a borough were to return two members, to feast its members, and to spend whatever property it owned.

While the county system had become a government by local gentry, and the boroughs a collection of privileged corporate bodies possessing no general law governing either their powers or their functions, the pressing needs of the early revolution in industry and transport had compelled the development of special Commissions created by Private Acts of Parliament promoted on the initiative of the local inhabitants to deal with the more urgent problems of Sewerage, Watching and Lighting and the Poor Law.

But by the passing of the Reform Bill of 1832 a drastic reform was made inevitable.   The change in the distribution of population which the industrial revolution had caused, had in many areas, completely shattered the working of the partnership between the Justices of the Peace and the traditional parish machinery. As in the United States in the nineteenth century the growth of small townships into great cities without any essential changes in their system of local government produced the administrative chaos in which the only principle of order was the law of the political boss, so in England in the early nineteenth century in many parishes which were swamped by a new industrial population an English Tammany replaced the Silences and Shallows of the past. The parochial system of compulsory unpaid service by the inhabitants of the maintenance of order, the repair of roads, and the cleansing of the streets and sites completely broke down and was replaced either by special Commissions created by private Act or by local political bosses who created whatever system their ingenuity could devise. But it was the inappropriateness of the parish for the administration of poor relief which precipitated the great reforms of the 'thirties. The Poor Law Act, 1834, was written in the purest milk of the Benthamite word.

Instead of 14,000 parishes there were to be less than 700 Boards of Guardians elected for administrative areas which were to be Unions of parishes grouped according to a plan made by a new central authority, the Poor Law Commissioners. Thus were the principles of rigid central control, governing bodies elected on a uniform franchise, and with areas appropriate to their functions introduced into English local government. This touch of reason was, its advocates believed, to make the whole population self-supporting. The poor would shortly no longer be with us. And it is worth recording that this Napoleonic touch of centralization was mainly responsible for the vigour of the Chartist movement in the North of England. In 1835 came the reorganization of the boroughs. Like the reform of the Poor Law it was the result of Benthamite inspiration. A Royal Commission studied under their inspiration the structure of 246 boroughs. Its Assistant Commissioners were sent on tours of inquiry; their

I

evidence was collected in five weighty volumes through which the constitutional historian may still cast a startled glance; and from this evidence there was culled a report which had the vigour of a brilliant political pamphlet. As a result the Municipal Corporations Act of 1835 provided a machinery of government consisting of a council three-fourths of which was to be directly elected by household suffrage and one-quarter indirectly elected—this aldermanic dilution of direct democracy being due to the caution of the House of Lords—and which was to have power to make laws for the good government of the boroughs and for the suppression of nuisances. But the Act of 1835 did not provide that the areas of the boroughs or their population should have any uniformity—Liverpool had 185,000 and Bradford 1,500; except that Treasury sanction was required for the alienation of any of their property, there was no central control by a Government department; and the Act applied only to 179 of the 246 boroughs which existed.

The result of these two Acts, the Poor Law Act of 1834 and the Municipal Corporations Act of 1835, was that there was for the whole country for one service only, that of poor relief, a uniform system of elected and directly controlled councils. In certain urban areas there was a machinery of elected councils which could form the nucleus of an effective local governing body. For while the Municipal Corporations Act did not directly confer many powers it was possible for the boroughs to acquire fresh powers and for the powers of various special Commissions to be transferred to them. They were centres round which local governing powers might be crystallized. But outside the towns to which the Municipal Corporations Act applied, except for the purpose of the Poor Law, the rest of the country had to rely on the old system of the Justice of the Peace and the parish. This meant that for nearly forty years outside the boroughs there was almost complete confusion. The balance of power between the political parties, and particularly the conflict between the Established Church and Dissent made it impossible that the powers of the non-elected Justices of the Peace should be greatly increased, while at the same time it was impossible that elected councils should be established for the rural areas. Whenever, therefore, there was an urgent need for the local administration of some new service it had to be provided by special bodies— ad hoc bodies—created for the purpose and composed partly of Justices of the Peace and local men of substance. In 1848 the Central Board of Health was given power to establish in certain circumstances local Boards of Health; in 1862 Highway Boards were appointed to attempt to straighten the tangle of the roads; while in 1871 School Boards were appointed to manage schools where religious bodies had failed to do so. It is because the elected principle could not then be extended to rural areas that the ad hoc principle of the Poor Law of 1834 was used to deal with each emergency as it arose. Instead of an elected council for the County to match the elected councils for the boroughs a variety of boards, commissions and such like whatnots made our local government in 1872 a chaos of authorities and a chaos of rates. That the confusion was not worse and that it was remedied at all was due to the interdependence of poor relief and sanitation. To prevent infection and to limit paupers to the crumbs which will not spoil the rich man's table are causes to bring good neighbours to sit upon committees. When the Sanitary Commission of 1869 reported that it was the chaos of areas and authorities in local government which was responsible for the prevalence of disease, Parliament in 1871 provided that there should be a central department, the Local Government Board, responsible for the control of local authorities and, in 1872, provided that every part of the country should be under a local sanitary authority. With the creation, in 1888, of elected councils for the Counties the outlines of our present system had been laid down.

[1] MSS. evidence before Haldane *Committee on Machinery of Government*, 1918. From material in the library of the London School of Economics. The phrase quoted is G. B. Shaw's.

[2] Miss Nightingale to Mr. Herbert, Nov. 18th, 1859, quoted Lord Stanmore : *Memoir of Sidney Herbert*, Vol. II., p. 369. For Army administration 1854-68 and subsequent reform see Sir Robert Biddulph : *Lord Cardwell at the War Office* (1904).

[3] J. W. Fortescue : *History of the British Army*, Vol. XI., p. 24.

[4] Lord Edmond Fitzmaurice's *Life of Granville* : Vol. I, p. 140, Jan. 10th, 1856.

[5] *Life of Lord Ripon*, Vol. I., p. 180-1.

[6] J. S. Omond : *Parliament and the Army*, 1642-1904 (Cambridge, 1933), p. 93.

[7] Stanmore's *Sidney Herbert*, Vol. I, p. 292.

[8] Omond : *Parliament and the Army*, p. 94.

[9] ibid., p. 99.

[10] ibid., pp. 111-112.

[11] ibid., p. 108.

[12] ibid., pp. 113-114.

[13] ibid., p. 114.

[14] ibid., p. 114.

[15] H. W. Richmond : *International Policy and Naval Strategy*, p. 241.

[16] ibid., p. 244.

[17] ibid., p. 244.

[18] Evidence of Sir James Graham Parliamentary Papers 1861, Vol. V., Q., pp. 804-6.

[19] H. W. Richmond : *International Policy and Naval Strategy*, p. 249.

[20] Harold Nicolson : *Political Quarterly*, 1936, p. 209.

[21] C. K. Webster : *Study of Nineteenth-Century Diplomacy*, p. 17.

[22] Cambridge *History of British Foreign Policy*, Vol. II., p. 106.

[23] Webster : *Study of Nineteenth-Century Diplomacy*, p. 17.

[24] Cambridge *History of British Foreign Policy*, Vol. III., p. 588.

[25] ibid., p. 577.

[26] ibid., p. 589.

[27] Maxwell's *Life of Clarendon*, Vol. II., p. 282.

[28] Parliamentary Papers, 1864, Vol. VII., Q. 2450.

[29] ibid., Q. 2581.

[30] ibid., Q. 2563.

[31] ibid., Q. 2581.

[32] From unpublished study of Dr. H. L. Hall on *Colonial Office*.

[33] Sir William Molesworth.

[34] H. L. Hall, op. cit.

[35] For Treasury control see A. J. V. Durell : *Principles and Practice of the System of Control over Parliamentary Grants* (1917) for full details and references to official papers.

[36] Andrew Lang : *Sir Stafford Northcote* (1891 ed.), pp. 73 and 111.

[37] These criticisms are to be found in the published memoranda on the Northcote and Trevelyan Report, 1853.

[38] 25th Feb., 1838. *Queen Victoria Letters*, 1837-61, Vol. I, p. 106.

[39] Lady G. Cecil's *Life of Salisbury*, Vol. III., p. 205.

[40] Algernon West : *Contemporary Portraits*.

[41] Greville : *Journal*, Sept. 29th, 1841.

[42] Fitzmaurice's *Life of Granville* : p. 177 and cf. p. 29.

[43] *Gladstone Papers* : Autobiography, 1897.

[44] Seton Watson : *Gladstone, Disraeli, and the Eastern Question*, pp. 4-5.

[45] *Quarterly Review*, Vol. 261, pp. 41-4.

[46] ibid.

[47] F. W. Maitland : *Justice and Police*, p. 21.

[48] ibid., p. 21-22.

[49] Justice Bowen in T. H. Ward's : *Reign of Queen Victoria*, Vol. I., pp. 282-3.
[50] ibid., p. 285.
[51] Viscount Birkenhead : *Points of View*, Vol. I., pp. 97-8. The Essay on the Ministry of Justice, pp. 92-129 would seem to be the official case against that institution.
[52] Selborne *Memorials*, Part II., 1865-1895, Vol. I., p. 298.
[53] ibid., p. 304.
[54] ibid., p. 305.
[55] ibid., pp. 314-315.
[56] Maitland : *Justice and Police*, p. 23.
[57] *Quarterly Review*, Vol. 262, p. 196.
[58] Justice Bowen in T. H. Ward's *Reign of Queen Victoria*, Vol. I, p. 323.
[59] ibid., pp. 324-5.

CHAPTER IV

THE STATE AND SOCIETY, 1870-1914

The economic condition of England after 1870—The action of the State which it required—To civilize where Industry had barbarized—To secure and to supplement the working of the market—The case of Land and Ireland—Capital, the Foreign Office and the Bank of England—The organization of the labour market—The provision of health, factory and educational services—Philosophical and popular ideas—Bradley and Herbert Spencer—The Empire in trust and the Empire in partnership—The foreign scene—Statesmen not at ease.

By 1870 the people of the United Kingdom seemed to be on the road to an abundant though dingy Utopia. The population had increased from about 21,000,000 in 1821 to more than 31,000,000 in 1870. This increase in population had been compatible with a fall in the price of food which had not been offset by a fall in wages. Men may not live by bread alone, but their larger loaf had secured the political support of the working class for Free Trade. In place of the despairing violence of Chartism they had concentrated on limited and specific reforms. The Reform Bill of 1867 enfranchising the urban working class was in a part a tribute of the middle class to the economic and moral progress of the " responsible working man ". Having made God in their own image that middle class hoped that He would help them to make all men in their image as well.

But the prevailing optimism was not very well grounded. For the position of England in 1870 was the result of special conditions which were soon to pass away. A variety of causes had contributed to the development of the industrial revolution in these islands. England's prosperity and political security were due to conditions as unique as those which produced the glory that was Greece, and time was to show that they were less stable than the grandeurs of Rome. Wool had given us cotton; cotton gave us factories; factories gave us foreign trade; and foreign trade brought more cotton.[1] For the application of science to industry fate had given us suitable climatic conditions, a fortunate distribution of coal and iron in relation to a then incomparable means of communication—a network of rivers navigable to an all surrounding sea. England's previous economic development had provided her with a machinery of capital investment, a market in land, and a mobility of labour which on the Continent had been delayed by feudal traditions or destroyed by war. Her previous political history had given her a unity and a social order favourable to the development of a vigorous economic life. " In the first half of the nineteenth century the industries of England present a picture of increasing production, rapid increase in the number of single undertakings and in each separate area of production the keenest competition between the various manufacturers, only giving way occasionally and under pressure of certain exceptional conditions to monopolistic organization ".[2] Her island position had enabled her to develop almost unhindered by war and revolution her special advantages for supplying the world with manufactured goods. In a generation from 1850 she had become the forge of the world, the world's carrier, the world's banker, the world's workshop, the world's clearing-house and the world's *entrepôt*.[3] Fortune had given to the British people the conditions necessary to the wealth of nations which Adam Smith had specified in 1776.

But with all these advantages there were circumstances in the position of this country before 1870 which might have given warning of difficulties to come. The world now well knows that improved communications may bring different cultures into such sudden contact that both may be destroyed; it knows too well the barbarizing effect of pioneering conditions on a migrant population, and that bloodshed and corruption result when an economic order outgrows its political framework.   It should not have required the pseudo science of Marxianism to predict the catastrophies which must ensue when the tortoise of political wisdom and social tolerance failed to keep pace with the hare of economic development.   Division of labour does not necessarily produce the intelligence its co-operation requires.   The forces which had produced the American Civil War and were later to produce the World War—the struggle of different political, social and cultural traditions to maintain themselves in an economic environment they could not control were present in England before 1870.   Though the repeal of the Corn Laws had not destroyed the prosperity of agriculture the struggle to secure that repeal had come near to disrupting our political system.   Had not the ownership of land been concentrated in comparatively few families united by ties of blood with the rising manufacturing interests; if the struggle over the Corn Laws had been a struggle, not between cousins but between separate geographical areas and different cultural traditions, our political structure might not have survived. Had not our peasantry already been destroyed and our proletarians not yet enfranchised English Liberalism might never have been born.   The case of Ireland shows on a small scale the problem which has since shaken the world.   England's industrial development produced a problem of mobility of labour from Ireland which undermined the system of local government in many English cities, nearly ruined our relations with the United States, shattered the great Liberal party led by Gladstone from 1868-85, nearly destroyed the procedure of the Mother of Parliaments and was ended only by civil war in the twentieth century.   The Irish Free State, which may yet prove the Achilles heel of the British Empire, was the outcome of a comparatively simple problem of the relation between an economic order and its political framework.   In Ireland an Englishman has a clue both to the political problems of the United States and the foreign policies of Balkan States.

Within Great Britain there were no separate nationalities which preferred poverty and their own political and social order to plenty and the political and social order of an alien culture.   Nor should it be forgotten that in the 'eighties the whole foreign-born population of the United Kingdom did not equal its emigration for a single year.   But had the Welsh all been Roman Catholics or had all our Nonconformists lived in Scotland the problem of minorities might have made democracy in Britain the hazard that it is in Europe.

But before 1870 not only the nationalism of Ireland, but the reduction almost to barbarism of the populations on the new industrial frontiers should have given warning of problems to come.   The prophetic eye of Disraeli had seen this problem of the two nations and the essence of his Conservatism was to secure not the abolition of rich and poor, but the reconciliation of these two nations—the hierarchical landed order and the anarchical industrial frontiers into a nation state.   Had this country not already become the centre of an international economic order Disraeli might have anticipated our contemporary autarchies.   As it was he was reduced to a spurious imperialism.   So the problem of Ireland and the problem of industrialism was to break the Liberal Party, to produce a Conservatism that dare not think clearly about economics and in the fullness of time a Labour Party whose inspiration was the memory of past wrongs rather than an understanding of the nature of politics.   The industrial revolution produced two parties who cannot forget the past— the Irish and the Labour Party.

After 1870 the real difficulties of this country were to begin.   Politically the overthrow of France by Germany in 1871 was a heavy setback to European Liberalism.   The political unity secured by the United States through civil war and the political unity of Germany secured by wars of aggression prepared the way for the decline of English agriculture and the loss of her supremacy in iron and steel. The depression of 1874, though it was world-wide, revealed the special vulnerability of the English economic order. Specializing for a world market they had given hostages to a fortune they were powerless to control. The opening of the American West found English farmers unprepared to meet the competition of wheat mined from the virgin prairies. In 1870 the United Kingdom provided half the pig-iron of the world. By 1913 the U.S.A. provided three times and Germany half as much again as we did. In 1890 the United States and in 1893 Germany passed this country in the production of steel. By 1913 the German production was twice and the American four times that of the United Kingdom. Britain's percentage of the world's international commerce dropped from nearly 22 per cent. in 1871-75 to little more than 15 per cent. in 1913. The loss of her supremacy in iron and steel and a decline in her percentage of world trade was inevitable as the industrial and commercial revolution spread round the world. The real grounds for anxiety were more subtle than a mere reduction in her share of world production and trade. They lay in the hesitancy with which she made adjustments which were forced upon her and in the fact that powers of science in the industrial order were to favour the great Continental land powers more than an island empire.

Although English agriculture had been the best in the world the land had not been wisely used. The tenure of agricultural land designed to protect the social interests of the landed aristocracy had meant that in a country overflowing with capital there had been little investment in the soil, because there was no security of tenure which would warrant men of capital investing their money in it.[4]   There

was a political factor in the prosperity of agriculture; and
when after 1886 the supremacy of landed wealth was lost,
their leaders gone, the smaller men and the farm labourers
had neither the political influence nor the commercial and
financial experience to secure the organization which was best
for themselves in a competitive world.   In the new age of
steel which followed the inventions of Bessemer in 1858,
and Thomas in 1878, Britain enjoyed no natural advantages.
England had been the pioneer in almost every phase of the
industrial evolution based on iron and coal.   But whenever
a great change in technique or organization occurs the older
seat of an industry has difficulty in maintaining its position.
England was to find herself severely handicapped in the
later revolution based on steel, electricity and the research
chemist.   The production of wrought iron depended on the
skill of experienced workers; steel on the scale of the producing units and the skill of metallurgists.[5]   With the discovery of aniline dyes in 1866 the chemist made his first
effective entrance into the field of industry.   The invention
of the internal combustion engine in 1876 made possible the
first motor car in 1887.   In the 'eighties the hunting of
the microbe began the opening of the tropics.   In 1894
Niagara would be harnessed to the service of electricity.   The
English discoveries in science and technology, 1800-70, had
been made by self-taught men who owed little to universities.[6]
The new chemical and electrical trades required technicians who could only be produced by an efficient system of
secondary education, possessed by Germany but not by us.[7]
In the United States not only was there a more open career
to talent, but a large home market offered every inducement
to the development of large-scale industry.   In this country
old established firms had old plants, nepotism in their
management and a disinclination to hustle for new
inventions.[8]
The volume of British foreign trade continued to increase

up to 1913.   But there was real ground for anxiety in the fact that in that increase the basic industries of coal, textiles and metals played the major part.[9] In the half-century before the War our output of coal was more than trebled.   In the same period following the opening of the Suez Canal and the substitution of iron and steel for wood in the construction of ships, we secured the supremacy of our Merchant Navy. But that supremacy was dangerously linked with the increasing part played by coal in our exports.   The export of coal was the basis of competitive power of our ships as carriers of the world's commerce.   In this we had given two hostages to fortune: the demand for coal depended upon technological conditions which might swiftly change; and the volume of trade depended on the political stability of the pre-war order.

What did these changes mean for the problem of government?   The economists we have seen tended to assume that there would be little difficulty in providing just that amount of government control and no more which was necessary to secure the material advantages of specialization and exchange. If there were some unbalanced enthusiasts who were prepared to say that all goes best when nothing is regulated, saner minds demanded " as much individual freedom as is consistent with the welfare of an organized society and the performance of self-imposed obligations ".   But this and similar formulæ assumed that there was agreement as to the nature of welfare and the conditions under which obligations could rightly be deemed to be self-imposed.   The problem of serving Mammon and whatever gods there be is more subtle than at first sight may appear.   Economic science derived its prestige from its discovery that there was an order in society which was due, not to the decision and power of an authority, but to the co-operation through the market of individual wills.   This economic order seemed to be the result of those natural laws which theology and reason had always assumed

Nature to observe.   The economists had shown how it was possible for there to be an ordered production and distribution of goods and services when individual choice was not politically dictated and when the means of satisfaction for every individual were not unlimited.   The laws of the economists were nothing more than the logical implications of certain assumptions as to the relation between means which were available and scarce, and the alternative uses to which they might be put.   In so far as they are correctly formulated these laws are never broken.   Whether a community is tottering on the verge of starvation or lolling in the lap of luxury economic law will be satisfied, as the law of gravity is satisfied, whether an economist speaks in comfort from a platform or dangles at peace from the lamp-post to which an ill-judged taste for abstraction may have brought him.

But, of course, any system of production and distribution with which we have to deal only works because it satisfies other laws besides those which the economists have so subtly abstracted.   The market of economic analysis assumes contract, and the idea of contract is only possible in a certain kind of society.   If there is to be contract violence must be taught its place.   And for violence to be taught its place the fundamental problem of politics—the right use of force—must also be solved.

And so we may say that the economists assumed an ideal State.   They assumed that it was possible to know and to secure just that amount of Government control which was necessary to secure the desired advantages of specialization and exchange.   They assumed that it was possible to secure within a given state that there should be no manipulation of governmental machinery in the interests of particular economic groups, and they assumed that the social and administrative conditions could be provided to supply that mobility of labour and of capital which the application of science to industry requires.   In a word they tended to assume that whatever the proportions in which the factors of production were combined and whatever the speed at which those proportions might be changed the political skill required would unfailingly arrive. The magnitude of these assumptions were hidden by the tacit alliance between economics and utilitarianism. For the latter by its confused assumptions that men both should and did pursue courses which would maximize their pleasures provided just the political thought the early industrial revolution required.

In the period after 1870 the importance of the social order which the economist had assumed was to be startlingly realized. The application of science to industry meant a rapid speeding up of the process of division of labour and of exchange. At first this was of enormous benefit to the particular area within which it occurred. But even in the area of a single State it meant the degradation of large classes of labour whose wits and sinews could not adapt themselves to the conditions of the market. For why should the rhythm of economic change harmonize with the rhythm of man's life. How can a man know that the change in demand for his skill may not occur when he is too old to learn afresh. What guarantee could there be that the mobility of labour which industrial progress requires can be harmonized with the social framework of the family. These difficulties were hidden for a time because the structure of industry was decentralized and the process of change still slow enough for the common virtues of honesty and frugality to secure their reward. At every point there was expansion. The structure of industry might be described as a system in which the centre was everywhere and the circumference nowhere. Still it was obvious that technological advance resulted in the sacrifice of one district or one class of labour to the benefit of the whole. Within a given country this sacrifice could be mitigated by private charity or a State Poor Law. But what would be the position where technological advance required the sacrifice of one country to the economic benefit of the world?[10]   It may be true that "there is no possibility of a world-wide arrangement of production or of a division of labour other than natural causes or chance dictates".[11] But it is too much to expect that every individual and every area will accept the fate which chance or nature dictate to them without themselves attempting to play the part of Fate.   And how do they play the part of Fate?   By the well-known political device of Protection.   " In its essence Protection is the effort to maintain the *status quo* even at the sacrifice of the greater wealth which might be secured by readjustment ".[12]   When in the period 1800-50 there semed to be developing a division of the world into new countries producing raw materials and old countries manufacturing them, the United States of America took steps to see that they were not limited to the production of raw materials.   In 1834 when, after the confusion of European wars, a national system was begun in Germany she took steps to secure that England should not be the only industrial country.   When, after 1870, the new wheat-growing areas of the American middle west were being developed, the agricultural groups in Europe took steps to protect themselves against the flow of wheat. And when after the war of 1914-18 the dislocation of European trade and industry would have caused large emigration to the United States, that country took steps to prevent the social consequence of too free a market in labour.   If the distribution of specialization is due to chance and natural causes why should the cultural and political systems submit to the dictates of chance?   Within a single political system it may be possible to persuade the threatened group that it is for the general interest that they should give way. Within a single political system it is possible to secure that a threatened group which prefers not to give way shall not be in a position to organize a damaging resistance to the force of change.   A common political loyalty will facilitate a healthy economic differentiation and provide the basis for the stresses and strains of continuous adjustment in the ways of work and life. The proper functioning of the market requires the supervision of the subtlest political skill; but if the economist can assume a State he cannot assume a world State. Without the latter the development of Protection when the rate of economic change is too severe for the cultural and political traditions concerned is inevitable.

By 1870 it was becoming clear that the new forces of industry were not necessarily in harmony with the national traditions on which the political systems of Europe were based. In the United States the economic exploitation of a continent was providing the material basis for the leading national power of the twentieth century; but in Europe it was not so easy to serve two masters—nationalism and plenty. To many nations Cobden's tidings of great joy that commerce was " a grand panacea which like a beneficent medical discovery will serve to inoculate with the healthy and saving taste for civilization all the nations of the world " was a message of political and social conflict. For it was not every country that could, like England, follow Cobden for its daily bread and Palmerston for its national pride. And even in England by the end of the century Chamberlain—a commercial Palmerston—was to feel " that the tendency of the times is to throw all power into the hands of the greater empires, and the minor kingdoms—those which are non-progressive—seemed to be destined to fall into a secondary and subordinate place ".

But these conflicts between national cultures were as yet only in their beginnings. Within the United Kingdom fresh and urgent aspects of the problem of the relation between the economic and the political order were being revealed. Originally *laissez-faire* had been a claim of pioneers for freedom to shape a new society unhampered by a corrupt and meddling political machine. New powers could only be put at the service of mankind if the dead hand of a tradition and the curse of privilege were removed. It promised a policy of plenty in place of a *politique* of power. This new freedom in the economic world had been enormously successful. But as the standard of living rose and the scale of the new industrial order swiftly grew the political problem took on a new urgency. A privileged aristocracy lost its responsibility; power was less mitigated by tradition; and the prosperous middle class were free to make a society in their own image. To Cobden this English " shopocracy " seemed to glory in being " the toadies of a clodpole aristocracy, only less enlightened than themselves ". To Matthew Arnold, of the three things necessary to civilization: a love of industry, of the things of the mind, and of beauty, it seemed that the new middle class only understood the first. Their freedom to get rich had produced neither right reason nor fine culture. If there was to be a rallying point for the intelligence and for the best instincts of the community it would have to be provided by the State. In the 'eighties William Morris was writing that " the present lower middle class are almost the worst in the community. They ape the bad habits of their betters and they despise those below them. Though they live in a kind of swinging comfort . . . they are ill housed, ill educated, crushed by grovelling superstition, lacking reasonable pleasures and entirely devoid of any sense of beauty ". The fact was that the combination of the vulgarity of a new rich with the traditional servilities of deeply class-conscious society had produced a snobbery and a vulgarity probably unparalleled in social history. If on the Continent an Englishman was a synonym for a gentleman it was only because the nobility had been the only Englishmen abroad. Had foreigners visited England in any numbers the blackguardism of the lower classes in this country would have been notorious throughout Europe. In 1878 W. S. Jevons, one of the soberest writers and observers of the nineteenth

J

century with no æsthetic axe to grind, said that while no Englishman was surprised when " a Frenchman surpassed us in politeness, and a German in profundity, and an American in ingenuity and affability ", we ought to feel ashamed that the Scandinavians " far surpass us as regards the good breeding and the general culture of the mass of the people ".[13] The American rowdy might be more dangerous with his bowie knife, but compared with the English blackguard he was a man of refinement.[14] The reason was that " the amusements of the masses . . . have been frowned upon and condemned and eventually suppressed by a dominant aristocracy. . . . It seems to be thought that the end of life is accomplished if there be bread and beef to eat, beer to drink, beds to sleep in, and chapels to attend on Sunday ".[15] In the past the rich had excluded the mass of the people even from the natural enjoyments of the air and sun that they might enjoy their shooting and other forms of sport. " It is hardly too much to say that the right to dwell freely in a grimy street, to drink freely in the neighbouring public house, and to walk freely between the high-walled parks and the jealously-preserved estates of our landowners, is all that the just and equal laws of England secure to the mass of the people."[16] J. S. Mill's essay on *Liberty* in 1859 was an attempt to demonstrate to the many-headed multitude that the idiosyncrasies of the highbrow ought to be tolerated if only because they would be found to pay in the long run.

The vulgarity of the middle and the blackguardism of the lower class were only a symptom of an underlying economic problem. Bagehot, one of the wisest of the Victorians, had realized that economists need not be opposed to the " legislative promotion of those industrial habits which conduce to the attainment of national morality or national happiness at a sacrifice of national wealth; to efforts at national education or compulsory sanitary reform; to all national aid from England towards the starving peasantry of Ireland; to every measure for the improvement of that peasantry which would not be the spontaneous choice of the profit-making capitalist ". Where there was no effective demand—that is to say a demand which it would be profitable to business men to meet—for some of the vital conditions of a healthy social life, those conditions would have to be provided by the use of political power. Just as J. S. Mill realized that political democracy was unworkable unless its members had reached a stage of development in which they were prepared to be persuaded by discussion,[17] so a free market in all things material and mental required that in things essential those who bought should understand their real needs. Those who had been excluded by a landowning oliarchy from the conditions necessary to their physical and mental development and then suffered all the barbarizing influences of pioneering industrialism, in which the conditions of the cities had the squalor and brutality of the camps of a barbarian and un-disciplined soldiery, could not be expected to create a civilized society by the exercise of their mere freedom to buy and to sell. But there was another and more threatening problem. The greater the success of industry the greater might be the specialization it might demand. What was to prevent the development of an industrial order in which the bulk of the workers were required to serve as mere living tools? The orthodox answer of the economists was that the rising standard of living would more than offset the disadvantages of increased specialization. It was tacitly assumed that if each were for himself the magic of the market would place even the hindmost beyond the devil's reach. But this optimism was unfounded. Living tools cannot be scrapped save by the hand of death; and the lingering taboos of Christian culture did not permit this drastic method should be applied to those who might miscalculate the demand for their particular kind of skill. The more intricate the web of industry the more difficult it became for any one individual or family to determine how best to prepare themselves to earn enough to live. Those who were fortunate enough to be employed in industries in which it was possible for them to combine to control the market value of their labour merely made more severe the pressure upon those who were not so fortunate. The development of the great Trade Unions indirectly increased the degradation of the unskilled labourer and the horrors of the sweated trades. But there was an even more radical problem which has since become clear to the eye of economic analysis—there is nothing in the theory of the market which shows how each individual tends to secure the hire of which he is worthy, that such hire will be sufficient for his needs as a citizen.

Herbert Spencer lamented that the artisan was able to obtain " from a fund raised by taxes certain benefits beyond those which the sum secured by his labour enabled him to purchase ". But we have seen that there is no reason to suppose that the market value of any individual's services in a system of complex division of labour will be sufficient to secure for him the goods and services which his development as a citizen requires. The inequalities of income which the development of division of labour produce may possibly undermine the social unity on which a peaceful development depends. The inequalities which are the product of freedom may destroy freedom itself. Whether this should be dealt with by a system of minimum wage legislation or by progressively raising the standard of those who are permitted to compete in the labour market cannot here be discussed. It is sufficient to note that the problem is implicitly present wherever there is production for more than subsistence. There is another problem which raises even more delicate political problems. Individuals may earn enough if those earnings are rightly spent to maintain in themselves and to provide for their children the necessary conditions of freemen. But what they earn may not be rightly spent. It is here that we touch the heart of the problem of individualism. It is doubtful whether anyone would maintain that he has a duty never to interfere with another individual for that individual's own good.   If anyone does seriously feel bound by that fearful duty it is extremely unlikely that the frailty of human sympathy will permit him to fulfil it.   Such quixotic indifference will only be possible when, a glorious angel in his own unique universe, he can contemplate his neighbours each in theirs moving to God or going to the devil as they shall freely choose.

The fact that we consider it our duty to interfere forcibly with children for their own good makes it difficult to be sure that it is our duty never forcibly to interfere with an adult for his own good.   And our doubt is strengthened when we remember that the principle that each is best taught by his own experience of going wrong is not applied by an advanced community to a backward one.   If this admission of the responsibility of the more developed or the more experienced individual or community for the less developed or experienced is felt to be an invitation to the bludgeoning of despotically disposed cultural despots it may be pointed out that the avoidance of such responsibility by those on whom it rests is the main cause of the despots themselves.

But however we may decide the difficult question of when we ought to interfere with others for their own good, we must always be interfering with them for the good of others and our own.   Education, health, insurance, safety regulations, must be imposed by some on others as the only way of avoiding their brutality, infection, or their clamorous demands for sympathy and help.   The greater the division of labour in a community and the more complex its organization the more often will such regulations be required.   In some cases it is impossible for anyone to enjoy the results of his own care unless others are restrained—health; in others it is impossible to provide a service for some without its being available to all—beauty of the countryside. These are obvious enough. But there are a vast number of others where experience has shown that either because most do not possess the means or because the service is not easily controlled by the demands of consumers in a market, public provision is desirable.

There is really nothing to prevent a society based upon freedom of contract producing a hierarchy more deeply divided than any in the past. Only an unfounded prejudice in the equal value of men as tools could lead anyone to suppose that each can earn what a man and a citizen requires to live. In 1886 Booth reported that " 32 per cent. of the population were living in a state of chronic poverty . . . incompatible with physical health and industrial efficiency ". Whether this was due to the fact that freedom of contract had not been properly secured—that there were forces of coercion on the side of the masters—or whether they were due to the market for labour being so well organized that it reflected only too truly the value of each man's work, a vital problem for the State was revealed. If the degradation were due to the existence of force and fraud the State must discover the legal and administrative machinery which freedom of contract requires. If it were due to the precision with which the markets sorted the productive sheep from the unproductive goats, the State had to decide how far payments according to the value of their work should be supplemented by payment according not only to the needs of individuals, but according to the needs of their fellow citizens that their sickness and indigence should not poison the whole social order.

After 1870 the State in England became more and more concerned with two main tasks: where there was reason to believe that the free play of individual choice and judgment would be of benefit to society it had to secure that the law would provide that there should be neither force, fraud nor the obstruction caused by obscure and dilatory legal forms

to hamper the creative urge of individual self-help; where
the free play of individual choice and judgment in the market
did not produce those things which individual choice and
judgment outside the market and in its considered political
judgment thought both necessary and possible, the State tried
to discover administrative methods for their production and
control.   For those things which the market could provide
a market had to be organized.   For those things necessary
to society which the market did not provide provision had to
be made.   Broadly speaking we may say that neither for the
ownership and use of land, nor the accumulation and application of capital, nor for the sale of labour was the market
properly organized.   And experience suggested that it was
unlikely that either education, health or safety or the provision of the statistics and fundamental research on which the
life of industry depend would be produced by those who live
by persuading others to buy.

Before passing to a brief consideration of some of these
problems of the State an obvious point must be mentioned.
The first condition of an intelligent individualism was lacking
when the existing law, whatever its content, was in form so
complex as to be unintelligible even to the expert.   In the
middle of last century not only was the statute law of great
bulk, but in the ordinary edition the contents formed one mass
without any systematic arrangement.   There was no thorough
severance of effective from non-effective enactments, nor did
there exist in a complete form any authoritative index or other
guide by which they might be distinguished.   The judicial
dicta and decisions were dispersed through upwards of 1,300
volumes comprising nearly 10,000 cases, exclusive of 150
volumes of Irish reports.   Well might Sir Henry Maine
write, " Such a system in the end beats all but the experts;
and we, accordingly, have turned our laws over to experts,
to attorneys and solicitors, to barristers above them and to
judges in the last resort ".[18]   He added, " that the very

small place filled by our own English law in our thoughts and conversation is a phenomenon absolutely confined to these islands ".[19]   In 1878 there began the revised edition of the statutes and Westbury began the authorized series of law reports.[20]

In 1829 the Real Property Commissioners had reported that " the law of England, except in a few comparatively unimportant particulars, appears to come almost as near perfection as can be expected in any human institution ".   That they were wrong is now generally admitted.[21]   The Land Law of England was in fact the law appropriate to an aristocratic state.[22]   The landowners constituted a powerful trade union able to enforce their rules of apprenticeship, rate of work and opportunities for leisure and amusement through their control of the machinery of Parliament.   In their development of the land economic advantage was subordinated to questions of political and social prestige.   A scheme of settlements which had been devised by certain ingenious lawyers at the Restoration had passed into the category of things immemorial and become one of the sacred bulwarks of Church and State.[23]   The defectiveness of the rules of Land Law had far-reaching effects.   It prevented the proper utilization of the land by discouraging investment.   It made the Parliamentary franchise incomprehensible to the layman.   " It may have been supposed ", wrote Maitland, " that one part at least of our law would be plain, the law relating to the Parliamentary franchise.   But it never will be plain so long as it depends on a real property law essentially nonsensical ".[24]   Proposals to establish a registry of titles were useless so long as the actual rules of the Land Law were themselves defective.   It is impossible to register what cannot be determined.   The depression of the 'eighties in agriculture and the change in its science compelled the landowners to abandon privileges which as a powerful trade union they had held at the expense of the community.   During the period of agricultural prosperity

1860-74 tenant-farmers had been discouraged from investment in improvements because of the fear of eviction. In
1875 they were protected by the Agricultural Holdings Act.
In the 'eighties, there was a popular outcry against settlements and the Settled Land Act of 1882 was passed. In 1880
the Ground Game Act entitled farmers to kill hares and
rabbits. In 1906 the Agricultural Holdings Act gave compensation for damage by game and freedom to determine the
choice of crops and the disposal of produce. But not until
after the War of 1914-18 during which the Lands Requisition
Committee had had brought home to them " the expense and
delays of land transfer in this country as compared with Continental countries "[25] was some of the dust of antique time on
an English title to landed property hoovered away.

In 1870 there began in Ireland a grimmer struggle than in
England over the relation between contract and civilization.
The creation of a peasant proprietorship in Ireland was begun
in that year. It was to be a magnificent lesson for English
statesmen in the relation of the State to the economic order.
In Ireland " all the circumstances, all the associations and all
the accretions " which had grown around the naked idea of
contract were different from England.[26] As about half the
country was owned by 700 persons,[27] the landlord was in
essence a monopolist. But he was a monopolist who differed
in religion from his tenant; who, dwelling out of the country,
had little or no idea of social obligations; and who before
1874 was the only part of Ireland represented in the British
Parliament. The Act of 1870 tried to make by law a
partnership which in England existed by custom.[28] It gave
compensation for disturbances, for improvements, and it
legalized the Ulster tenant right custom.

It failed because of the great variety of its exceptions, the
lowness of the compensation and the tenants' insecurity of
tenure[29] when prices rose as they did until 1878 the farmer
preferred to pay the increased rent his landlord demanded

rather than be evicted and take his compensation. But when
after 1878 prices fell and evictions grew the agrarian question
was amalgamated with a national movement and developed
into a national and class war. By 1881 Mr. Gladstone was
convinced that a " further degree of State intervention with
the holding of land was the only solution. When her institutions permitted it Ireland would doubtless benefit by a system
of free contract, but the conditions then existing did not allow
it ".[30]   The Act of 1881 carried further the experiment of
1870. The Ashbourne Act of 1885 made the first real attempt
to settle the land question in Ireland by creating a peasant
proprietorship. It enabled the entire purchase money of a
holding to be advanced by the State.[31] By this time the Irish
had their war chest in the United States and could produce
arms, men, dynamite and assassins.[32] In 1891 Balfour introduced a new system under which the landlord or vendor was
paid in a specially-created Guaranteed Stock. In 1903 Wynd-
ham's Act, and in 1904 Birrell's, laid the foundation for the
complete abolition of landlordism in Ireland.[33]

We have seen in Chapter I the difficulty which the principle of limited liability had to overcome. From 1872 the
spread of the company system took about thirty years to
complete.[34] In the nineteenth century each unit of British
industry was on a comparatively small scale. " Its basis was
in the main a family basis; its capital was provided privately
and it was built up and extended out of profits; in so far as it
required banking facilities, it found them from independent
banks, often family banks, which in general had their headquarters in the provinces, and particularly in the Midlands
and the North, where the new industries flourished."[35]   In
Germany, the great industrial developments after 1870 were
due in a large measure to the assistance of the banks; in
France the individual investor, being very small, relied almost
entirely on the investments suggested to him by the big banks;
and in the United States the banks devoted themselves to the

development of American industry rather than to international finance; in this country London's financial organization adapted itself to the needs of a world-wide commerce,
but industry maintained its independence of financial control.[36]
But by the end of the century in the sphere of foreign investment the demand for political aid was felt. It had been
assumed that the industrial structure might be left to
individual foresight. The structure of industry was left to
the individual judgment and savings of innumerable small
capitalists. In the case of foreign investments though the
machinery was separate and specialized there was no formal
regulation of capital investments except to prevent fraud and
to prevent activities judged socially unwholesome.[37] The
savings of the *rentier* and professional classes were invested
through the London market in foreign enterprises and
Government stocks.[38]

The power to act without complications of official formality
was considered to be one of the secrets of supremacy.[39] The
State was reluctant to interfere. It wished neither to check
investment operations nor to call on banking institutions to
give assistance to some governmental purpose.[40] But in the
small circle of the ruling minds, financial was united with
political power in a community of similar ideas.[41] Towards
the end of the nineteenth century our rulers were not only
those with an estate in the country but also those with investments in the wide-wide world. The Government was pressed
and yielded to the demand that it should aid British industry
to secure openings and contracts abroad.[42] With the development of German competition, the Foreign Office became more
active in the promotion of the interest of commerce. In
1897, Great Britain denounced the commercial treaties which
prevented her from granting imperial preferences. In 1898,
the Imperial Department of Agriculture, and in 1899, a
School of Tropical Medicine was opened. In 1899, also, the
first development loans were given to the Colonies. In

1900 the Colonial Stocks Act was passed. Fortunately for the peace of Europe the important objects of British policy usually lay outside Europe. But when they were touched, the British Government renounced its attitude of non-interference between itself and the financial forces of the country.[43] There was developed a powerful and subtle tradition of co-operation between them and a " skilful and determined combination of self-interest and national interest secured ".[44]

In every advanced financial organization there is a market in which funds available only for very short periods are lent out. This market for short period loans—the call loan market—was provided by the ordinary commercial banks. The capital market dealt with the supply and demand for long period loans. The Stock Exchange dealt with the transfer of rights in already existing securities. Savings of a special character were dealt with by insurance companies, savings banks, and agricultural mortgage banks. Given a sufficiently long period and given an international gold standard, harmony between these diverse forces might be secured by the rate of interest. But by the middle of the nineteenth century it was clear that there " resided in the financial structure a tendency not only to harmony but also to disharmony ". The necessity " was gradually realized for some agency capable of acting as a brake upon the system ". This was the Bank of England acting as a central bank. That there is a distinction between the code of behaviour, appropriate to a commercial bank, and that appropriate to a central bank, was recognized as early as 1797. It was a bone of contention between practical authorities for nearly three-quarters of a century afterwards, and was finally established by Walter Bagehot in 1873.[45] Whereas the object of a commercial bank is to make a profit, a central bank must often undertake operations which are not only not profitable but result in losses. Its aim must be the safety of the financial system and the economic welfare of the country. It must hold the account of the Government because the latter's financial operations are conducted on such a scale that unless special measures are taken they may seriously derange the money market. It is responsible for the management of the monetary system of the country.

The Bank of England is almost unique as a central bank, in that it is a private institution practically independent of any form of legal control, save in regard to its power of issuing banknotes and granting loans to the State. It is practically free to do whatever it likes except that in order not to oppress His Majesty's subjects, it is debarred by the Tonnage Act of 1694 for all time from using any of its funds in dealing in merchandise or wares of any description. Independent of political influence, yet functioning solely in the public interest, it showed the knowledge, judgment and authority of individuals placed in a position of unchallengeable independence with great resources and every technical device at their disposition. Before the War, as London was the most powerful financial centre in the world, the automatic operation of the gold standard, under the supervision of the Bank of England, was comparatively satisfactory.[46]

After 1870 the problem of the proper organization of the labour market was to grow and grow until it has become perhaps the major problem of government. The dominant opinion before 1870 was that any tendency to destroy the freedom of individual action was " directly contrary to the undoubted truths of economical science" which must be "unflinchingly upheld at the peril of unmeasured evils ".[47]   It was recognized that true freedom of action could only exist if individuals were free to combine to secure these things which singularly they could not.   " The workman has a right to guard his own health, convenience, comfort and safety, and this he cannot effectively do while he remains an isolated individual. The reason is evident: the employers form a small class, between whom communication and concert are much more easy than between their men, and who have usually a strong disinclination to alter for the benefit of their men, any custom or regulation which seems to be for their own advantage. The single workman, dependent for his living upon his week's wages, is utterly incompetent to enforce any concession from his wealthy employer. Union is the natural remedy."[48] But if collective bargaining was desirable in order to secure conditions of safety, leisure and health, collective bargaining for the raising of wages was condemned as either futile or immoral. Futile because it was extremely unlikely that with their comparatively small numbers they could have any permanent effect on the rate of wages. " The most that could be done was to moderate or delay the adjustment of wages to conditions of bad trade by the enforcement of standard rates ".[49] Immoral because a union could only succeed in maintaining a high rate of wages by PROTECTION, that is by levying contributions from other classes of labourers and from the population in general.[50]

But this appeal to the altruistic sentiments of Trade Unions was open to the fatal retort which laid bare the radical confusion at the heart of all individualism, that the effect on others was no concern of theirs. How could any person make any contract with an easy conscience if it was his duty to consider whether his gain was not another's loss. " If ", wrote Edgeworth in a famous pamphlet, " it is attempted to enforce the argument against Trade Unionism by the consideration that it tends to diminish the total national produce, the obvious answer is that unionists, as ' economic men ', are not concerned with the *total produce*. Because the total produce is diminished, it does not follow that the labourer's share is diminished ".[51] In this matter " the untutored mind of the workman had gone more straight to the point than economic intelligence *misled by a bad method*, reasoning without mathematics upon a mathematical subject ".[52] In fact it was obvious that Trade Unionism in so far as they spread a knowledge of the conditions of the market and tended to break down the pools of labour bargaining in isolated ignorance, would render competition nearer the normal which economists assumed in their analysis of its benefits. But in so far as there were undoubtedly combinations of employers enjoying advantages of wealth and knowledge which gave them a superiority of bargaining power, and combinations of workers which gave them a temporary monopoly as compared with the unorganized workers, there was no reason to suppose that the actual contracts made were in the interests of the community as a whole. It was theoretically tenable that there was " an adjustment of contracts more beneficent than that which the mechanical play of competition tends to establish ". In a word in so far as competition was perfect—i.e. satisfied the conditions of the multiplicity of the bargainers, and their knowledge of the condition of the market—it might produce the greatest sum total of advantages for all. But in so far as competition was imperfect, due to the existence of monopolies on either side, there was no reason to accept its result. It was extremely unlikely that in a community in which " the whole structure of our wealth and refined civilization " was " built upon a basis of ignorance and pauperism and vice " that the requirements of a mathematically-perfect competition would be approximated to.

Prior to 1870 the Legislature and the Courts, in so far as they were not defending the privileges of the owners, were wrestling with the problem of reducing the element of coercion in the making of contracts. While they were opposed to the use of violence by strikers against blacklegs they could not ignore the opportunities for victimization and fraud which the masters enjoyed. If, as Jevons admitted, the collective bargaining of the Trade Unions was a more flexible and subtle instrument than the use of paternal legislation for securing health, safety and leisure, it was not clear that they might not be better for the prevention of intimidation and fraud.

Whether Trade Unions were attacked as creating monopolies of particular kinds of labour skill which could be exploited at the expense of the rest of the community; or defended as securing a closer approximation to a properly organized market for labour, it was clearly revealed by the Poor Law Commission of 1905-9, that the market for labour was so defective that it was one of the main causes of pauperism.[53] " The system of odd jobs was the most certain, the most extensive, cause or condition predisposing to pauperism." The significance of the unorganized nature of the labour market was revealed in the study of Unemployment, first published by Sir William Beveridge in 1908. He showed that " while the teaching of Adam Smith had secured the abolition of the visible and legal obstacles to the mobility of labour, such as laws of settlement and of apprenticeship, nothing had been done to remove the impalpable but no less real barriers of ignorance, poverty and custom ".[54] While it had been assumed that the demand for labour was single and concentrated and the supply of labour infinitely mobile and adaptable, investigation showed that while the markets for other commodities were increasingly organized that for labour was still left to ill-informed individual action.[55] The prevailing method of obtaining employment was still that of personal application at the works. The prevailing method of selling labour was to hawk it from door to door.[56] The consequences of this dispersal of demand in a variety of local places and the lack of knowledge on the part of the individuals composing the supply, was to turn making a livelihood into a gamble. For in all trades, just in proportion as the market was unorganized and labour immobile, there was a possibility and a tendency for fresh men to enter under the influence of local developments at one place though men of the same trade were standing idle elsewhere.[57] This unorganized condition of the labour market resulted in (1) each employer or small district contriving to maintain a separate reserve of labour;[58] (2) the recruitment of trades not in accordance with their real growth, but by local accidents;[59] (3) the longer men were in one occupation the less they would know how to find work outside;[60] and (4) a swelling of the casual labour market by every form of human weakness and misfortune and from every point of industrial unrest.[61]   In a word the increasing pace of industrial change required that the market for labour should be so organized that changes in demand for different forms of labour, due either to changes in demand for goods and services or in the methods by which they were produced, should be made known to those concerned.   The spread of information was a matter which cried out for organized rather than for individual action.[62]   Only by such an organization of the labour market could boys and girls be guided in their choice of a career or educational authorities plan the technical training which they would require.[63]   The beginnings of such an organized market for labour was provided in 1909 by the Labour Exchange Act.   In 1911 a scheme for compulsory insurance against unemployment was begun.   This involved a recognition of the principle that the general interest in the flexibility of the industrial structure involved an incidence of unemployment on individuals for which they could not be fairly held responsible.   The unemployment which was due to the mobility of labour required by industrial efficiency could be fairly charged to the working cost of industry itself.

An essential condition for the development of a market in commodities is the provision of statistics.   The census had been established in 1801; a census of production was commenced in 1906.   In 1886 a voluntary system under the Board of Trade was begun for the collection of annual returns of acreage, cropping and livestock, but compulsion was resisted by the agricultural community on the ground that it might be made the basis for increased taxation.   So that it was not until 1917, when the Corn Production Act passed in the emergency of War offered a subsidy for certain crops,

K

that it was possible to secure the inclusion of agriculture in the census of production. In 1882 the word " Unemployed " first appears as a noun and in 1886 there is the beginning of a systematic collection of labour statistics. In the same year the Board of Trade began to supply traders with an account of the movements of overseas trade and tariff changes, extracts from consular reports and information as to the opening for British trade and industry abroad.

The development of our public health services, bewildering in detail, is simple in principle. Attempts to reduce the cost of pauperism in the 'thirties led to an investigation into the prevalence of epidemic disease and its relation to poverty. In 1843 a Royal Commission had recommended legislative and administrative action to deal with a serious national evil of bad sanitation and ill-health. In 1869 the Royal Sanitary Commission summarized the minimum sanitary conditions necessary for civilized social life. In this early period the driving force was the dread of the spread of infection.[64] But in the next fifty years to the fear of infection was to be added a motive of economy. Sickness was found to be a terrible hidden charge upon industry. The ignorance and ill-health of the England of the pioneering industrial revolution could not be afforded by an England in competition with the vigour of the United States and Germany after 1870. At the same time the development of medical science after 1850 brought a vision of a preventative medicine which concerned not merely with the unseen drains beneath the house but with an " understanding of those unseen processes of attack and defence which find their sphere in the cells and fluids of the body, and their influence upon the infecting or disturbing agent ".[65] From the vision and technique of Pasteur's work on the causes of fermentation in 1858 there followed between 1871 and 1894 the discovery of the bacilli of leprosy, typhoid, tuberculosis, cholera, diptheria, tetanus and plague. From the discovery of the unseen bacilli research passed to the discovery of its agent, the toxin and the antitoxin by which it could be met.[66] With the hunting of the microbe the doctor took his place beside the engineer in questions of health administration. Whereas in 1869 water supply, sewerage, streets and highways, housing, the removal of refuse, consumption of smoke, public lighting, inspection of food, provision for the burial of the dead, registration of death and sickness were recognized as necessities for a civilized life, a generation later the study of animal and vegetable parasites, infection by bacteria, disinfection and causes of specific diseases were equally necessary. In the twentieth century infantile mortality, school hygiene, tropical medicine, tropical disease, industrial hygiene, and venereal disease were vital parts of the work of public health authorities. Preventative medicine entered a biological setting which comprehends the nature of the organism, the nature of their environment and their inter-relation.[67] In 1908 the systematic examination of school children was begun. In 1911 the National Insurance Act provided a system of insurance against ill-health for all employed persons between certain ages and with certain financial limitations. Ten million persons in England became eligible for the care of over 10,000 doctors. These panel patients could seek medical advice the moment that they felt the need; while their doctor could multiply his attentions without fear that his motive would be misunderstood. This meant that disease might be studied at the beginning and treatment continued until it was effective.[68] This change was largely the result of the Poor Law Commission of 1905-9, which had laid bare the contradictions of the existing system. " While poor law principles might approve a generous establishment of sanitary provision for the prevention of disease and destitution, on the other hand, medical relief for the individual, as a form of relief, had to be grudging or even deterrent in order to avoid pauperization, and it thus deprived itself of effectiveness. . . . So long as it dealt only with sickness as an outcome of economic destitution, it was obviously debarred from affording medical treatment as a *preventative* measure against potential destitution." The National Insurance Act of 1911 brought the great mass of the less obtrusive forms of sickness into prominence as a necessary field of public health activity.

As early as 1833 supervision of some of the conditions of industrial employment had been made part of the business of government. The Factory Act of that year began an important development by providing that there should be four paid inspectors responsible for the policy it imposed. But they were at first hampered by the fact that, as the registration of births was not made compulsory until 1837, they had no evidence of the age of the children whose conditions of work they were supposed to control. At first also they were appointed with powers to make " such rules, regulations and orders as may be necessary for the due execution of the Act " and with power to try offenders, impose fines and in default to commit to prison. Such a heroic combination of legislative executive and judicial powers was not then to be endured. In 1844 the rule-making powers were transferred to a Government department. By 1878 the whole manufacturing field had been brought under control. The staff was organized into districts with district inspectors and grouped into divisions each under a superintending inspector and the whole staff placed under a chief inspector at the Home Office. After 1890 there was a rapid improvement. In 1891 it was made compulsory to give particulars of earnings to all piece workers in textile factories; in 1895 the Home Office secured power to apply special rules to dangerous trades. Four industrial diseases were made notifiable by employers or by doctors who learnt of their existence. A reasonable temperature was for the first time required in the factory. In 1901 it was decided that ventilation must be satisfactory. When Asquith was at the Home Office special medical

engineering and electrical branches were added to the inspectorate and women inspectors were appointed for the first
time.[69]

The development of our public health services most clearly
shows the intricacy of the relation between the individual and
the community. In so far as Christian tradition imposes
upon the State the duty to strive officiously to keep alive any
member of the community who might otherwise die the
State finds itself involved in a responsibility for an understanding and an application of the forces which determine
life and death. In 1801 the first census, and in 1836 the
registration of births and deaths, put the State upon a course
which may only end with the supervision over the exits and
entrances of life and death that Plato proposed for his
guardians. The privilege of procreation may yet have to be
controlled—for if it may be made a crime to make two blades
of grass grow where one had grown before it is difficult to see
why it should not be made a crime to make two mouths be
where one had been before. Nor can the State rest content
with its control of the size of the population. It may be
immediately concerned with the age distribution of whatever
population it decides upon. As the expectation of life increases and the proportion of the population over working
age increases the ceremony of making way[70] may become a
part of our national pageantry. The anthropologists have
shown us that primitive man was so often right where the
godly thought him wrong that his prescriptions for senility
may enjoy the same prestige as his prescriptions for puberty.
In any case the possible fusion of Eastern indifference to death
with the Western technique of experiment and investigation
may produce startling results. The partnership of the living
with the dead and those yet to be born may grow closer than
even Burke could wish.

Down to 1870 schools in England were provided by private
persons, endowments or joint stock companies. The assistance

of the State was limited to the meagre grants which Parliament provided to be administered by religious bodies. By 1870 it was clear that private enterprise had failed to provide the elements of education for even half the children of the country. A census report of 1851 put the number of children in England between three and fifteen years at 5,000,000, of whom only 2,046,848 were at school, 49 per cent. staying till eleven and 28 per cent. till thirteen. In 1869 two-fifths only of the children of the working classes between the age of six and ten were on the register of Government aided schools and only one-third of those aged ten to twelve. In the private schools, with a few brilliant exceptions, the quality of the teaching was almost worthless. In London a Royal Commission had found that in the uninspected schools among the teachers " none are too old, too poor, too ignorant, too feeble, too sickly, too unqualified in one or every way, to regard themselves, and to be regarded by others, as unfit for school-keeping ".[71] No fundamental improvement was possible before 1870 because, as Cobden wrote in 1850, " the Liberal party, the soul of which is Dissent, are torn to pieces by the question, and it is not easy to heal a religious feud. The Tories, whatever they may say to the contrary, are opposed to the enlightenment of the people. They are naturally so from an instinct of self-preservation ".[72] After the Reform Bill of 1867, which enfranchised the sceptical and thinking artisans, the Government in 1870 took the step of providing that where the religious denominations had specifically failed a local school board was to be elected. These school boards might compel attendance if they wished and pay the fees of necessitous children. The object of the Bill was " to complete the present voluntary system, to fill up the gaps, sparing the public money where it can be done without, procuring as much as we can the assistance of the parents and welcoming as much as rightly can the co-opera-tion and aid of those benevolent men who desire to assist their neighbours ".[73] In 1873 the children of parents receiving poor relief were obliged to attend. In 1876 a motive for absence was removed by forbidding the employment of children under ten. In 1880 attendance was made universally compulsory up to ten. In 1891 school fees were abolished in most schools. But not until 1918 was universal full-time attendance up to fourteen and the abolition of all fees secured.[74] In the meantime while it had been recognized, as Lowe put it, that we must educate our masters, it was even more obvious that we must train our workers and educate our industrial leaders. It was not only that, as Forster said when introducing the Bill of 1870, despite their powerful sinews and determined energy our uneducated labourers were in danger of being overmatched by the well-taught workers of other countries,[75] but that in the 'nineties it was clear that " Englishmen must take business as seriously as their grandfathers had done, and as their American and German rivals were doing: that their training for business must be methodical like that of their new rivals and not merely practical on lines that had sufficed for the simpler world of two generations ago ".[76] To meet this need for technicians chairs in the older universities were provided for the natural sciences, provincial universities were developed, the new County and County Borough Councils were empowered to develop technical education. In 1899 the Board of Education was created and in 1902 the skill and cunning of Morant and Balfour secured the abolition of the school boards, a compromise on the question of religious teaching in schools and the responsibility of local authorities under the supervision of the State for the development of both elementary and secondary education.

As the experience of the need for intelligent co-ordination of the complex specialization which industry imposed compelled the abandonment of *laissez-faire,* the political problems was made more difficult by the varieties of intellectual experience which science was bringing to the different social classes. As the contradictions latent in the seeming simplicity of the utilitarian creed were revealed academic minds were encouraged to examine with some Socratic skill the nature of society. In his *Ethical Studies* Bradley gave to Utilitarianism a mortal wound from which it has never recovered. He once more united England with the Continental thought from which it had so long been sundered. He recalled some political thinkers to a consideration of the problem that it is the function of the State to promote the good life; that there is a reason in morality which is something more than a calculus of pleasures. What Bradley taught with one of the finest English metaphysical minds, in some of the most lucid of English prose, T. H. Green persuasively lectured, though with theological pre-suppositions which made his exposition needlessly obscure. But it is significant that the best philosophical minds were driven to consider once again that the social order was a moral order and that the problem of politics was not a simple antagonism between a party of persuasion and a party of coercion, but the discovery of those institutions which should best provide for the transition from coercion to consent. At a time when one of the major political problems would be the development of a technique by which the continent of Africa could be civilized, as Rome had once civilized the German forests and the English marshes, this was a vital gain.

But if the philosophers had their intimations of developments to come the general public was hopelessly bewildered by the impact of the new science of biology on their dying creeds and common-sense morality. In 1859 Darwin's *Origin of Species* came to convince the world of two propositions: that the origin of man himself was of the same nature as that of all other living things; that the varieties of living things could be explained without the assumption of a miraculous and incomprehensible design. To many his work was the occasion for confusing every political and moral issue they had heard of and misunderstood. Though they must have known even before 1859 that babies were neither moral nor rational, Darwin's evidence that their own morals had a natural history nearly sent them to the dogs. A return to the jungle was by many thought to be the only way of maintaining their present freedom from it. For a time the more barbarous superstition of self-help was reinforced by the belief that science showed that mutual aid was the enemy of progress. Darwin himself in the *Descent of Man* repudiated these puerile vulgarities. He wrote: " Important as the struggle for existence has been and even still is, yet as far as the higher parts of man's nature is concerned there are other agents more important. For the moral qualities are advanced either directly or indirectly much more through the effect of habit, the reasoning powers, instruction, religion, etc., than through natural selection: though to the latter agency we owe the social instincts which afford the basis for the development of the moral sense ". As soon as the conception of evolution was carefully studied it became obvious that the important thing was the duty it imposed on each individual to consider how he himself in his intimate life might serve his kind and his duty in fellowship with others to control the environment which influenced them all.

Unfortunately the real significance of Darwin's vision was largely lost by the fact that the English middle class paid for its contempt for things of the mind by its acceptance of Herbert Spencer's confused ideas about evolution and the nature of society. He tried to reconcile a conception of evolution, which owed more to engineering than to biology, with a conception of rights, derived from Thomas Hodgkin's conception of society as a natural phenomena to which the universal spirit had assigned natural laws. He seems to have believed with the Utilitarians that pleasure is the sole good, and that to consider the direction of evolution is by far the best criterion of the way in which we shall get most of it (Moore). For a generation he prevented clear thinking by his followers on any of the problems involved in the interdependence of living things and their environment or on the problems of the nature of duty. This was particularly unfortunate, because towards the end of the nineteenth century the new contacts and conflicts of culture which the swift development of communications was producing required the most careful philosophical criticism and control. Seeley's *Expansion of England* which showed the development of the Empire in a fit of absence of mind gave to the English doctrine of muddling through an almost cosmic significance. If an empire could be built up in a fit of absence of mind a society might be created in the same way. There were here symptoms of that attack on reason which was later on the Continent to have such devastating effects but which might be expected first to have appeared in England where the bewilderment caused by the impact of science on ancient customs was first severely felt. Towards the end of the century there must have been many who like Lord Salisbury " had never known what it was to doubt the truth of Christian doctrine " but " had all his life found a difficulty in accepting the moral teaching of the gospel ". This must have produced in others as in him " a very profound sense of the obscurity of things ".[77]

If the importance of religion waned as more and more of the sceptical and thinking artisans became a political power Protestant bigotry was replaced by a nationalism so virulent and pervasive that it could destroy nearly every gift which science offered to man. In England it had been possible to believe that there was no essential conflict between the development of Free Trade, the growth of Liberalism and the sense of national unity. England was to save Europe by her example of freedom broadening slowly down from precedent to precedent. Our politics were the dispute of a family over individual morals and individual shares in one increasing revenue. The Irish troubles could be put down to the Papist aberrations of the bad boy of the family. But in the third quarter of the century the force of nationalism was to show itself in disturbing ways. Instead of a cultural and spiritual tradition, nationality became a self-conscious pose. A spiritual heritage became a creed to be taught; to some a business to be developed. Beginning with Seeley's *Expansion of England* there was steadily developed a new and vulgar imperialism which hoped to see the frontiers of suburbia advance to the equator. To Chamberlain our tropical possessions were England's undeveloped estates, which can never be developed without imperial assistance. It was to seem to Kipling that " God has arranged that a clean run youth of British middle class shall, in the matter of backbone, brains and bowels, surpass all other youths ".

The worst ravages of this racial megalomania were prevented by the traditions of the Colonial Office itself, the integrity of all those who were capable of sustained economic analysis, and the national tradition which was firmly opposed to military adventures.[78]   Before 1871 three Permanent Secretaries of State for the Colonies had expressed separatist views—Stephen, Merivale, Blatchford. If they were retained it was because " the authority of the British Crown " was " the most powerful instrument under Providence of maintaining peace and order in extensive regions of the earth and . . . in diffusing amongst many millions of the human race the blessings of Christianity and civilization ".[79]   When in 1872 Disraeli was saying in his grandiloquent way that " the Colonies have decided that the Empire shall not be destroyed; and in my opinion no Minister in this country will do his duty who neglects any opportunity of reconstructing as much as possible of our Colonial Empire ",[80] the structure of that Empire had so developed that we were saved from the dangers of pursuing an imperial will-o'-the-wisp.

It had already split into the Empire in partnership and the Empire in trust. Between 1837 and 1867 over three-quarters of a million had left Great Britain and Ireland for British North America and nearly another million for Australia and New Zealand. In Canada in the critical period between 1839 and 1854 a silent revolution had taken place. It was carried out by mere instructions from the Crown, conveyed by dispatches to the Governor. Whereas in 1839 Lord John Russell, as Colonial Secretary, could hold that responsible government—the acceptance by the Governor of such policy as a colonial cabinet responsible to a colonial legislature might produce—was " entirely incompatible with the relations between the mother country and the colony ", in 1846 the Colonial Secretary, Lord Grey, was writing that " it cannot be too distinctly acknowledged that it is neither possible nor desirable to carry on the government of any of the British possessions in America in opposition to the opinion of the inhabitants ".[81]   The powers of the Crown were never formally abolished. But by the growth of constitutional conventions there was a progressive expansion of the sphere of colonial self-government from limited autonomy to the complete self-determination of the present Dominion status.[82] Responsible government once established in British North America was extended to Australia and New Zealand. In 1852 the colonies were allowed to devise their own constitutions. In 1859 the Government of Canada asserted its right to " adjust the taxation of the people in the way they deem best, even if it should unfortunately happen to meet with the disapproval of the Imperial Ministry ". Dominion tariffs were to grow unpruned by any imperial and Free Trade hand. In 1867 the British North America Act was the legal embodiment of a federal constitution devised by the self-governing colonies of British North America for the conduct of their national affairs. From that time on the rapid evolution of the Overseas Dominions involved many complicated adjustments of old political machinery to changing conditions. The tendency to equality of status was both right and inevitable. Geographical and other conditions made this impossible by the way of federation. The only alternative was by the way of autonomy; and along that road it was steadily sought.

The more or less casual meetings of the self-governing colonies at the Jubilees of 1887 and 1897 and the Coronation in 1902 developed into an Imperial Conference with rules of procedure and a regular constitution. In 1907 Imperial Federation was specifically rejected and a formal constitution was drawn up. " It will be to the advantage of the Empire if a conference to be called the Imperial Conference is held every four years, at which questions of common interest may be discussed and considered as between his Majesty's Government and his Governments of the self-governing dominions beyond the seas." By 1926 every self-governing member of the Empire was master of its destiny. In fact if not always in form it was subject to no compulsion whatever.[83]

Entirely different from the Empire in partnership was the development of the Empire in trust. The opening of the Suez Canal in 1869, the final triumph in 1875 of the steam-ship over sail, the rapid development of railways with the new forms of steel, the discovery of the microbe, made the partition of Africa by the European Powers as inevitable as the early stages of the industrial revolution had made the occupation of the Mississippi Valley. When science had removed the barriers of disease to the course of trade, either the existing political organization had to accept responsibility for the control of the racial and cultural conflicts which inevitably ensued or they would see the establishment of a black feudalism ravaged by greed, superstition and lust. With what skill the delicate task of the partition of Africa was carried out by a Europe, which possessed no central authority, the diplomatic records now show. A divided continent had to partition a new world on pain of seeing the re-establishment of slavery, and the extinction of the small tapers of culture it had painfully kept alight on the edge of a dark abyss.

In Canada the presence within a British colony of a politically conscious alien community, French and Catholic, and the existence on its borders of the powerful influence of the Republican institutions of the United States had hastened the development of responsible government. So far as the white colonies were concerned, their eventual independence was considered desirable and inevitable. In 1836 Cobden had regarded the colonies as but one accessory to the army, navy, the church and the Corn Laws, which were the unjust privileges of aristocracy. In 1841 Sir G. C. Lewis in a classic discussion had argued that neither for tribute or military assistance, nor for trade facilities or outlets for immigration, or penal settlements, were the colonies of any possible value as possessions. In 1860 Cairnes wrote that " in commercial policy, in territorial policy, in military defence, the colonies, in the teeth of example, advice and remonstrance, have pursued their own way. We have abandoned all the objects for the sake of which our colonial empire was founded. We are unable to impress our will upon our colonies in any particular, however in itself reasonable or just or apparently necessary for their safety or ours. We retain the privilege of spending yearly £4.5 millions on their protection and receive in requital prohibitive tariffs and ironical allegiance ". An English colony was not worth the sacrifice of a single American contract. In 1861, when a powerful committee inquired into the existing system of colonial defence, the outlook was so dominated by the idea of colonial self-reliance that it was sometimes difficult to differentiate those who favoured imperial co-operation from those who looked forward to imperial disintegration.[84] Godley, the Assistant Under-Secretary for War, considered that the presence of the British flag all over the world added very much to our weakness.[85] Lowe, the Chancellor of the

Exchequer, considered that as the thirteen colonies had once revolted from us so we might separate from our colonies because we were taxed for their benefit.

But the fact was that outside Canada, Australia and New Zealand we had incurred commitments which it would be morally shameful and psychologically impossible to abandon. As Sir J. Stephen had once said, " we emancipate our grown-up sons and keep our unmarried daughters and children who may chance to be rickety in domestic bonds ".[86]   We had become responsible for many " detached islands with heterogeneous populations—wretched burdens to this country which in an evil hour we assumed, but which we have no right to lay down " (c. 1848).

The experience and responsibility of the Colonial Office had grown in many " repulsive controversies " in which no member of the Cabinet but the head of the Colonial Office could ever be persuaded to devote any time.[87]   The abolition of the slave trade had made it responsible for the recreation of a society in the West Indies.   For the first five years after its annexation New Zealand had been the scene of an important experiment in the art of native government.   In 1830 the term " Crown Colony " was for the first time applied to the tropical possessions under the direct control of the home Government.   The retention of the Cape of Good Hope had embarked us in a continent where no frontiers could be drawn and in contact with the Boers, whose native policy would make either withdrawal or peaceful settlement impossible.[88]   In West Africa small forts retained to suppress the slave trade provided the starting-point for a commercial and political expansion once the economic value of the tropics was realized.   In India the mutiny of 1857 had led to the inauguration of a new era of public works undertaken by the central or provincial governments, which was profoundly to modify the *laissez-faire* tradition.   As soon as inland penetration became possible the policing of coastal districts by a

navy was no longer sufficient.   If the natives were to be protected at all the Government had to become a road maker,
a railway builder, and a constructor of ports.   For it was
only by the development of a commerce in tropical products,
such as palm-oil, rubber, cotton and gum that the trade in
men or slavery could be suppressed.   The Congo showed
the danger of shirking Empire when trade had already connected two unequal civilizations.[89]

That interplay of economic and political factors is clearly
shown in the work of Salisbury.   Speaking in the House of
Lords in 1890 he said, " Up to ten years ago we remained
masters of Africa, practically, or the greater part of it, without
being put to the inconvenience of protectorate or anything
of that sort, by the simple fact that we were masters of the
sea and that we have had considerable experience in dealing
with native races.   So much was that the case that we left
enormous stretches of coast to the native rulers in the full
confidence that they would go on under native rulers, and
in the hope that they would gradually acquire their own
proper civilization without any interference on our part.
Then suddenly we found out that that position, however convenient, had no foundation whatever in international law.
We had no rights over all those vast stretches of coast
—we had no power of preventing any other nation
from coming in and seizing any portion of them ".[90]
Was he to allow a struggle for supremacy between white
traders of different nationalities, with the degradation of the
natives which must ensue and the possibility of national sentiment provoking war?   He decided that a selective regulation
of the British advance, the transmutation of independent
movements into an expansion of Empire was to be preferred.
" The rights of the black man that he recognized were:
the right to a rescue from the curse of the slave trade; the
black man's right to share in the religion and civilization of
which the white races were the trustees; the right to be

well governed. But there was no questioning of the right of European absorption and no idea of a right to independence or sovereignty. And for the reason that his generation had knowledge of what Africa for Africans meant. Their dilemma was, were they justified in placing fresh burdens of cost and responsibility upon their own people at home? "[89] When chartered companies were resorted to—the Niger Company in 1886, the East African Company in 1888 and the Rhodes South Africa Company in 1889—though they received monopolistic rights in trade and administration, their fiscal powers were limited; the Imperial Government reserved the right to supervise their native policy; exclusive control over their foreign policy and the right to withdraw their charter. Before 1870 a harder, more emotional generation had believed either in extermination by the sword and natural causes or assimilation by the gospel. After 1870 neither assimilation nor extermination were feasible. It was then a question of the technique of control. Where there was to be indirect rule the Government and not the trader had to take the responsibility. In 1869 the Suez Canal altered the trade route of the world. In 1870 the cheapening of railways by Bessemer steel made possible the penetration of the Continent; in the 'eighties the chartered companies offered profitable investments; in 1897 the mosquito was discovered to be the cause of malaria. At the same time a new conception of the duties of government emerged. The colonial authorities became responsible for the economic as well as the political welfare of the lands they governed.[91] Lord Harcourt, when Colonial Secretary, said that " the position of the Colonial Secretary on the Crown Colony side of his department carried with it the powers, duties, responsibilities and anxieties of a practical and laborious despot controlled only by the forces of nature, by his own discretion and by the sporadic curiosity at question time of friends or opponents, inspired either by imagination or information ".[92]

L

It had to provide a policy with regard to vacant lands, irrigation, methods of cultivation, transport, health. It had to experiment in a variety of political methods.[93]

The essential element in all this was the necessity of the State to keep pace with the development of trade, if only to prevent the bloodshed and degradation of uncontrolled private traders and the exclusion of the area from Free Trade should other countries have got control. To preserve the open door for all comers was after the 'fifties the aim of policy of Great Britain, and one great motive of her expansion was to prevent her own commercial exclusion.

After 1870 in foreign relations English statesmen had to consider that the absolute supremacy of the British navy was threatened by the potential power of any industrial power with access to the sea to challenge it by the new weapons science was producing. Russia in the Black Sea, France in the Mediterranean and the new Germany in the North Sea were all potential rivals. Though the two-power standard at sea was proclaimed in 1889, it had to be recognized that it was impossible to increase our army proportionally to those of the great land powers' nationalism and the industrial revolution had produced. There was an almost universal conviction that for Constantinople to pass into the hands of Russia would be a disaster for the British Empire. But it was also the conviction of English statesmen that it was futile to spend any more English blood in sustaining the Turkish Empire. She was too feeble for independence and her vassalage to Russia would be too dangerous for our route to India. But if she were eliminated as a sovereign power, government of some kind would have to be found for the wretchedly oppressed multitudes of European Turkey. The Balkans could not be left as a no-man's-land. " But ", wrote Salisbury in 1876, " division of that kind of jetsam is peculiarly difficult. If the Powers quarrel over it, the calamities of a gigantic war must be undergone. If they

agree people call it partition and denounce it as immoral."[93]
If the approaching demise of Turkey threatened the
European balance of power that balance had been even
more profoundly disturbed by the Prussian defeat of Austria
and of France. " Austria's existence ", wrote Salisbury, " is
no longer of the importance to us that it was in former times.
Her vocation in Europe has gone. She was a counterpart
to France and barrier against Russia: but France is gone,
and the development of Russia is chiefly in regions where
Austria could not, and if she could would not, help us to
check it."[95]

It seemed in fact that in 1870 the only political structure
on the Continent was the league of the three Emperors of
Russia, Prussia and Austria, while as a threat to the Mediterranean route to India there was the possibility of an alliance
of France and Russia. Such was the general background of
the diplomatic drama which culminated in the Congress of
Berlin. Beaconsfield succeeded in driving a wedge between
the three emperors, whose autocracy was incompatible with
British Liberalism and strategically a threat to British
imperialism. " Next to making a tolerable settlement for
the Porte " our great object at the Congress of Berlin " was
to break up and permanently prevent, the alliance of the three
Empires ".[96] The breach thus opened between Germany and
Russia by this masterpiece of diplomacy was never again
completely closed.[97] But if England had divided her enemies
her system of responsible government made it impossible
for her to assure the support of possible friends. While she
wished to assure herself of the armed assistance of Germany
against Russia she was not prepared to support Germany in
the event of a second Franco-German war.[98] Bismarck
always thought that serious negotiations with England were
dangerous because they were impossible without secrecy, and
if secret the absence of Parliamentary sanction would make
them worthless.[99]

To the difficulties of the shifting balance of power on the continent of Europe between the great land powers was added in the 'eighties the triple drama of the continent of Africa. In the south the impossibility of drawing any settled boundary between the crumbling native states and the British and Boer colonists with their conflicting native policies. In 1880 Black Michael complained that in Africa many thought that Zululand should not be a border at all, but should be included in His Majesty's possessions. " But if Zululand, why not Swaziland and so on northward to the Equator? . . . I don't think it is for our interest to continue this kind of advance, while we are responsible for the cost of it."[100] Thus spoke the voice of mid-Victorian finance before the problems of economic imperialism silenced it perhaps for ever. In 1882 the Gladstone Government began our long occupation of Egypt " from a love of peace and on the principle of peace "[101] with the hope and intention of withdrawal provided only that " the order of things to be established shall be of a satisfactory character and possess the elements of stability and permanence ".[102]   In 1885 French rivalry in Egypt and West Africa together with the Russian threat in Central Asia compelled England to recognize Germany's right to colonization in Africa.[103]   In these complexities the policy of splendid isolation was pursued by Lord Salisbury. Although in 1898 Chamberlain, supported by Lansdowne and Devonshire, was in favour of an Anglo-German alliance openly sanctioned by Parliament as opposed to an alliance with France or Russia, Salisbury felt equally little confidence in Russia, Germany or France.[104]   By 1900 the position of Britain might well seem precarious.   " Your Majesty ", wrote Bulow, " is quite right in feeling that the British must come to us. They have just lost a good deal of hair in Africa; America is uncertain; Japan is not to be depended upon; France is filled with hate; Russia is perfidious; public opinion is hostile in all countries. . . . At present it is beginning to dawn gradually on the minds of the British that they will not be able to hold their world empire merely by their own power against so many opponents."[105]

But in 1894 Britain had already moved towards Japan as the one Power capable of holding Russia in check.[106] In 1902 the Conservative Government made a treaty with Japan, though it involved a surrender of the tradition of the constitution that the British Government would not pledge itself to take part in war before public opinion had decided for itself.[107] In Manchuria, Russia was seeking to extend her authority, while in the Yangtse valley England was using her influence to exploit her commercial interests.[108] Russia's tightening political and economic hold over Persia provoked a statement from the British Foreign Secretary in the House of Lords in 1903 that there must be no foreign naval base in the Persian Gulf.[109] In 1904 the Tangier crisis between France and Germany produced the *entente cordiale,* which though for Lansdowne it was mere colonial agreement having no threat for Germany,[110] laid the basis for a working partnership which the German naval threat to British sea power ripened to an alliance in war. From 1902 it was necessary that England should win France, hold Russia, agree with Italy, and prevent the German naval menace and the threat of her strategic railways in Asia Minor.[111] In this task her diplomatic brains were " far superior to those of Germany, both in the clearness with which they perceived their goal, and the logical accuracy with which they carried on their negotiations ".[112] By 1907, the opinion in the inner English political circles was that Germany was going to contest with us the command of the sea and our commercial position.[113] Though this may have been a delusion of some courtiers and bureaucrats, it should be recorded that in 1908 Asquith told Balfour that " the Government could form no theory of the German policy which fitted all the known facts except that they wanted war ".[114]

What effect had the changing face of industry and trade, the new worlds of science, and the mutations of society upon the art of politics? The diaries and speeches of the traditional leaders are eloquent with their growing distress. In 1884 Hardy is writing of the " revolutionary race which Gladstone has started and Chamberlain will run ".[115] Goschen tells the Eighty Club that " the dethronement of orthodox political economy seemed likely to be signalized by the appearance of a swarm of quacks ".[116] To Selborne, in 1886, it seemed that we were approaching a time " when the real contest will be between revolution and the English Constitution such as we have known it ".[117] In the 'nineties, Chamberlain is demanding a Red Cross service for the competitive industrial system.[118] The eternal laws of supply and demand and the sanctity of private right in property are mere phrases, " the conventional cant of selfish wealth ".[119] In 1895, Salisbury writes despairingly " Governments can do so little and prevent so little nowadays. Power has passed from the hands of statesmen, but I should be very much puzzled to say into whose hands it has passed. It is all pure drifting ".[120] And the true full note of a dying age in Rosebery's speech at Glasgow in 1909. " In my opinion the deep, subtle, insidious danger which underlies all is the danger of Socialism. . . . I may think Tariff Reform or Protection an evil, but Socialism is the end of all, the negation of faith, of family, of property, of monarchy, of empire."[121]

We may sympathize with these masterful administrators of the unforeseen. For, by 1880, human affairs had reached such a state of complexity that they required the aid of mathematical analysis. " The lights of unaided reason— though sparkling with eloquence and glowing with public spirit—are but a precarious guide unless a sterner science fortify the way."[122] In Government departments the simple decimal dots which dukes had sometimes damned, gave place to formulæ, rich and strange. But statistics' artful aid and mathematics' magic spells, though they might reveal, they could not solve the problems of the State. To the extensive but backward view of history, the importance of the period 1870-1914, might seem to lie in the attempts made by a growing democracy to master the plutocratic powers which held it in thrall.   It might seem to be an attempt by publicity and measurement to cure the sickness of an acquisitive society. But the contemporary politician could enjoy no such simplicity of vision. For he has not merely to decide on which side he stands in some dispute; but which disputes will justify his leaving colleagues with whom, in other things, he is agreed. The more numerous and more urgent the issues which arise, the more must he strive to retain the method of persuasion in conditions which threaten force.

Was the conflict between rich and poor to be solved as Disraeli had flamboyantly proposed by securing a " union of the cottage and the throne ", or as Gladstone had so often preached, by developing in the unprivileged the moral integrity he assumed the privileged to possess.   Or must it, as the Radicals proposed, be slowly mitigated by the growth of reason and measurement in State affairs at the expense of tradition and privilege.   And how was this domestic problem related to the changing balance of power in Europe and the spreading network of a closely woven world economic order in which it seemed that markets might not open to the merely " economic man ", but only to be the Machiavellian use of political power?   And how again was it related to those religious issues which to some statesmen were of equal importance with the quantitative economic adjustments they were called upon to make?   In 1868 Disraeli had made his main appeal to the Protestantism of the nation.   " The ultimate triumph, were our Church to fall, would be to that power which would substitute for the authority of our Sovereign the supremacy of a foreign prince."[123]   The youthful Esher shrewdly remarked in 1880 " if the Irish were

Mahommedan or Hindus we should have no difficulty with them. Every consideration would be then shown to their religious prejudices. Because they are Catholics they have been treated like dogs and are borne down by the vulgar bigotry of English Evangelicalism ".[124] " I should consider ", wrote Selborne in 1885, " the maintenance of the Established Church of much greater importance that the predominance of my own or the defeat of any other political party ".[125]

By the middle of the 'eighties, the traditional Conservatism was facing the destruction of the economic basis of their order. The vision of a Tory democracy based on a union of the cottage and the throne, was already the baseless fabric of a dream. It had had to yield to the realities of an industrial order in which wealth could no longer be held merely on the understanding that traditional obligations would be gracefully performed, but by its power to manipulate the springs of human action in a still imperfectly educated electorate and its willingness to serve when it could not cajole. It was saved partly by the fact that the world-sweep of the industrial revolution already gave indications of its challenge to the splendid isolation in which the English economic heritage had been so shrewdly developed. Salisbury's policy of splendid isolation is anticipated in the sphere of foreign affairs, a desire which was steadily to grow in all cultural groups until in the decades after the War it destroyed the economic order the nineteenth century had achieved. It was saved also by the fact that the Irish question disrupted the Liberal Party by raising the ghost of all those questions, religious and national, it was their belief that peace and plenty had for ever laid. In these circumstances it was understandable that the new most vital political movement at the end of the nineteenth century should have been the rise of the new Labour Party. Its leaders turned their backs on all the mighty issues which were preparing a challenge to the world, and sought in the domestic morality of their countrymen and their common-sense capacity in common tasks to develop a simple form of economic Nonconformity. It had its origin in three main sources: the new professional classes which the growth of science and the increased functions of the State had called into being; the humanitarianism which, with the decay of traditional Christianity, now sought to save the slums as it had once sought to save the world; and the unions of organized labour whose leaders desired something more than to be the mere promoters of collective bargains. The professional classes who were not entirely specialized in the natural sciences had intimations of the challenge which science offered to the traditional art of politics. It was only by research, and above all by quantitative measurements, that the problems of society could be solved. They realized that only the educated classes could lead a peaceful revolution. They recognized that " the middle and upper classes are the revolutionary element in society; the proletariat element is the Conservative element as Disraeli well knew ".[126] Their humanitarianism was Puritan and peaceful. It was Bernard Shaw who made the Puritan in the Englishman face the question of the real place of property in the social order. Suppose that private property was demonstrably not reliable evidence that its owner possessed the Christian virtues of thrift and honesty, but only of the uncertain operation of economic forces, natural, amoral and capricious. Suppose that it could be shown that it was as difficult for a poor man in an industrial society to be a good citizen as for a rich man to enter into the Kingdom of Heaven. If these things were so, then the humanitarianism which had had its Radicalism mitigated by religious faith would, with the decay of that faith, be faced with an absolute obligation to abolish inequalities which were no longer justified by any spiritual law. It was peaceful because they realized the " ordinary citizen's desire for gradual and peaceful change as against revolution, conflict with the army and police and martyrdom ".[127]

[1] A. L. Bowley's *England's Foreign Trade*, 1922 edition, pp. 112–113.
[2] For the most systematic eulogy see Leone Levi : *History of British Commerce* 1872.
[3] L. C. A. Knowles : *The Industrial and Commercial Revolutions in Great Britain during the Nineteenth Century.*
[4] Morley's *Cobden* (1883 edition), p. 205.
[5] G. C. Allen : *British Industries*, p. 92 (1935 edition).
[6] R. C. K. Ensor : *England, 1870–1914*, p. 151.
[7] ibid., p. 110.
[8] ibid., p. 110.
[9] *Britain's Industrial Future.* (The report of the Liberal Industrial Inquiry 1928), p. 9.
[10] A. L. Bowley's *England's Foreign Trade*, pp. 15–16.
[11] ibid., p. 146.
[12] G. C. Allen : *British Industries*, p. 13.
[13] W. S. Jevons : *Methods of Social Reform* (edition 1883) Essay on Amusements of the People, published 1878, pp. 20–21.
[14] ibid., p. 5.
[15] ibid., p. 6.
[16] ibid., p. 3.
[17] *Representative Government*, 1861, *passim.*
[18] Sir Henry Maine : *Village Communities* (1871 edition), p. 60.
[19] ibid., p. 59.
[20] Report of *Cranworth Commission*, 1867.
[21] Holdsworth : *Introduction to the Land Law*, p. 309.
[22] A. V. Dicey, L.Q.R. XXI., p. 221.
[23] Frederick Pollock : *The Land Laws*, p. 189.
[24] Maitland : *Collected Papers*, Vol. I, p. 191.
[25] Holdsworth : *Introduction to the Land Law*, p. 319.
[26] cited Thomas : Unpublished *Study of House of Commons*, 1832–1867.
[27] Bonn : *Modern Ireland and her Agrarian problem*, p. 60.
[28] Dicey : *Law and Opinion in England*, pp. 265–6.
[29] Bailey : *Irish Land Acts*, p. 18.
[30] Thomas : op. cit.
[31] Bailey : *Irish Land Acts, passim.*
[32] Dec. 24th, 1885, Harcourt to Hartington. A. G. Gardiner : *Life of Sir William Harcourt*, Vol. I, p. 553.
[33] Bailey : *Irish Land Acts, passim.*
[34] Ensor : *England 1870–1914*, p. 113.
[35] Cmd. 3897 of 1931. *Committee on Finance and Industry*, pp. 162–3.
[36] ibid.
[37] H. Feis : *Europe, the World's Banker* (Yale 1930), p. 83.
[38] Allen : *British Industries*, p. 11.
[39] H. Feis, op. cit., p. 83.
[40] ibid., p. 85.
[41] ibid., p. 87.
[42] ibid., p. 96.
[43] ibid., p. 87.
[44] ibid., p. 117.
[45] Cmd. 3897, pp. 14–15.
[46] ibid., *passim.*
[47] W. S. Jevons : *Methods of Social Reform*, p. 124.
[48] ibid., p. 108.
[49] J. R. Hicks : *Theory of Wages*, p. 165.
[50] W. S. Jevons : *Methods of Social Reform*, p. 111.
[51] W. Y. Edgeworth : *Mathematical Psychics*, 1881, pp. 44–5.
[52] ibid., pp. 44–5.
[53] Sir Wm. Beveridge : *Unemployment* (1930 edition), p. 256.
[54] ibid., p. 216.

55 Sir Wm. Beveridge : *Unemployment* (1930 edition), pp. 216 and 198.
56 ibid., p. 197.
57 ibid., p. 209.
58 ibid., p. 200.
59 ibid., p. 209.
60 ibid., p. 211.
61 ibid., p. 202.
62 ibid., p. 199.
63 ibid., p. 212.
64 Cmd. 363 : *An Outline of the Practice of Preventive Medicine*, by Sir George Newman, 1919, p. 13.
65 p. 18.
66 ibid., p. 10.
67 ibid., p. 60.
68 Article, *Times*, 15-7-35.
69 Mess H. A. : *Factory Legislation and its Administration*, 1891-1924 *passim* and cf. Times 20-7-33.
70 Sympathetically described by Max Beerbohm in *Christmas Garland*.
71 *Newcastle Report*, 1858-61, Vol. 1, p. 93.
72 Morley's *Cobden* (1883 edition), p. 352.
73 Thomas : Unpublished *Study of House of Commons*.
74 Helen Wodehouse : *The History of Education*, p. 202.
75 Thomas : *Unpublished Study of House of Commons*, p. 604.
76 R. C. K. Ensor, op. cit., p. 501, citing Marshall in 321 of 1908.
77 Lady G. Cecil's *Life of Lord Salisbury*. Reference mislaid. Might one not say *passim* ?
78 See H. F. Egerton : *History of British Colonial Policy, passim.*
79 cf. Sir James Stephen : *Letters with Biographical Notes*, (1906), pp. 49-52.
80 Buckle's *Disraeli*, Vol. V. p. 195.
81 and 82 For the development of Colonial Self Government, see Chap. 5 of R. L. Schuyler : *Parliament and the British Empire*.
83 *Report of the Inter Imperial Relations Committee Imperial Conference*, 1926.
84 See *Colonial Military Defence Committee* 1861, XIII. (No. 423).
85 ibid., Q. 2093.
86 Morrell W. P. : *British Colonial Policy in the Age of Grey and Peel.*
87 ibid.
88 ibid.
89 Lady G. Cecil : *Life of Lord Salisbury*, Vol. 3, Chapters 8-11 on the Partition of Africa.
90 ibid., Vol. 3, pp. 225-6.
91 L. C. A. Knowles : *Industrial and Commercial Revolutions*, pp. 332-59.
92 ibid., page 328 footnote.
93 ibid., p. 341-59.
94 Lady G. Cecil : *Life of Salisbury*, Vol. 2, p. 80, Salisbury to Sir Louis Mallet, Jan. 14th, 1876.
95 ibid., Sept. 23rd, 1876, Salisbury to Beaconsfield, pp. 85-6.
96 Buckle's *Disraeli*, Vol. 6, p. 367. Beaconsfield to Drummond Wolff.
97 A. F. Pribram : *England and Europe*, 1871-1914, p. 14.
98 ibid., p. 18.
99 ibid., p. 28.
100 Lady V. Hicks Beach : *Life of Sir Michael Hicks Beach*, Vol. 1, p. 162. Jan. 15th, 1880, Hicks Beach to Sir Bartle Frere.
101 Bernard Holland : *Life of the Duke of Devonshire*, Vol. 1, p. 368.
102 Granville to the Great Powers 1883, cited *Cambridge History of Foreign Policy*, Vol. 3, p. 174.
103 A. F. Pribram : *England and Europe*, 1871-1914, p. 31.
104 Gooch : *Before the War*, Vol. 1, p. 5.
105 A. F. Pribram, op. cit., pp. 87-8.
106 ibid., pp. 55-6.

[107] Gooch : *Before the War*, Vol. 1, p. 22.
[108] Pribram, op. cit., p. 83.
[109] Gooch, op. cit., Vol. 1, p. 10.
[110] ibid., p. 54.
[111] Pribram, op. cit., p. 94.
[112] ibid., p. 118.
[113] Esher : *Journal*, Vol. 2, p. 267.
[114] Balfour to Lord Lansdowne, Nov. 6th, 1908.
[115] A. E. Gathorne Hardy : *Gathorne Hardy* : A Memoir, Vol. II., p. 193.
[116] Elliot : *Life of Goschen*, Vol. 1, p. 307.
[117] 17th June, 1886, to Sir Arthur Gordon.   Selborne : *Memorials*, Part II., Vol. II., p. 227.
[118] Garvin : *Chamberlain*, p. 512, Vol. 2.
[119] Holland.   *Life of Devonshire*, Vol. 2, p. 71.
[120] *Gathorne Hardy*, Vol. 2, p. 345.
[121] Crewe : *Lord Rosebery*, Vol. 2, p. 623.
[122] Edgeworth : *Mathematical Psychics*.
[123] Buckle's *Disraeli*, Vol. V., p. 88.
[124] Esher : *Journal*, Vol. 1, p. 76, Sept. 30th, 1880.
[125] Selborne *Memorials*, Part II, Vol. 2, p. 182, Nov. 5th, 1885.
[126] Godfrey Elton : *England Arise*, p. 94.
[127] ibid., p. 113.

CHAPTER V

THE Reform Bill of 1867 gave to the working men a pre-
ponderance of voting power. " Will they ", asked Lord
Cranborne, " do that which no class armed with power has
hitherto done in the history of the world ".[1] Would they
not use their new-found power to further their own interests.
" What an unknown world we are to enter ", wrote Hardy
in his diary.[2] " If the gentry will take their part they will
be adopted as leaders. If we are left to the demagogues,
God help us! " Goschen wrote, " we believe that the
new electorate will . . . attribute an importance to senti-
mental questions which these questions have not hitherto
been able to secure . . . that in social questions they will
require more vigorous action, a fiercer warfare against abuses,
more Government intervention; that in economical matters
they will be less faithful to political economy . . . and that
there may even be a tendency to take a somewhat different
view of the right definition of national prosperity ".[3] But
he thought that the classes who had hitherto exclusively
wielded political power " will retain ample strength to prevent their being overwhelmed by numbers on questions
where they have a right and justice on their side ". Humpty
Dumpty had certainly had a great fall, but the frying-pan and
the fire might yet be postponed.

The classes who had hitherto exclusively wielded political power were not left defenceless. In the boroughs the new Reform Bill provided a lodger franchise. But in the counties it added to the existing £50 rental qualification a new occupational franchise for tenants of property rated at £12, and it reduced the freehold qualification to £5. These secured great indirect influence to the large landowners. Politically, there were now two Englands: a democratic England of the cities and an aristocratic England of the shires. In the boroughs the number of electors was more than doubled. In Birmingham it was tripled, in Leeds, Blackburn and Bolton, quadrupled.[4] But save in London, the difficulties of registration prevented the lodger franchise from having any influence upon the elections. In the counties neither the small tradesman, nor the miner, or the peasant had the vote. Conservatism was further strengthened by the very unequal distribution of seats. Even though the Redistribution Act of 1868 disfranchised 52 seats the small rural boroughs with an aggregate population of 500,000 were of greater weight than the 10,000,000 of the Metropolitan, Midland and Northern boroughs. The Lake District had a representation in the House of Commons equal to six times that of the mining and shipping North-East.[5]

Such confusion and complexity could not continue, however subtly defended. In 1872 the Ballot Act was passed in spite of the hostility of the House of Lords and the secret disapproval of the House of Commons. The secret ballot for which it provided was opposed by Disraeli as a retrograde step, divorcing political life from publicity.[6] It had been opposed on similar grounds of principle by many Liberals. But the power which the open ballot gave to the larger landowners to exercise compulsion on their tenants, and the more physical compulsions employed in the towns, made reform inevitable. Of the election of 1868, Bright wrote " . . . the corruption, bribery, compulsion, tumult of this General

Election have probably never been exceeded—the whole country is disgraced and ought to be shocked, and no man who has no other remedy to offer can with any show of reason resist the ballot ".[7]   The blow given by the Ballot Act to the indirect influence of the landowners made possible the development of the Nationalist Party in Ireland.

Nor could the distinction between the urban and rural franchise produced in 1867 long survive. Selborne might argue that there were natural differences between rural and urban communities justifying and making expedient a difference in their franchise: that the first was dependent upon territorial ownership and the possession of land; the second an organized unity with an opinion of its own.[8] But the distinction became more arbitrary and unreal with the passage of time. Areas entirely urban in character were treated as though they were rural. Towns more flourishing and populous than neighbouring boroughs were denied representation. By 1884 there was no one to oppose the principle that the householders of the counties should be given the £10 occupational household and the lodger franchise of the boroughs and the third Reform Bill was passed. The real fight was over distribution. The House of Lords feared that if distribution were not settled by the existing Parliament a new Parliament with a Radical majority might create equal electoral districts, so they refused to pass the Franchise Bill until redistribution had been agreed upon. Gladstone declared that he would not dissolve on the issue of the Franchise Bill, but that if forced to dissolve, he would raise the question of the position of the House of Lords in the Constitution. By the influence of the Queen, the party leaders were brought together and " with incredible facility and rapidity " they produced " a larger ... more symmetrical and consistent scheme for a rearrangement of all the electoral districts in the United Kingdom than had before been thought of by any practical statesman ".[9] The essence of the scheme was that all cities and towns with less than 15,000 inhabitants were thrown into the counties; and the counties and the big towns were broken up into single-member constituencies.[10] The Conservative principle of the representation of communities was replaced by the Radical principle of the representation of majorities. The redistribution seemed to Hardy a revolution, quite cast down Goschen, and made Sir Henry Maine very gloomy.[11]

What was the effect of these changes in the franchise? It is difficult to say because the problems of government are determined by the course of industry, the march of science, and the decay of religion as much as by the extension of the franchise. Education, health, and social legislation would have had to be developed by any Government whether or not there had been an extension of the franchise. The vital effect of the extension of the franchise was to alter the whole machinery of government; and to provide a different environment to which the subtle mutations of party leadership and constitutional practice had to be adapted.

It seemed to Goschen that " the whole centre of gravity of the Constitution had been displaced " by the Act of 1867. Mill had pointed out that before the Bill, it was impossible in the House of Commons for the interests of the working classes to be represented or understood.[12] Bright that through our defective representation " the scandalous abuse " of the Church of England put on the character of a national and useful institution, though five-sixths of Ireland and two-thirds of Scotland, and 14,000 chapels in England and Wales were Dissenting.

The reforms of 1867 and 1884 did not suddenly transform the House of Commons. The numbers of members who could claim close relations with peers and baronets only gradually diminished; while the number of those concerned with industry and commerce gradually increased. In 1860, 108 Members of the House of Commons were either sons of peers or heirs to the peerages; in 1897 there were 51. In 1865, 90 Members of the House were engaged in manufacturing and mercantile operations; in 1880, 112. From 1874 to 1900 the number of brewers, ironmasters, armament makers and manufacturers increased from 61 to 120. Both in 1865 and 1880 there were 80 Members who had served in the Army or Navy, 250 had attended one of the great public schools or gone up to Oxford or Cambridge. Not until the rise of the Labour Party and the Liberal victory of 1906 was there a drastic change in the character of the House.

The enlarged electorate led to the development of an entirely new technique of political leadership. The Constitution required a Prime Minister and a leader of the Opposition who could touch the springs of action in the common man. Persuasion and propaganda were to replace patronage and corruption. The necessity of appealing to the new and many-headed Cæsar was repugnant to statesmen of the old school. In 1868 Derby is writing of the " balderdash and braggadocio in which Gladstone has been indulging on his stumping tour ".[13] In 1874 Selborne is perturbed that Gladstone as Prime Minister should propound in an election address a popular budget.[14] While the Midlothian campaign of 1879 seemed " a precedent tending in its results to the degradation of British politics, by bringing in a system of perpetual canvass, and removing the political centre of gravity from Parliament to the platform ".[15] By 1880 Gladstone is himself uneasy at the use which was being made of his own technique by the Radical Chamberlain. In the 'nineties Rosebery will shock the Queen by addressing a popular meeting on a policy not previously discussed with herself. In 1900 an election will be fought on the initiative of a Minister—Chamberlain—not the Prime Minister, and in a manner to make a fitting prologue to this century of propaganda; while in 1910 where Gladstone had sowed and Chamberlain watered Lloyd George will reap and

M

glean the increase. By then a General Election will be considered by a large proportion of the electorate as practically
a referendum on the question which of two Governments shall
be returned to power.[16]

The doctrine of the mandate was gradually developed.
In 1868 when Gladstone carried resolutions against the
Church of England in Ireland, Disraeli claimed that the
House of Commons had no right to deal with a question un-
discussed at the previous election. In 1886 Hartington
writes " although no principle of the mandate may exist there
are certain limits which Parliament is morally bound to
observe. . . . The House of Commons has no right to initiate
legislation especially immediately upon its first meeting of
which the constituencies were not informed and of which they
might have been informed ".[17]

The swing of the pendulum became a cliché of the
politicians' vocabulary. For the electorate seemed to show a
preference for the party whose defects it had had most time
to forget. And for a time its verdict promised to be decisive.
Before 1867 Cabinets had been dependent upon the subtle
calculations of groups and were defeated or successful by very
small margins. Peel, in 1841, had turned out the Whigs by
one; Russell, in 1852, was displaced by nine; Derby in the
same year by nineteen. In 1866 the second reading of the
Finance Bill had been carried by five and Ministers were
afterwards defeated by eleven. In 1868 Gladstone carried
the Irish Church Bill by 118 and this majority was the sign
of a new political era. Governments could now look to
majorities of a hundred and more. The number of constituencies which were contested at a General Election was
greatly increased. Before 1867 it was common for half the
seats to be uncontested.[18] In 1859, 101 constituencies had
been fought; in 1865, 204; in 1868, 277; in 1880, 352.[19]

In the period 1868 to 1880 there were two great
ministries: the Gladstone Ministry, 1868-74, with a majority

of over 100, followed by the Disraeli Ministry of
1874-80. The swing of the pendulum in 1874 might perhaps be ascribed to the fact that all the powerful interests
affected by five years of legislation: the landed interest; the
Church of England and those who desired religious education
in elementary schools; the brewers and licensed victuallers
went over to the Conservatives. As Disraeli put it with his
artist's insight into the coming technique of propaganda:
the Ministry had " harassed every trade, worried every profession, and assailed or menaced every class institution and
species of property in the country ". The electorate were
invited to close " this career of plundering and blundering ".[20]
More concretely the public houses were mobilized against the
chapels and the Government " borne down in a torrent
of gin and beer ".[21]   In 1880 it was the Conservative turn
to be borne down by a torrent—this time of Gladstone's Midlothian denunciation—" from day to day, under a Ministry,
called, as if in mockery—Conservative, the nation is per-
plexed with fear of change ".[22]

But a simple alternation of Liberal kettle and Conservative
pot was not to be. The Gladstone Government of 1880-85
marked the transition to a new era, for it was hopelessly
divided between the Old Whigs under Hartington and the
new Radicalism of Chamberlain. The peaceful substitution of
Radicalism for Whiggery was not to be. In 1886 when Gladstone dissolved after the rejection of his first Home Rule Bill,
316 Conservatives, 74 Liberal Unionists, 195 Liberals and 85
Nationalists were returned. The Home Rule issue enabled
the Conservatives to hold office—except for the short Glad-
stone-Rosebery Administration 1892-95—until 1906. It
enabled the House of Lords to avoid the adjustment of its
powers to a changed political and social era until the split of
the Conservatives themselves over the mirage of imperial
economic unity enabled the Irish Party and the new industrial
democracy educated by the Independent Labour Party

since 1893 to demand the passage of the Parliament Act in 1911.

An analysis of the election results from 1885 to 1910 enables us to trace some of the forces which were shaping the political scene.   Ireland was committed to the continuous return of her eighty unchanging patriots—until the Home Rule issue should be solved they were simply a weapon of Nationalism and not a possible instrument of government. Liberalism of the Gladstone tradition was only firmly secured in the Celtic fringe of Wales and Scotland.   The south-east of England was almost overwhelmingly Conservative except at the election of 1906.   The industrial north was mainly Liberal, London, on the whole, Conservative, while the full swing of the pendulum was to be seen in the Midlands and the West.   With the rise of the Labour Party we can trace the disintegration of the older political traditions, and the emergence of new political forces.   From 1874 the public house was an important election agency for the Conservatives and the chapel for the Liberals.   By 1900 the inspiration of Nonconformity and temperance are finally exhausted and the Liberal Party draws deeply upon Fabian springs.   Meanwhile the Conservative Party has lost the battle for the unity of the United Kingdom and has failed to agree or persuade to an imperial unity.

The enlargement of the electorate altered the relation of the member to his constituency and the party machinery had to be reorganized.   Though after 1835 the Carlton Club for the Conservatives had provided the initiative in scrutinizing the electoral rolls the connection between the central organization and the local party committees was very loose.[23]   Elections to the Tories when they took place were little more than an unseemly though necessary formality to enable the natural leaders to assume control.[24]   But after the Conservative defeat of 1852 Disraeli had employed a solicitor, Rose, to undertake a revision of the party organization.   The Central

Conservative Office in Whitehall kept a register of approved candidates and tried to get the local people to make their own selection from among them. In 1868 these local associations were affiliated to a National Union.[25] In 1873, for every borough election, Disraeli had " an expert to visit the scene of action and prepare a confidential report so that he might as far as possible be acquainted with the facts ".[26] But in 1880 the Central Office seems to have been quite ignorant of the mind of the electorate.[27] Later under Akers-Douglas as Whip and Captain Middleton as chief agent its organization seems to have given satisfaction.[28] The Conservative Central Office remained " a handmaid to the party " and was never allowed to usurp the functions of leadership. Neither the Union nor its council had any executive power. In the last resort power lay with the leader of the party and his self-selected committee of M.P.'s called the central committee.[29]

After 1867 the organization of the Liberal Party, too, was changed. In Birmingham Schnadhorst organized the New Model for Chamberlain. This became the inspiration of the National Liberal Federation. " The Birmingham plan is perhaps the only one on which the Liberal Party can be sufficiently organized in a great constituency ", wrote Hartington, in 1877.[30] But the Whig leader feared that a federation of such local organizations would put the management into the hands of the most advanced men. And indeed by 1877 the Federation was a Liberal Parliament outside Parliament, a weapon of Radicalism providing for the direct participation of all members of the party in the determination of policy. Local associations chose their candidates on condition that they adopted the party programme determined by the periodical meetings of the Federation. The power of the Liberal machine severely taxed the Liberal leaders. In 1891 Schnadhorst had to point out that delegates attended, not to express opinions, but to hear what measures the leaders of the party could adopt with reasonable hope of remaining a united party.[31]   Hartington felt that Chamberlain had organized an outside power to the belittlement of Parliament.   Harcourt wrote to Morley that it was " absurd that we should leave the Federation to formulate a creed and then go down to swear to all its articles ".[32]   The machine, complained Rosebery, was a permanent force jealous of and an enemy to whatever was extraneous to it.[33]

After the passing of Sir Henry James's Corrupt Practices Act, 1883, the cost of a contest for almost any seat was within the means of men with moderate means or no means at all if they represented a cause for which subscriptions could be raised.[34]   In 1885 Joseph Arch secured a 600 majority over the Duke of Portland's brother.[35]   It was to this election that Rosebery subscribed £50 because it seemed to him to be a farce to give the agricultural labourer the vote and then not to allow their chief representative to sit in Parliament.[36]

On the nature and source of party funds the biographies of statesmen are usually discreet.   We catch occasional glimpses of collecting activities.   In 1868 " What we want ", Disraeli wrote to Stanley, " is to raise one hundred thousand, which it is believed will secure the result.   It can be done if the Cabinet sets a good example ".   He induced his colleagues in the Cabinet to subscribe a minimum of £10,000.[37]   In 1879 Esher tells us " we made out a list of peers and M.P.'s who may be asked to subscribe to a General Election fund.   There are 114 of them.   An average of £500 a piece would, Harcourt thinks, enable us to win twenty county seats ".[38]   With the development of the large federations the money affairs of the party funds were supposed to be entirely in the hands of the Chief Whip, the Prime Minister knowing nothing of them unless in some particular case the facts came out.[39]   Sometimes they did.   In 1891 Rhodes gave Schnadhorst £5,000; later, alarmed at certain speeches of Gladstone and Labouchere, he asked him to divert the money to charity. Schnadhorst exceeded his functions and reassured him.   By

1901 *Spectator* was suggesting that Rhodes had given £5,000 to the Liberal Party in return for a promise that Uganda should not be evacuated.[40]

After 1832 some progress had been made with the task of adapting and modifying the procedure of the House of Commons for its new work as a legislative machine controlled by an executive based on popular power.   Between 1840 and 1870 the average length of a session had actually declined from 131 to 115 days.[41]   Procedure had been simplified and an increasing control by the Government secured.   Further tightening of the Government's control of the procedure of the House would in any case have been necessary with the great increase of legislation that came with the growth of collectivism after 1870, but the first important changes were the result of Irish obstruction in 1880.   The Ballot Act of 1872 resulted in the return in 1874 of fifty-nine Home Rulers.   In 1875 Parnell, their leader, began a policy of systematic obstruction, not as a method of debate, but as a weapon to destroy the Parliament of the United Kingdom as a constitutional assembly.[42]   He intended to destroy the Union by paralysing its political organ.   The Speaker and the Government had now to discover how to raise the state of siege in which the Commons were involved.   In 1881, after a sitting lasting forty-one and a half hours, the Speaker announced that he considered that he would best carry out the will of the House and might rely upon its support if he declined to call upon any more members to speak, and at once put the question from the chair.[43]   This emergency use of the prestige of the Chair could not be a permanent solution.   In 1882 an autumn session of six months was devoted to the reform of the rules.[44]   It resulted in the introduction of the closure by which on the initiative of the Speaker 200 members agreeing the question under debate could be at once put to the vote.   This was useful enough to stop obstruction on a particular question or to prevent a Bill from being talked out, but was little use for meeting full and informed debate on the details of a Bill.[45]   For this the Guillotine (first used as an expedient in 1881 and 1887), by which a certain number of days is allotted to each of the remaining stages of a Bill was developed.   This was a brutally efficient weapon for carrying legislation, but clumsy and unsatisfactory for the improvement of debate.[46]   It tended not to hasten Parliamentary debate but merely to dispense with it.[47]   In 1909 the Speaker was first given the power to select amendments so that time might be spent on those which the House wished to consider.   The " Kangaroo " was made an inherent instead of an occasional power in 1919.   Its disadvantage was that it added " omniscience to the many qualities already demanded of the Chair ".[48]   In 1902 Balfour laid a complete scheme of reforms before the House of which the parts adopted secured the application of closure to Supply, a fixed distribution of the time of the session between the Government and private members and the allocation to the Government business of the earlier part of each day's sitting. Rules which had once been framed to " promote a fertilizing flow of eloquence " were now modified " to dam up its vast and destructive floods and keep them within reasonable limits ".[49]

By 1910 the average length of a session had increased to 140 days.   Of these finance took 38; another 25 went to debates on the Address various motions and formal business, leaving only 77 for legislation.   Allowing 14 days for private members, little more than 60 were available for Government legislation.   During the ten years ending 1909, 388 Government Bills passed the House in 483 days.   The ten most important occupied 207 days leaving 276 for the remaining 378.   In the same period the average time in general debate each session was 24 for English supply services and procedure; 19 for the Empire, including the Army and Navy; 16 for finance (exclusive of supply and consolidated fund); nine for Ireland; two for Scotland; one for Wales.[50]

In this general background it will be convenient to consider the development of the Cabinet system and the subtle conventions by which it is governed in the three periods, 1868-1880, 1880-1906, 1906-1914.

1868-1880: it is now impossible to recapture the inner spirit of these strange politics. We should be nearest doing so if we could understand the technique by which Disraeli led simple squires in their halting quest of democratic power. With no science (he was " on the side of the angels "), with exotic morals (" the man ", said Gladstone, " is falser than his doctrines ") Disraeli had an artist's insight into the problems of political power. " In legislation ", he wrote, " it is not merely reason and propriety which are to be considered, but the spirit of the times ".[51] But what to him was the spirit of the times? He made Sidonia say " the tendency of advancing civilization is in truth towards pure monarchy. Monarchy is indeed a government which requires a high degree of civilization for its full development. It needs the support of free laws and manners and of a widely diffused intelligence. Your House of Commons that has absorbed all other power in the State will in all probability fall more rapidly than it rose. Public opinion has a more direct, a more comprehensive, a more efficient organ for its utterance than a body of men sectionally chosen. The printing press absorbs in a great degree the duties of the Sovereign, the priest and Parliament; it controls, it educates, it discusses. That public opinion when its acts would appear in the form of one who has no class interest ". This adumbration of the totalitarian state within the chaos of Victorian economic plenty and spiritual poverty should warn us on what depths the frail bark of the democratic state is launched. In 1873, when Disraeli was seriously considering the future of the Conservative Party, he said, " all the questions of trade and navigation, of the incidence of taxation and public economy are settled. But there are other questions not less important and of deeper and higher reach and range which must soon engage the attention of the country. The attributes of a constitutional monarchy, whether aristocratical principles should be recognized in our Constitution, and if so in what form, whether the Commons of England shall remain an estate of the realm, numerous but privileged and powerful, or whether they should degenerate into an indiscriminate multitude ".[52] When in office he secured an influence over the Queen and used the monarchical tradition for party ends. " I do think Dizzy has worked the idea of personal government to its logical conclusion ", wrote Lady Ponsonby to her husband.[53] And she continued, " that superstition . . . can be worked by an unscrupulous Minister to his advantage and the country's ruin ".

It was Gladstone's opinion that since 1874 " her mind and opinion had been seriously warped "; that she had been deliberately misled by a mind more powerful than her own and by one who " owed everything to woman "[54] cannot be doubted. In 1867 when the Queen was trying to settle the Reform Bill dispute Disraeli wrote to Northcote, " the Royal project of interposition with our rivals is a mere phantom, it pleases the vanity of a court deprived of substantial power ".[55] But in 1872 he is saying that " the principles of the English Constitution do not contemplate the absence of personal influence on the part of Sovereign, and if they did the principles of human nature would prevent the fulfilment of such a theory ".[56] In 1881 he told the Queen " that the speech of the Sovereign is only the speech of the Ministers is a principle not known to the British Constitution. It is only a piece of Parliamentary gossip ".[57] His influence with the Queen led her to the constitutionally perilous experiment of continuing a correspondence with him after his resignation. Did not the Queen express the hope and belief " that this shameful heterogeneous union—out of mere folly—will separate into many parts very soon and that the Conservatives will come in stronger than ever in a short time—the sort of mad and unreasoning flow of Liberal success as is so unnatural that I feel certain it can't last ".[58]

No doubt it may be argued that Disraeli merely lied to the Queen for the good of his country; that his flattery was like the courtesy of the barrister to a prejudiced and incompetent judge. But in the time of Gladstone and Disraeli not to be a gentleman was a ground for political criticism. " The aristocracy, said Albert was no gentleman; Albert said it of Disraeli; Disraeli said it of Gladstone."[59] Gladstone considered that a gentleman was necessary at the War Office to deal with the Commander-in-Chief. In 1878 Disraeli, attacked separately from his colleagues, said that in the old days such efforts at dividing a Prime Minister from his colleagues were " not only deemed unfair and unjust and unconstitutional, but ungentlemanlike ".[60] In 1874 Disraeli told Lady Bradford that he had broken the Irish ranks " by keeping my temper and treating Butt and his intimate colleagues as gentlemen, which they certainly are not; but their vanity is insatiable ".[61] To prove the Liberal Party gentlemen Granville in 1874 challenged the Tories to a race across country.[62] Attacked by Chamberlain in 1876 Disraeli described the attack as " one of the coarsest and stupidest assaults I well remember. No intellect, no sarcasm or satire or even invective: coarse and commonplace abuse such as you might expect from a cad on an omnibus ".[63] To Derby he wrote that Gladstone was an " unprincipled maniac . . . extraordinary mixture of envy, vindictiveness, hypocrisy and superstition; and with one commanding characteristic— whether Prime Minister or leader of the opposition, whether preaching, praying, speechifying or scribbling, never a gentleman ".[64] Gladstone, he told Lady Bradford, was a " vindictive fiend ".[65] Gladstone considered that Disraeli

" demoralized public opinion, bargained with diseased appetites, stimulated passions, prejudices and selfish desires that
he might maintain his influence ".[66]   Without venturing to
understand the code of a gentleman in those exacting days
the student may feel that it did not cover the writing of some
of the letters by which Disraeli fooled the Queen.

If Disraeli stooped as no gentleman should to lead a Queen
by the nose, Gladstone, with the greatest respect for the
Constitution as he had been trained to understand it by Peel
and by Palmerston, was driven after 1874 into violent opposition to the Queen, the House of Lords and the power of
aristocracy.   His position as a popular leader was clearly
revealed when, though he had retired from the leadership
of the Liberal Party in 1874, it was found impossible for any
other Liberal to accept office while he should remain in
politics.   " There is not room for argument about the
proposition that the man who leads the Liberal Party out
of doors ought to lead it in Parliament ", wrote Hartington,
who had borne the burden of the leadership in Opposition
of the Liberals in the Commons to Granville, who had carried
the same burden in the Lords.   " It is only fair to the Queen,
to the country, to the party, that this should be acknowledged
at once ".[67]   And so in 1880 the Queen had to accept Gladstone as Prime Minister with a Cabinet which in her view
contained " all the worst men who had no respect for kings
and princes or any of the landmarks of the Constitution ".[68]

In considering the working of the Cabinet system we must
note: the procedure by which a change of Government was
brought about—for this is a vital test of the efficiency of a
political system; the forces which determined the choice of
Prime Minister; and the organization and working of individual Cabinets.   In the period 1868-80 there was an
important modification of the method by which the Government was changed.   For it was established that a Government would be acting in the spirit of the Constitution if, after

a defeat in the Commons it asked for a dissolution, and if, after a defeat at a General Election it resigned without meeting Parliament. It is important to see the way in which the problem appeared to the Ministers concerned; for it is not the conventions of the Constitution at any given point of time which are so important as the process by which the conventions come to be changed.

When in 1868 Disraeli was defeated on the Irish Church resolutions put forward by Gladstone the Queen would not hear of his resigning. Gladstone was of the opinion that the Cabinet ought not to dissolve without a reasonable chance of success. Disraeli argued that the House had no right to deal with a question which had not been discussed at the previous election. He said that he would " indicate what I think is the duty of the Cabinet as regards themselves and their party and then by Her Majesty's special desire I shall refer their duty under the circumstances to the Queen personally ".[69] Having secured his Cabinet's consent to a dissolution he went to the Queen ten days later without again consulting his colleagues because he felt that their resolution to dissolve might have weakened.[70] This was resented as a departure from precedent. Defeated at the election he immediately resigned, putting into practice the theory he had stated in 1841 in opposition to Melbourne. His actual reasons for resignation at the time are not clear. The Queen was anxious to get the business over before December 14th.[71] Disraeli talked the matter over with Stanley, Cairns and Hardy and the Cabinet agreed, though with some fear that the Conservative Party would be offended and alienated.[72] In 1873 there was a complicated exercise in Constitutional niceties. The Gladstone Government (1868-74), with a normal majority of ninety, was defeated by three votes on an Irish Universities Bill which had offended the Protestants, the Irish Roman Catholics and the educationalists—that Cerberus which always blocked the road to knowledge. Gladstone was for dissolution. Hartington, the Whig leader, was not, thinking a change of Government would be bad for Irish administration. After two Cabinet meetings it was decided to resign.[73] Disraeli then declined to take office. Gladstone held that by defeating a Government you lay under an obligation to replace it; Disraeli that because a Minister has a majority which can prevent another parliamentary leader from forming an administration likely to stand he did not " thereby acquire the right to call on Parliament to pass whatever measures he and his colleagues think fit ". It was, the Conservatives considered, neither their duty nor their interest to dissolve Parliament for Gladstone. They would not admit the right of any Government " to make any question they please vital, and if a combination negatives it force upon one portion of it all responsibility ".[74] Gladstone was in fact compelled to take office again. The crisis revealed on what nice agreement and complex understandings the seeming simple two-party alternation depends.

In 1874 the Gladstone Government impulsively dissolved. Defeated at the election like Disraeli in 1868 Gladstone resigned without meeting Parliament. But he was careful to state that such a resignation was not always proper. He considered it " more agreeable to usage that the expiring Government should await its sentence from Parliament by meeting it while in possession of office ".[75] He wrote to Granville " it is Parliament not the constituencies that ought to dismiss the Government and the proper function of the House of Commons cannot be taken away from it without diminishing somewhat its dignity and authority ". But this time he resigned for reasons of convenience.

In 1878 the Disraeli Cabinet (1874-80), in spite of the peace with honour their leader had brought back from the Berlin Congress, decided that, possessed of a good majority, they would not dissolve.[76] But by 1880 the persistent obstruction of the Irish under Parnell was making the con-

duct of necessary business difficult.   The Queen, anxious for
the continuance of a Conservative Government and alarmed
at Gladstone's Midlothian oratory, proposed that Beaconsfield should come to some agreement with " some of the
sensible and reasonable and not violent men on the other
side ".   Disraeli tactfully replied " that there were no
sensible and reasonable men to appeal to "; " the nominal
leaders have no authority; and the mass . . . are animated
by an avidity for office such as Lord Beaconsfield after more
than forty years' experience cannot recall ".   But the time
would come " when the interposition and personal influence
of Your Majesty may most beneficially be exercised in bringing about a more satisfactory state of the House of Commons
than now prevails ".[77]   In March, misled by by-elections in
Liverpool and Southwark and by rumours of Whig secession
he dissolved.   Before the decision was taken the Cabinet sat
two and a half hours and every member of it was required
to give his opinion: the members of the House of Commons
having the priority.[78]   Defeated, he resigned without meeting
Parliament.

How had the Gladstone and Disraeli Cabinets been formed
and worked?   Great informality marked the method by
which a political leader was then selected.   Disraeli said
" the leader of a party in a House of Parliament is never
nominated: the selection is always the spontaneous act of
the party in the House in which he sits.   Lord Derby never
appointed me to the leadership, but the party chose to follow
me and the rest ensued ".[79]   The Queen, it was recognized,
could exercise her discretion as to which of the possible leaders
she would invite to form a Ministry.   When Derby had
resigned in 1868 he " ventured to submit that as there is no
question of political change Your Majesty should apply to
the Chancellor of the Exchequer ".[80]   But she could have
sent for Richmond or for Stanley instead of sending as she
did for Disraeli.[81]

When Disraeli resigned the same year the Queen had no hesitation in sending for Mr. Gladstone. She recorded of their first interview after he had consented to form a Government that " he was most cordial and kind in his manner, and nothing could be more satisfactory than the whole interview ".[82] There were certain difficulties about the Cabinet which Mr. Gladstone proposed to be adjusted. Lord Clarendon as Foreign Secretary—with " his temper, his manner, his want of discretion, etc. ", could not Mr. Gladstone by dwelling upon his bad health get him, without compromising her, to take any other office? Lord Russell, the Queen said, " ought surely not to be thought of ", and Mr. Gladstone felt that " he had for the last few years done nothing but injure a brilliant reputation ". The rather peculiar person, Mr. Lowe, " of a very angular mind ", might be difficult to manage. Should the kind and genial Mr. Bright be included (and Gladstone thought India would do for him) as he and Bright disliked each other.[83] But the Cabinet was formed without difficulty. Clarendon went to the Foreign Office; Russell gracefully declined office, and Bright became President of the Board of Trade.

Gladstone considered that his Cabinet of 1868-74 was " one of the finest instruments of Government that ever were constructed ". It was really a working Cabinet and not an assemblage of departmental Ministers.[84] It seemed to him to approach closest to the perfection once achieved by Peel. Gladstone had serious limitations as a Prime Minister. He was utterly unlike the colleagues with whom he had to work and his own supporters in Parliament. No one, it was said, ever knew quite what he meant.[85] His fullest statements were to some uniformly obscure.[86] The chiefs of the Liberal Party had hitherto been either pure Whigs with Liberal or even Radical leanings, or Canningite converts whose Liberalism was more in foreign than in home affairs. Lord Russell was a type of the first and Lord Palmerston of

the second.[87]   In Gladstone all the contradictory elements
seemed to move together with equal power.[88]   His combination of a belief in political liberty and High Church principles was a mystery to the Tories, and his belief that to our
system of landed property we owed the kindly and intimate
relations between our higher and lower classes an exaspera-
tion to the Radicals.[89]   His appreciation of working men
puzzled the patrician Whigs.   In 1878 Granville was
astonished to meet him in Regent Street coming from a
meeting of working men.[90]   In the 'seventies the landed
magnates and the leaders of commerce and industry were with
the middle classes prepared to support the Liberal Party.
But beneath the surface there were serious divisions.   On Disestablishment, household suffrage in the counties, education,
and the land laws the Whigs and the Radicals were completely divided.   When Gladstone temporarily retired in
1874 the Whigs would follow one leader, the Radicals another and the Irish a third.[91]

Gladstone was better in his influence on legislation than in
the executive part of his work.   The only departments of
State in which he was naturally interested were the Treasury
and the Board of Trade.   The Foreign Office he regarded as
task work, and he was only interested in the Army and Navy
in so far as they affected the Estimates.   He was " disposed to
regard the heads of departments as to a great degree autonomous in their own provinces, and entertained great doubts
as to the right of a Prime Minister to require a Cabinet
Minister to resign.[92]   He denied the right of the Queen to
know what were the individual opinions of members of the
Cabinet.   He did not stoop to manipulate the Queen for
his party's power, nor did he, as he might, make party capital
out of his knowledge of her political bias and petty
obstructions.

Disraeli's Cabinet of 1874-80 was a masterpiece of a
different political art.   He adopted with the Queen a

N

combination of deference and *camaraderie* which served to make her a tool to his designs while she felt herself to be his partner in the highest problems of the State. While forming his Cabinet he prayed Her Majesty " to permit him to observe that in forming an administration, it is necessary to make some offers, which you are almost certain will not be accepted. Powerful personages are conciliated by the offers of great posts, and might be estranged were they not made, even though it may be impossible that they should be accepted ".[93]   His Cabinet was a small Cabinet. He " proposed having only twelve in the Cabinet—six in each House ". Pursuing his intention of changing back the oligarchy into a " generous aristocracy round a real throne " he placed round the person of his Sovereign the heads of the house of Cecil, Seymour, Bridgeman and Lygon, the heir of the Percies, a Wellesley, a Somerset; while in the Cabinet and in important positions outside there were the representatives of the Stanleys, Hamiltons, Lennoxes, Herberts and Cecils, besides a Manners, a Lowther, a Bentinck and a Bourke.[94]   But he recognized the Conservative debt to Lancashire by putting R. A. Cross, the director of a Lancashire bank, at the Treasury and " he recommended very highly a Mr. Smith of Westminster, a rich and most respectable clever man who always maintained that the working classes were not Republican ".[95]   When in 1878 the resignation of Derby over the Eastern question imperilled the Government, Disraeli secured both the confidence of Lancashire and the adhesion of the House of Stanley by promoting Derby's brother and heir to be Secretary for War,[96] while Northumberland, the head of the Percies, was taken into the Cabinet as Lord Privy Seal.[97]   It was not fitting to Disraeli's mind that a Tory Cabinet should lack on its front bench in the Lords a due representation of the old families.[98] Whereas Gladstone denied the right of the Queen to know what were the individual opinions of members of the Cabinet, Disraeli

made her feel that she was its most important member.   On
the Eastern crisis he kept her accurately acquainted " with
the views and feelings of the various members of the
Cabinet ".   At one time those views were seven, and the
seventh was " the policy of Your Majesty which will be
introduced and enforced to the utmost by the Prime
Minister ".[99]   But though he might control the Queen with
unscrupulous ease Disraeli, in Salisbury's opinion, as head of
a Cabinet lacked firmness.   " The chiefs of departments got
their own way too much, the Cabinet as a whole got it too
little . . . with all his great abilities he was unable to decide a
general principle of action . . . his final political principle of
action was that the party must on no account be broken."[100]
He could not in office, as he had in Opposition, skate so
boldly over the thin ice between his own reforming ideas and
the property interests of those who had made him their
champion.[101]   He adopted the practice of leaving his
colleagues to manage by themselves the conduct of Bills
affecting their own departments and only intervened himself at critical moments.[102]   The Cabinet decided that the
invasion of Afghanistan should take place through only one
pass.   Lytton objected, because Lytton did Hardy did,
because Hardy did Disraeli did.[103]   Determined not to lose
Hardy, the representative of the Oxford clergy, a Bill for
consolidating the Burial Acts was lost.[104]   But the decision
to purchase the Suez Canal shares (1875) was his own, carried
in the Cabinet against strong opposition.[105]   The decision to
stand by Frere in South Africa, who had committed the
country to war not only without leave but contrary to his
instructions, was Disraeli's supported by Hick-Beachs in the
Cabinet and the Queen outside.[106]   And in the Eastern crisis
he stood between the Queen eager for war and a divided
Cabinet unable to realize that firmness was the only way to
peace.[107]

    1880-1906: To the Conservatives the Liberal victory of

1880 seemed portentous. " The hurricane that has swept us away is so strange and new a phenomenon that we shall not for some time understand its real meaning . . . it seems to me to be inspired by some definite desire for change and means business. It may disappear as rapidly as it came or it may be the beginning of a serious war of classes ", wrote Salisbury.[108] The Radical programme sponsored by Chamberlain in 1880 professed to sound the death knell of the *laissez-faire* system . . . and the intervention of the State on behalf of the weak versus the strong, in the interest of Labour versus Capital, of want and suffering versus luxury and ease.[109] The predominance of the Radicals made the " Whig Party a mere survival kept alive by tradition after its true functions and significance have passed away ".[110] Halifax wrote to Goschen that " it used to be an article of the Liberal creed to get rid of all legislative interference with what men did in the way of business, with two exceptions only: (1) if it was injurious to the public; (2) to protect those who could not protect themselves. All the Bills introduced by the present Government run counter to this principle.[111]

The Gladstone Cabinet of 1880-85 is the bridge between two political worlds. The conflict between the pretensions of the Crown and the power of a popular leader could no longer be concealed; the Irish question was threatening the very basis of peaceful government; Gladstone stood out as the popular leader, but in him, the new leader was shackled by the old priest. His ecclesiastical mind could not reach down to " the sceptical and thinking race of artisans " whose present discontents were the real basis of the reformers' zeal. With a passion for justice and financial purity he could not see that the financial technique of government was merely a means to whatever necessary conditions of social justice inquiry might lay bare. He could see that the condition of Ireland was incompatible with both the religious and economic assumptions of the English middle class; he did not realize that the condition of the English working class was as incompatible with his economic assumptions as the Irish peasantry itself.

The Constitutional crisis had been clearly revealed, immediately Disraeli resigned.   During Gladstone's retirement, Granville in the Lords, and Hartington in the Commons, had borne the dust and heat of Opposition. The Queen, who considered that Gladstone's " whole conduct, since 1876, had been one of violent, passionate, invective against and abuse of Lord Beaconsfield ",[112] was anxious that anyone but he should be Prime Minister. It had to be explained to her that Gladstone as the leader of the Liberal Party in the Country, ought to lead it in the House: that he would be more dangerous outside the Cabinet than as its leader. " For if the Government were overthrown by him he would come to power, relying on the more advanced section of the party, whereas if called upon by the Queen now it would be necessary for him to obtain the support of as large a number as possible of its more moderate members."[113] As Hartington said, " the spirit of the Constitution is that the ablest and most powerful member of the Opposition should be called on to take the position of the retiring Government ".[114] So as neither Granville, the leader in the Lords, nor Hartington, who had been chosen leader in the Commons, could form a Government with safety to their party or without danger to the Crown the Queen acquiesced. She was advised by Disraeli as to the attitude she should adopt. He suggested the words she might use in her interview with Gladstone: " the Opposition having succeeded in defeating my Government, I have in the spirit of the Constitution sent for their leaders, who have confessed their inability to form a Ministry and have advised me to send for you. I wish, therefore, to know whether you are prepared to form an administration ". Characteristically, he added, " Mr. Gladstone will probably be diffuse in his reply, which will give Your Majesty an advantage in ascertaining his real intentions ".[115]

This Gladstone Cabinet (1880-85), when shattered by internal dissensions and the tragedy of Gordon, with a majority of twelve in the Commons and defeated in the Lords, debated the question of their resignation at one of the longest Cabinets ever held. Granville was for resignation, but Bright persuaded Gladstone against.[116] In 1883 Granville had written to Hartington " that it would be a great responsibility to turn Gladstone out and destroy the coherence of the Liberal Party. The effect upon the position of the aristocracy and the richer classes may be very great ".[117] When, in 1884, the Government finally resigned after a defeat on their own Budget, caused by a combination of Tories and Irish, there was a prolonged crisis. Dissolution was impossible, because the old constituencies had by the Act of 1884, ceased to exist, and the new were not yet created. Salisbury refused, for some time, to take office until assured by the Queen that Gladstone's guarantees for the conduct of Parliamentary business were satisfactory. The election of 1886 returned 249 Conservatives, 335 Liberals and 86 Parnellites. Randolph Churchill, Smith and Hicks-Beach were for resignation, but Salisbury decided to meet Parliament, compelling the Opposition to combine for his defeat.[118] The political situation was unparalleled. Lord Carnarvon on behalf of Salisbury had secretly negotiated with Parnell and Parnell, through Mrs. O'Shea, with Gladstone. The latter had been converted to Home Rule and, pondering the precedents of 1827 (Catholic Emancipation), 1846 (Corn Laws) and 1867 (Reform), was prepared to support a Conservative leader who would carry it through. Parnell cared not with whom the deal was made, but ordered the Irish vote in English cities to be given to the Tories, as they controlled the House of Lords, and he did not know of Gladstone's conversion until too late. The electorate in the counties supported the Liberals in return for the Reform Bill of 1884 and therefore, though the Irish vote in the cities had given some twenty to forty seats to the Tories,[119] Parnell now allied himself with Gladstone. It was this complex of circumstances which led Salisbury to meet Parliament (January, 1886) before he resigned. When Gladstone, defeated on his Home Rule Bill, dissolved and was defeated at the election, he resigned without meeting Parliament, holding that it was best for Ireland that the strongest party should at once face its responsibilities.

The Queen now vigorously intrigued to secure a Government composed of all those most opposed to Gladstone. But she could do little. Hartington urged by her to support Salisbury that the country might not be perpetually exposed to changes of Government, tactfully replied that " . . . there remains on the part of the large majority of the constituencies so strong an attachment to party organization and associations, that no such fusion of parties could at present take place ".[120] The new Prime Minister, Salisbury, had succeeded to the leadership of the Conservatives in the Lords, on the death of Beaconsfield, in 1881. He held that it was for the Queen to choose between him and Northcote, the leader in the Commons.[121] His Cabinet was in office until 1892. There is a unique record of his decision to dissolve in 1892;[122] 269 Conservatives were returned, 46 Liberal Unionists, 81 Irish and 273 Liberals. Meeting Parliament the Government fell to a vote of no confidence, moved by Mr. Asquith. Once again the Queen had to accept Mr. Gladstone, and he, when the Lords rejected the Home Rule Bill of 1893, would have dissolved on the issue of the position of the House of Lords in the Constitution, but his colleagues were not to be persuaded. In 1894, blind and deaf, and at odds with his Cabinet over Naval Estimates he resigned for the last time and his successor, Rosebery, was the Queen's choice. In 1895, after two Cabinet meetings, and much difference of opinion, the Rosebery Government decided on resignation. Lord Salisbury held that it ought to dissolve. But Rosebery, while admitting " that it may be unusual that the same House of Commons should declare a want of confidence in two succes- sive administrations " refused.[123]

The dissolution of the Salisbury Government in 1900, marks the beginning of a new political age. Disraeli had shown what a little unscrupulousness could do with a Queen; there were many who thought that Gladstone repaid the lesson by showing how unconscious hypocrisy might secure the devotion of a people. Had not a Yorkshire correspondent written to Hartington in 1885, that in their eyes " whatever Mr. Gladstone proposes must be right and to differ from him (even in company with Bright) is deadly sin?" Chamber- lain was to show the power which was latent in the exercise by a powerful Minister of the prerogative of dissolution. He had deliberately studied the means between the old rhetoric and the new colloquialism. His speech had been so direct that the Queen had said that unless it were modified he could not remain in the Cabinet. Now, in 1900, though not Prime Minister, he was the most powerful member of the Cabinet and determined to capitalize success in war as a party majority. He did not feel inclined to undertake the respon- sibility of a settlement . . . without a popular mandate.[124] For the first time in generations a General Election was to turn on the personality of a single Minister, who was not Prime Minister.[125] Salisbury came round with reluctance to the opinion that it was expedient and necessary to do what he dis- liked. Chamberlain's word to the nation on the eve of the polls was " patriotism before politics ".[126] The implied antithesis was ominous for representative Government in the new century.

The formation and working of the Cabinets between 1880 and 1906, must be briefly considered. In 1880, Gladstone was no longer the law-giver of an obedient Cabinet, but the moderator between forces that clashed violently on nearly every issue of politics. The Queen looked to the Whigs, Granville and Hartington, to blanket his fires. But Gladstone understood little more than the Queen, the basis of the electoral verdict. He formed his Cabinet, three-fourths of Whigs and one-fourth of Radicals, while the Liberal Party in the country was three-fourths Radical and one-fourth Whig. Hartington, the Whig leader, only held on at the War Office because he felt that his resignation would mean Radical leadership. He was " terribly sick of office and seldom found himself in real agreement with his colleagues ".[127] Granville was intriguing with the Queen as to the best moment to turn Gladstone out. On the other side were the Radical twins, Dilke and Chamberlain. Gladstone was, with great difficulty, persuaded that he must admit Chamberlain (aged forty-two). Dilke was not included, but was kept informed by Chamberlain of everything that went on. " In the matter of leakages ", wrote Gladstone, " our State is little short of disgraceful ". Had not Chamberlain and Dilke had an unusual influence with the Press, and had behind them the power of the Radical caucus, they could not have held their own for five years against a Cabinet of peers. After the passage of the Reform Bill in 1884, this Cabinet was in dissolution. It seemed like a man afflicted with epilepsy, and each fit was worse than the last.

The Salisbury Cabinet, 1886-92, taxed the resources of its Premier. In the formation of their Cabinets, Prime Ministers have the most complex of problems. They have to consider the exacting sense of political proprieties ruling in the small world of clubs, to deal with voracious appetites for power—the Carlton Club resembled when a Government was being formed the Zoo at feeding-time[128]—to placate the prejudices of the Queen, political and personal, and to secure than an unwritten constitution is adapted without disaster to a changing social order. For Salisbury, his problems were

more than usually complex. He felt that the country was
" on the inclined plane leading from the position of Lord
Hartington to that of Mr. Chamberlain, and so to the depths
over which Mr. Henry George rules supreme ".[129]   Gladstone's conversion to Home Rule had lost him and secured
to Salisbury, the Queen, society, and the great Whig families,
and the Radical Chamberlain.   Salisbury thought that the
Government should have been formed by Hartington, the
leader of the Liberal Unionists, a sportsman whose leisure
was mostly spent in the hunting-field, at his club, or on the
racecourse, but who embodied for the time the feeling that
justice to Ireland must not mean injustice to one-third of her
population.[130]   But Hartington would not form a Government, nor would he join the Cabinet, because to have done
so would have left Chamberlain with so small a following,
that he might have slid back into Gladstonianism.[131]   The
conflicting claims of his aged and shakey team forced Salisbury to take the double burden of the Foreign Office and the
Premiership, so that the Government suffered by having a
peer Prime Minister absorbed in foreign affairs, while its
leader in the Commons, Smith, was unable to control a dis-
tracted party.

The revolt and resignation of Randolph Churchill, who as
leader of the Tory democrats, was as much a thorn in the side
of Salisbury as Chamberlain had been to Gladstone, opened a
place for Goschen as the accredited representative of
Liberal Unionist opinion.   Salisbury himself " was by
temperament and opinion, incapable of becoming a great law-
maker.   He did not believe in any good to be effected by
inspired ventures in legislation.   Legal provision had to be
made for the accommodation of existing institutions to the
constantly changing social conditions of the people; practical
evils had to be remedied as they appeared ".[132]   " To those
who know English politics well ", he wrote, " they are not
attractive "; their highest rewards confer no real power.

Their strongest men have to carry out ideas that are not their own ".[133]   In 1886 Hicks-Beach wrote to him, " I confess much doubt whether the country can be governed nowadays by persons holding opinions which you and I should call even moderately Conservative. But I feel pretty certain that the only chance of its being so governed is by those who hold such opinions combining to do so ".[134]   So we find the Salisbury Government under the influence of Chamberlain carrying out much of the Radical legislation which Gladstone had regarded with distrust: the extension of local govern- ment to counties and free education, and measures to keep agricultural workers on the land.[135]

The Gladstone Cabinet of 1892 was one of the strangest in English history. The Queen accepted him as Prime Minister because to come to him after others had failed would elevate him into a dictator. But the Grand Old Man was, at eighty- two, " a very alarming outlook ". She would, she said, in no way " interfere in the formation of this iniquitous " Govern- ment. So, through the Prince of Wales, she persuaded Rose- bery to take the Foreign Office and she vetoed the inclusion of either Dilke or Labouchere. The Cabinet included Morley as Chief. Secretary for Ireland, Campbell-Bannerman as Sec- retary of State for War, Asquith at the Home Office and Sir Edward Grey as Under-Secretary for Foreign Affairs. In his diary, Sir Algernon West has left us a picture of this Cabinet: Gladstone with the doors of the senses gradually closing, Rosebery, incapable of co-operating with anyone, Harcourt, rowdy and quarrelsome. In the Commons, even with the support of the Irish—who were now divided into two groups—it had a bare majority of forty. In the Lords there was an overwhelming majority against them, and when the Home Rule Bill arrived there, though the shooting season was in full swing, 419 peers were present to defeat its forty-one supporters. Patriotism was more than grouse. On the House of Lords in 1892 Gladstone had sent the Queen

220 YEARS OF ENGLISH GOVERNMENT

a memorandum which she had found " very curious ". He pointed out that on the three previous occasions that he had been in Office his party had been largely, though unequally represented in all orders of the community; that now, though Liberal views were supported by a majority of the English-speaking people, they were hardy at all represented, and were imperfectly known in the powerful circles with which the Queen had personal intercourse. There was a widening gap between the upper and more numerous classes. The present Government had a bare tenth of the membership of the Lords and possessed not one acre in fifty.[136]

Rosebery, who was sent for by the Queen on her own initiative to succeed Gladstone, described his own difficulties in a letter to the Quen. " He has inherited from his predecessor a policy, a Cabinet and a Parliament, besides a party of groups one of which is aimed against himself. All this is kept in existence by a narrow majority which may at any moment break away. He, himself, is only able to guide this tumultuous party through a leader, bitterly hostile to himself and ostensibly indifferent to the fate of the Government. Lord Rosebery in the meantime is shut up in a House almost unanimously opposed to his Ministry and for all political purposes might as well be in the Tower of London."[137] The relations between Harcourt and himself were, in fact, so strained that in the end they only communicated through a third party. Harcourt complained that he was expected to accept beforehand and defend a policy of the Prime Minister and Foreign Secretary in the Lords without having been consulted beforehand;[138] that the situation of a leader of the House of Commons called upon to defend appointments of which he knew nothing and did not approve was impossible.[139] He told Rosebery that the Secretary for Foreign Affairs ought to be in the House of Commons and that the leader of the House of Commons should have constant opportunity of communication with him. He complained that all those on whom depended the issue of peace or war—the Prime Minister, the Foreign Secretary, the Admiralty and the Colonies were in the Lords.[140]   Rosebery as Prime Minister, was not pleased when Harcourt asked that he should be able to make independent decisions in the House of Commons, see all official despatches, have some control over patronage, and that a Cabinet should be called at his request.[141]   Rosebery and Harcourt, being poles asunder on the fundamentals of government, could not make the adjustments that Disraeli and Northcote and to less extent, Salisbury and Smith had achieved.   But the days of a peer Prime Minister were numbered.

Imprisoned in the Lords, Rosebery was plagued by the Queen.   She had her own views " as to the Constitution that was fifty-seven years ago, delivered into her hands " and found some of Lord Rosebery's views " Radical to a degree, almost Communistic ".   At one time he had respectfully to refuse to admit the need for the Queen's sanction before submitting a question to a popular audience, for " such a principle would tend to make the Sovereign a party in all the controversies of the hour and would compromise its neutrality ".[142]

In the Salisbury Cabinet of 1895 the Conservatives, old Whigs and Radical imperialists formally coalesced.   What in 1885 seemed impossible—Salisbury, Goschen and Chamberlain in the same Cabinet—was secured.   But Cabinet making was a delicate task.   The high Tories complained that deserving Conservatives were sent empty away while Liberal Unionists and the Birmingham gang seized the loaves and fishes.[143]   Devonshire was offered the Foreign Office, but preferred to be Lord President of the Council; Chamberlain, invited to be Chancellor of the Exchequer, preferred the Colonial Office; Goschen went to the Admiralty; Hicks-Beach became Chancellor of the Exchequer because he was, after Balfour, the only debater fitted for the House of Commons; Lansdowne was made Secretary for War because he had served under Cardwell; James wanted to be Lord Chancellor, but because of Halsbury's claims he had to be content with the Chancellorship of the Duchy. The Cabinet contained eight peers, three of them the heads of great families, but its inner life was determined by Salisbury, Balfour and Chamberlain.[144]   Salisbury, aloof in the Lords, " did not exercise the control over his colleagues either in or out of the Cabinet that Beaconsfield did "; he " frequently allowed important matters to be decided by a small majority of votes, even against his own opinion " and " left his colleagues very much to themselves unless they consulted him ".[145]

The development of imperialism and the course of the South African War made Chamberlain by 1899 stronger than the Prime Minister and probably stronger than all his colleagues together.[146]   He was able to secure the Khaki election of 1900.   In 1902 Salisbury resigned and Hicks-Beach decided to leave office with him.   The Duke of Devonshire, who had in the past thrice been offered the Premiership, was now passed over because he was a Liberal Unionist; Chamberlain was laid up by a serious cab accident and the King sent for Balfour.[147]   He found himself in a position requiring the fullest exercise of the powers of his office to secure reforms which he considered to be essential against the opposition of his colleagues on the one hand and before the return of the Liberals on the other.   Coached by Morant he secured the compromise of the Education Act of 1902; he supported the Irish Land Purchase Scheme of 1903 and the Licensing Act of 1904; he was responsible for the Committee of Imperial Defence; backed Lansdowne at the Foreign Office when he concluded an alliance with Japan and the Anglo-French Convention of 1904.   It was his concern for the reorganization of the military and naval forces and for an understanding with France and Japan which led him to remain in office long after a dissolution had become necessary. The centrifugal nationalism of the colonies had thrown Chamberlain back on Imperial preference.[148]   By 1903 the Cabinet was divided between the Free Trade policy of Ritchie, the Chancellor of the Exchequer, and the Chamberlain programme of Tariff Reform.   In this situation Balfour defended a policy of agreement to differ so long as party convenience required.   Though Hicks-Beach said that Chamberlain's tariff proposals had divided, and if persisted in would destroy the Unionist Party.[149]   Balfour claimed the right to an open mind.   " I should consider that I was ill performing my duty, I will not say to my party, but to the House and to the country if I were to profess a settled conviction where no settled conviction exists."[150]   He wrote to Devonshire, " whatever be the merits of the questions . . . why should the fact that some of us differ and many of us hesitate about it, break up or tend to break up the present Cabinet . . . our resignations must produce an immediate dissolution and this is not a felicitious moment for putting the party fortunes to the hazard. . . .   I think in this connection we ought to bear in mind that through many Parliaments Catholic Emancipation was an open question in the Tory Party; and a generation later the some was true of Free Trade.   I suppose that Disestablishment occupies at the present moment a similar position among the Radicals.   I cannot conceive why we are not to allow ourselves a liberty of difference which we allow to our opponents and which is in strict conformity with constitutional tradition. . . .   It should be agreed that the question is an open one; that we should be allowed officially to collect information upon the effects of the proposed policy, that we should discourage explicit statements of individual opinion."[151]   In September, 1903, he summarily dismissed Balfour of Burleigh and Ritchie, though he had, unknown to the Cabinet, Chamberlain's offer of resignation in his pocket.

The next day two other Free Traders, Hamilton and the Duke of Devonshire, resigned also. Balfour then accepted Chamberlain's resignation and persuaded the Duke of Devonshire to withdraw his. But later, when Chamberlain and the Free Traders complained not unnaturally that they had been tricked, Devonshire felt compelled to resign.[152] Balfour was determined to hold power until the treaty with Japan was signed; he was determined to reorganize the War Office and to establish the Committee of Imperial Defence before Campbell-Bannerman should take office. So he carried out the " fine idea of Joe freely operating outside, Arthur sympathizing with him and co-operating inside and Mr. Austen holding the keys of the safe ".[153]

By December, 1905, Balfour could no longer avoid resignation or dissolution. He resigned hoping that the dissensions of the Liberals would be their destruction. Most of the constitutional experts were agreed that precedents were against the formation of a Government by an Opposition in the last months of an expiring Parliament. But Campbell-Bannerman accepted office. " Personally ", he said, " I am strongly against refusing office; it would be ascribed to divisions or to cowardice . . . refusal is not in keeping with the clamour we have made for the last year or two."[154] At the election of 1906 the long Conservative reign was ended. In the next eight years the Constitution was to be tested to the verge of civil war as an instrument for the preservation of order, a tool of social reform, and a state of mind able to administer the unforeseen. The struggle of English democracy to avoid that despotism which is the price of empire had commenced.

1906-14: It is impossible to give even in outline the political events which tested and moulded the prewar constitution between 1906 and 1914. For the first time since Napoleon the condition of foreign affairs imposed on those responsible for defence preparations for a war which might involve the life of the English political and economic system. A Foreign Secretary had to negotiate in a European anarchy on behalf of a democracy which could only decide for peace or war on the very eve of Armageddon. The Ministers for the Army and Navy had to secure the essential minimum for safety from a Parliament preoccupied with problems of social reconstruction. For the first time since the hungry 'forties there was a failure of real wages to rise, and with the collapse of the landed aristocracy the issue between competitive industrialism and the elements of social justice was clearly set. But the issues of war or peace and of social reform or social revolution could not be squarely faced until a problem of race —Ireland—and an anachronism—the House of Lords—had been dealt with. A political history would have to lay bare the interplay between the problem of the Lords and Ireland and the political education of an industrial proletariat under the shadow of a deepening European crisis. Here we can only consider the nature of the Constitution as shown by the crisis of the Parliament Act, of the Home Rule Bill which followed, and the difficulties of a democracy when the issues are war or peace which the crisis of 1914 laid bare.

The formation of the Campbell-Bannerman Government in 1905 was a fine example of the complexities of that art. Balfour had no doubt that the King would send for Campbell-Bannerman as the recognized leader of the Liberal Party since 1908[155] in the Commons, while Spencer, the leader in the Lords, was followed by only about twenty peers.[156] Edward VII had already taken the precaution of establishing friendly personal relations with the Premier-to-be.[157] In forming his Cabinet Campbell-Bannerman had to harmonize a diversity of creatures. Grey, Asquith and Haldane considered that effective government required that Campbell-Bannerman himself should not lead in the Commons. He had mentioned to Asquith that " that ingenious person R. B.

o

Haldane proposed to dump him on the Upper House ".[158] When he refused this courteous elimination there was a possibility that Grey, Asquith and Haldane might refuse office. But Asquith wrote to Haldane, " Grey is resolved to refuse office.   I have come to the conclusion that it is my duty to accept.   If I refuse to go in either the attempt to form a Government fails or a weak Government would be formed entirely or almost entirely of our colour ".   Grey's real difficulty was that of joining a Government in which Rosebery was not included.   But he was persuaded by Acland that he ought not to imperil the whole Liberal cause.[159]   But with the Foreign Office (Grey) and the War Office (Haldane) held in suspense Cabinet making " was attended with more than ordinary difficulties.   Alternative plans had to be made on the assumption that the two recalcitrants would come in or that they would stay out ".[160]   Campbell-Bannerman remained in the Commons, but with Asquith at the Treasury, Haldane at the War Office and Grey at the Foreign Office the Liberal Imperialists were strongly entrenched.   Among the new men were Lloyd George, who as the President of the Board of Trade, was to vivify that office as Chamberlain had vivified the Colonial Office; Birrell at the Board of Education; Sidney Buxton at the Post Office.   Outside the Cabinet as Under-Secretaries of State were McKenna, Winston Churchill and Herbert Samuel.

The election of 1906, on the surface a victory for Free Trade and Nonconformity, was at bottom a victory for a new industrial democracy.[161]   " Unless I am greatly mistaken ", wrote Balfour to Knollys, " the election of 1906 inaugurates a new era."[162]   " Something more than the ordinary party change is going on before our eyes, and I do not think the full significance of the drama can be understood without reference to the Labour and Socialist movements on the Continent."[163]   The new Government did not singe a king's beard, but they caused his eyebrows to rise when they " ' presented him ' with a gracious speech promising twenty-two Bills in the new session ".[164] To its three most contentious Bills—Education, Trade Unions, Plural Voting—the Government added a Merchant Shipping Bill and private members a dozen more, of which some, like the Land Tenure Bill, were adopted by and pushed forward by the Government. Innumerable committees and commissions were appointed to explore Canals and Waterways, the Feeding of School Children, the Miners' Eight-Hour Day, Metropolitan Police, Vivisection, the Welsh Church and Small Holdings.[165] For a long time afterwards it was unusual to meet anyone in London who was not a member of some committee of investigation. But Governments do not live by research alone. And Oppositions also serve who only stand and wait. For the Unionists the resources of the Constitution were not yet exhausted. " There has certainly never been a period in our history in which the House of Lords will be called upon to play a part at once so important, so delicate and so difficult," wrote Balfour to Lansdowne.[166] The Government " will bring in Bills in a much more extreme form than the moderate members of their Cabinet probably approve: the moderate members will trust to the House of Lords cutting or modifying the most outrageous provisions; the left wing of the Cabinet, on the other hand . . . will be consoled by the reflection that they will be gradually accumulating a case against the upper house ". And so it came to pass. But the ultimate results of this cool advice to exploit the Constitution were to be a transformation Mr. Balfour did not foresee. The Lords were led to challenge the new democracy and its leaders on ground where the challenger was certain to be destroyed. Campbell-Bannerman said that Balfour's course " left no room for doubt . . . that the second chamber was being utilized as a mere annexe of the Unionist Party ".[167] It was said that Balfour signalled to it to come to his rescue, not on great emergencies affecting national interests, but on measures which touched only the ordinary interests of the Unionist Party.[168]   Lloyd George said it was not the watchdog of the Constitution but Mr. Balfour's poodle.   But for a time the poodle could bite.   In a Cabinet which contained the Catholic Lord Ripon and the Nonconformist Lloyd George unanimity on educational policy was not possible.[169]   Lloyd George spoke of the Education Act of 1902 as " riveting the clerical yoke on thousands of parishes ".[170]   As English opinion was not ripe for the abolition of State religious instruction, and as provision for all the sects was not possible because they were so numerous, the Government's Education Bill in 1906 was its most difficult task.   But the House of Lords so transformed the Bill that for the Commons to have recovered its original form would have been a labour of weeks.[171]   When the Commons rejected their amendments the Lords were persuaded that the Cabinet dare not dissolve when the issue might be made one of Church versus Chapel instead of Lords versus People.   Though Campbell-Bannerman was for dissolution the majority of the Government were against risking their majority.

But while destroying the Education Bill the Lords passed the Trades Dispute Bill of 1906, though it was a private members' bill which the Government accepted in place of that prepared by their own legalists because it gave clearer recognition to the right of combination and the liberty to strike.   They rejected a Plural Voting Bill, a Land Valuation Bill and a Licensing Bill, in spite of the intercession of the King and Lord Milner.   They were to accept from Asquith and Lloyd George a Workman's Compensation, the Eight-Hour Day, Trade Boards and Labour Exchanges.

Asquith had been summoned by the King to succeed Campbell-Bannerman in 1908.   Lloyd George took Asquith's place as Chancellor of the Exchequer.   Court circles felt that they were at last overwhelmed by the middle classes.[172]   By the end of 1908 Asquith felt that the Lords had effectively blocked the road in education, temperance and land reform, Welsh Disestablishment and Irish Home Rule. Then the Lloyd George Budget of 1909 tempted the Lords to their destruction. Its provision for a more steeply graded income tax and for taxing the landlords was necessitated by the needs of the Navy. But because the former might remove the revenue motive of a tariff and the Land Value Duties would require a complete survey and valuation of their land the peers, who were more property-minded than politically inspired, opposed.[173] It was in vain that their intellectual leaders counselled caution. Hicks-Beach, Cromer and Balfour of Burleigh because they were Free Traders were not listened to.[174] In vain the latter pointed out that though they had an abstract right to reject a Budget, " usage, precedent, national convenience were arrayed against its exercise ". " Finance ", he told them, " differs from all other legislation in this respect. If a Bill is rejected either by the Lords or by disagreement the *status quo* remains and survives . . . it is not so in finance. A referendum in finance would destroy the control of the House of Commons over the Government." The Lords, blind to the fact that their rejection of the Budget would enable Lloyd George to pillory them as rich and selfish irresponsibles, rejected the Budget by 350 to 75 (30th November, 1909). The Constitution was now to be tested for its capacity for fundamental self-amendment. It fell to the Prime Minister Asquith to manipulate the complex conventions of the Constitution so that neither the King Edward VII in the Court, nor Lloyd George in the constituencies should strain the delicate fabric to a hopeless collapse.

Before the rejection of the Budget by the Lords Edward VII had seen the Opposition peers with the agreement of Asquith. So anxious was the King that the Budget should pass that he asked Asquith to sanction his promising them a dissolution in January, 1910. This would have given away the principle at stake and Asquith refused.[175]   After the rejection Parliament was dissolved, and at the election in January the Liberals lost a hundred seats, but the Government, so long as it was supported by the forty Labour and eighty-two Irish members, had a majority of 124.   The Government was dependent for its existence on the Irish and they were determined to destroy the power of the Lords to veto Home Rule.   What followed is a classic example of the complex working of Constitutional niceties in time of crisis and of the underlying forces which may destroy a State.

Before the election Asquith knew that Edward VII considered that he would not be justified in creating new peers until after a second General Election.   For the King to pledge himself to create peers to pass a Bill dealing with the House of Lords, a Bill which had not even received the assent of the House of Commons, would be a breach of his duty.   That the King should place permanently in the hands of the Prime Minister of the day the prerogative to create peers was considered in Court circles to be an outrage.[176] According to Esher, Balfour was of the opinion that as Lansdowne, the leader in the Lords, was pledged to pass the Budget if the Liberals were returned there was no crisis. Asquith knew before the first election that two elections would be necessary if the Lords were to be reformed.   The passing of resolutions limiting the Lords veto was the first business of the new session.   Asquith had to explain to his followers that he had received no guarantee that the Royal prerogative for the creation of peers to pass a Bill for the reform of the Lords had been given.   When the resolutions were passed he told his followers that " if we do not find ourselves in a position to ensure that that statutory effect will be given to this policy in this Parliament we shall then either resign our offices or recommend a dissolution of Parliament ", and he added, " that in no case would we recommend dissolution except under such conditions as will secure that in the new Parliament the judgment of the people as expressed in the election will be carried into law ". Asquith was striving to keep the King's name out of politics. At the height of the struggle Edward VII died, and his death was followed by a conference between the parties to discover a compromise. But this failed, as it was bound to do. For the vital issue was Home Rule, and this could not be settled by any adoption of joint sessions between the two houses, nor were the leaders prepared to settle the Home Rule issue separately by referendum. With the failure of the conference Asquith decided that for the sake of the Monarchy itself a dissolution must take place at once. Had he resigned the Opposition could not have lasted, and a dissolution granted to them would have brought the King into politics. The King was between the devil of the Tory Party who considered him to be their natural head, and the deep sea of the Radical press. On November 11th he saw George V, explaining that he could not advise a second dissolution unless he had reasonable assurance that the King would use his prerogative if the Government secured a sufficient majority. He secured not a guarantee but a hypothetical understanding.[177] Asquith's view of the functions of the Crown were clearly stated. " It is to act upon the advice of the Ministers . . . whether the advice does or does not conform to the private and personal judgment of the Sovereign. . . . It is not the function of a Constitutional Sovereign to act as arbitrator or mediator between rival parties and policies; still less to take advice from the leaders of both sides with a view to forming a conclusion of his own."

At the election the position of the Government was practically unchanged. The Government was returned with a majority of 126, Labour providing forty-two and the Irish eighty-four. In July, 1911, the Cabinet submitted a Minute to the King that it would be their duty to advise the Crown to exercise its prerogative for the creation of peers. Asquith insisted that he himself and not the King should inform the Opposition, so that there might be no doubt that the responsibility was the Government's.   There was a real danger that the Tory Party might regard the King as their natural ally who was deserting them in a crisis.

The Parliament Act was finally passed by the Lords in spite of the efforts of Halsbury, F. E. Smith and Lord Willoughby de Broke to secure its rejection.   But it seemed to many of the Conservatives that single chamber Government had been imposed upon England by pressure from Ireland.

The Parliament Act of 1911 provided a temporary settlement of a conflict within the Constitution which had been steadily increasing since 1868.   For when the Conservative Party realized that the Liberal Party under Gladstone was a trinity of three unequal parts—old Whig, new Radical and Irish patriots—they naturally developed the idea of demanding a dissolution whenever their views and those of the House of Commons conflicted.   In the absence of a written Constitution embodying a theory of democratic government they had a plausible case.   For the vital problem of all constitutions is the procedure to be adopted for securing a peaceful change in the policy or membership of whatever body exercises the supreme power in the State.   In the British Constitution, once it became impossible for the Monarch to exercise his or her discretion as to who should be entrusted with the formulation of the policy of the State, the problem was acute.   Was the only check to the policy favoured by a majority of the elected House of Commons to be their interpretation of the public mind and their respect for the possible punishment for any indiscretions at a possibly remote election the very date of which they themselves could determine?   How was the power of the people to cashier their rulers to be secured? The people elects the legislature; a majority of the legislature empower some of their number to exercise every power of the State subject only to the limitation that they, the majority, do not object and that the people do not rebel. Further, as the power of the legislature extended to the very framework and fundamental principles of the Constitution itself, it could transform the organs through which the people's will was expressed. This difficulty could be met in part by the theory of the mandate. But there could be no provision that a mandate would be sought on any issue except that which seemed desirable to the party which was seeking a majority when an election did occur. Unless there is a non-elected power in the State the mandate might establish a dictatorship.

In 1868 the House of Lords passed the Irish Church Bill because its principles had been approved by the country at the polls. But their amendments led to a protracted deadlock broken only by negotiations between the two parties aided by the personal influence of the Queen. In their first use of their newly-discovered weapon the Lords were advised by the skilful Disraeli. But with his death in 1881 and the succession of Lord Salisbury the relations between the two houses deteriorated. Even before 1867 Granville, then the Whig leader in the Lords, had found them as hostile to a Liberal policy abroad as to reforms at home. During the Gladstone Government, 1868-74, he had had to recommend an Education Bill and the abolition of university tests in an assembly hostile to any religious equality; the Irish Land Act of 1870; a great scheme of Army reform to those who considered that the military forces of the Crown were the natural preserves of the Upper classes. He had had to justify the abolition of purchase by warrant, secret voting, the legal status of Trade Unions and the complete alteration of the structure of the Supreme Court.[177a] Over the Reform Bill of 1884 the Lords had hoped to force a dissolution, but Gladstone had refused to dissolve except on their own position in the Constitution.

But it was the split on Home Rule in 1886 which made the position of the House of Lords impossible. For the number of Liberals in the Lords now shrank to pitiable proportions. It was not merely that the great majority of the lords were opposed to Home Rule. In that they might have claimed to be expressing a national will as opposed to a passing combination of petty interests. But the development of the need for social legislation after 1886 coincided with the development of the House of Commons as a legislative machine that could not endure the brake of privilege the Lords applied.

A new machinery of party organization had been made to meet the new political conditions which the enlargement of the electorate and the spread of popular education produced. Disraeli had some insight into the new art of leadership which was required; Gladstone with conscious skill or unconscious cunning had achieved the arts which leadership requires. But the general attitude of the aristocracy to the new electorate was to be fatal to their order.

A study of the elections which followed the third Reform Bill of 1884 show that the doctrine of the swing of the pendulum was little more than a comforting superstition held by the Opposition and a bogey by which a Government could discipline rebellious back benchers. The real problem was much more subtle and complex.

It was true that a Government which relied entirely on its record in office to secure the support of the electorate at its next appeal would be likely to suffer disappointment. Benefits conferred would not mean power renewed. A Government would not be warmly supported in the heat of an election by its benefits being recollected in tranquillity. It was not the record of the Government, but the occasion of the election which would determine the result. When Disraeli in 1878 did not resign and fight while Peace with Honour still echoed in the public ear, he went down two years later

to surprised defeat.   Chamberlain, by forcing an election in
1900 while the passions of war were still stirred, secured a
second term of office for the Salisbury Government.   But
the most subtle example of this skill in seeking the right
moment for electoral victory was the dissolution of 1886.
For the Gladstone Government, by refusing to dissolve in
1885 on the technical ground that the constituencies were not
yet in existence and resigning office to Lord Salisbury,
deprived the latter of the advantage of being the Opposition and yet secured the support of the agricultural
labourers whom they had enfranchised in 1884.   But not
only was the occasion for dissolution of the utmost importance: the nature of the issues and their presentation were
found to be all-important.   The issues must be simple and as
little complicated by detail as possible.   Careful preparation
of the public for the acceptance of new ideas, and on the
other hand sudden appeals to old prejudices in conditions
making it difficult for your opponent to mobilize an appeal
to reason, were the arts to be mastered by the party agents.
In 1886 Gladstone failed because the issue of Home Rule was
presented before it had had time to be developed; in 1906
the Liberal case against Tariff Reform succeeded because it
had had full time to be developed. The same election provided
a perfect example of the use of political prejudice.   Not only
was the Conservative Party hampered by a confused presentation of the case for Tariff Reform while the Liberal
opposition had ample time to develop the logical appeal of
the Cobdenite case; they also had the misfortune to have
arrayed against them the instinctive fears of the populace.
Their education policy of 1902 had " stirred into life one of
the fundamental fears of Protestant England: was ' Rome to
be on the rates? ' "; Balfour's Licensing Act of 1904 enabled
beery " Mr. Bung the Brewer " to leer from Liberal posters;
prejudice and virtue thus enlisted, Imperial Preference was
attacked as threatening a " Dear Loaf " and a return to " the

Hungry 'Forties "; finally, as a crowning mercy to the Liberal cause, the introduction of indentured Chinese labour on the Rand made possible a virtuous repudiation by their supporters of a threatened slavery.

From Sedan to the outbreak of war in 1914 the British Cabinet system provided an enigma to our enemies and friends. Whether it be true that our diplomatists secured the essentials of a policy which self-preservation required, the very spirit of Cabinet government bewildered foreign powers. Not only was there the oscillation between Conservative and Liberal Governments, which our system of resignations and dissolutions made it impossible for the most subtle diplomat to predict, but there was the existence within each Cabinet, however unanimous on matters of urgency standing for immediate decision at home, profound divisions on the very basis of foreign policy save the ultimate and most disturbing principle of all that England should reserve complete liberty to act as she choose.

Before the Congress of Berlin not a few of Disraeli's own followers had serious misgivings concerning the wisdom and morality of the policy which he was pursuing.[178]   In 1877 a section of the Cabinet under Derby was against war at any price, Lord Salisbury was against war at the present moment, while several supported by the Queen were bitter Russophobes.[179]   The Queen, in January, 1878, denounced "the great barbarians " and even talked of abdication in her shame of the " low tone " of the country and the Cabinet.[180]   The threats to Russia were in fact a gigantic piece of bluff.[181]   The Bulgarian atrocities were such a burning question between the two parties that for two years the major issue of foreign policy could not be considered on its merits.[182]   Gladstone's relentless flow of moral precepts were for two years the main business of his life.

Bismarck frequently complained that it was difficult to conclude a reliable agreement with England.   The public negotiations required if a binding agreement were to be made exercised a detrimental influence upon the majority of all other European relationships.[183]   In 1898 Chamberlain favoured an approach to Germany, but Salisbury felt as little confidence in Germany as in Russia or in France.[184]   Only with the Japanese Treaty of 1902 was there a conditional surrender of our traditional privilege of self-determination, and to secure that Balfour hung on when normally his Government would have resigned or dissolved.   In the growing deterioration of European relations from the Moroccan crisis of 1905 to 1914 the British Cabinet believed that they had retained their freedom of action to act as they choose when a crisis for France should occur.   Actually in 1907 military conversations had begun with France and Belgium. They were not revealed to the Cabinet until 1912, and though the situation was then formally defined, Sir Edward Grey believed that England was still free, while Poincaré was convinced that she was committed beyond recall.[185]   In the years immediately before the war of 1914-18 Lloyd George has stated that " the Cabinet as a whole was never called into general consultation upon the fundamental aspects of foreign relations ".[186]   It was of course preoccupied with the dying embers of sectarian passions in education, the Disestablishment of the Church in Wales, the menacing problem of Irish Home Rule and the Constitutional niceties of the Parliament Act.   The Government's right hand in domestic affairs did not know what its left was doing in foreign affairs.   All the things that mattered were conveyed in private and confidential letters from our diplomatic representatives abroad to the Foreign Secretary personally, in his private and unpublished replies and in the interviews which he held with the ambassadors at the Foreign Office in Downing Street.[187]

Grey, the Foreign Secretary, had been appointed in 1905 because he satisfied the Foreign Office by being an aristocrat and party tradition by being a commoner.   We may assume that whatever the underlying causes of the war they could not have been removed by the action of one Government. We may assume that the outbreak of war was effected by no one Government.   But we must admit that the general condition of Europe revealed remediable weaknesses in our system of government.   It is the considered judgment of one of the most sober historians of pre-war diplomacy that Grey's " great fault was what has been regarded as the great virtue of British constitutional leaders—the preference for practical compromise for the present instead of theoretical perfection for the future.   He was content in foreign affairs to meet situations as they arose and deal with them according to the most practical and common-sense needs of the moment ".[188]

[1] Hansard, Vol. 186, 3rd series, pp. 1568–73.
[2] cf. Gathorne Hardy, Nov. 12th, 1867.
[3] A. Elliot : Life of Goschen, Vol. I., p. 161.
[4] Seymour : Electoral Reform in England and Wales, Chap. X., p. 283.
[5] ibid., p. 348.
[6] Buckle's : Disraeli, Vol. V., p. 141 and see A. G. Gardiner's Life of Harcourt, Vol. I., p. 239.
[7] Williams : Rise of Gladstone to leadership of Liberal Party, p. 173.
[8] Selborne : Memorials, Part II., Vol. 2, p. 99.
[9] ibid., p. 122.
[10] Lady G. Cecil's Salisbury, Vol. III., pp. 122–4.
[11] A. E. Hardy's Gathorne Hardy, Dec. 3, 1884.
[12] In Representative Government.
[13] Derby to Disraeli, Nov. 22, 1868.   Buckle's Disraeli, Vol. V., p. 92.
[14] Selborne : Memorials, Vol. I., p. 330.
[15] ibid., p. 470.
[16] Cd. 5163, pr. 126.
[17] Holland's Devonshire, Vol. II., p. 142.
[18] Disraeli to Corry : Buckle's Disraeli, Vol. V., p. 89, Nov. 3rd, 1868.
[19] Maxwell's W. H. Smith, Vol. II., p. 26.
[20] Buckle's Disraeli, Vol. V., p. 262.
[21] Gladstone.
[22] Buckle's Disraeli, Vol. VI., p. 518.
[23] Hill : Toryism and the People, p. 38.
[24] ibid., p. 81.
[25] Buckle's Disraeli, Vol. V., p. 184.
[26] ibid., p. 185.
[27] ibid., p. 520.
[28] Lady Cecil's Salisbury, Vol. 3, p. 197.
[29] C. S. Emden : The People and the Constitution, p. 137.
[30] Holland's Life of Devonshire, Vol. I., p. 245.
[31] C. S. Emden, op. cit., p. 135.
[32] A. G. Gardiner : Life of Harcourt, Vol. II., p. 407.
[33] Crewe's Rosebery, Vol. II., p. 595.

34 Selborne : *Memorials*, Part II., Vol. II., p. 189.
35 ibid., p. 189.
36 Crewe's *Rosebery*, Vol. I., p. 246.
37 Buckle's *Disraeli*, Vol. V., p. 57.
38 Esher : *Diary*, Dec. 4, 1879.
39 J. A. Spender : *Life of Campbell-Bannerman*, Vol. I., p. 206.
40 ibid., p. 204.
41 Article in *Round Table*, 1911.
42 Redlich : *Procedure of the House of Commons*, Vol. I., p. 140.
43 ibid., p. 159.
44 ibid., p. 170.
45 *Round Table*, 1911.
46 ibid.
47 ibid.
48 ibid.
49 Redlich, op. cit., pp. 193-4.
50 *Round Table*, 1911.
51 To Hicks-Beach, Dec. 17, 1874. Lady Hicks-Beach's *Hicks-Beach, I.*, p. 46.
52 Holland's *Devonshire*, Vol. I., pp. 121-2.
53 F. Hardie : *Political Influence of Queen Victoria*, p. 55 (in 1878).
54 Zetland : *Letters of Disraeli to Lady Bradford and Lady Chesterfield*, Vol. I., p. 92.
55 Buckle's *Disraeli*, Vol. 4, p. 457.
56 F. Hardie, op. cit., p. 245.
57 ibid., (citing *Queen Victoria Letters*.
58 Buckle's *Disraeli*, Vol. VI., p. 528 (1880).
59 H. H. Bolitho has, I think, pointed this out.
60 Buckle's *Disraeli*, Vol. VI, 241.
61 ibid., Vol. V., p. 337.
62 Fitzmaurice : *Life of Granville*, Vol. II., p. 121.
63 Buckle's *Disraeli*, Vol. V., p. 480.
64 ibid., Vol. VI., p. 67.
65 ibid., VI., p. 239.
66 Acton's *Letters*, p. 78.
67 Holland's *Devonshire*, Vol. I., pp. 260-2, Dec. 7th, 1879.
68 cf. *Queen Victoria Letters*, 2nd series, Vol. III., Chap. 2, *passim*.
69 Buckle's *Disraeli*, Vol. V., p. 28.
70 ibid., Vol. V., p. 33.
71 ibid., Vol. V., p. 94.
72 ibid., Vol. V., p. 95 (Disraeli to Queen, Nov. 28th, 1868).
73 Holland's *Devonshire*, Vol. I., pp. 117-9.
74 Buckle's *Disraeli*, Vol. V., p. 206.
75 His reason for resignation *Queen Victoria Letters*, 2nd series, Vol. II., p. 317 Mem. 17 Feb., 1874.
76 Buckle's *Disraeli*, Vol. VI., p. 369.
77 ibid., Vol. VI., p. 511.
78 ibid., Vol. VI., p. 514.
79 ibid., Vol. V., p. 114.
80 ibid., Vol. IV., p. 586 (see *Queen Victoria Letters*, 2nd series, Vol. I., pp. 492-509).
1 *Queen Victoria Letters*, 2nd series, Vol. I., pp. 492-509, for the actual change-over.
2 *Queen Victoria Letters*, 2nd series, Vol. I., p. 564, Qu's Mem. 3 Dec., 1868.
3 ibid.
4 Morley's *Gladstone*.
5 Parker's *Graham*, Vol. 2, p. 2 and Holland's *Devonshire*, Vol. 2, p. 77.
6 Hardy's *Diary*, Vol. 2, pp. 364-5.
7 Fitzmaurice's *Granville*, Vol. 2, p. 2.
8 Selborne : *Memorials*, Part II., Vol. 2, p. 348.

[89] Knaplund : *Gladstone and Britain's Imperial Policy*, pp. 167–70.
[90] Fitzmaurice's *Granville*, Vol. II., p. 175.
[91] ibid., Vol. II., pp. 1 and 150.
[92] A. G. Gardiner : *Life of Harcourt* (App. II., being Harcourt's Mem. on Morley's chapter on the Cabinet in his *Walpole*).
[93] *Queen Victoria Letters*, 2nd series, Vol. II., p. 323.
[94] Buckle's *Disraeli*, Vol. V., p. 295.
[95] *Queen Victoria Letters*, 2nd series, Vol. II., pp. 321–2.   Mem. of 20th Feb., 1874.
[96] Buckle's *Disraeli*, Vol. VI., p. 272.
[97] ibid., p. 280.
[98] ibid., p. 280.
[99] Buckle's *Disraeli*, Vol. VI., pp. 194–5.
[100] Balfour : *Autobiography*.
[101] Ensor : *England 1870-1914*, p. 30.
[102] Buckle's *Disraeli*, Vol. V., p. 370.
[103] Balfour : *Autobiography*.
[104] Buckle's *Disraeli*, Vol. VI., p. 163.
[105] Ensor : *England 1870–1914*, p. 39.
[106] ibid., p. 106.
[107] ibid., p. 47.
[108] Lady Cecil's *Salisbury*.
[109] Introduction to *Radical Programme*.
[110] *Quarterly Review*, Oct. 1883.   Article *Disintegration*.
[111] Elliot's *Goschen*, Vol. I., pp. 252–3.
[112] *Queen Victoria Letters*, 2nd series, Vol. 3, pp. 75–6, 8 April, 1880.
[113] Holland's *Devonshire*, Vol. I., 260–2 and 274.
[114] ibid., Vol. I., p. 276.
[115] Buckle's *Disraeli*, Vol. VI., p. 538.
[116] Fitzmaurice : *Granville*, Vol. II., pp. 421–2.
[117] Holland's *Devonshire*, Vol. I., pp. 397–8.
[118] Lady Hicks-Beach : *Hicks-Beach*, Vol. I., p. 258.
[119] Ensor : *England 1870–1914*, p. 95.
[120] Holland's *Devonshire*, Vol. II., p. 173.
[121] Lady Cecil's *Salisbury*, Vol. III., p. 137.
[122] Garvin's *Chamberlain*, Vol. II., p. 538.
[123] Crewe's *Rosebery*, Vol. II., p. 507.
[124] Garvin's *Chamberlain*, Vol. III., p. 585.
[125] ibid., Vol. III., p. 593.
[126] ibid., Vol. III., p. 583.
[127] Holland's *Devonshire*, Vol. I., p. 397, Dec. 1883.
[128] Lady Cecil's *Salisbury*.
[129] ibid.
[130] Elliot's *Goschen*, Vol. II., pp. 50 and 87.
[131] Lady Cecil's *Salisbury*, Vol. III., p. 310.
[132] ibid., Vol. III., p. 167.
[133] ibid., Vol. III., p. 111.
[134] Lady Hicks-Beach : *Hicks-Beach*, Vol. I., p. 302.
[135] Garvin's *Chamberlain*, Vol. II., p. 423.
[136] *Queen Victoria Letters*, Vol. 2, 3rd series, pp. 172–5, Oct. 28, 1892.
[137] Crewe's *Rosebery*, Vol. II., p. 456.
[138] Gardiner's *Harcourt*, Vol. II., p. 337.
[139] ibid., Vol. II., pp. 338–9.
[140] ibid., Vol. II., p. 270.
[141] Crewe's *Rosebery*, Vol. II., p. 441.
[142] ibid., Vol. II., p. 462.
[143] Garvin's *Chamberlain*, Vol. III., p. 6.
[144] ibid., Vol. III., p. 7.
[145] *Hicks-Beach*, Vol. II., App. A., pp. 359–63.

146 Garvin's *Chamberlain*, Vol. III., p. 295.
147 Ensor : *England*, 1870–1914, p. 354.
148 ibid., p. 372.
149 J. A. Spender : *Campbell-Bannerman*, Vol. II., p. 101.
150 ibid., Vol. II., p. 102.
151 Holland's *Devonshire*, Vol. II., pp. 307–9.
152 ibid., Vol. II., pp. 340 and 352.
153 ibid., Vol II., pp. 352–3
154 J. A. Spender : *Campbell-Bannerman*, Vol. II., p. 192.
155 Ensor : *England* 1870–1914, p. 239.
156 Esher : *Diary*, Vol. 2, p. 56.
157 Spender : *Campbell-Bannerman*, Vol. II., p. 176.
158 Halevy : *History of the English People*, Vol. 5, p. 6.
159 Spender : *Campbell-Bannerman*, Vol. II., p. 197.
160 ibid., Vol. II., p. 200.
161 Halevy, op. cit., Vol. 5.
162 Lee : *Edward VII.*, Vol. II., p. 449.
163 Esher : *Diary*, Vol. II., p. 136.
164 Spender : *Campbell-Bannerman*, Vol. II., p. 270.
165 ibid., Vol. II., p. 281.
166 Newton's *Lansdowne*, p. 352–3.
167 Spender's *Campbell-Bannerman*, Vol. II., p. 356.
168 ibid., p. 357.
169 ibid., p. 275.
170 *Life of Birkenhead*, Vol. I., p. 171.
171 Spender's *Campbell-Bannerman*, Vol. 2, p. 311.
172 Esher : *Diary*, Vol. II., p. 303.
173 Ensor : *England* 1870–1914, pp. 413–14.
174 ibid.
175 Spender-Asquith : *Life of Asquith*, Vol. I., pp. 257–8.
176 Esher : *Diary* Vol. II., p. 424.
177 Halevy, op. cit., p. 333, and Ensor, op. cit., p. 424.
177ᵃ Fitzmaurice's *Granville*, Vol. 2, p. 4.
178 Cambridge : *History of Foreign Policy*, Vol. 3, p. 99.
179 ibid., Vol. 3, p. 120.
180 ibid., Vol. 3, p. 120.
181 ibid., Vol. 3, p. 126.
182 Seton Watson : *Gladstone Disraeli and the Eastern Question*, p. 57.
183 Pribram A. F. : *England and the European Powers*, p. 28.
184 Gooch : *Before the War*, Vol. I., p. 5.
185 Nicolson : *Lord Carnock*, pp. 372–3 and 383.
186 Lloyd George : *Memoirs*, p. 46.
187 ibid., p. 49.
188 Fay, *Origins of the World War*, Vol. 1, p. 30.

P

CHAPTER VI

THE MACHINERY OF ADMINISTRATION, 1870-1914

Efforts of the departments concerned with Defence, Health, Home, Trade and others to adjust themselves—Politics and administration—The Treasury tradition—The problems of Civil Service recruitment and promotion—The development of delegated legislation—The making of Local Government.

THE problem of the organization of the defence departments was radically changed by the shift in the economic forces which pressed upon the world and by the changes in the political and social structure of England at which we have glanced. In the Army the anomaly of a royal claim to more than titular supremacy, the anachronism of ranks recruited from criminals and officers too gentlemanly to acquire professional skill, could not remain. But the changes could only be brought about by the methods which the Constitution provided and in the spirit which inspired the political parties and their leaders.

The swiftness and precision of the Prussian victories of 1866 over Austria and in 1870 over France produced sufficient anxiety about army administration to secure that the Cardwell reforms were carried through. By the War Office Act of 1870 the Secretary of State for War secured formal recognition of his responsibility for all aspects of army administration. The Army Enlistment Act of 1870 introduced " the modern system of short service with the colours, followed by a period in the reserve, which provided the army with a pool of trained men, who could be recalled for service at any moment ".[1] Humanity had first appeared in the treatment of soldiers after the Crimean War, when the Prince Consort secured that there should be separate quarters for wives and

children of common soldiers in barracks.[2] Now the enlistment of criminals was forbidden and the discharge of men of
bad character authorized. In 1871 the abolition of the
system of purchase of commissions killed the conception that
only those who were possessed of property could be trusted
to defend the honour and liberty of those who had none.

But the struggle over the Army Regulation Bill which
proposed the abolition of purchase shows the obstacle which
constitutional niceties and political prejudice might oppose to
administrative reform. The Commander-in-Chief in the
Lords was opposed to the course recommended by the Secretary of State for War in the Commons. The delaying action
of the Lords was met by Gladstone advising the Queen to
cancel the warrant under which purchase had been made legal.
The Lords were then compelled to pass the Bill in order to
secure for the officers concerned the compensation which it had
provided. The struggle had a wider significance than its bearing
on army reform. The opposition of a group of colonels in
the Commons led them to try to baffle the majority by mere
consumption of time—an early experiment in parliamentary
obstruction; while the Peers were brought sharply into conflict with the Commons on an almost naked class issue.[3] The
discipline of the Army as Gladstone recognized was " a subject so grave, so delicate and associated at such a multitude of
points with the interests and feelings of the governing class,
that it should be as little as possible exposed to the influence
of parliamentary pressure ".[4]

The root difficulty of the division of power between the
Commander-in-Chief as representative of the Crown and the
Secretary of State responsible to Parliament was not yet
properly resolved. " You cannot," wrote Disraeli in 1879,
" get a Secretary of War to resist the cousin of the Sovereign
with whom he is placed in daily and hourly communication.
I tremble when I think what may be the fate of this country
if, as is not unlikely, a great struggle occur with the Duke

of Cambridge's generals ".[5]   In 1881 a claim by the Duke of Cambridge that " the command of the Army rested with the Commander-in-Chief as representing the Sovereign ", and that he could not be " merged in the Secretary of State " drew from Childers, the Secretary of State for War, a clear statement that the latter was responsible for the exercise of the Queen's prerogative and not a mere financial officer who had " gradually intruded on the province of the Crown by means of the power of the purse ".[6]   By an Order in Council, February 21st, 1888, the work of the War Office was distributed between a military division under the Commander-in-Chief responsible for everything connected with the efficiency of the soldier and a civil division under the Financial Secretary, responsible for expenditure and the control of the manufacturing departments.[7]   But this intense centralization of responsibility under which the Commander-in-Chief alone " would be accountable to the Secretary of State, even for such a matter as the defective design of a heavy gun ", could not conduce to efficiency,[8] and the Hartington Commission proposed that the War Office should be remodelled on the lines of the Board of Admiralty.   They proposed that the Secretary of State should be advised by a War Office Council consisting of the heads of the various departments individually answerable to him for their administrative work; that the office of Commander-in-Chief should be abolished and replaced by a general officer responsible for the command of troops and stationed at home and a Chief of Staff to advise on the fundamentals of military policy as a whole.[9]

To the Queen these " reckless changes and incredibly thoughtless proposals were ' really abominable ' ".   The evidence given before the Hartington Commission was suppressed " because the difference of opinion in high quarters was so acute as to render publication indiscreet ".[10]   When the Duke of Cambridge was finally induced to retire in 1895 the new scheme retained the Office of Commander-in-Chief, though with altered duties and responsibilities. Instead of an Army Council as the Hartington Commission had recommended the Secretary of State was to preside over a War Office Consultative Council composed of the Commander-in-Chief, the Adjutant-General, the Quartermaster-General and the Inspectors-General of Fortifications and Ordnance. The Commander-in-Chief was made the principal adviser of the Secretary of State on all military questions, and military opinion was to be focused by means of an Army Board, presided over by the Commander-in-Chief.

This scheme, for which Campbell-Bannerman was mainly responsible, was an unfortunate compromise, for it involved the simultaneous responsibility of the heads of departments to both the Parliamentary and military heads, while the Commander-in-Chief was in an anomalous position, not having full authority over the heads of the military branches for which he was responsible.[11] As neither the Council nor the Army Board had clearly defined responsibilities, it is not surprising that in 1899 Chamberlain dreaded our War Office more than the Boers,[12] or that " military calculations of requirements proved utterly inadequate to meet grossly misjudged situations and betrayed also in their detail a lack of coherent organization or forethought ".[13] The Esher Committee of 1904 pointed out that the War Office had been administered from the point of view of peace, and that it was necessary " to make a complete break with the past, and to endeavour to reconstitute the War Office with a single eye to the effective training and preparation of the Military Forces of the Crown for war ".[14] The Committee recommended the establishment of an Army Council on similar lines to the Board of Admiralty, but modified to meet the special conditions of the Army; the creation of a Chief of Staff; and the abolition of the Office of Commander-in-Chief. In 1904 an Army Council was established consisting of seven members (four military and three civilian) with the Secretary of State answerable to Parliament for everything connected with the Army. The Commander-in-Chief was bowed off a scene which he had confused for over half a century and the Army was at last controlled by a responsible statesman, advised by soldiers.[15]

Compared with the War Office, the Esher Committee saw the Admiralty as an administrative paragon. " The Admiralty system is sound in principle. It has been handed down without material change from the period of the great naval wars. It may be said to have been founded on the proved requirements of war. . . . It conforms closely to the arrangements under which the largest private industries are conducted."[16] The Board had been extensively reorganized in 1869, and after some minor changes in 1887 consisted of a First Lord; four Naval Lords (one being controller); the Civil Lord, the Financial and Parliamentary Secretaries, and the Permanent Secretary. The First Lord was head of the department and directly responsible to Parliament. But with the coming of steam and steel even for the Admiralty events were to take a questionable shape. Naval supremacy resting on wooden ships, " which took a long time to build; which no Power had the materials to multiply indefinitely, and which once built were serviceable for sixty years ", could rest at ease.[17] But steel, steam and many inventions made it more practicable for foreign Powers to build on level terms. And it is significant that Great Britain originated none of the nineteenth-century naval changes. Neither armour nor turrets, or breech-loaders, neither mines nor torpedoes, or submarines were British ideas. The service did not favour inventions.[18] Perhaps their inventiveness was damped by the rigours of Treasury control. The Gladstonian tradition that the cost of any particular service should be the decisive factor in deciding upon its desirability was there firmly enshrined.

first hint of Combo services

Intelligence in experts was not encouraged by politicians. " If soldiers were allowed full scope they would insist on the importance of garrisoning the moon in order to protect us from Mars ", said Salisbury.[19] Of the Admiralty Hicks-Beach said, " their experts' way of dealing with subjects deprived me of all confidence in them. . . . I believed their demands were based, not on what was really needed, but upon what they thought they could get us to give ".[20] The pressure of Treasury control produced a wasteful struggle for pence instead of an expense of thought.   " More than half the difficulty between the Admiralty and the War Office arises from personal feelings, distrust and jealousy where there ought to be hearty co-operation and this is really a serious mischief . . . the Admiralty say almost in as many words that the War Department want to do them out of stores."[21]   Neither the Army nor the Navy had any organs of thought to relate and co-ordinate their demands on the public purse to the public needs.

After 1870 the self-governing colonies had become partly responsible for their own defence, and the development of the steamship by changing conditions for moving troops had altered the basis of strategy.[22]   In 1885 a Colonial Defence Committee was organized.   In 1890 the Hartington Committee had advocated " the formation of a Naval and Military Council which should probably be presided over by the Prime Minister, and consist of the Parliamentary heads of the two services and their principal professional advisers ".   But Campbell-Bannerman was not prepared for a thinking and planning war machine, holding that in this country there was no room for general military policy in the larger and more ambitious Continental sense.[23]   In 1894 a conference was held in Downing Street on the co-ordination of the fighting services—Spencer from the Admiralty, Campbell-Bannerman from the War Office and Rosebery, at which the latter introduced what he afterwards considered to have been the germ of the Committee of Imperial Defence.[24] In 1895 Devonshire was asked by Salisbury to preside over a Defence Committee of the Cabinet. But the scope of this committee was " ill-defined and uncertain. The War Office and Admiralty and other departments were inclined to refer questions to it as little as possible. . . . It did not often meet, had no permanent secretariat and kept no records. Its functions consisted in settling now and then controversies between the War Office, the Admiralty and the Treasury, which would formerly have led to interminable correspondence or would have been brought before the Cabinet as a whole ".[25] In the South African as in the Crimean War the Cabinet had no means of obtaining a reasoned opinion on which to base its policy. In 1901 Balfour established the Committee of Imperial Defence. It consisted of the Prime Minister, the Secretary of State for War, the First Lord of the Admiralty, the Secretary of State for India, the Chancellor of the Exchequer and such persons—including the Dominion Prime Ministers—as from time to time the Prime Minister chose to summon. To this fluidity in its composition much of its efficiency and usefulness was due. It was, and remained, not an executive but a consultative body. But it was provided with a secretariat and considered strategical schemes affecting every aspect of imperial defence.[26] It was a committee of this C.I.D., appointed in 1911, which produced the famous war book in which there was worked out for each department every detail of what they must do in the event of war.[27]

The Royal Sanitary Commission of 1869 had urged the need for a strong Government department to deal with Public Health. A timid and unconvinced Cabinet decided to create a new Ministry, the Local Government Board, containing the Public Health powers of the Privy Council, the Local Government Act department of the Home Office and the Poor Law Board itself. " Whether the Government ever intended, as the sanitary enthusiasts were led to believe, to establish a sort of twin Ministry with separate departments for Public Health and Poor Relief under a single political chief cannot now be determined ".   " The Bill for the constitution of the new authority was originally in the hands of W. E. Forster, Vice-President of the Committee of the Privy Council for Education . . . but education was competing with public health for the attention of the Minister most competent to deal with both."   Goschen was promoted to the Admiralty before the measure could be got through Parliament.   A weaker and less experienced administrator, J. J. Stansfield, brought in and carried a weaker Bill and became the first President of the Local Government Board. An internecine feud followed between the civil servants of the Poor Law Board interested in Poor Law and those interested in Public Health, in which the latter were worsted.[27a]

There were two functions warring within the bosom of a single department.   Sir J. Simon has described how from being an executive officer of the Privy Council he became a mere advisory officer who could do little or nothing without the sanction of the Secretary of the Board.   The Minister backed the Secretary, and the medical adviser went to the wall.   In 1876 his branch, " the Medical Department ", was broken up and dispersed among the branches of the former Poor Law Board.   For nearly half a century the Poor Law side of the Local Government Board maintained its predominance.   But the Public Health services of the more enterprising local authorities were developed by local Acts, by successive Public Health Acts, Isolation Hospital Acts, Artisans' Dwellings Acts, Sale of Food and Drugs Acts.   When, in 1913, the Board of Control succeeded the Lunacy Commissioners in the supervision of persons of unsound mind they increasingly emphasized the Public Health aspect of this service and were brought into closer relation with the Local Government

Board. From 1911 there was the vast new system of Public Health Insurance under separate Boards of Commissioners for England, Scotland, Ireland and Wales. The Royal Commission on the Poor Law, in 1909, proposed that the Boards of Guardians should be abolished; that the conception of a deterrent Poor Law should be abandoned; and proposed a " vast extension of the best possible provision for the sick from whatever disease they might be suffering; the removal from the Poor Law of all kinds of mental deficiency, from the dangerous lunatic to the feeble-minded ". It approved the provision of Employment Exchanges; national pensions for the aged and unemployment insurance.[28] As the new science of medicine and the new demands of a democracy for social services developed expert medical staffs were attached to many Government departments. The Local Government Board as the department administering the Poor Law was responsible for " a composite system embracing the care of the destitute of all categories, including sick persons, mothers and infants, lunatics, mental defectives, children of school age, and aged persons so far as any of these may happen to be destitute ".[29] The National Health Insurance organizaton supervised the administration of medical and sanatorium benefits and of cash benefits in the form of sickness, disablement and maternity benefits; there was a division of authority between the Board of Education and the Local Government Board in relation to maternity and child welfare. The Privy Council under the Midwives Act, 1902, was responsible for the approval of the rules of the Central Midwives' Board governing the qualification and conduct of midwives. The Home Office supervised the administration of Part I of the Children's Act, 1908, which related to infant life protection. Such a system could not be economical and had an obvious tendency towards departmental rivalry and friction. With the development of public health services in various directions —nursing, diagnosis of disease, medical treatment—it was of great importance that it should be controlled by a single Minister.

The War Office and the departments concerned with health—the lords of death and life—are excellent examples of the way in which the functions of the State in the nineteenth century attached " themselves to the office in which the need for them happened to be first imperatively felt, or which had to provide money for them, or which was the department of the Prime Minister or the Court or whatever power in the State had dealt with them before they were regularly organized ".   At any time we shall find that some departments will have outgrown the purpose for which they were originally established, while others will have been established hurriedly to meet some passing emergency without due regard to their permanent duties or to the relation which those duties might bear to those of existing departments.[30]

The Ministry of Agriculture and Fisheries reveals the furtive and often infertile commerce of science with politics which our Constitution compels.   An Agricultural Department of the Privy Council first appeared in the estimate for the Privy Council in 1868-69 under the title of Cattle Plague Department.[31] In 1881, on the eve of the economic changes which were to wipe away the supremacy of agriculture in our business and our counsels, it was complained that if one wanted to get any information about disease of cattle one was referred to the Minister who looked after art, science and religion; if one wished to hear something about agricultural statistics or corn returns one was referred to the Minister whose duty it was to look after railways and ships; while the President of the Local Board, to whom one looked for information with regard to public highways, roads and bridges, had for his main duty the care of paupers.   However, on April 20th, 1883, a Committee of the Council—the Agricultural Department—was established for the consideration of all matters relating to agriculture. In 1889 the Board of Agriculture took over the powers and duties of the Privy Council under the Destructive Insects Act, 1877, and various Acts relating to the contagious diseases of animals; the powers and duties of the Commissioners for Land and Tithe Rent Charge; the powers and duties of the Commissioner of Works under the Survey Act, 1870. But at the head of the new department were placed country squires acceptable to the unimaginative majority of their order—Chaplin and Walter Long.[32] In 1903, mindful of the miracle of the loaves and fishes, the Board became the Board of Agriculture and Fisheries. By 1914 it was an aggregation of the ghosts of extinct bodies of commissioners and sections detached at intervals from other public departments and discharging services more or less subsidiary to agriculture, but not exhibiting any central interest or understanding in relation to the art and science of agriculture as a whole. Its powers had grown out of departments established to administer restrictive or fiscal laws; the animal branch was concerned not with the science and art or breeding of animals, but with police measures or the humanitarian prevention of the export of old war horses; while the livestock branch was mainly concerned with the breeding of cavalry horses. The care of land remained with the Office of Crown Lands, Woods and Forests and the Land Valuation Department. In 1917 the exigencies of war produced a Food Production department. By then the Board occupied twelve distinct sets of scattered premises grouped in five areas: an administrative open field system.

When the theory and practice of government is in process of rapid change it is inevitable that some departments should have the vestigial, others the experimental, functions of the State; some will be used as lumber-rooms; others as potting-sheds. But over their infinite variety it is the custom of the British Constitution to leave the dust of antique time unswept.

Why the Local Government Board, " following the precedent of the more ancient Board of Trade, should have been made to pretend to the world that it was a corporation of five high dignitaries, members of the Privy Council, who never met and were never intended to meet, and whose functions were carried out, and were always intended to be carried out, by the one among them who was named as their President, has never been explained ".[33]   A serious obstacle to reorganization lay always in the question of immediate cost.   A report on the Customs and Inland Revenue Department in 1889 said, " it is notorious that large reorganizations have seldom realized the expectations of economy . . . when two services are consolidated the tendency is inevitable for the higher rates of salary where there is a difference to be generally adopted ".[34] A further barrier to reorganization was the practice of paying the heads of new departments less than half the sum paid to the offices of traditional distinction.   In the case of the Board of Agriculture, the Board of Education, Board of Trade and Local Government the salaries were less than half those of the Chancellor of the Exchequer and the Secretaries of State. This hierarchy of Government departments had an appreciable effect on the prestige of the newer departments. Administrative rationalization was sometimes impossible because of the actual variety of the duties to be done or the political opposition to be overcome.

The Privy Council, formally the most important, is in practice the least differentiated of the organs of the executive.[35]   By 1880 its functions could only be classified alphabetically.   It was responsible for assizes, burial boards, charters of boroughs, clergy returns, coinage currency, contagious diseases of animals, convocation, county courts, Dentistry Acts, Education Acts, gas company amalgamations, etc., etc., to the end of the alphabet.   The Home Office was the residuary legatee of the departments which had branched off from the original office of the Secretary of State.   With

the development of the groping collectivism of State legislation after 1870 it was loaded with many cares. Harcourt,
in 1883, said that its work had increased five times in twenty
years.[36] Early State regulation of industry had been reconciled with individualism on the grounds that the powers
exercised were merely police powers—the protectors of inno-
cence or the enemies of vice. So the Home Office was made
responsible for the early Factory Acts, the safety and hours
of work of women and young persons in factories, industrial
diseases, manufacture of explosives, safety in mines. After
1870 it developed a tendency to be consulted on industrial
questions other than safety. It was made responsible for the
Workmen's Compensation Act, 1906, the Shop Acts and the
Employment of Children Acts. Before the war it had also
acquired responsibility for the protection of wild flowers,
advertisements and money lenders. Since the war it has
acquired Northern Ireland and the tote. The Office of
Works has remained the Cinderella of the Government
departments, performing the menial services for all the rest.
Rosebery in 1884 refused the Commissionership of Works as
he considered it " the least of all the offices, being only a sort
of football for contending connoisseurs ".[37] This snobbery
of office had bad effects on the appearance of London. In
1912 the Office of Works had so overridden and ignored the
London local authorities that relations between them were
practically non-existent.[38] For constitutional reasons the
Office of Works was not allowed undivided control of the
public estates: for the property of the Government is
managed by the Office of Works at a dead loss defrayed out
of the general pool of taxation while the Crown Lands are
managed like any private estate as trustees for the Crown.

The development of the Board of Trade most clearly
marks the growth of Government action. Deprived by the
triumph of free trade of its powers over commercial policy it
became the instrument for whatever regulation of industry

the State might undertake. Its growth was swift but un-
planned. In 1786 it had seven clerks; in 1840, thirty; in
1853, sixty, and by 1914 there were over three thousand. In
1851 the powers of the abortive Railroad Commission,
1846-51, were transferred to the Board of Trade. As a
large proportion of our merchant ships were found to be
" commanded and navigated in a manner reflecting discredit
on our national intelligence and injurious to the interest of
Great Britain " it had acquired the multifarious duties under
the Merchant Shipping Acts (1854). In 1866 the administration of fisheries had been transferred to it from the Office
of Works. In 1872 it received from the Emigration Commissioners responsibility for the administration of the
Passenger Acts. By 1880 it had become evident that the
Bankruptcy Acts had failed to distinguish between the judicial
and administrative aspects of the control of bankruptcy, and in
consequence the law's delays had prompted recourse to
private arrangements in which collusion and fraud were
alarmingly prevalent. In 1883 the control of the administrative side of this vital aspect of a competitive and changing
social order was transferred from the courts to the Board of
Trade. In the first half of the nineteenth century the method
of granting letters patent for inventions and manufactures did
not differ from the procedure applicable to all other kinds of
patents such as grants for nobility. As late as 1852 every
application " passed through nine stages in seven separate
offices situated in different parts of the town at a distance from
one another, and in all these stages fees were exacted ". In
1852 the first Patents Commissioners were appointed; in 1883
they were swept away and replaced by a Comptroller-
General.[39]

As late as 1890 the President of the Board of Trade scarcely
ranked as a leading position in the Cabinet. It was an abode of
peace for Hicks-Beach when he was too sick to take the Irish
Office.[40] But from 1886 it was to be become more and more

involved in vital issues of industrial organization. For in that year the House of Commons adopted a resolution on the motion of Charles Bradlaugh that labour statistics should be collected and published. In the same year also the Board of Trade Journal commenced a system of commercial intelligence. The department was well-nourished by statistics, for its statistical branch had been organized by Porter (1832-76), and after 1876 by Giffen. When after 1900 the hitherto steady advance of real wages was stayed and the social reconstruction of the country after its headlong rush to wealth and power was due, the Board of Trade under Lloyd George became one of the most important departments of the State.

Like the Board of Trade the Board of Education too had its origin in a Committee of the Privy Council. The application of the first meagre grants in aid of education were given to a committee of the Privy Council appointed in 1839 by Order in Council to avoid discussion in Parliament. By 1847 the " business of the Education committee had absorbed the greater part of the staff of the Privy Council Office ".[41] In 1848 although Kay Shuttleworth, the assistant secretary, was really doing the work of an Under-Secretary of State, the members of his department still regarded the clerk to the council as their official head. In 1853 the Northcote and Trevelyan Report remarked of the Education Department of the Privy Council that " to bring together under the charge of a single establishment business of a wholly incongruous character tends not to efficiency but to confusion ". In 1865 Lingen, the Permanent Secretary, said that the Council except as a merely consultative body was of no account. Full parliamentary responsibility rested on the Lord President and the Vice-President. The usual practice of the office was that the committee was only convened to ratify what the President and Vice-President had prepared beforehand. But the passion for phantom committees or boards seems to have been due to the desire of Governments to avoid awkward questions as to the prestige and possible cost of a new department. *Laissez-faire* morality required that each new department of State should be only a little one.   To grow and blush unseen was the best way to escape the Treasury massacre of innocents. In the case of education policy so great were the passions latent in religious rivalries that it was found desirable not to define too closely the character of the Committee of the Council. Although a Department of Education had been advocated by Disraeli in 1855[42] Lowe justified the retention of the Committee on the ground that it was a very good check against individual corruption or indiscretion.   Minutes upon which public money was to be distributed should not, he thought, be left entirely to one Minister.   He did not think that the office required a Minister of high rank.   " It is not analagous to the Secretary of State's Office; we do not administer important affairs; we merely follow the public where it leads and pay out money.   That is a much lower occupation altogether than the administration of great transactions which is vested in every Secretary of State ".[43]   It was considered a further convenience that while the Lord President of the Council could answer for the Committee in the House of Lords the Vice-President could answer in the Commons.   Although W. E. Forster, nominally Vice-President, was a real Minister of Education inspiring the great increase of work after the Education Act of 1870, it was not until 1899 that the Department was cut adrift from the Privy Council and set up as an independent Board.   This was made possible by the urgent need to bring into some organized relation the shreds and patches of our education system.   The Act of 1870 had been passed to remedy the failures of the voluntary system.   It seemed that the decay of religion was necessary for the growth of education.   An effective compromise between the State and the religious bodies was not secured until 1902. Meanwhile, religion apart, the relation in the curriculum between the rudiments to prevent barbarism and the essentials

Q

to make efficient workers and trained industrial leaders had to be decided. In 1886-87 the Education Department laid down that " the course suited to an elementary school is practically determined by the limit of fourteen years of age and may properly include whatever subjects can be effectively taught within that limit ". Following this lead many School Boards developed a " higher elementary " education which overlapped with the secondary education provided after 1888 by the new County Councils. The Bryce Commissions found that for education other than elementary there were two authorities: the Department of Education, the central authority responsible for the work of the local School Boards; the Science and Art Department, which financed the technical education provided by the County Councils. They recommended the formation of a " Department of the executive Government presided over by a Minister responsible to Parliament who would obviously be the same Minister to whom the charge of elementary education would be entrusted ". This was secured in 1899.

The Treasury was the centre of the administrative machine. The system of audited accounts inaugurated by the Act of 1866 had taken away the unlimited discretion which the Treasury had in the past enjoyed and blindly used. An enlightened tyrant replaced a capricious despot. For the system of reports prepared by the Comptroller and Auditor-General and considered by the Public Accounts Committee of the House of Commons not only told the Treasury what the departments were doing but subjected the Treasury itself to the discipline of impartial audit. But the traditional antagonism between the Treasury and the departments was not removed until after 1914-18.

In 1887 Sir R. E. Welby, then Permanent Secretary to the Treasury, considered that " the theory of the control exercised by the Treasury was complete ". He did not know " in what sense it could be improved by formal power or by

any formal document ".[44]   The essence of the theory lay in
the distinction drawn between policy and finance. The
Treasury was " responsible for financial order throughout the
service " . . . it had " to give its assent to every measure
. . . of every kind which was proposed and which had for
result the increase or tendency to increase the public expenditure ".[45]   This right of the Treasury to determine what the
departments of State might spend rested upon an unbroken
principle which had the force of law.   By that principle the
Treasury possessed the power to determine by what means
the controlling authority of the Crown over the public expenditure could best be maintained and its decision as to what
expenditure was or was not sufficiently authorized was final
and without appeal.[46]   But this power of the Treasury was
purely financial.   " From the moment it interfered in any
shape or kind with policy it was departing from its proper
sphere."[47] The Treasury could compel a department to state a
prima facie case for any proposed change which involved an
increase of expenditure and if that case were unsatisfactory the
Treasury could compel reference to the Chancellor of the
Exchequer and through him to the Cabinet.[48]   This power of
the Treasury by which " all acts of administration requiring
money " came before the Treasury " as a sort of shadow "
gave it control also over all questions as to the staff required
to carry out the work of the departments.[49]

It is obvious that skill and patience would be required to
divide the substance of policy from its financial shadow.
Unless there was the closest co-operation between the departments and the Treasury they would fail to agree as to where
the division lay.   For the officials responsible for advising
the Chancellor of the Exchequer on the financial aspects
of proposed policy were also responsible for advising him in
his criticisms of the policy of his colleagues in relation to the
general financial policy of the country.   In fact for many
reasons there was a traditional antagonism between the

Treasury and the departments throughout the nineteenth century. The struggle of Peel to prune away the vested inefficiencies of eighteenth-century departments had passed into the Gladstonian tradition that to take care of the pence was policy enough. This was a mere shadow of the underlying conflict between the technique of business with its preoccupation with costs and the eighteenth-century tradition that the patronage of gentlemen was at once the defence of the privileges of their order and the liberties of common men. After 1870 this contest between patronage and efficiency became a contest between the policy of *laissez-faire* and the new collectivism.

The antagonism between the Treasury and the departments caused serious inefficiency. For the Treasury " did not interpose their veto at the beginning of a policy when they might prevent it, but at the tail of the policy when they can only spoil it ".[50] So long as there was no close co-operation between the Treasury and the departments the former could not initiate reforms; they could only criticize reforms which involved increased expenditure. They adopted the policy of automatically reducing the estimates of a department as a blind way of encouraging economy. It was their practice to cut down the education estimates by £10,000.[51] This irritating hint to departments to think again, of course, led them to think ahead, asking more than they need and not reducing expenditure when they might. The Treasury could not resist an application for expenditure from a powerful administrative department strongly represented in the Cabinet. They were forced to secure their economies by resisting all administrative reforms which involved an initial cost, by cheese-paring on the salaries of civil servants, particularly the lower grades, and by resisting the development of all new departments. It was the constant business of the Treasury when any new proposal was made " to see if they could not suggest something else which was cheaper ".[52]

So long as policy and finance were regarded as two antagonistic powers, two incompatible loyalties, there could be no sound finance. The special difficulties of army finance led to the clearest statement of the principles involved. " There are two totally different conceptions of financial control . . . the first and more or less traditional one, based on constitutional analogies, is that administrative departments are to be distrusted, watched, and checked, and the function of finance . . . is confined to watching, criticizing and checking their expenditure. . . ." This means the " creation of two twin antagonistic powers . . . the expenditure which should be directed solely to secure efficiency tends to degenerate into extravagance and economy which should check waste to result in incomplete efficiency. . . . The second, and more modern notion of financial control, means the union of finance and administration so that financial consideration may attend and determine administrative policy from its inception as well as control it during its progress, and review it in anticipation of each new financial year. The latter theory . . . attributes higher functions and a more real and profitable control to finance than the older and more limited theory of its functions appropriate to times of imperfect administrative organization. . . . The one would make finance a mere critical division of . . . administration the other recognizes the function of finance as that of governing the whole policy of administration ".[53] This policy of co-operation between the Treasury and the departments in the common and related duties of efficiency and economy was reaffirmed by the Haldane Report of 1918. It said that " the superiority of the spending departments in knowing what is required for the execution of their several services, in accordance with the policy with regard to them which has been determined by Parliament or the Government, must necessarily limit the scope of any useful exercise of the restrictive authority of the Chancellor of the Exchequer. On the other hand, the wider experience and expert knowledge which his department should possess, not of all the details of each particular service, but of all its financial incidents and implications, and of the methods by which administrative efficiency can be ensured and increased will enable the department of finance usefully to criticize the methods of other departments ".[54]

The decision to recruit the Civil Service by competitive examination was the beginning of its reorganization. In 1854 it was a fragmentary and disjointed service of some 16,000 officials distributed among departments whose relations to one another were as remote and prickly as those of separate States. Over this Balkanized service the Treasury exercised only an uneasy suzerainty. The confusion was due to the necessities of an oligarchic constitution in a changing world. For aristocracies often retain an administrative confusion as a tribute to their own antiquity and a defence against the probe of vulgar curiosity. Many nineteenth-century administrators took the same pleasure in the nodulosities of their departments that a second-rate lawyer takes in the obscurity of the law by which his own importance is magnified and his pay increased. But to the confusion inherited from a past unswept by revolution there was added the chaos of rapid and unco-ordinated growth due to the creation of departments in response to casual emergencies when neither political principles nor financial policy would permit a systematic plan.

The essential problem of staffing was to decide whether the Civil Service should be one or many. Was the Civil Service to be made into a unit so that the separate departments might think themselves to be merely sections of a single service, or were the critics of the Northcote and Trevelyan Report right when they claimed that the Civil Service " was a thing so heterogeneous in its nature that it required the application of special rules and principles suitable to its different parts?" Was each department to have its own system of recruitment or was there to be a system common to the whole Civil Service?

Owing to the independent action of the different departments there was by 1874 a chaos of functions, a chaos of grades and a chaos of rates of pay among the personnel of the service. " There were utterly incongruous arrangements as to number, classes, rates of pay and prospects of promotion in the several departments and in the various offices within the same department. The advancement of any particular member of the service was governed not so much by his ability or conduct as by the accidental circumstance of his having originally entered in one office rather than in another." Instead of the two classes of civil servants those responsible for policy and those trained for routine work common to the whole service which the report of 1853 had proposed, there had developed a litter of shattered grading schemes. A continuous struggle was found to be necessary if the ideal of the service as a profession with definite prospects was to be retained against the tendency to differentiate the conditions of work and rates of pay in different departments. For this tendency there were obvious reasons rooted in the nature of Government service.

The report of 1853 had argued that only by having two separate and distinct schemes of examination for two separate and distinct grades of clerk could the State offer a definite career and avoid the waste due to using men of ability on the drudgery of the routine work of an office. But this principle of separate recruitment for policy and routine work was bound up with another, namely, that the State should gather the fruits of the educational system as they matured. Such were the imperfections of the English educational system that the Government, by its competitive examinations, recruited men whose potential capacity was greater than they had had any opportunity to develop at the age when economic necessity compelled them to sit. Boys were taken into the service for routine work who, but for the imperfections of the educational system might a few years later have competed for entrance to the policy-forming grade.   In private enterprise the handicap of an imperfect educational opportunity may be overcome in the rough and tumble of competition.   But the State was pledged to offer a career with definite prospects to the recruits into each grade.   So the method of recruitment by competitive examination raised the awkward problem how to provide for promotion within the service from a class recruited at one stage of the educational system to a class recruited at another without either damaging the attractiveness of the higher grades to the best minds that the universities could produce, and without giving such discretion to the heads of departments as might threaten once more a development of patronage.

It was not merely a question of providing for the recruitment of the right proportion of entrants to two grades and their subsequent relations within the service.   The Civil Service quickly became an organization too complex to be run by such a simple division of labour as a policy and a routine grade of clerks.   As the functions of the State were extended the structure of the service became more complex. Between the civil servant responsible for policy and those who did the routine work there was inserted an Intermediate grade who did the executive and audit work required in the new departments concerned with the administration of complex social service; while below the routine grade boy and girl clerks were recruited in increasing numbers to do the manipulative work of the departments.   This changing character of Civil Service work interacted in a complex way with the changes which were taking place in the educational system.

The first demand for a division of the service into policy-forming and routine grades was met by a classification of the service into First and Second division clerks.   But by 1890 the State was recruiting from the elementary schools a group of boy clerks below the Second division to do the increased routine work of the State, though in so doing they were creating blind-alley occupations. By 1912 the development of the new social services created a demand for executive officers and to secure them an Intermediate class was inserted between the First and Second divisions recruited from among the ablest products of the secondary schools who for economic reasons could not go to a university. Further, while it has been held desirable to use general classes common to the whole service in all departments wherever possible so that the conditions of pay and the prospects of promotion might be as clear and wide as possible, such simplification has not been possible. Of the three classes into which Civil Service work has come to be divided—administrative, executive, and clerical—the proportions in which they are required varies widely in different departments. In some there is no place for administrative grades, in others no place for executive. Special departmental classes have had to be created because in some branches of clerical work a supervisory grade is required at a lower point in the organization than in others. There are complications caused by the sudden creation of new departments. This often means the recruiting of staff outside the normal examination system and the assimilation afterwards of some of the recruits surprisingly high in the service. Further, there is a steady mutation of grades due to the action of the Treasury. For the Treasury is often tempted to press for a departmental class (paid on a lower scale) to be appointed for some duties; though this may be a temporary economy at the cost perhaps of discontent in the service due to a gradual obstruction of the channels of promotion and the difficulty of any entrant to the Civil Service clearly estimating the prospects of the life career he is adopting.

From the very beginning of the competitive system there was no shortage of candidates for Government service. But once a man was in the service he found that he had given hostages to fortune because there might be little demand for his services in the open market. The conditions of their service might be modified and it might not pay them to protest. Until the development of Whitleyism after the war of 1914-18, all negotiations could only take place through the head of their department. The Treasury were not prepared to recognize a trade union structure or the technique of collective bargaining. It exercised a steady pressure for economy in administration. The principles of permanence and pensions designed to secure the freedom of the Civil Service from patronage made it chary to "establishing" more civil servants than was absolutely necessary. It secured the recruitment of temporary or unestablished civil servants for work which was not clearly permanent. These were often kept on as temporaries long after they should have been established. By 1914 nearly 50 per cent. of the Civil Service consisted of unestablished grades. The chaotic organization of the service made it difficult for the Treasury even had it wished to do so, to secure any precise relation between remuneration and service. In the lower grades the wage paid barely reached subsistence level. In the higher grades in return for undoubted privileges of security and a pension the civil servant was expected to forego claims for overtime which would have been given in private enterprise. However pressing the grievance of a particular grade the Treasury was reluctant to remove it because of the possible demand for proportional changes from the other grades. As the scale of State activity grew the Treasury was forced more and more to make the conditions of pay and service follow those of commerce. It could not allow the conditions within the service to differ too widely from those prevailing in private enterprise. As the Civil Service was neither a caste above suspicion nor an order which had renounced the world; as it did not live of its own nor by the proceeds of

private charity but by those of compulsory taxation, a rela-
tivity (blessed word) had to be maintained between its conditions and those of the outside world.   The Treasury had
the difficult task of holding the balance between the conditions
of an order in the service of the State and the employees
of a private enterprise.   It did not wish the service to adopt
the methods of collective bargaining and the strikes common
in private enterprise; it did not wish the worker in competitive
industry or the public to attack those privileges of the public
servant which were the safeguards of its purity.   The civil
servants on their side, regarding themselves as a public profession, strove to secure a fairness in promotion that no trade
union in competitive industry would have attempted to
demand.   As the conditions of recruitment and promotion
were determined by general rules laid down and applied by
the Treasury, the civil servant was immune from the direct
operation of the forces which in private enterprise determine
the wages and conditions of service, but they were not immune
from the sporadic demands of Parliament for economy.

The new bureaucracy was developed to carry out the
policies which Parliament approved.   This it could not do
unless it exercised wide discretionary powers.   The problem
of the scope and control of " delegated legislation " now
appears.   Delegated legislation it has been said is a " natural
reflection, in the sphere of constitutional law, of changes in
our ideas of government which have resulted from changes
in political, social and economic ideas, and of changes in the
circumstances of our lives which have resulted from scientific
discoveries ".[55]   Delegated legislation is only a special
aspect of the problem of the relation between the tradition
of democracy and the scientific spirit.   " Behind all delegation of legislative power lies the desire to reconcile democracy and despatch, the interested but always illuminated
innovation of the amateur with the disinterested research of
the expert."[56]

All Governments, however simple, must exercise a discretionary power. For it is impossible that laws should be framed with a complete knowledge of all the circumstances in which they will have to be applied. Provision to temper the rule to future conditions is made by all Governments— whether it is the discretion of a single man like Solomon, the surreptitious legislation of a bench of judges, or the rule-making power of a Government department charged with the duty of developing a particular policy. The price of justice is the flexibility of law. For justice it is said consists in the impartial application of a known rule. But in a changing world the application of an unchanging rule will produce hardships likely to undermine the very habit of obedience. It has been suggested that we should distinguish between the special commands or Acts intended to carry into effect a pre-existing law and special commands or Acts not intended to carry into effect a pre-existing law, calling the first executive and the latter arbitrary. But this distinction begs the question at issue, which is how far the law should provide for modifications of itself necessary to secure the purpose for which it was framed. If the law is to remain unaltered while circumstances are changing, individuals and whole classes have to bear the burden of a growing disharmony between the law and the social structure. Where changes in the social order have been very slow, the cost of maladjustment between the law and the facts can be borne by individuals until sufficient experience has accumulated to justify the cumbrous intervention of the legislature. The legislature had to modify the common law rules about property and contract; a further increase in the rate of social change requires that provision for elasticity in the laws of Parliament themselves should be provided. What the legislature used to do for the courts the departments must now do for the legislature.

In England before 1832 there was ample if unsystematic provision for the exercise of discretionary power by those in authority. The machinery of Local and Central Government consisted of officials and bodies possessing a large measure of autonomy.[57] In the sphere of Local Government, Quarter Sessions, Borough Corporations and Poor Law Authorities; in the sphere of Central Government, such departments of State as the Exchequer and the office connected with the revenue, the office connected with the Army and Navy, and the office of the Secretaries of State were left to carry out their duties in their own ways subject only to the legislative control of Parliament and to the control of the law as interpreted by the courts. Subject to that control these officials and bodies possessed independent powers of action, and a capacity for development along their own lines. The King exercised the discretion of his prerogative; Parliament took its part in the changing functions of the King in Parliament and devoted most of its time to administrative detail and to innovating legislation; the courts applied the common law and in applying changed it. Bribery itself was a system of conventions by which elasticity was given to the rigidity of the rule of law. Parliament had already delegated some rule-making power to the Crown, Government departments, and special commissions. The whole system of Local Government depended upon the discretionary use of legislative executive and judicial powers by the Justices of the Peace. This confused condition in which local custom, the artificial reason of the common law, and the sovereignty of the King in Parliament existed side by side might be compatible with the habit of obedience, but it did not further a clear understanding of the problems involved.

After the passage of the Reform Bill (1832) the House of Commons found that it could not exercise as before its powers of detailed regulation and supervision. The social problem of poverty compelled the delegation of rule-making powers to officials of the Central Government because the traditional machinery of the Justices of the Peace had broken down. But there was no order or system in this growth of delegated legislation. Parliament would delegate in one case and not in others without any clear grounds for the difference. It regarded the Navy as a permanent institution and therefore took the trouble to make a code, whereas the Army, which it considered a temporary evil, it left to be regulated by the Crown during the short period for which Parliament licensed a standing Army.[58]   After 1870 the parliamentary draftsmen found it possible to relieve Parliament from some of its congestion of business by providing that the details of Bills should be settled departmentally. But the limits of delegated power, the methods of Ministerial procedure in their exercise, and the safeguards for the protection of the public and the preservation of parliamentary control were determined by the emergencies of the occasion.[59]   Power was delegated by Parliament to officials because the topic involved some detail or because it was technical or because there were other demands on Parliament at the time when the new policy was being considered.   Since 1832 the English system of government has been transformed: the confused and conflicting powers of Kings, Lords and Commons has been transformed into the menacing simplicity of a Cabinet dictatorship mitigated by professional experts, organized interests, and electioneering progaganda.   But these fundamental changes were brought about almost absent-mindedly by men engaged in matters they considered more attractive.

Two factors may be distinguished as responsible for the confused development of our delegated legislation: (1) the *laissez-faire* tradition of the reforming politicians before 1870 with lack of any urgency in the need for administrative and legal reform because of our political isolation and industrial supremacy; (2) the powerful and subtle traditions of the Constitution.

(1) Before 1870 reformers were mainly concerned with

the promotion of humanitarianism, the extension of individual
liberty and the reform of a fantastic legal procedure.   They
were more concerned to remove the evils of a bad Government than to consider the planning of a good.   Their theory
of democracy was astonishingly naive.   In its classic statement by Mill it is assumed that if all interests were represented
in a legislature the balance of power would be held by the
intelligent and disinterested minority.   Parliament was
simply the common room and the club writ large.   Fortunately they were never called upon to apply in practice
this theory of conflicting interests harmonized or subdued
by common sense.   For until 1867 political power was
limited to an electorate supposed to be large and intelligent
enough to identify its own interests with the interests of the
greatest number without the latter being troubled for the
formality of voting their approval.   Except for the legal
reforms necessary for the working of a system of contract,
the reorganization of Government was due to the pressure of
casual emergencies.   Factory legislation was due partly to
humanitarianism and the political antagonism of the agricultural and manufacturing wings of the governing class.
The control of shipping and railways was due to a seeming
failure of the principles of *laissez-faire* in a key position of
the economic order.   Civil Service reform was due to the
shock of 1848; War Office reform to the disgrace of the
Crimea and the rise of Prussia; while in the Colonial Office
there was a confused interaction between economic theory,
humanitarianism and the recognition that in dealing with
diverse civilizations the technique of each for himself and
the devil take the hindmost was not enough.   Even after
1870 when the extension of the suffrage to include all
householders, the rise of organized labour, and the growing
competition of foreign States with large, trained bureaucracies,
compelled the State to provide elementary education, to investigate the root-causes of poverty and disease which

threatened public order and health—even then the continuance of sectarian passions, the inherited cancer of Anglo-Irish hostility, the passions of the South African War, and the muddled struggle over the tariff, prevented any systematic reorganization of the machinery of Government.

(2) The influence of the traditions of the Constitution has affected every detail of the machinery of Government. The innate conservatism of English political practice has been as mixed a blessing as the legal rigidity of the constitution of the United States. Clouds of antique statutes and the dust of out-moded forms have obscured the majesty of the law. The position of the Prime Minister would have been very different but for the lingering death of effective monarchy; the procedure of the House of Commons has been as much a pageant of the past as a code of rule for effective debate; that there is no Civil Service but only servants of the Crown has had far-reaching effect on the structure of our Civil Service; and the " rusty curb of old father antique the law " has prevented the development of our administrative law. In no other country are lawyers more powerful and in no other is the law less understood by the ordinary citizen.

It is not therefore surprising that the last Committee on Ministers' powers reported that " the system of delegated legislation has been built up haphazard without plan or logic, and that the extent and limits of delegation have been determined by accident and expediency and not upon any system ". Political and legal tradition have prevented a clear recognition of what was really being done. As Parliament became responsible for what had previously been done or left undone by local agencies, it had to provide some method by which its general rules could be adapted to local conditions. As Parliament came to deal with subjects which involved a technical and scientific knowledge it had to recognize its own incapacity to deal with the details; finally, as Parliament passed from merely laying down the conditions of competition to an attempt to determine the purpose and the methods of co-operation, it has had to provide a machinery by which schemes may be prepared, developed and enforced. The advance of science has increased the number of problems which are best dealt with by fashioning a remedy and then applying it where experience dictates. The increasing unity of the community compels in time of crisis an ever-increasing delegation of power to the executive.

Only after 1850 was there any great increase in delegated legislation. It was a necessary instrument for carrying out the collectivist policy which industrial progress and scientific knowledge made inevitable. The development of large business corporations made the old procedure of control by the criminal law or the common informer inadequate because a corporation could not go to gaol and financial penalties might be less than the cost of complying with the regulations. The new codes of health and safety could only be applied by employing inspectors, analysts, and in the last respect in the power of Government departments themselves to act in default. The great development of delegated legislation begins with the establishment of the Board of Agriculture in 1889 and the Board of Education in 1899, and takes on something of its modern scope with the social legislation of the Liberal Government 1906-14, which provided Old Age Pensions, National Health Insurance, Labour Exchanges, and the germ of a Ministry of Transport and a Department of Scientific and Industrial Research.

One effect of the Reform Bill of 1884 was the creation of the framework of our present system of Local Government. The urgent problem of drains had secured that in 1872 all parts of the country should be under some sanitary authority. Unfortunately the areas chosen for this important duty were formed by making the urban part of a poor law union the urban sanitary district, leaving the rural fragments

R

—sometimes in three separate pieces—to be the rural sanitary district. This pulling of sanitary rabbits out of poor law hats did not make for that adjustment between area and function which effective Local Government requires. In the 'eighties a vital reconstruction of Local Government was considered but only a debilitated compromise emerged from the conflict of parties and traditions. The time had come to provide an elected authority to exercise those administrative powers which the non-elected Justices of the Peace had hitherto controlled. As Lord Salisbury told the House of Lords in 1888 it could not except the people who exercised a voting power in all the most important questions of the Empire to acquiesce in the doctrine that they are not fit to manage their affairs.[60] The Local Government Act of 1888 provided that the administrative powers of the Justice of the Peace should be transferred to councils elected for each county. This provided that there was now a system of local authorities of wide enough area effectively to develop the new powers which were becoming important. It could take over main roads and bridges, provide those services of preventative medicine as distinct from drainage which the development of medicine was to make possible, and when higher education should be thought necessary provide an authority for its administration. The areas were the areas of the historical counties with certain modifications to make them a workable administrative system.

The original plan to transfer the powers of the Justice of the Peace to an elected authority for the county was so modified as to cause grave future difficulties. In the first place the larger Municipal Boroughs objected to the new counties being responsible for any services within their area. Their objection was not unreasonable, for in the existing conditions of transport and local social organization it was very unlikely that the ordinary worker, whether rural or urban, could afford to secure election, or if elected to serve upon the new

County Councils. As Selborne wrote: " In most English counties I think the country gentlemen are likely to hold their own so long as they choose to do so . . . (there is) very remote danger that the county government would be worked for revolutionary purposes."[61] Their objection was met by the provision that the largest Municipal Boroughs should themselves have all the powers of a county and be called County Boroughs. The result of this compromise was that instead of a system of local government providing a national division of powers between the larger area responsible for those services which required a large area for their proper administration and the sub-divisions of that area responsible for its appropriate services there was created a dual system. In the large towns (roughly some sixty County Boroughs with a population of 50,000 and over) there were County Borough Councils responsible for all the functions of local government within their area, while outside the County Boroughs there was a county system within which power was divided between the county and its sub-divisions, the urban and rural districts. This provided the next fifty years with two obstinate problems: in an age of rapid transport changes the County Boroughs would change their frontiers (for the Act had provided that after suitable inquiry their boundaries could be changed by Provisional Order) while (which the Act also provided) Municipal Boroughs would grow large enough to be made into County Boroughs; secondly, as the areas of the urban and rural districts were themselves based on no principle of function the county would have incompetent authorities to co-operate with. These two problems, the struggle of the unified system of the County Boroughs with the federal system of the counties and the unsuitability of the areas into which the counties themselves were divided—were to plague Local Government till the present day.

It should be remembered that this structure was set up before the coming of either the motor car or electricity. It meant that the coming age of H. G. Wells was to be faced in the county by the traditions of Barchester and in the smaller urban districts with those of Bumbledom and Gradgrind.

The Government of London provides an extreme example of the almost unsolvable complexity of the Local Government problem. The Act of 1888 created a new county, the County of London, and provided it with an elected governing council, the London County Council. Whereas in the case of the other counties there were in existence historical counties which could be modified into workable administrative areas, London had to be created by carving out its areas from the five counties that were contiguous to the City. But the area so carved out was an area of some 117 square miles, which in 1855 had been thought suitable for the administration of water, fire, drainage, and building lines, by an indirectly elected authority, the Metropolitan Board of Works. In 1855 that area had only been half built-up. In taking this area for the new County of London the situation developed by 1918 that the 117 square miles of the London County Council was not only completely built-up, but included only some 4,000,000 of the 8,000,000 of London's population. The London County Council found itself responsible for the administration of services of roads, transport, housing, fire, drainage, which required for their effective operation co-operation with some dozens of local authorities which outside the Administrative County operated in the area of what is known as Greater London.

[1] Omond : *Parliament and the Army*, p. 119.
[2] Temperley : *Victorian Age in Politics*, p. 34.
[3] Ensor : *England 1870–1914*, pp. 10–11.
[4] Gladstone.
[5] Buckle's *Disraeli*, Vol. VI., p. 474, to Lady Bradford, Dec. 20th, 1879.
[6] Omond : *Parliament and the Army*, pp. 129–30.
[7] ibid., p. 132.
[8] Hartington Commission.
[9] Omond, op. cit., pp. 136–7.
[10] ibid., citing *Wolseley's Life*, p. 241.
[11] ibid., pp. 145–8.

[12] Garvin : *Chamberlain*, Vol. 3, p. 452.
[13] Lady Hicks Beach's *Hicks Beach*, Vol. 2, p. 148.
[14] Omond : *Parliament and the Army*, p. 152.
[15] ibid., p. 154.
[16] *Report of the Committee.*
[17] Ensor : *England 1870-1914*, p. 287.
[18] ibid., 121
[19] Lady Cecil's *Salisbury*, Vol. 3, p. 218, Feb. 5th, 1892.
[20] Lady Hicks Beach : *Hicks Beach*, Vol. 2, p. 57.
[21] Elliot's *Goschen*, Vol. 2, p. 180, Oct. 1888, W. H. Smith to Goschen.
[22] Omond : *Parliament and the Army*, p. 110.
[23] Spender : *Campbell Bannerman*, Vol. 1, p. 118.
[24] Crewe's *Rosebery*, Vol. 2, p. 497.
[25] *Royal Commission on War in South Africa.*
[26] Asquith, *Genesis of the War*, p. 113.
[27] Ensor : *England 1870-1914*, p. 433.
[27a] Material and quotations from Webb : *English Local Government*, Vol. 8. *English Poor Law History*, Part II., pp. 197-9.
[28] ibid., pp. 530-2.
[29] Haldane : *Report on Machinery of Government*, 1918.
[30] See MSS. of Evidence for Haldane Report at London School of Economics.
[31] For development of Ministry of Agriculture, see MSS. evidence above and *Report of Agricultural Tribunal Investigation*, 1923.
[32] Ensor : *England 1870-1914*, p. 286.
[33] Webb : *History of Poor Law*, p. 191.
[34] C. 5748.
[35] John Willis :. *Parliamentary Powers of English Government Departments* (Harvard Studies in Administrative Law, Vol. 4, 1933), p. 96.
[36] Crewe's *Rosebery*, Vol. 1, p. 170.
[37] ibid., p. 212.
[38] Sir Lionel Earle : *Turn over the Page*, 230.
[39] Llewellyn Smith : *Board of Trade*, pp. 173 and 195.
[40] Lady Hicks-Beach : *Hicks Beach*, Vol. I., Chap. XII.
[41] Frank Smith : *Life of Sir James Kay-Shuttleworth*, p. 216.
[42] Buckle's *Disraeli*, Vol. 4, Chap. 2.
[43] In Evidence before Commission.
[44] 1887 XIX, Q. 12.
[45] ibid., Qu. 2.
[46] 1865 X App. 1, 70
[47] 1888 XXVII Qu. 10,623.
[48] ibid., 10,639.
[49] 1914, XVI., Qu 35,757.
[50] Lady Cecil's *Salisbury*, Chap. IV., pp. 176-7.
[51] Hamilton : *Parliamentary Reminiscences*, 1868-85, p. 304.
[52] In general on the Treasury, see Durell : *Parliamentary Grants.*
[53] 1870 XII.
[54] Haldane : *Report on Machinery of Government*, 1918.
[55] *Report on Ministers Powers*, Cmd. 4060.
[56] Willis : *Parliamentary Powers of English Government Departments*, p. 153.
[57] Cmd. 4060.
[58] ibid.
[59] ibid.
[60] Ensor : Article in *Politica*, 1936, on County Councils.

CHAPTER VII

THE INTERREGNUM, 1914-18

The three problems of war: Constitutional; Political; and Administrative—The development of the War Cabinet—Its organization—The unsolved problem of leadership in war—Some examples of State control: Man-power—Munitions—Food—Shipping—The Air Ministry—The general character of Government control in time of war—Elasticity and decentralization—The real root of power—Problems of democracy in war.

THE power of a Government in war is dependent upon the resources which it has accumulated in peace.   Representative Governments have the advantage that there will probably be widespread agreement that the war is just and should be pursued.   They have the great disadvantage that the machinery they must use for the making of the vital decisions war demands will be geared to party groups and loyalties irrevelant in a state of war.   Representative Governments are likely to be unskilled in the ruthless pursuit of the means to a limited and specific end.   In time of peace they have been organized to discuss policy until there is little opposition to whatever action is finally taken.   Every detail of their machinery of Government will bear the marks of that compromise which is the spirit of the whole.   In peace the loyalty of the politician is to his party as the means by which society may be improved; the duty of the Civil Service is to run that part of the machinery of Government which is at any time outside politics and to give to the party in power the best service it can.   In peace Government is partly technical routine and partly an education of the people in a way of life.   The Administration is concerned with what is agreed, the political with a search for what may be agreed.   But in war policy cannot be adapted to an intellectual condition of the people; it has to be adapted to a physical condition at the seat of war.

For the performance of her traditional rôle in a European war the political organization of the Cabinet and the machinery of the Civil Service had been effective. " The Committee of Imperial Defence had elaborated a war book which set forth the emergency legislation needed and the action required of every Government department. All this stood well the test of experience."[1] But as the nature of the struggle was revealed the machinery of Government had radically to be transformed. In a few months we can see changes in the spirit and the machinery of Government which normally would have taken many years. They provide over-whelming evidence that the health of political institutions depends upon the existence of tolerated differences of opinion as to the end as well as to the means which society should pursue. The war reveals a sickening of the State because all its institutions had to be adapted to a purpose which was imposed—though the compulsion came not from a despot but from an enemy in arms.

It was not possible it was found to combine rapid and effective action in the various theatres of war with the main-tenance of Cabinet responsibility and control. When the Cabinet was deposed in favour of a small and select group of its own members based on the political support of a coali-tion, the new body had to discover if they could the principles and the machinery which should determine the relation between politicians and soldiers in war. To the solution of this the central problem of Government in war the Committee of Imperial Defence had made no advance.[2] Finally, what-ever the supreme authority might be it had to provide for the administration of materials and men which in peace had been outside the sphere of the State. The war showed three problems: the Constitutional, which required a modification of the law and the conventions of Cabinet responsibility; the

problem of leadership, which required that the relation between soldiers and politicians should be determined; and
the administrative, which required that the life of the country
should be administered for the needs of war. It is significant
that a healthy popular Government found little difficulty in
solving the first and the third. But the second remained to
the end insolvable; and it did so because there is a fundamental incompatibility between the disease of war and the
life of democratic States.

The first pressure of the business of war was dealt with by
the time-honoured precedent of a committee of the Cabinet.
The Prime Minister and those heads of departments who
were responsible for the day to day operations of war consulted
with the Committee of Imperial Defence on serious questions
involving new departures in policy or joint strategical operations. But the force of constitutional tradition made it impossible without serious friction to draw a hard and fast line
between an inner and an outer Cabinet.[3]

By November, 1914, however, a special committee of the
Cabinet or War Council for the conduct of the war was
established. This absorbed the Committee of Imperial
Defence. But the Cabinet as a whole did not abdicate its
authority. All important steps were reported to it and at
times it took an active part and asserted its overruling
authority.[4] But by this time the need for drastic changes
was becoming clear. Asquith, the Prime Minister, was a
great parliamentarian, who had shown in his handling of the
Parliament Act all the gifts that peace could demand of a
Constitutional statesman. These same gifts had secured that
we entered the war united and not divided. He had realized
" that the break-up of the Cabinet involving his own resignation, would " have meant " a war conducted by a Conservative Government . . . the country divided . . . an unknown
number of people determined to stop the war at the earliest
possible moment ".[5] But for him the war would have found

us divided with a Cabinet in disorder or dissolution and impotent to take any decision.[6] But the qualities which could launch us smoothly into war could not teach us to weather its storms. In the Cabinet " he waited on others. He no doubt often averted conflict but he never contributed a suggestion ".[7] But it was not simply that Asquith was not a man born to lead in war. The principle of a responsible Cabinet drawn from one party was itself unworkable in war. In a few months the opposition found that their position was intolerable. If they criticized the Government they were thought to be unpatriotic; if they did not it was assumed that they shared with the Government responsibility for what was done.[8] The graceful party minuet of peace could not be danced to the drums of war. The first coalition was formed on May 26th, 1915. This was an unwieldy coalition of twelve Liberals, eight Conservatives, one Labour, and Lord Kitchener, twenty-two in all. Asquith said that its formation was one of the most uncongenial jobs that he had ever had to carry through.[9] It was made especially unpleasant because the Unionists had pegged out their claims, and suffering already from that terror of the mob and its leaders which was later to destroy the peace which war secured, they compelled the omission of Lord Haldane.

This first coalition did little either to solve the problem of creating an inner Cabinet or to determine the right relation between the civilian and military spheres. In June, 1915, the inner War Cabinet was replaced by the Dardanelles Committee. This was a dropsical body consisting of the Prime Minister, the First Lord of the Admiralty, Churchill, Sir Edward Carson, Bonar Law, Lord Crewe, Lord Curzon and Lord Lansdowne, and such experts as they might consult. Whereas in the War Cabinet all important matters connected with the war had been dealt with by four or five Ministers, now at least a dozen powerful, capable and distinguished persons who were in a position to assert themselves had to be consulted. " At least five or six opinions prevailed on every topic and every operative decision was obtained only by prolonged discursive and exhaustive discussions."[10] The decisions of the Dardanelles Committee had often to be re-debated in the Cabinet."[11] As the operation in the Dardanelles developed to include the many operations undertaken in the Near East the Dardanelles Committee developed into the War Committee. But the main defects remained. It was too large; it was overcharged with duties and it was often kept in ignorance of essential and vital information of a technical kind upon the problem which came before it. There was delay, evasion and obstruction in giving effect to its decisions.[12] It was hampered by the necessity of obtaining Cabinet approval, while the Cabinet was responsible for what it could not really control.[13]

It is not possible here even to outline the process by which Lloyd George displaced Asquith in December, 1916. " In the preparation of the ground, the gradual marshalling of forces, the swift changes of front, the handling of the Press and all else that goes to the make-up of modern political strategy " it " stands as the classic example of this kind of warfare ".[14] Without attempting to judge the fairness of the actions taken it is possible to see the problem which was involved. Asquith was not temperamentally fitted for the conduct of the war. He was the embodiment of a peace-time tradition which had to be transformed for the war and perhaps for ever. The peace-time processes for securing a change of government were unthinkable in war. There could be no appeal to an electorate. Political leaders were like an advance guard which, cut off from the main body must act as best they can. It was a tide in the affairs of men for which no pilot could be found save among those already on the bridge. Lloyd George knew (1) that Asquith seemed to be wedded to a tradition and a technique that could only bring disaster; (2) that Bonar Law, the leader of the

Unionists, would regard any coalition as a temporary co-
operation of parties which left unprejudiced the position of
the leaders of the separate forces.[16]   With Carson, Beaver-
brook and Northcliffe to assist him Lloyd George detached
the Unionists from Asquith and forced them to co-operate
with him.   The usual Constitutional devices for a change of
Government not being available, he had to use intrigue and
the Press barons as dictators have since had to use prison
and the assassin.   According to Chamberlain the Unionists
desired to work with Asquith, distrusted Lloyd George, and
believed that Asquith's influence with the Liberals, the Irish
and the Labour Party was necessary.[17]   They had little confidence in Bonar Law's judgment and none in his strength of
character.[18]   It seems that Asquith was misled by Bonar Law
as to the attitude of the Unionists.   When he resigned the
King sent for Bonar Law and when he failed to secure the
support of either Lloyd George or Asquith (whom he consulted in that order) the King sent for Lloyd George.[19]
Before the latter accepted office the King invited Asquith,
Bonar Law, Lloyd George, Balfour and Henderson to confer
with him and with each other at Buckingham Palace.[20]   It is
said that Lloyd George became Prime Minister because
inquiry had elicited that a Ministry under Bonar Law would
not be sustained on a division.[21]

But Lloyd George, having accepted office, was not free
to choose his Cabinet without reference to party politics,[22] and
to politics which could not be modified by an appeal to the
electorate.   He had not that freedom of choice which belongs
to the leader of a united political party.   Out of 260 Liberals
only 136 were prepared to support him.   The majority of
the Tories in Asquith's Cabinet were opposed to his premiership.   Bonar Law insisted that his political colleagues should
have posts in the Cabinet, posts which Lloyd George would
have preferred to give to men of business.   Only the refusal
of the Liberal Ministers to join his Cabinet enabled him to

include a few non-political men—Sir Joseph Maclay as Shipping Director; Lord Devonport for Food; Prothero as Minister of Agriculture; Lord Cowdray as Chairman of the Air Board and Fisher at the Board of Education.[23] The Tories would have neither Churchill nor Lord Curzon.[24]

Lloyd George as Prime Minister was certain of two things: that a Cabinet of twenty or more was a futile instrument for the conduct of business which required immediate action[25]; and that no Prime Minister could possibly undertake the task of running Parliament as well as running the war.[26] The Parliamentary Constitution would have to go into cold storage for the duration, where it was to be hoped that it would not decay. In December he formed his War Cabinet of five. This was the central organ for the direction of the war. Other Ministers attended when required and brought their expert advisers if they wished. In practice the Cabinet room was often overcrowded with Ministers and their officials.[27] With the representatives of the Dominions and of India the War Cabinet formed the Imperial War Cabinet. In May, 1917, General Smuts was made a member. The Constitution had proven flexible enough to provide a Public Safety Committee.

But this War Cabinet was only the nerve centre of an elaborate organization. Individual Ministers were made responsible for specific interdepartmental administrative problems, e.g., Lord Curzon for the provision of unsinkable ships. *Ad hoc* committees were detailed to report on specific problems to the Cabinet, e.g., man power and food production. Standing Committees were appointed on special problems such as War Priorities, Eastern Affairs, Economic Development, Home Affairs and Demobilisation. These standing committees enabled Ministers who were not members of the War Cabinet regularly to meet.[28] The Economic Committee, consisted of ten Ministers and met at least once a week; the Committee for Home Affairs consisted of nine.

So complex a system could not be run with the informalities of a Gladstonian Cabinet. An agenda, a time-table, and some method for recording decisions and communicating them to the people concerned were now essential. These were provided by the Cabinet Secretariat, which was a small staff of civil servants, and an extension of the Secretariat to the Committee of Imperial Defence. " The subjects " for the War Cabinet " were placed on the agenda by the Prime Minister or by any member of the War Cabinet or at the request of any Minister or department concerned. . . . At the beginning of each week a list of the outstanding subjects ripe for consideration and awaiting decision were circulated by the Secretariat and this list was usually worked off in the first two or three days of the week."[29] An elaborate time-table was prepared and Ministers were summoned by special telephone to the Cabinet. Where Ministers disagreed they could circulate in advance a statement of their cases. The Secretariat had its own conventions. It did not consider it the duty of its members to initiate or to perform administrative acts. It avoided any interference with the responsibility of the departments. It dealt direct with the Minister and left it to him to decide whether his business should be brought before the Cabinet or not. In practice Ministers who were concerned with problems of national policy, such as India, not directly relevant to the immediate problem of war found it difficult to secure the attention of the War Cabinet.

So far the Constitution had given proof of a flexibility adequate to the stresses of the war. The War Cabinet solved the problem of adjusting an executive whose roots were in party and whose life in time of peace lay in its relation to the House of Commons to the unity required by war. But the War Cabinet did not really solve the problem of leadership in war. The unsolved problem of the relation between the politician and the soldier remained.

Asquith had only with extreme reluctance crossed the boundary between the civilian and the military spheres.[30] He could not play the part of an amateur strategist or foist his opinions upon men who had made soldiering the study of their lives.[31] But to Lloyd George the fact that a man had made a life's study of anything meant that he might love his opinion in despite of new and bitter truth. " In an emergency the able but unimaginative expert is a public danger. On the one hand their thorough knowledge of the details of the business, and their high reputation, give them an authority which it is difficult for the amateur to set aside. While in a situation for which there is no precedent experience often entangles the expert."[32]

In all human affairs there is a sharp conflict between the knowledge of the expert and the wisdom of common sense, between scientific or demonstrative thinking and deliberation. " When questions are submitted to deliberation, scientific thinking is in constant demand; but in the last resort we come to issues that cannot be scientifically settled or the parties would agree; these are matters we say for judgment; and the wise counsellor is the man of good judgment." Of matters for judgment there are two main sorts: there may be agreement as to the result desired, but deliberation as to the means, e.g., will a strike produce the desired rise in wages? There may be a dispute as to whether the result which can be achieved is worth securing, e.g., is the successful strike worth the suffering involved?[33] These difficulties are well known in peace and they are dealt with by the understandings which exist between the civil servants and the political heads of the great departments. But war provides a special case for which the practices of peace provide no guidance. As the conduct of war involves the direction for a special purpose of the whole power of the nation it is the statesman who must ultimately be responsible. The nation in arms requires that the supreme command should be the Cabinet as the supreme authority in the State. " It is for the statesman, with such advice as they can command, to survey the battle area as a whole on land and sea, to examine the needs and possibilities, to make their plans and to dispose of their resources to the best advantage."[34] But the handling of armies and navies must be left to professional experts.[35] But those experts are very different from the kind of experts which the statesman uses in time of peace.[36] " The civil servant can be trusted to carry on the plan of the Government even when he does not agree with them . . . but a soldier in war cannot do the same."[37] For the advice of the expert soldier and sailor, unlike the advice of the expert financier, involves action which they alone can take.[38] What then should be the relation between the statesman who must make vital decisions and their experts who alone can carry out the policy decided? It has been suggested that it should be of " the nature of a partnership, in which the statesman becomes the senior partner ".[39] But the terms of that partnership when armies and navies should have been mobilized had not been considered before the war.[40] Ministers like Churchill considered it to be part of the business of a civilian Minister to prepare plans of campaign. An expert like Kitchener was not only Secretary of State for War, but also the chief military adviser of the Government, and to a great extent his own Chief of Staff.[41] A military view detached from all political considerations was not really available for the civilian Cabinet.[42] The experts " did not conceive it to be their business to inform the War Council of the Cabinet where and why they differed from their civilian chiefs.[43]

In December, 1915, Sir William Robertson was made Chief of the Imperial General Staff. He proceeded clearly to define the respective functions of Ministers and soldiers in war. The War Council, composed exclusively of civilian

Ministers, was to be the supreme directing authority in the position of the Commander-in-Chief of the imperial land forces. But it was to receive all advice on matters concerning military operations through one authoritative channel only. That channel was to be the Chief of the Imperial General Staff. Robertson secured that " all military operations required to put into execution the policy approved by the War Council should be issued and signed by the Chief of the Imperial General Staff under the authority of the Secretary of State for War, *not* under that of the Army Council ". The Cabinet could not therefore act through the Army Council without the knowledge of the General Staff.[44] The effect of these changes was " to bring about an immediate improvement in the business of conducting the war ".[45]

But the problem of the terms of the partnership between statesmen and soldiers was not thereby solved. Lloyd George has made the specific charge that Sir William Robertson signally failed to realize what his duty as an independent adviser to the Imperial Cabinet on military matters required.[46] He withheld from the Cabinet essential facts about politics which he supported and believed that they would oppose.[47] " The truth that mattered was wilfully and skilfully kept from their cognisance."[48] Nor were the statesmen in a position to compel them to co-operate. " On land the High Command had its way. As far as the general strategy of the land fighting was concerned it was their policy. The only exception was the campaign in Palestine, which they deprecated."[49] But in the case of the Admiralty, the Government compelled the Admirals to take measures necessary to meet the submarine menace. " Had they not overruled the Sea Lords the submarines would have won and the Allies would have been beaten."[50]

Not only was the British Government at the mercy of their Commanders-in-Chief, whose ability and prestige were far greater than that of the military advisers attached to its War

Ministries, but every Allied Government was in the same predicament. It has been said that an Allied strategy did not exist. " Instead of one great war with a united front there were at least six separate and distinct wars with a separate, distinct, and independent strategy for each."[51] The only way out of this impasse was to set up an authoritative inter-Allied body which would have its own staff and its own intelligence department who, working together, would review the battlefield as a whole and select the most promising sector for concerted action.[52] When the disasters of 1917 secured the Allied Supreme War Council in November of that year the difficulty remained that the military experts were merely advisory. The proper relations between the military and the civilians remained to the end undiscovered.

Behind the front line of strategy the record of the Government was good. As the nature of the struggle was not at first realized by anyone there was unavoidable delay in developing the machinery of government which the war required. But as soon as any policy was determined the administrative skill for its application was quickly forthcoming. Some of the problems to be solved must be briefly glanced at.

As the whole idea of conscription was alien to our political tradition and its necessity not realized there was from the first a fatal misdirection of our man-power. So long as voluntary enlistment continued men left industries where later they were to be desperately wanted to join the ranks. The essential interdependence of the army and the factory was not recognized. There was a false distinction between the home front and the front of war. Psychologically this may have been valuable. The war was always kept at a distance. But it seriously impeded the proper organization of the country's strength. Trade Unionists who would themselves have gladly died in the trenches would not allow changes in their

s

working rules which might have saved those already there. The very emotions which steeled the country to war supported this obstruction. The war was a war for freedom and freedom involves the right of a man to work at the conditions he can secure by contract. So in demanding higher wages and in resisting the rationalization of industrial processes the worker was fighting the same battle as his military brother. Should a country of industrial *laissez-faire* ever be in conflict with a country despotically organized this would seriously weaken it. There is a vital psychological and administrative problem for democracies to solve. How are they to extend to the whole of their industrial order the military psychology of discipline—the humorous acceptance of the fact that the Army has the whip-hand. The Army is psychologically a totalitarian state. Does its *morale* depend upon there being in the background a civilian population that is free to enjoy advantages even at the expense of those who are in the Army itself?

That industry must be deliberately organized for war production was realized by a Government whose political tradition was Free Trade and individualism only under the pressure of startling events and dangerous crises.[53] No scheme had been prepared to settle the order in which men should be withdrawn from industry.[54] In 1914 there was no central State machine fully equipped with experience, knowledge or power for the organization of labour in a national emergency. The three departments then concerned with the organization of labour—the Local Government Board, the Home Office and the Board of Trade—had little control over or relations with the recruiting departments of the War Office or the Admiralty.[55] Few could realize the length of the struggle that was before them; even those who did could hardly realize that the demand for men for the Army would be so great that it would require careful husbanding of the civilians left to supply the essential needs of the Army in the field and the civilian population at home. In the United Kingdom out of an estimated male population of 14,350,000, some 5,500,000 were finally serving with the armed forces. The larger the army in the field grew, the larger was the number of men and women at home required to equip them. Nor was it merely a question of providing the man-power for the supply of the armies, but of supplying the labour required to feed the civilians and to produce those exports on the sale of which our financial security was dependent.[56] None of these problems could be dealt with at once. The nation was not willing to submit to unquestioning discipline. The authorities had no machinery with which to handle the problems. It was impossible to estimate " during the astonishments of war " what was the degree of importance to be attached to each of the different demands. There was the ineradicable complexity of modern industry.[57] Only gradually was the authority necessary created. Through the various stages of a Man-Power Board, the Ministry of Munitions, the Department of the Director-General of National Service to, in August, 1917, a Ministry of National Service.[58] The Ministry of Labour created in 1916 provided the basis for the whole supply of labour. It was deliberately removed from the immediate executive responsibilities involved in the administration of the Munitions Acts and rendered as far as war would permit neutral in labour matters. It was principally occupied in preparations for peace.[59] It was the Government's main instrument for conciliation.

The demand for munitions combined with the rush of skilled workmen to the colours created by March, 1915, a situation in which firms were living mainly by taking in one another's employees.[60] The Government was faced with the problems of limiting the movement of workmen, making one workman do the work of one and a half and preventing by persuasion or coercion industrial strife. The foundations of

labour regulation were laid down by the Munitions of War
Act of July 2nd, 1915.   Faced with the industrial traditions
of masters and men, the psychology of war which " with
magnificent impartiality stirred up the best and the worst
human passions ",[61] and with the limitations imposed upon
swift and dramatic changes by the actual structure of
industry,[62] the Government by this act laid the foundations
of labour control.   The fundamental principle of the Bill
was that while the worker remained a civilian, with all the
rights and privileges of civil law, his industrial rights were
severely limited.   In those controlled establishments where
the worker was required to surrender some of his industrial
rights the profits of the employer were also limited.   Lock-
outs were made crimes and arbitration compulsory.[63]   The
Act, which was the culmination of a long period of negotiations commencing in November, 1914, provided a definite
statutory basis for the development of a dilution programme.[64]
Dilution was not secured by persuading the skilled man to let
the unskilled take his job—because the unskilled could not
do the work.   It had to be divided into its component parts
and fool-proof machines introduced.[65]   Before long " the
ugly shape of war was to intrude into every part of the
workman's life ".[66]   His freedom of movement was checked,
his wages controlled, strikes forbidden and his work defined.
His recreation was limited, his consumption of liquor and the
building of his homes curtailed.[67]   In August, 1917, the
struggle between workers and fighters was composed by
bringing recruiting for both services under a common
control.[68]   The Ministry of National Service (August, 1917)
was instructed by the War Cabinet to be in a position to give
the meaning in terms of man-power of all department
proposals; to make arrangements for transfers from the
civilian to fighting and vice versa when necessary.   A War
Priorities Committee of the Cabinet was to decide what were
the most pressing industrial needs and to give instructions to

the Ministry of National Service as to the channels into which labour was to be directed.[69]

For the supply of munitions of war the functions of the Army Contracts Department (which had been reorganized before 1907) was limited before 1914 to the breaking up of rings. Army factories were only allowed to produce one third of Government guns and ammunition and half the army clothing, so that a prosperous private enterprise might be a vital part of our defence.[70] The War Office machinery was adjusted to the needs of peace; the resilience of private industry, it was believed, would meet the needs of war. By October, 1914, the buying machinery of the Army was paralysed. It was easier for manufacturers to do business with our Allies indirectly through the Board of Trade than with the War Office.[71] In November, 1914, Mr. Wintour, of the Board of Trade, was made Director of Army Contracts. By his efforts the Army was secured its essential supplies of beef, jute, food, textiles and leather. But by May, 1915, it was clear that essential supplies would not be forthcoming merely from the incentives provided by rising prices. National factories were built; raw materials were monopolized and distributed by the Government at fixed prices and manufacturers were required to produce shells at prices based on an analysis of cost.[72] By requisitioning practically the whole output of the engineering industry and making use of nearly all the iron and steel available, the Government virtually suppressed private trade and ignored civilian needs.[73] But in the case of textiles and foodstuffs civilian needs could not be ignored. The intervention of the War Office to meet the needs of the troops led inevitably to the development of a Ministry of Food. Starting with an effort to protect the Government against high charges, the stage was finally reached of a national and international organization to secure supplies at reasonable prices for the whole nation.

There was no general food problem until the end of 1916. The policy of the Government had been to trust as far as possible to private enterprise for the maintenance of civilian supplies.[74] Since 1870 our whole farming technique was based on the assumption that transport had made available cheap corn for the towns, cheap manures for the land and cheap feeding stuffs for livestock.[75] Whereas Germany could feed her whole population for six out of seven days in the week we could only feed ourselves from Friday night until Monday morning. We could feed fifteen out of our forty-seven milions, or all of them for 125 days out of 365. In the spring of 1915 the difficulties of the Government over munitions produced the first Coalition; in the autumn of 1916 the problem of food control produced the fall of Asquith. On October 10th Runciman explained that the importation of wheat into the United Kingdom would have to be undertaken by a Royal Commission, of which the chairman would be the Minister of Agriculture.[76] The idea of a Food Controller was even then a pleasant jest, but in November it was admitted that we " had been driven bit by bit against our will . . . to suspend the easy flow of purely voluntary action ". In the House of Commons Churchill made a prophetic speech. " I believe that before the end of this war . . . all shipping will certainly be taken over by the Government and regulated in one form or another. . . . I believe that all important employment will be regulated by the State for the purposes of war. I believe that ration tickets for everything that matters will be served out to every one of us. I believe that prices will have to be fixed so as to secure to the poorest people in this country . . . the power of buying a certain modicum of food sufficient to keep up physical war-making efficiency at prices which are not outside the scope of the wages they receive. . . . I am sure that we shall come to a national organization of agriculture like there is a national organization of munitions."[77]   When the Government failed to find and appoint a Food Controller it fell.   When the new Lloyd George Government was formed in December Lord Devonport was made Controller.   On December 2nd, 1916, the New Ministries and Secretaries Act gave statutory authority for the creation of three new Ministries—Labour, Food and Shipping.

So great was Lord Devonport's appetite for work and belief in his knowledge of food that Lord Rhondda, who took over in June, 1917, had to create a Ministry of Food out of a one-man business.[78]   " The Ministry of Munitions were then in charge of oils and fats, including the materials for margarine.   The Board of Trade controlled the import of meat and cheese and had made a beginning with frozen fish . . . the Admiralty, the War Office and the Navy and Army Canteen Board obtained most of their supplies independently. The War Savings Committee undertook a large part of the Food Economy campaign.   The Board of Agriculture undertook food preservation, and the control of oats was shared between the Board of Trade and the War Office."[79]

All these powers (except the importation of refrigerated meat from South America, Australia and New Zealand, which remained with the Board of Trade) were taken over by the Ministry of Food or the Wheat and Sugar Commissions. Wintour, a former official of the Board of Trade, became Rhondda's right-hand man.   The Ministry had not only to buy, sell, transport and distribute on the largest scale, they had to secure fair distribution at fair prices to ten million separate households.   For the first they secured men with the widest experience of the special trades concerned.   For the second they created a special staff with an interest in economic laws and experience in the arts of public administration.   The genius of Rhondda organized an administrative machine which was centralized for thought but decentralized for action.[80]   He saw that freedom from detailed Treasury control was necessary and that the Minister should give to publicity what in peace would have been given to parliamentary duties.[81]   He fully used the knowledge of the physiologists.   Calories were counted as carefully as rifles and shells.   Every million calories represented the food required by one person for a year, every billion reduced by some 500,000 tons the demands made on our shipping; and that meant in 1918, 100,000 additional American troops on the Western Front.[82]   To reach the homes and daily lives of forty million people there were two administrative organs. In each of the fifteen areas into which Great Britain was divided there was placed a Food Controller, the representative of a central executive department.   In nearly 2,000 separate areas there were established representative Food Control Committees.   Finally a National Food Council run by a competent journalist, pursued the policy that it was more blessed to persuade than to command.

By respect for scientific advice, by combining the traditions of the Civil Service with the experience of business experts, by decentralization of machinery and by a scrupulous attention to fairness in distribution the Ministry of Food was able to secure both peace and plenty.[83]

Shipping of all industries was the one in which the success of the ordinary machinery of commerce had been most conspicuous.   Although the State had been forced to undertake the protection of the sailors in the signing of their contracts, the control of safety conditions, and although there was a strong case for further State intervention to secure a humanitarian minimum in shipping conditions, yet the free play of economic forces " with their ruthless automatic checks on inefficiency and error " had secured an elastic and responsive system among the various organizations responsible for the purchase, finance, transport and marketing and consumption of goods which entered into international trade.   But as it was the system most subtly organized so it was the system in which, once State control was introduced, it would have to go the furthest. For " control of shipping depends upon control of commodities and must be international in character. Unless the State is to decide what is to be imported and the priority in which different cargoes are to be shipped it will be compelled to leave a free freight market in operation, for it is impossible for the shipowner himself to exercise an arbitrary selection . . . for shipping is the handmaid of commerce and unless the commercial interests are allowed to make known their requirements in the ordinary way the requirements must be fixed by the State itself ".[84] It was the effect of a partial State control of tonnage on the freight rates of that part which it did not control which was the cause of the demand of a Ministry of Shipping. " The task of the Ministry of Shipping and Allied Maritime Transport Council was to concentrate the available tonnage on the shortest route as a corollary to the purchase of supplies on the credit of the State, in the nearest markets." The necessary concentration would not have been accomplished without an extension and centralization of control. But it was a last expedient and one made possible only by the financial assistance of the United States. It enabled the necessary minimum of supplies essential for war purpose to be maintained, but at a price in adverse exchanges, indebtedness and commercial dislocation which added immensely to the burden of war.[85] It would have been impossible without international control. No single State could fix the freights on cargoes carried under foreign flags and dictate the movements of foreign tonnage. As it was, with their overwhelming strength the Allies had to pay neutral shipowners rates three or four times as great as those allowed to British owners.[86]

In the early stages of the war the introduction of State control was opposed by the greater part of the shipping industry on the grounds that it would imperil the flow of essential supplies.   It was the effect of partial control on ship-ping rates for those who were uncontrolled, and the growing pressure for the allocation of essential supplies, which forced the creation at the end of 1916 of a Controller of Shipping. By that time there was a chaos of authorities in which order could only be introduced by a concentration and extension of power.   In 1916 the Admiralty Transport Department were responsible for providing ships for naval and military service, tonnage and space for the Wheat Authority, and for the carriage of a large proportion of British and Allied imports. But the Admiralty " had no definite power to criticize or re-fuse the demands of any of the departments or to limit the allocation of tonnage. The Board of Trade were responsible for the employment of all insulated space in liners with a modified right of diverting the ships themselves ".   A Ship Licensing Committee controlled, on the instruction of the Board of Trade on very broad lines, the employment of all ships not on full requisition.   Various committees set up by the Board of Trade controlled the running of all British ships in the French and Italian coal trade.   " The official ore broker chartered for the Ministry of Munitions British and neutral tonnage to bring ore from Spain and the Mediterranean." The Port and Transport Executive Committee appointed at the joint instance of the Board of Trade, Admiralty and War Office was responsible for all measures necessary to improve the turn-round of shipping at all ports.[87]   And this problem of the turn-round was at least as important as the problem of tonnage itself.[88]   The whole shipbuilding resources of the country were subject to an absolute Admiralty priority.   The Board of Trade issued under the Munitions of War Acts certificates for such ships as they desired to see completed, but they had no power to obtain the necessary allocation of labour and material for their completion. Over the whole field a Shipping Control Committee " exercised a general super-vision, but possessed neither an administrative staff nor direct

executive powers, though they were generally able to obtain
Cabinet backing for their more important decisions ".[89]

The Shipping Controller, when he was at last appointed,
was a shipowner. He had not only to coerce those who put
profits before patriotism; it was necessary that he should be
able to command the support of those who distrusted the
extension of State control.[90] A close association of shipowners
with the Ministry was essential to its success. Not only was
" their knowledge and experience required in the practical
work of the Ministry, but their services were of the utmost
importance in conducting negotiations with their fellow shipowners ".[91] The rapid extension of Government requisition
of tonnage was followed by a decision to build and run ships
on Government account. With the Admiralty, War Office
and Ministry of Munitions freely competing for the material
available, merchant shipbuilding received in practice only
what was left over after their claims had been satisfied.[92]
Only a strong department definitely responsible for building merchant ships could secure the materials required.
When in three months, February to April, 1917, the submarine campaign sank 1,200,000 tons, which equalled the
Controller's estimate of the largest output he could secure in
a year, and the Admiralty could hold out little hope of a
substantial reduction in the sinkings, the situation was so
desperate that the Government in May transferred the control
of Merchant Shipbuilding to the Admiralty.[93] But the
problem of men and materials was not yet solved. There
were five overlapping authorities: the Shipyards Labour
Department at the Admiralty, the Labour Department of the
Ministry of Munitions, the Ministry of National Service, the
War Cabinet Labour Department and the Ministry of
Labour.[94] On the one hand the War Office refused to release
skilled men; on the other organized labour was opposed to
dilution until they were released.[95] For steel the War Office
and the Ministry of Munitions and the Allies had claims which

none of them would reduce.[96]   In May, 1918, therefore, the
Department of Shipbuilding was transferred to Lord Pirrie,
an experienced shipbuilder, with the title of Controller-
General of Merchant Shipping, a seat on the Board of
Admiralty and the right of direct access to the Cabinet.[97]

In the development of the Air Ministry we have an excellent example of the interplay between technical, administrative and constitutional forces.   In the stress of war the
new department passed rapidly through stages which otherwise might have taken decades.   In 1912 the establishment
of a permanent consultative committee called the Air Committee, with the duty of co-ordinating the efforts of the
Admiralty and the War Office formed the nucleus of the
future Air Ministry.[98]   But there was no central policy for
air.   Fisher and Churchill at the Admiralty might have their
vision of aerial navies fighting in the central blue, but the
War Office could only think of aircraft as aids to recon-
naissance—a not quite gentlemanly Pegasus.   In July, 1914,
the separate existence of a Naval Air Force was recognized.

In the early days of the war there was no clearly defined
policy.   There was, for example, uncertainty as to whether
the naval or the military planes should be responsible for
defence against Zeppelins.   The development of a separate
Air Ministry was the result of the technical problems connected with the supply of aero engines and aircraft.   For the
equipment of an air force could not be organized on mass
production lines along with the ordinary munitions and
instruments of war.   In February, 1916, Lord Derby's Air
Committee was appointed to collaborate in arranging the
supply and design for the material of the Naval and Military
Air Services upon such points as might be referred to them by
the War Committee, the Admiralty, the War Office or any
other department of State.   With no executive powers and
no authority to override Admiralty obstruction, the Derby
Committee collapsed within two months.   In the spring of

1916, Lord Curzon, the Lord President of the Council, was exploring the possibilities of reorganization and suggesting an Air Board as the preliminary to an Air Ministry. Mr. Balfour, for the Admiralty, conducted the opposition. On May 11th the War Committee decided to establish an Air Board consisting of Lord Curzon as Chairman, two naval and two military representatives, Lord Sydenham as independent expert and Major Baird as Parliamentary Secretary. But the Air Board, like the Committee, was without executive powers and, though charged with the duty of organizing the supply of material and preventing competition, possessed no authority to determine a policy for the placing of orders. Lord Curzon claimed for the Air Board the control in both the air services, of invention, research, experiment, design, production and finance. Balfour claimed for the Admiralty the separate control of these functions as far as the Naval Air Force was concerned, while the Ministry of Munitions wished to undertake the design and supply of aeroplanes for both Army and Naval Air Forces. This was one of the grandest departmental disputes of all time, only drowned by the noise of battle itself. In December the War Cabinet decided that the powers of the Air Board should be enlarged. The New Ministries and Secretaries Act provided that the President of the Air Board should be deemed to be a Minister and the Board a Ministry. In relation to aircraft the Board was to have such powers and duties of any Government Department in authority, whether conferred by statute or otherwise as His Majesty may by Order in Council transfer to the Board or authorize the Board to exercise or perform concurrently with or in consultation with the Government Department or authority concerned.[99] The Ministry of Munitions was to undertake the design and supply of aeroplanes for both the Army and the Navy. The Air Board was to be responsible for allocating the available resources between the Admiralty and the War Office. This division of responsibility for design and responsibility for supply between the Air Board and the Ministry of Munitions might have been fatal had they not both been housed in the Hotel Cecil.[100] Propinquity secured what politics could not.

In August, 1917, the Smuts Committee pointed out that the Board was more a conference than a Board, that with no technical and advisory personnel of its own it could never form an independent air policy, and said that in their " opinion there is no reason why the Air Board should any longer continue in its present form as practically no more than a conference room between the older services, and there is every reason why it should be raised to the status of an independent Ministry in control of its own war services ". On November 29th, 1917, the Royal Assent was given to the Bill creating an Air Ministry. Miraculously Admiralty and War Office agreed to its terms. The new Air Council was based on the organization of the Army Council.

Three things clearly emerge from the experience of the State in the administrative problems of the war: (1) that the Government would have been powerless without the co-operation of organizations of the industrial and commercial interests with which they were concerned; (2) that their legal powers were a matter of slight importance compared with the force of opinion both of the general public and the groups concerned that co-operation was a duty; (3) that the conditions of war throw little light on the problem of State control of the life of a community in time of peace save that they bring out clearly the difficulty of combining a policy of plan with one of no plan.

In agriculture the Food Controller was " a constitutional monarch who could only govern with the support and approval of the majority in any particular trade. The voluntary co-operation of traders and manufacturers was at least as important as the compulsory powers conferred by D.O.R.A." All the innumerable Boards, Councils, Associations and Advisory Committees were associated with the work of the controlling departments and functioned to some extent as representative governing bodies of the trade or industry concerned.[100a]

In the first week of the war the President of the Board of Agriculture and Fisheries had set up a consultative committee of experts—agriculturalists drawn from all parts of the country and in touch with local opinion.[101] When in January, 1917, a Food Production Department was created with power, in consultation with the Food Controller, to make orders bearing on the better cultivation of agricultural land, England and Wales were divided into twenty areas, for each of which a local Commissioner was appointed as the Food Production Department's representative on the committee for that area. These Agricultural Executive Committees were given a free hand. The department said, " this is what we want done; you know how it can be done ". To this policy much of the success achieved was due.[102]

In the case of industry problems of man-power, production, exports and imports were so closely connected that they could be dealt with by industries as a unit. It was essential for the State to have the closest co-operation with all the interests concerned.[103] In the case of shipping the Ministry of Shipping looked to the liner companies to run their vessels with the same zeal and efficiency as if they retained a pecuniary interest in the success of the voyages. This trust would have been impossible had not the terms of requisition been arranged with bodies which were fully representative of the industry and organized strongly to speak for it.[104]

In all problems of industrial labour the Government relied upon the co-operation of the employers and the Trade Unions. In March, 1915, letters were sent to the Trade Unions asking them to consult with the Chancellor of the Exchequer and the President of the Board of Trade.[105] When the immense discouragements and disarrangement of war caused the inevitable industrial unrest the Government could only show its willingness to deal with remediable grievances and trust to the will to win.[106]

In spite of the wide powers conferred by D.O.R.A. (August, 1914) on the Government to make regulations for the public safety and defence of the realm they did not give it power to exercise a complete control of trade, to regulate dealings and to prescribe maximum prices.[107] It was only by the use of the absolutist theory of the Royal Prerogative that the subject has no legal right to compensation against the Crown that the tyranny of the market prices was overthrown. " It was because compensation for property requisitioned need only be made *ex gratia* that the costing system could be and was legally enforced." The principle that no compensation was payable for losses inflicted by measures which were of general application alone made a regime of maximum prices and the prohibition of private dealings possible.[108] But in the great majority of cases what was lawful and what was not did not very much matter. What mattered was the extent to which any measure commanded general support and was applied impartially all round. Measures of State intervention which went beyond what the best opinion in any particular trade regarded as necessary and possible were practically certain to fail, however valid their legal sanction.[109] The control of shipping was carried on largely by and through the leading representatives of the industry itself and rested at bottom on a basis of agreement.[110] In one case the shipowners, having established in court that a liner requisition scheme which was the pivot of the whole supply system of the country was *ultra vires*,[111] did not press their advantage, desiring only recognition of the fact that their co-operation was voluntary and not enforced.[112] " There was a strong feeling that the Government should not be hampered in the prosecution of the war by too close an inquiry into the strict legality of its administrative action." And of course a well-founded legal objection could be overridden by an Amending Act.[113]

The development of war-time control of the economic life of the nation was due almost entirely to the pressure of emergencies and " hardly at all to a deliberate policy of State intervention consciously thought out and consistently pursued ".[114]   With the outbreak of war certain interests saw their only salvation in the assistance of the State.   In their case there was no conflict between the particular and the general interests.   The Government guaranteed the solvency of the banks and discount houses by placing the credit of the nation behind approved commercial bills payable by debtors who could not meet their obligations.[115]   Where the military necessity was obvious the Government took over the railways of the country by an agreement which guaranteed their pre-war dividend.   As the refiners were paralysed by the failure of sugar imports from Central Europe, the Government took control of the purchase and importation of sugar. But when it became necessary for the Government to fix prices, control and centralized purchase had to be extended from the finished article back to the raw material.   From the devising of machinery for the purchase of raw materials it was driven to experiment with the control of the production of essential foodstuffs.[116]   Its control of commodities drove it to the control of shipping.[117]   And in shipping at least it was clear " that it must be all or nothing; . . . private trading actuated solely by economic motives and State trading liable to be deflected by political considerations could not exist side by side ".[118]

The extension during the war of State control in every aspect of the national life provides certain simple lessons in the nature of government and the technique of administration. In the first place the whole party system was practically suspended.   In so far as it existed, it existed rather as an embarrassment to the development of policy and the discovery

T

of talent. Yet but for the party system the spirit and the talent which were available would not have been there at all. It is doubtful whether democracy could wage war for any length of time without a serious impairment of its political life. The attempt of the English aristocracy to resist the domination of Napoleon was paid for by a degradation of our political life for twenty years after the Battle of Waterloo. It is in the hour of victory that the most serious blow is likely to be struck at the life of the party system. The Liberal Party, which alone could secure unanimity for our entrance into the war, was destroyed by the peace it had made possible. Secondly, the control of the State was more successful in those spheres where publicity and measurement could give the results which were required. Given the simple problem of rationing and the control and purchase of raw materials, we had only to give the available experts a free hand and the power to impose whatever costs they could not limit on posterity to get what was required. An enormous new sphere was discovered for the use of statistics and the use of publicity where co-operation of the public was essential. Where they could be told what it was they were required to do, and where what was required could be related to some dominant emotional aim only common honesty and technical skill were required, which is not to say that the arts of administration were not taxed to their utmost. Never was it more clearly demonstrated that the success of administration lies in the centralization of knowledge and the decentralization of power. Elasticity and decentralization were the secrets of success.

In the case of wool purchase and meat control uniformity and a common policy were secured as much by periodical meeting between subordinate officers as by central direction.[119] Every controlling department had its advisory committees of experts and forceful critics. It was found possible to combine the expert experience of those trained in competitive industry and bargaining with the control and planning of the civil servants. " The initiation and direction of schemes rested with the permanent officials, who had no previous experience of commercial affairs . . . the execution, the technical capacity and the personal influence . . . were the contribution of business men."[119] But it was in the realm of business where results are measurable that the most success was achieved. " Elasticity and decentralization are easier to introduce in business administration than in the administration of law . . . business looks forward, law looks backwards . . . though fairness demands similar treatment for similar cases at any one time, completely new principles may be followed at different times without injustice."[120] From this judgment it may be inferred that to those who consider that the domination of the material environment is now a limited and calculable problem it is possible to secure an administrative technique which shall secure the abolition of scarcity, though it may involve an abrogation of the traditional legal rights of liberty and property. Were the four years of war a rehearsal for a future five years' economic plan? Fundamentally the answer to this is that the coercion necessary was provided by the enemy. The whole system of co-operation was a product of the fear of defeat. If it ever should be possible for men to feel for an idea as they felt for the complex of national feeling in the war, then the same degree of control would be possible; only the battle front would be within the State against all those who were not converted to the ideal held by the dominant group. Nor should the enormous inefficiency, viewed over a period, of the methods used be forgotten. A scale of priorities was given by the dictates of the enemy. That shells might be made the whole equipment of our industries was distorted; it was found impossible to impose the cost in any equitable way. What men could see and feel that had to be fairly divided; but the unseen costs could be allowed to accumulate as they would. Nor must the peculiar exaltation of spirit and steady degradation of moral be forgotten. The existence of the army in the field and the threat of death in nearly every home provided a stimulus and an emotional appeal in time of crisis which was very real even among those who would have been careful to disguise its presence. But it is equally true that there was a steady degradation in the character of our public men throughout the period. No human being could stand up to the ordeal of responsibility and keep his sense of proportion. The Lloyd George who drove Asquith from office for his country's good was mightier in power, but smaller in essential political stature when he called the General Election of 1918. If the experts and the professional civil servants escaped this corrupting breath of power and responsibility the whole of the ordinary population were deprived of any essential education in political realities. For they had not to choose the way that they would live, but only to lend a hand in whatever way they could to a common cause.

[1] Sir Frederick Maurice : *Governments and War*, p. 120.
[2] J. A. Spender and C. Asquith : *Life of Asquith*, Vol. 2, p. 123.
[3] ibid., Vol. 2, p. 124.
[4] ibid., Vol. 2, p. 127.
[5] ibid., Vol. 2, p. 95.
[6] ibid., Vol. 2, p. 100.
[7] A. Chamberlain : *Down the Years*, p. 116.
[8] Ronaldshay : *Life of Lord Curzon*, Vol. 3, p. 124.
[9] *Life of Asquith*, Vol. 2, p. 171.
[10] Churchill : *World Crisis* 1915, p. 391.
[11] *Life of Asquith*, Vol. 2, p. 130 and 180.
[12] Asquith to Lloyd George, Dec. 1, 1916, *Life of Asquith*, Vol. 2, p. 253.
[13] Chamberlain : *Down the Years*, p. 111.
[14] *Life of Asquith*, Vol. 2, p. 273.
[15] Chamberlain : *Down the Years*, p. 116.
[16] *Life of Asquith*, Vol. 2, p. 248.
[17] Chamberlain : *Down the Years*, p. 113 and 121.
[18] ibid., p. 121.
[19] It is possible that the King did not ask or that Asquith declined to tender advice as to who should be his successor. Chamberlain, op. cit., pp. 125–6.
[20] *Life of Asquith*, Vol. 2, pp. 273–4.
[21] Addison : *Politics from Within*, Vol. 2.
[22] Lloyd George : *Memoirs*, p. 1039.
[23] ibid., pp. 1077–9.
[24] ibid., p. 1043.

[25] Lloyd George : *Memoirs*, p. 1073.
[26] ibid., p. 1051.
[27] Chamberlain : *Down the Years*, p. 132.
[28] *Empire Review*, 1923 & 1924, Articles by C. Jones.
[29] ibid.
[30] *Life of Asquith*, Vol. 2, p. 122.
[31] ibid., Vol. 2, p. 121.
[32] Lloyd George : *Memoirs*, p. 1155.
[33] Joseph : *Logic*, pp. 184-5.
[34] Lloyd George : *Memoirs*, p. 2341.
[35] Sir Frederick Maurice : *Governments and War*, p. 124.
[36] ibid., p. 127.
[37] ibid., pp. 155-6.
[38] ibid., p. 128.
[39] ibid., p. 128.
[40] ibid., p. 130.
[41] ibid., p. 134.
[42] *Life of Asquith*, Vol. 2, p. 132.
[43] Sir F. Maurice : *Governments and War*, p. 132.
[44] *Life of Asquith*, Vol. 2, p. 190.
[45] Sir Fr. Maurice : *Governments and War*, p. 139.
[46] Lloyd George : *Memoirs*, p. 2272.
[47] ibid., pp. 2221, 1825.
[48] ibid., p. 2192.
[49] ibid., p. 2333.
[50] ibid., p. 2333.
[51] ibid., p. 2347.
[52] ibid., p. 2344.
[53] E. M. H. Lloyd : *Experiments in State Control*, p. 22.
[54] Humbert Wolfe : *Labour Supply and Regulation*, p. 12.
[55] ibid., p. 3.
[56] ibid., pp. 1 and 2.
[57] ibid., p. 3.
[58] ibid., p. 3.
[59] ibid., p. 297.
[60] ibid., p. 217.
[61] ibid., p. 120.
[62] ibid., p. 99.
[63] ibid., pp. 101-2.
[64] ibid., p. 158.
[65] ibid., p. 154-5.
[66] ibid., p. 136.
[67] ibid., p. 153.
[68] ibid., p. 52.
[69] ibid., p. 52.
[70] E. M. H. Lloyd : *Experiments in State Control*, p. 16.
[71] ibid., p. 21.
[72] ibid., p. 23.
[73] ibid., p. 25.
[74] Sir William Beveridge : *British Food Control*, p. 6.
[75] T. H. M. Middleton : *Food Production in War*, p. 35.
[76] Beveridge L *British Food Control*, p. 22.
[77] cited Beveridge, *op. cit.*, p. 27.
[78] Beveridge, *op. cit.*, p. 47.
[79] ibid., p. 52.
[80] ibid., p. 335.
[81] ibid., p. 336.
[82] T. H. Middleton : *Food Production in War*, p. 328.
[83] Beveridge : *British Food Control*, p. 73.

[84] C. Ernest Fayle : *The War and the Shipping Industry*, p. 404.
[85] ibid., p. 405.
[86] ibid., p. 404.
[87] ibid., p. 199.
[88] ibid., p. 402.
[89] ibid., p. 199.
[90] ibid., p. 205.
[91] ibid., p. 217.
[92] ibid., p. 239.
[93] ibid., p. 245.
[94] ibid., p. 248.
[95] ibid., p. 247.
[96] ibid., p. 247.
[97] ibid., p. 254.
[98] *Official History of the War in the Air*, Vol. 1, p. 211.
[99] Section 8.
[100] *War in the Air*, Vol. 3.
[100a] E. M. H. Lloyd : *Experiments in State Control*, pp. 352–3.
[101] Middleton : *Food Production in War*, p. 167.
[102] ibid., p. 168.
[103] Lloyd : *Experiments in State Control*, p. 272.
[104] Fayle : *The War and the Shipping Industry*, pp. 409 and 337.
[105] H. Wolfe : *Labour Supply and Regulation*, p. 151.
[106] ibid., pp. 120 and 141.
[107] E. M. H. Lloyd : *Experiments in State Control*, p. 50.
[108] ibid., p. 52.
[109] ibid., p. 64.
[110] Fayle : *The War and the Shipping Industry*, p. 221.
[111] *China Mutual v. Maclay*, 1918, 1.K.B. 33.
[112] Fayle, *op. cit.*, p. 237.
[113] ibid., p. 216.
[114] E. M. H. Lloyd : *Experiments in State Control*, pp. 260–2.
[115] ibid., pp. 261–2.
[116] ibid., p. 264.
[117] Fayle : *op. cit.*, p. 401.
[118] ibid., p. 337.
[119] E. M. H. Lloyd : *op. cit.*, p. 390.
[120] ibid., p. 394.
[121] ibid., p. 390.

CHAPTER VIII

THE STATE AND SOCIETY SINCE 1918

The influence of the war in the post-war World—The new economic
functions of the State—Currency and the Bank of England—Trade and
overseas investments—The abandoment of Free Trade—The problem of
the labour market—Theories of the relation of the State and industry—
The pressure of emergencies in Coal; Iron and Steel; Agriculture—
Some aspects of State action in relation to the standard of living—The
organization of Education—Public Health—And Police.

MANY of the problems which may threaten the existence
of democratic government in this country would have
existed had there been no world war in 1914-18. Without
the war the development of Free Trade, which is an attempt
to make use of the maximum territorial division of labour,
would have led to a conflict between the economic and all
the other aspects of man's estate. In particular the division
of labour which the progressive application of science to
industry requires would have conflicted with the psychological
forces of nationalism. In the nineteenth century the largest
Free Trade area in the world, the United States of America,
was only created by the destruction in civil war of the slave-
owning South. Nor would the wounds of that conflict have
been healed had there not been a territory as large as the
Roman Empire west of the Mississippi empty for occupation
by victor and vanquished alike. In Central Europe a
political system which was to be the framework of the most
powerful European industrial power was only created by a
policy of blood and iron. Not one of the colonies settled
by Englishmen failed to develop a system of tariffs for the
development of their political and social life. If the early

stages of the industrial revolution produced in England, which had boasted a cultural unity since the Conquest, the Luddites and the Chartists, it was hardly to be expected on the world stage it would not produce convulsions of enormous violence. Without the war the United States would have closed her paradise to the hungry hordes of Europe. Without the war textiles, because they are one of the simplest forms of manufacture, catering for an almost universal demand, would have developed in the East. The revolution in agriculture, which must have such far-reaching consequence for the political and social structure of the future, destroying as it does the traditional framework in which civilization— the life of cities—has hitherto been set, was inevitable without war. Nor was the war responsible for the demands made on the art of politics and the science of administration when specialization of labour made the market value of most workers less than the minimum income the performance of their civic duties required. Finally, the war did not create all those conditions, strategic and economic, which are now so much more favourable to the great land powers than they are to a democratic island empire.

But all these conditions have been modified by the effects of the war. Possessing " the most delicate and most elaborate trade system ", we offered " the largest possible target to dislocation because it sprawled all over the world ".[1] We were an octopus in a sea of sharks. The war was won by the two great sea powers of the world blockading the most formidable of land powers. The Allied blockade and control of shipping acted as a tariff wall behind which infant industries grew to sufficient maturity to enable them, when peace was signed, to secure that tariffs and subsidies should be in peace what the blockade had been in war. The great trade routes of the Pacific had been left open to the competition of the Americans and Japanese, while Scandinavian countries had learnt to build their own ships. The political disturbances of China and of India injured British trade when they left other countries unmoved. The reduction in the volume of the world trade by the dislocations of war and the fears and passions of the peace struck an almost mortal blow to British shipbuilding.

The interplay between the growing sweep of the industrial revolution in the world and the particular dislocations of the war it is not possible to follow. The ultimate effect of their joint forces on the future of this country we can only surmise. After the Napoleonic wars it took twenty years for this country to recover its political and economic stride. The fact that the chaos and misery of the period after Waterloo to the hungry 'forties was a prelude to the complacent 'sixties is to some a promise now of ease and plenty yet to come. But the comparison is superficial and misleading. For in the early nineteenth century one thing was sure. Whatever the political and social stresses caused by wars, the war itself and a combination of geographical and economic factors had thrust the industrial leadership of the world upon us. Whatever the political dislocation caused by the misery of the war itself and the uncertainties of peace it was mitigated by the rapidity of an economic advance which brought not only plenty but the power to live in peace. Moreover as the expedient of popular government had not then been tried the weaknesses of our political system could be envigorated by extensions of the suffrage. Not new parties only, but new political forces, could be called to the service of the State. The anæmia of aristocracy could be remedied by a transfusion of blood from the rising middle class. So long as the goal of manhood suffrage lay ahead political deadlocks could be broken by an extension of the suffrage. In our relations with foreign powers it could be plausibly argued that our own profits were the world's gain. Our internal politics were like a series of successful strikes by workers in a factory for whose output there is an increasing demand.

Underlying all the activities of the State in this country since 1918 have been two anxieties: first, that the standard of living possible before the war might no longer be possible, while the insistence of the newly enfranchised people that it should might destroy the recuperative powers of the economic system; second, that a decline in our economic strength in relation to the world had to be prevented from causing the collapse of the political and administrative orders for which we were responsible.   If the general set of industrial and financial forces were against the continued supremacy of these islands what was to become of the political arch of which they were the keystone?   It is by now fairly clear that the despotic system of government will generally prevail if the democratic experiment of the British Commonwealth of Nations were to fail.   Who can suppose that either the Scandinavian democracies or the democracy of France or even that of the United States would survive the confusions which would follow the struggle for China, India and Africa when the British political order had collapsed?   To say this is to claim no superiority for the British in the art of politics.   For a variety of reasons a system of constitutional and administrative devices have been developed with their centre in these islands and the collapse of that system would shake the world.   It may be that it would be better for the world that the English political tradition should live hereafter only in her political literature—that she should be a word without the sword.   But the end of that political system would be a turning-point in the history of the world.   In four of the world's five continents it would mean that the application of natural science to the life of man would be made by force and not by persuasion.

Some of broader outlines of the economic context of State activity since the war must here be given.   In 1913 about 30 per cent. of our industrial population was engaged directly or indirectly in the production of goods and services for sale

outside Great Britain.   British coal mines exported 40 per
cent. of their output; the cotton trade sent more than half of
its exports to Asia.   About 60 per cent. of all our foodstuffs
were imported.   Great Britain built 60 per cent. of the
world's ships; while British ships carried 50 per cent. in
volume of the entire sea-borne trade of the world.[2]   Shipping and other services to the value of £129 millions together
with an income from overseas investments of £210 millions
converted an excess of imports of £158 millions into a balance
of £181 millions available for overseas investments.[3]
In the five years 1907-11 of the total loans raised about
20 per cent. had been for home investment, 35 per cent. for
investment in the Empire, and 45 per cent. for investment
in foreign countries.[4]   London was the undisputed monetary
and financial capital of the world, enjoying an almost effortless superiority which required no State-controlled machinery
for its exercise.   This position of Britain had been attained
" not by the pursuit of any preconceived plan, but by a process of almost unhampered evolution based on trial and error
and aided by the practical aptitudes and instincts of our race,
as well as by certain fortunate accidents in the way of natural
resources and geographical position ".[5]

The war and the increasing impetus of the industrial
revolution throughout the world between them transformed
the conditions to which British industry and commerce had to
be adjusted if her political and social order were to survive.
In finance our previous effortless supremacy passed for ever;
in commerce the principle of free trade proved for the world
stage as parochial as once had proved the peace of Rome; in
the organization of industry the distortions of war and the
technical revolutions which continued through the peace imposed a problem of reorganization impossible to solve without
the assistance of the State.   In particular whereas before the
war the mean figure, round which unemployment moved, was
in the neighbourhood of $4\frac{1}{2}$ per cent., since the war it has only

been less than 10 per cent. (in 1927) and has at times been
more than 21 per cent.[6]

We may briefly consider the problems of the State in
relation to (1) prices, (2) trade and commerce and (3) industrial organization.

All economic activity is carried on in an environment of
law which imposes conditions on the manner in which all the
factors of production become available.[7] But the central
function of any economic system that is based upon individual
judgment and choice of occupation and enjoyment is
" the continuous comparison of all sorts of prices and
rewards for service including the profits of enterprise."[8]
The State had therefore the task of helping to keep the
movement of prices within the limits to which industry and
the social order can be adjusted without collapse. For " to
allow prices to fall, whilst social forces maintain wage costs,
obliterates profit, and the attempt to reduce contractual incomes without power to abate contractual incomes
immediately jeopardizes both nationally and internationally
the sanctity of contracts ".[9] The maintenance of the sanctity
of contracts recognized by the most ardent individualist as
a function of the State is now seen to involve the solution by
the State of the most intricate problem of applied economics—
the control of the price level. Because the seamless web of
pre-war finance had been rent first by the war, then by the
burden of war debts, and again by the protective policies of
national cultures threatened by industrial revolutions,
Government action in the monetary field had by 1934-35
developed to an unprecedented scale.[10] After 1918 " a very
violent depreciation of money in the immediate post-war
period destroyed over a large part of the continent of Europe
all rational calculation and all orderly social and economic
development. This was followed by a period of relative
stability in which material well-being progressed markedly.
This was followed by a violent turn-down of prices . . . the

problems thus raised transcend in importance any others of our time and generation ".[11]

In this country the control of our currency is exclusively a matter for the Bank of England. In determining its policy it has to weigh the interests of group against group in relation to the interests of the country as a whole. It has been held that it should not be required to submit to political pressure and that economic analysis should not be distorted by party obligations.[12] So far it has remained an autonomous regulator of one of the most vital conditions upon which economic activity depends. So far as civilization depends upon " the expectation of normal profits to individual concerns and the sanctity of contracts " the banks have since the war had the care of civilization thrust upon them. For their important duties the Bank of England has developed an inner Cabinet —the Committee of Treasury, consisting of the Governor and seven other directors elected by secret ballot of the whole court.[13] The need for continuous consultation with other foreign banks has led since the war to the growth within the bank of a higher Civil Service.[14] The pre-war supremacy of London has been replaced partly by co-operation between the central banks of the world but also by conflicting national policies about the objects and methods of an international monetary system.[15]

The most important decision made by the Government on financial policy in the post-war world was that of April 28th, 1925, to return to the Gold Standard. Severely criticized by many experts at the time and disappointing in its subsequent results, it was forced upon the Government by the expiry, 1925, of the Act which then forbade the export of gold. To renew that Act the Government considered would have " destroyed our rising credit in every country of the world ".[16] Though the pound was thus overvalued by about 10 per cent., causing a decline in Britain's share of world exports in the period 1925-29, the Balfour Committee of 1929 was of the opinion that it was " unthinkable that any appreciable body of opinion would favour a fresh departure from the Gold Standard "; and three months before the country did come off gold the Macmillan Committee recommended " that this country should continue to adhere to the International Gold Standard at the existing parity ".[17]   When in September, 1931, the Gold Standard was suspended, the relationship between the Treasury and the Bank of England became closer than ever. The whole policy, the whole management of sterling is now discussed continuously between the representatives of the Treasury and the representatives of the Bank of England.[18]   In 1932 the Finance Act created an Exchange Equalization Account of £150 millions to be operated secretly for the protection of the sterling exchange against seasonal fluctuations, speculative operations and the movements of refugee capital. This account involved a further extension of Government responsibility for the monetary policy of the country which is, however, still regulated by the Bank of England.[19]   The destructive speculative attacks on currencies which developed after 1929 had to be beaten off by defensive measures undertaken by central banks which as they were attacked raised their discount rates and limited credit for speculative purposes.

Government responsibility for the stability of the currency has always been admitted by the most radical supporters of *laissez-faire*. But the post-war world was to impose on the Government a concern for the development of trade and of overseas investments which was to lead them to the acceptance of the most thorough going policy of protection and to experiments in economic imperialism.

Down to 1925 there was no real cause for pessimism about the position of British trade. It seemed that the recovery of world trade from the impediments of war would restore our prosperity. We should enjoy an increasing proportion of one increasing trade. Though aground we were not yet on the rocks and would be floated off by the returning tide.   But with the return of this country to gold in 1925 there was no substantial diminution of unemployment and our export trade failed to maintain its progress and lost ground to its competitors.[20] The year 1927, which was the nearest approach to normal in the post-war years, brought to light problems which were not merely the residual difficulties of the war period but symptoms of a new industrial and commercial era.   In 1929 we suffered from trade depression in many of our great industries at a time when other countries were enjoying a considerable degree of prosperity.[21]   Between 1929 and 1934 when the volume of world trade shrank by nearly a quarter the share of the United Kingdom slightly rose (from 13.03 per cent. to 13.85 per cent.), but this was partly due to a temporary improvement in our favour of the terms of trade. Owing to the collapse of the price of raw materials in 1933, a bale of exports bought nearly 23 per cent. more then than it would in 1929.   This advantage was not likely to be permanent.   The labour and equipment set free by the improvement in the terms of trade were not transferred into other forms of production for the home market.   The internal organization of finance and industry did not prove flexible enough to adjust itself to the changes in the markets of the world.

Before the war there had been available for overseas investment a surplus of between 130 and 180 million pounds. In 1913 an income of over £200 millions from overseas investments and £130 millions from shipping and commissions had not only paid for the importation of some 60 per cent. of our food supply but had left £180 millions for investment abroad.   By 1926 that surplus had been nearly wiped out. In 1929 it had recovered to £139 millions, but in 1931 it had become once more an adverse balance of £104 millions. In these conditions of violent variations it was impossible that the British Government could alone of the great

Governments of the world renounce the use of tariffs as a
defensive weapon or a constructive tool.

In the immediate post-war years of optimism, Mr. Keynes
had written " we must hold to free trade in its widest interpretation as an inflexible dogma to which no exception is
admitted. We must hold to it even when we receive no
reciprocity of treatment and even in those rare cases when by
infringing it we could obtain a direct economic advantage ".[22]
Although the war had made the first breach in our Free
Trade policy with the McKenna Duties which were continued
after it, and although the post-war years produced a mild
imperial preference and the safeguarding of key industries,
in 1927 only 2 to 3 per cent. of British imports were liable
to safeguarding or other protective duties and only one out
of every 200 British workers was employed in safeguarded
industries.[23]   But in 1930 the Manchester Chamber of Commerce and the Economic Committee of the Trade Union
Council both declared for the abandonment of our traditional
policy. In November, 1931, the Abnormal Importations
Bill was passed by the House of Commons in three days and
in February, 1932, the Imports Duties Bill in six.[24]

The former was a temporary measure giving to the President of the Board of Trade power to impose duties to check
an abnormal stream of imports. The latter was the real
foundation of the new Protectionism. It gave Protection to
home industries, provided a basis for preference within the
Empire and for reciprocal agreements with or retaliation
against foreign countries.[25] To a basic 10 per cent. *ad valorem*
tariff on imports the Treasury were empowered to make
additions on the recommendation of an Import Duties
Advisory Committee.[26] In the summer of 1932 the Ottawa
Agreement widely extended the principle of Imperial
Preference. At the World Economic Conference of 1933
the representative of the British Government held that tariffs
might be imposed for revenue, the maintenance of a country's

standard of living, and the encouragement of forms of in-dustry and production regarded as essential to the economic life of a country.[27] The Government was embarked on the difficult task of co-ordinating the threefold policy of Protection to British agriculture, trade agreements with countries in the sterling area, and Imperial Preference.

The regulation of trade thus imposed upon this country by the planning policies of the countries of the world involved also the control of external investments. Before the war 20 per cent. of new capital raised was for home and 80 per cent. for foreign investment. In 1928 the proportions were 60 per cent. and 40 per cent. respectively. After 1931 foreign lending came almost to a standstill. Restrictions were adopted as a deliberate policy. In 1935 of £182 millions raised nearly 89 per cent. were for home, about 9 per cent. for the Empire and less than 2 per cent. for foreign countries. The State was becoming responsible for the deliberate allocation of British capital resources.

In 1907 Campbell-Bannerman could claim that the sea-power of this country implied no challenge to any single State, because of our adherence to the principles of independence for all nations and freedom of trade made our fleet not a threat of violence but a messenger of good will.[28] In 1860 the whole Empire had been thrown open to world trade. In 1897 the British Government withdrew its opposition to the preference policies of those colonies which had full responsible government. Though by 1907 these had all developed a policy of Imperial Preference, the open door was maintained in the colonial empire. In 1917 a Royal Commission on the natural resources, trade and legislation of certain parts of His Majesty's Dominions concluded that it was vital that the Empire should be in a position to resist any pressure which foreign powers might exercise through their control of raw materials and commodities essential to our well-being.[29] In 1919 Great Britain began to grant

U

preferential rates in her tariff for the products both of the Dominions and the Empire and through the Colonial Office to secure preferences for British goods in the non-self-governing colonies and protectorates. By 1936 only in a small part of these was the open door still maintained.[30]   These colonial agreements were among the most successful attempts to expand trade within a given area.   Between 1929 and 1936 the " whole structure of British finance had been transformed ".   Free Trade, no taxation except for revenue, lowering the cost of living by every means; the gold standard, the enormous sinking fund, the strict and punctual discharge of international obligations all had gone.[31]

In 1840 the revenue was about £52 millions, of which almost exactly three-fourths was derived from customs and excise.   Tea, sugar, tobacco, spirits and corn produced two-thirds of this customs revenue.   From 1842 the income tax was developed as an instrument to make the reform of the tariff possible.   In 1853 Gladstone proposed to secure the extinction of the income tax by 1860. But the Crimean War disposed that it should be raised from 7d. to 1s. 4d. in the pound.   It was maintained at 10d. in 1860 in order to secure the revision of the tariff.   In 1865, on the eve of the General Election, it had been reduced to 4d.   In 1874 Gladstone again offered to abolish it.[32]   In 1890 72 per cent. of our national tax revenue was obtained from indirect taxation.[33]   In 1894 the reorganization of Death Duties—the graduation of the main tax according to the amount in the pool and not to sums drawn by particular beneficiaries—gave a great new direct tax comparable to the income tax and yet independent of it.[34]   In 1907 Asquith's Budget differentiated for the first time between earned and unearned income, levying 1s. for the latter and 9d. for the former on those with less than £2,000 a year.[35]   By 1913-14 46 per cent. of our tax revenue was indirect.

A total expenditure of about £50 millions in the 'thirties

had risen to £90 in the 'nineties and to nearly £200 in
1913-14. In 1932-33 expenditure was £859 millions. In
1914 the highest rate of income tax was 1s. 2d. in the £ and
supertax was 1s. 4d. In 1932-33 the figures were 5s. and
8s. 3d. Before the war the richest taxpayer was not called
to pay more than 1s. 8d. of his income to the State; in 1933
he might pay as much as 2s. 3d.[36] Indirect taxation provided about 39.8 per cent. of our national tax revenue.[37]

We have considered first some of the facts which deepened
Government responsibility for currency as the life-blood of
a competitive system and compelled a reversal of its traditional policy of Free Trade. It is possible to argue that the
decline in our exports being due to a change in our favour of
the terms of trade was a matter for congratulation. Our daily
bread could be earned by brows which sweated less. But this
is to ignore the necessity of transferring the resources so
released to the provision of other needs. After the war we
can now see that our task was to transfer our energies to meet
the different character of the external markets and the satisfaction of different domestic needs. But the problem was
difficult and its real character obscure. The political forces
of nationalism, the technological forces of scientific research
and the economic problems inherent in the changing scale of
industrial production presented to the business man uncertainties he had never known and to the State administrative
problems of an entirely new scale.

In the early nineteenth century it had seemed to Malthus
that the root problem of human organization—the flaming
sword that barred the gate of any earthly paradise—was the
tendency of any easing of the task of filling stomachs to
encourage also an increase in their number. Priapus would
always outstrip Ceres. This Malthusian fear was exorcized
by the discovery that the fruit of men's labour and the fruit
of their loins could vary independently. Nature ploughed
by science could be more fertile in goods than was man in his

own image.   But in place of the old problem of subsistence thus resolved a new problem of organization now appeared. Increasing supplies of goods depended upon a division of labour, and the greater the supplies the more various they must be and the more various they were the more subtle the division of labour required.   The assembling of the factors of production began to overshadow all other human problems. Among the factors of production was labour, and so the problems of the organization of the labour market began to overshadow all others.

In this country before the war our labour had been trained and our capital sunk in old industries; our population was clustered at the mines, at the shipyards, or in Lancashire. Our whole industrial life had grown into a mould.[38]   We were specialists in the job of supplying the world with coal, textiles and other manufactured articles.   The supremacy of our shipping was dependent partly on the fact that as great coal exporters we had the economic advantage of possessing a saleable ballast for out-going ships in search of foreign trade. When, after the war, oil and electric power were developed as alternatives to coal, the cotton industry made rapid strides in the Far East, and the shrinking volume of world trade withered the shipyards, the problem of unemployment was most menacing precisely in those industries where our development had been greatest in the past.   From 1923 to 1935, though the number of persons insured in the coal industry had decreased by 22 per cent., the unemployment figure was in the latter year 32 per cent.; in shipbuilding, in spite of a contraction of numbers employed by 40 per cent. unemployment was 42 per cent.; in cotton a shrinkage of 21 per cent. had still left 22.2 per cent. unemployed.[39]

Fundamentally the policy of economic nationalism has been a " protest against interdependence and an attempt to protect group interests in each country from the disturbing effects of external change ".[40]   It has been the policy of trusts and trade unions which could command the powers of the State. This has been stigmatized as " a flight from reality " on the ground " that every improvement in communications makes the interdependence of the world more real ".[41]   But it too would be a flight from reality to ignore the fact that as a consequence of the depression which began in 1929, by 1934 " never before had so many Governments intervened so actively to protect particular producers or to regulate the functioning of the price system ".[42]   The essence of the matters would seem to lie in the fact that to make use of the maximum territorial division of labour would impose on particular groups a flexibility which they may not be prepared to endure.   In the case of the industrial revolution in this country an expanding population and a rising standard of living could only impose on labour the mobility required by such methods as the Combination Acts and the Poor Law Act of 1834.   When the first primitive suppression of combinations had been abandoned the complex legal and political adjustments of the laws relating to Trade Unions had to be worked out.   Even then within this homogeneous community it was found necessary by State action to complete that organization of the labour market which the Trade Unions and employers' organization had only raggedly secured.   It has been necessary to provide for changes in occupation too sudden to be met by individual judgment.   Those who protest against the madness which has driven the world from freedom of trade are ignoring all the forces which in fact do determine industrial and commercial organization.   In this country it is admitted that powerful Trade Unions and price-fixing associations with their multitude of contractual obligations have made the problem of " wage adjustment capable of no obvious solution ".[43] There are wide diversities in the relative position of workers in different industries and occupations.[44]   The heavy fall in world prices imposed a particularly heavy burden on the wage earners in the export industries.[45] There has been since the war a shift in demand from productive activities to services. The numbers of employed in the South has increased 28 per cent. and in the North there has been a decline of 3 per cent. But the proportion of unemployment is four times as great in the North as in the South of England.[46]

The relation of the State to industry since the war has been one of the greatest confusion. Roughly there have been three phases of the discussion and practice: (1) in the first five years after the war discussion was dominated by the influence of the experience of State control during the war and by the naive theories of nationalization and of industrial democracy. It was perhaps not surprising in a country which though it had had no experience of universal suffrage, yet as the traditional home of Parliament should be prepared to consider the possibility of the application of democracy to industry. The tendency was further strengthened by the fact that not only was the country highly industrialized, but that the railways, miners, and transport workers seemed to hold a dominating position while the employers' side was admittedly chaotic, due to the fact that the structure of industry before the war had been individualistic. During the war also the Trade Unions had been taken into partnership with the State in the conduct of the industrial side of the war; further, in the post-war years the leaders of industry were misled by the post-war boom into undertaking unwise expansions. The shipping industry widely miscalculated the demand for shipping just after the war; cotton indulged in an expansion which an elementary knowledge of the facts might have prevented; while the coal industry exploited the temporary post-war shortage in such a way as to hasten the very development of alternative sources of power which were to be its doom. Just as everyone in the war thought of peace as a return to a brighter pre-war world, so everyone engaged in industry thought of the future of industry as being an extension of those developments which had been noticeable before the war. Before the war the Webbs had shown democracy in industry broadening slowly down from precedent to precedent, and it was believed that the democratization of industry would after the war be extended in the way that the franchise had been extended. So for some time the war of pamphlets turned rather on the question whether the new world of order and plenty was to be introduced by persuasion or by a little well-placed violence. The technicians of the strike believed in the mines for the miners, the railways for the railwaymen, and no doubt if pressed would have agreed that cows should belong to cow-men and ganders to geese. The rift in this simple lute of federal harmony appeared with the gradual awakening of the older Trade Unions to the fact that their dominating position was being undermined by economic forces over which their political power gave them no control. It was no use their running up the Jolly Roger of nationalization on an industrial ship which the economic tides had left high and dry. Further, it was gradually realized that the impact of science on industrial structure and the flexibility which the rapid changes in demand imposed required a much more complex organization than most nationalizers could conceive. The clearer-sighted leaders in industry began, not to demand nationalization pure and simple, but appropriate constitutions for industry. And so gradually the dream of nationalization passed into the hope of rationalization. In 1919 the Sankey Commission advocated for the coal industry " either nationalization or a method of unification by national pur-chase ". In 1926 the Samuel Commission condemned nationalization as a " vast and hazardous experiment ", and held that " the variety and freedom of private enterprise was more likely to conduce to the progressive development of this particular industry than control by the State ". But if the bureaucratic reach-me-down of nationalization was found unsuitable for any of our major industries the traditional antagonism before the war to the principle of combination had to be modified. " The individualism of the British character (had) often led the manufacturers to retain personal control over a small and relatively inefficient works, rather than pool his brains and capital to the greatest advantage of the industry."[47] But during the war some industries had to be dealt with as a whole, while after the war the prestige of certain occupations, such as the iron and steel industries, or shipping, or agriculture itself,[48] was to compel the intervention of the State. But the method of that intervention was determined by a series of almost casual emergencies and conditioned by a sound judgment that the varieties of industrial organization must be at least as various as those of the political world. A community which had avoided the straight-jacket of a rigid constitution for its political organization was not likely to impose crippling restraints upon its industrial organization. Nationalization might, as Mr. Tawney wrote, be simply a question of constitution-making, but constitutions were, his countrymen knew, the most kittle cattle in the world.

In 1928 the Liberal Industrial Report demonstrated the " unreal character of the supposed antithesis between Socialism and Individualism ", and suggested that the abuses of private capitalism and unrestricted individualism could be reformed only on the lines already set.[49] In the first place there was " a necessary and important place for the public concern in the national economic system ". These were " undertakings of great national importance which require large amounts of capital yet fail to attract private enterprise on an adequate scale, either because of the necessity of limiting profits or for some other reason ", or they were undertakings " where unavoidable conditions of monopoly would render unregulated private enterprise dangerous, or where the private shareholder had ceased to perform a useful function.[50]

Public concerns consisted of (1) national undertakings operated by the Central Government—the Post Office, the Telegraphs, and the Telephones; the dockyards and manufacturing establishments of the War Department; the Office of Works; the Royal Mint; the Commissioners of Crown Lands; the Stationery Office; the State Management Districts under Licensing Act, 1921; the Roads under the Ministry of Transport; (2) National Undertakings operated by officially appointed *ad hoc* bodies—the British Broadcasting Corporation, the Central Electricity Board and the Forestry Commission; (3) local undertakings operated by the Local Authorities themselves—those public utility undertakings whose growth had been the inspiration of Fabian Socialism; (4) the variety of local undertakings operated by officially appointed *ad hoc* authorities, e.g., the Port of London Authority, the Metropolitan Water Board, the London Passenger Transport Board; (5) companies whose profits are regulated or restricted, e.g., building societies; co-operative societies and parliamentary companies; (6) numerous charitable undertakings not run for profit. Outside these public concerns was the whole world of large-scale business operated by joint stock companies. Of these some had passed out of the effective control of their shareholders, while others were still managed or effectively controlled by their proprietors. Some had attained something of monopoly position, while others were still subject to normal competitive conditions. " Where neither diffused ownership nor monopolistic tendencies were present it was only necessary for the State " to establish an environment in which normal competitive conditions " could flourish with the greatest efficiency and the least possible waste ".[51] Where there was diffused ownership the abuse to be remedied was the inadequacy of the balance-sheet legally required which was " the cause of loss and deception for the investing public by placing a premium on inside information, gossip and breach of confidence ".[52]   " The honest financier spends his time in getting hold of true information to which he is not entitled, and the less honest in spreading false information for which, under cover of general darkness, he can obtain credence."[53] This last judgment was strikingly confirmed by the Mac-millan Report of 1931, which reported that " in general the individual investor can hardly be supposed to have himself knowledge of much value either as to the profitable character or of the security of what he is offered ".   In 1931 the total market value of the £117 millions subscribed for capital issues, whether of shares or debentures, of 284 companies was £66 millions, a loss of over 47 per cent.[54]   They proposed that there should be better publicity by requiring that the information given should be more accurate, that the responsi-bility of the auditors to see that the publicity provision of the revised Company Law was fully satisfied in the letter and in the spirit, and that " the Board of Directors should be subject to the criticism of a supervisory council consisting of members directly representing shareholders and in some cases employees ".[55]   In a word, unless the State were to concern itself in the future much more subtly with the legal forms of competitive industry, the investor, like the unemployed before the establishment of labour exchanges, would remain " a stranger and afraid in a world he never made ".

It was the opinion of the wiser economists that the working of self-interest was " generally beneficial, not because some natural coincidence between the self-interest of each and the good of all, but because human institutions are arranged so as to compel self-interest to work in directions in which it will be beneficial ".[56]   But post-war experience showed that the existing human institutions were not so arranged that the industrial order was compelled to work for even a shadow of the general good.   A feature of modern industrial progress due partly to the effect of scientific discoveries on the scale of the plant which it requires, and partly to the growing complexity of the markets which it serves, is that it proceeds discontinuously in leaps and jumps.[57]   It seemed that neither the search of individual investors for profit nor the powers of the most enlightened bankers could administer the stimulus to reorganization that was so obviously required.[58]   In 1930 the Bankers' Industrial Development Company was established by the efforts of the Governor of the Bank.   It had a capital of £6 millions, of which £1.5 millions was subscribed by the Bank of England and £4.5 millions by the Deposit Banks, Merchant Banks and finance houses. Its Board consisted of six members with the Governor as Chairman.   Its purpose was " to receive and consider schemes for the reorganization and re-equipment of the basic industries of the country when brought forward from within the particular industry and if approved to procure the supply of the necessary financial support for carrying out the scheme ".[59]   But it met with little success.   It was unable to decide whether the provision of aid for one part of an industry might not do harm to the rest.   The official Treasury view was that Government assistance for the reorganization of our basic industries was dangerous.   For while " Government money was available it is not natural to suppose that all the necessary sacrifices would be readily made ".   For rationalization is " a difficult and painful process involving the full recognition of losses, cutting down of creditors' claims, wiping out of whole classes of shareholders ".[60]

In practice the Government was compelled by considerations of policy spasmodically to interfere with the organization of many of our basic industries.   For whatever the limitations and problems of Government control, they were unavoidable so long as the problems of the industries concerned were themselves produced by political activity in the rest of the world.   But the Government's action was necessarily distorted by the political pressure which each industry could bring to bear and by the responsibility for the conditions of any industry which might be laid upon it as a result of Government action in the last war and Government fears for the next. Three industries may be briefly considered: Coal; Iron and Steel; Agriculture.

In the case of coal, the industry was not freed from the abnormal influence of temporary demands and subsidies until 1927.[61] " By reducing the length of the legal working day in 1919 the Government had attracted fresh labour into the industry; by increasing the hours in a period of depression it enlarged the volume of the industry's unemployment. During the post-war boom it permitted coal to be sold at an exorbitant rate to the foreigner, with the result that the development of alternative sources of power was stimulated. In 1925 it adopted the opposite policy of subsidizing the industry so that the foreigner could be provided with coal cheaply at the expense of the taxpayer. In 1930 it proposed to achieve the same end at the expense of the domestic consumer."[62]

The Coal Mines Act of 1930 attempted both an immediate palliative for the partial suppression of competition, and a permanent cure for the evils of the industry by reorganization. For the first Parliament granted wide discretionary powers to a central elected council to arrange district schemes subject to the general supervision of the Board of Trade. For the second a permanent Coal Reorganization Commission was appointed by the Board of Trade, not directly responsible to any Government Department, for the purpose of promoting reorganization by amalgamations, arrived at if possible by permission and if not by coercion. The plans of the Commissions have met with strong opposition from the industry.

During the war extensions of the iron and steel industry were designed for the needs of war and not for the markets of the peace. In consequence we acquired many first-class works, but they were in the wrong place and they were not

balanced for ordinary commercial business.[63] Investigation
revealed that the concentration of heavy steel industry
required to be gradually rebuilt on a national scale with plants
larger than any yet built.[64] While in 1932 the Import
Duties Advisory Committee recommended the imposition of
a temporary duty of $33\frac{1}{3}$ on many classes of iron and steel
the Government extended the operation of the duty until
October, 1934, on the understanding that the industry would
proceed with schemes of rationalization. But the high tariff,
by increasing the industries competitive in the home
market, thereby weakened the previous inducement to
reorganization.[65]

The relation of the State to agriculture reveals in
the most vivid way the pitfalls and the snares that must dog
a Government once it takes, under whatever compulsion, to
the economic road. In the first place agriculture is the
occupation most directly threatened by the advancing
industrial revolution in the world. Agriculture is the
occupation of two-thirds of mankind and the application of
science to its methods will involve the greatest displacement
of labour in the history of the world. Secondly, because it
is the occupation of the great majority of the world's workers
it occupies in most political systems a preponderating influence
in the councils of the State. Thirdly, in this country its
position is peculiar and complex; as we were the first
industrial country in the world, agriculture occupies a position
less politically powerful than in any other first-class power,
and as we are strategically no longer an island, the
wisdom of accepting its comparative subordination has been
questioned. Agriculture is a fine example of the possible
conflict between the interests of the national groups and the
interests of the world considered as a whole.

In this country before the war the agricultural industry
had lost its natural leaders. In the nineteenth century down
to the depression of the 'nineties farm relief had been supplied

by the land-owning class.   But that depression wiped them out as an economic and political power and the actual control of British agricultural production had passed almost entirely to the farmers themselves.[66]   The system was one midway between the peasant system of the Continent and large-scale capitalist undertakings for plantation crops.   Investigation prompted by the needs of war suggested it would be possible to organize the industry to feed half instead of one-third of our population.

The essential figure was that 28,000,000 acres would under any circumstances be under grass, and 12,000,000 acres under crops, but there was a margin of 6,000,000 which by subsidy or protection could be turned from grass to crops.   But this simple analysis was complicated by fact that the natural field for development of British agriculture—war apart—was in livestock, dairying, poultry, fruit, flowers and vegetables.[76] Even in the corn-growing area of East Anglia the sale of livestock and livestock produce amounted to 68 per cent. of the total.[68]   If the economic advantage of the development of the livestock industry were sacrificed to the strategic need for crops, one-half of the food supply would still depend upon our ability to pay for it abroad and to protect the routes by which it must be carried.

In these circumstances it is not surprising that the agricultural policy of the Government has since the war been most haphazard.   There have been, of course, many reasonable extensions of Government action to secure increased efficiency. Plant and animal diseases have been controlled; education and research provided; special credit facilities provided which the preoccupation of the banks with foreign trade and investment before the war had failed to provide.   But there have also been confused and conflicting policies of protection and subsidy.   In 1924 the sugar beet industry was started and has been artificially stimulated ever since.   In ten years it received £39,500,000 and in 1934 employed 32,000.[69]   In 1932 the Wheat Act provided a guaranteed price for a specified quantity of wheat grown in the United Kingdom. The amount paid in 1934 was £4.5 millions. In the same year £1.5 millions was paid to milk and £3 millions to beef.[70] The methods have included "quantitative regulation, subsidies, levies, guaranteed prices, tariffs, and marketing schemes ".[71] In 1933 the Marketing Act associated internal marketing arrangements with the regulation of imports by quotas. As a result of the adoption of a policy of Imperial Preference the percentage of her food supplies imported from Empire countries has increased from 38 per cent. to 50 per cent.[72] But while Empire self-sufficiency in most foodstuffs is possible, it would deprive British manufacturing industries of large markets in foreign countries and would prevent them from meeting their obligations on British investments.[73]

It is not surprising that to many we seem to be wandering between two worlds, the one not dead but senile, the other monstrous but not stillborn. On the one hand the Government has had to provide a far more subtle legal framework for the working of competitive industry than the nineteenth century could have foreseen; on the other the conflict between industrialism and nationalism has compelled a direct intervention of the State in regions Cobden hoped it would never know. The form of State intervention in industry has been determined by the particular emergencies and the political forces which in each prevailed. There is a mighty maze and still without a plan. It is, of course, the argument of *laissez-faire* that this monstrous institutional complexity will in the long run exact a far heavier price than would be the simple conflicts of competitive industry. With the State no longer umpire, but combatant and judge, where is justice to be found in Israel?

However this may be we must observe that in its treatment of those social aspects of the industrial order which most would admit to belong to the sphere of Government the same conflict of principles and administrative complexity is to be found. Let us glance briefly at State action in relation (1) to the standard of living; (2) the provision of services which it is generally agreed require collective action.

(1) At the end of the last century the enquiries of Booth (London, 1894) and Rowntree (York, 1899) revealed the startling probability that from 25 to 30 per cent. of the town population of the United Kingdom were living in poverty.[74] Of this poverty bad habits accounted for only 13 per cent., unfortunate circumstances for 19 per cent., and about 68 per cent. was due to the inadequacy and irregularity of the wages paid. Since then the increasing productivity of industry, the organization of the unskilled into Trade Unions, and the supervision of the unorganized by the State through Trade Boards has reduced the percentage of poverty to about 11 per cent. and of this poverty less than one in five is due to the insufficiency of the wages paid. Unemployment and not the insufficiency of wages is now the major cause of poverty.[75] On the eve of war real income per head had not shown for some years any tendency either to increase or to decline. The effect of the war was to increase the earnings of the unskilled as compared with the skilled and of the worker in sheltered industries as compared with those in unsheltered. It is difficult to estimate the real earnings of any class of worker, because the direction of his expenditure has been greatly changed. It has, however, been estimated that wage earners as a whole have, in spite of the heavy increase in unemployment, secured substantially enhanced real earnings per head during the last ten years.[76] At the same time expenditure on the social services has risen from £100 millions to £400 millions between the periods 1909-14 and 1932-35. The ratio of expenditure on social services to ages it is estimated has risen from 3.4 per cent. in 1880 to 10.4 per cent. in 1913 and about 18 per cent. in 1930.[77]

But the action of the State in relation to the standard of

living has been marked by a confusion and a war of principles. In the case of Workmen's Compensation it was decided that the employer should be held responsible for all accidents, whether they were due to his negligence or to acts of God.[78] This may have been justified by the administrative impossibility of discriminating between the accidents due to negligence and those due to unforeseeable circumstances. But the result was that the employer insured himself against liability, thus freeing himself from any incentive to initiate or to introduce safety measures, while the worker had no guarantee that he would get anything at all from an employer who had failed to insure.[79] The desire to distinguish Unemployment Insurance Benefit from Public Assistance led to family needs having no place in the original benefits decided. But the character of post-war unemployment compelled the introduction of family allowances first as a temporary expedient and then as an essential part of the system.[80] The National Health Insurance scheme made no provision for family needs, so that a man unemployed through inability to find work will find his family needs taken into account, but if his unemployment is due to sickness they will not.[81] The most notorious of these confusions was that the legally deterrent Poor Law was by pressure of circumstances compelled to provide a variety of preventative and curative services which overlapped with others provided for men and women who were not paupers.

The administrative chaos which can be produced by the pressure of unforeseen emergencies upon schemes born of confused principles is shown by the fate of the Unemployment Insurance scheme since the war. Compulsory Unemployment Insurance could be justified by the fact that while a risk might be overwhelming and impossible to estimate by an individual worker or a particular industry, it might be measurable when considered from a collective standpoint.[82] While unemployment due to personal qualities and defects

v

could not be foreseen unemployment due to industrial fluctuations could. So the initial scheme of 1911 developed by a brilliant group of civil servants was limited to a particular group of industries—building, constructions of works, shipbuilding, engineering—which were thought suitable because, while they were liable to fluctuations they were not likely to decay. It was compulsory to avoid the predominance of bad risks; required a definite relation between contributions paid and benefits received in order automatically to exclude bad risks; made the State a contributor so that it might provide stability and exercise the necessary controls. Its framers knew that fire insurance would fail if there were no protection against arson. But the extension of the scheme to the greater part of the field of industrial employment in 1920 led to the abandonment of nearly every principle which a sound insurance scheme must observe.

The original scheme had been intended to provide specific benefits to meet a measurable risk. The benefits provided were not supposed to meet every need of those who drew them. The scheme assumed a normal working of the labour market. It could not meet the needs of those who were unemployed because a series of industrial and political revolutions had devastated our economic system. With the extension of the scheme to cover nearly the whole of industry it was found first that the benefits legally due in accordance with the contributions made would not save those who were unemployed through decay of their industries from the Poor Law. But as soon as benefits were given beyond the amounts actuarially due the whole insurance character of the system was imperilled. Actually it became a system of Public Assistance for those who were considered to be available for work. It was a system of outdoor relief for the able-bodied poor. This was fair neither to the unemployed themselves nor to the community as a whole. What was required was that an insurance scheme should cover certain calculable risks of normal industrial fluctuations; that those who were displaced from industry permanently because of the decay of the industries in which they had been employed should be trained for new occupations; while those, if any, who were not capable of benefiting from the training offered should be regenerated by whatever health, educational or disciplinary measures which were necessary. The adoption of the principle of " work or maintenance " involves the acceptance of compulsory allocation of jobs. But a free labour market can be organized if Labour Exchanges provide the conditions of a market, compulsory insurance gives protection against calculable risks, and if an authority for the able-bodied poor provides that maintenance and education of which the need by any individual or group cannot be foreseen because it is the result of revolutions in industry which no one can foretell.

(2) In the case of those social services which in the nineteenth century were clearly recognized to be within the scope of Government action there has been added to the difficulty of conflicting principles the confusions of a legal and administrative system needlessly complicated. In the case of education the question of the age to which the State should provide that its future citizens must be educated has been complicated by the mazes of the local educational administrative scheme. The Education Act of 1902, while it provided that in those towns which were County Boroughs the direction of whatever public education was provided should be under a single authority, divided the responsibility in the counties between the county council and the municipal boroughs and urban districts. The former it made responsible for secondary education in all their area, but elementary education it was to control only where the latter were not themselves the authority. As these elementary educational authorities are responsible for a large number of post-primary schools whose work overlaps and conflicts with the post-primary and secondary education for which the county is responsible, the

Director of Education of the county may have a task beyond the wit of man. He may have to adjust his system to the diverse elementary and post-primary schemes of thirteen different authorities.[83] The administrative organization which was determined by the balance of power, administrative, financial and sectarian, in 1902, has been a handicap to educational reform. The fundamental reform proposed by the Hadow Report of 1926, that post-primary education, i.e., education after the age of eleven, should be systematically organized to meet the needs of adolescence has been hampered not only by the inability of the electorate to realize that it should be their privilege to train those who must come after them, so that the school-leaving age is not yet raised to fifteen, but also by the confusion of educational authorities inherited from 1902. In Public Health, after a generation of talk, the confusions laid bare by the report of the Poor Law Commission of 1904-9 was removed in 1929. The counties and county boroughs of England and Wales can now operate the health services once provided by the Boards of Guardians for the sick poor and are in a position to provide skilled institutional treatment for all classes of the population. Only in London, however, have the possibilities of the new system been fully realized. There the transfer of the Poor Law Institutions to the London County Council has made possible a clearly marked division between the field of local action concerned with the detection of disease and the local measures necessary for its prevention. Here again, as with education, the inspiration which the advance of knowledge has provided has been cribbed, cabined and confined by the administrative anomalies Parliament cannot find time or temper to remove. Not until 1929 was a serious attempt made to deal with the fantastic inappropriateness of the smaller urban districts for their duties as a health authority. The unified control of all health services under a single County Medical Officer of Health has not yet been secured.[84]

Finally, the organization of the police force provides an interesting example of that Bumbledom which breeds eternal in the English breast. " The local authorities upon whom it was originally necessary to force a police system have come to regard their government as a privilege which ought not to be taken away or modified."[85]   A Department Committee on the Police Service in 1919-20 recommended that all non-county borough forces should be merged in the county. This would seem common sanity, for in a small police force, experience, specialization, and freedom from patronage are impossible.   Inspector Frenchs cannot be trained at Bridling-ton-in-the-Mud.   Efficient policemen must not only be stronger than lions but swifter than eagles.   But such speed and strength come only from modern equipment and the power of concentration and dispersion which it gives.   One day the force must patrol a distant racecourse, another control a busy fair, and all the time watch malefactors as they fly.   For this it had been estimated in 1919 that 100,000 population is the minimum size of a borough which should claim a separate police force.   In 1932 the Home Office proposed that all forces in boroughs with populations under 75,000 should be merged.   But there are still twenty-six boroughs with under 30,000 which have separate forces.[86]

[1] Minutes of Evidence to Committee on Finance and Industry, 1931, Cmd. 3897, Qu. 6673.
[2] Sir W. T. Layton : Economic Situation of Great Britain, 1931, pp. 6–7.
[3] Fayle : The War and the Shipping Industry, p. 6.
[3] Layton, op. cit., p. 15.
[4] Evidence Cmd. 3897, Niemeyer Qu. 6818.
[5] Cmd. 3897, p. 4, para. 7.
[6] A. C. Pigou and Colin Clark : Economic Position of Great Britain, p. 34.
[7] D. H. Macgregor, p. 94.
[8] League of Nations : World Economic Survey, 1934–5, p. 66.
[9] Cmd. 3897, p. 116.
[10] League of Nations, World Economic Survey, 1934–5, pp. 65-6.
[11] Cmd. 3897, p. 92.
[12] Cmd. 3897 Minutes of Evidence, Qu. 3.
[13] ibid., Qu. 95.
[14] ibid., Qu. 120.
[15] J. H. Richardson : British Economic Foreign Policy, p. 33.

[16] Sir B. Mallet : *British Budgets*, 3rd Series, p. 267, citing Horne's Budget, 1929.
[17] J. H. Richardson, *op. cit.*, p. 36.
[18] ibid., citing Chamberlain, House of Commons, Dec. 21st, 1934.
[19] ibid., pp. 44–50.
[20] Cmd. 3897, p. 7.
[21] Cmd. 3897, p. 48.
[22] Quoted J. H. Richardson, *op. cit.*, p. 20.
[23] J. H. Richardson, *op. cit.*, p. 22.
[24] ibid.
[25] ibid., pp. 94–5.
[26] ibid., p. 100.
[27] ibid., p. 100.
[28] J. A. Spender : *Life of Campbell Bannerman*, Vol. 2, p. 330.
[29] Cd. 8462.
[30] S. H. Bailey ; article, *Economica* 1932. *Political Aspects of Discrimination in International Economic Relations.*
[31] Churchill, House of Commons, 23rd April, 1936.
[32] Ward : *Reign of Queen Victoria*, Vol. 1, pp. 331–49.
[33] Gertrude Williams : *The State and the Standard of Living*, p. 335.
[34] Ensor : *England 1870–1914*, p. 217.
[35] ibid., p. 396.
[36] F. Hirst, *Consequences of the War*, p. 235.
[37] Gertrude Williams, op. cit., p. 335.
[38] Sir W. T. Layton : *Economic Situation of Great Britain*.
[39] Pigou and Clark, *op. cit.*, Tables, pp. 14–15.
[40] League of Nations *Economic Survey* 1934–5, p. 192.
[41] ibid., p. 92.
[42] ibid., pp. 65–6.
[43] G. C. Allen : *British Industries*, 2nd edition, pp. 283–5.
[44] Pigou and Clark, *op. cit.*, Tables, pp. 14–15.
[45] ibid.
[46] Ministry of Labour Report, 1936.
[47] Committee of 1917.
[48] D. H. Macgregor : *Enterprise, Purpose and Profit*, pp. 49–55 for analysis of causes of State control.
[49] *Britain's Industrial Future* (report of the Liberal Industrial Enquiry), p. 75.
[50] p. 75.
[51] p. 85.
[52] ibid., p. 85.
[53] ibid., p. 85.
[54] Cmd. 3897, p. 166.
[55] *Britain's Industrial Future*, p. 91.
[56] Cannan : cited Gertrude Williams : *The State and the Standard of Living*, p. 321.
[57] D. H. Robertson in Minutes of Evidence to Cmd. 3897, Vol. 1, p. 323.
[58] ibid.
[59] ibid., Qu. 9029–36.
[60] ibid., Hopkins Qu. 5690.
[61] G. C. Allen : *British Industries*, p. 35.
[62] ibid., p. 45.
[63] Layton : *Economic Situation of Great Britain*, p. 21.
[64] H. S. Jevons : *British Steel Industry*, p. 25.
[65] ibid., p. 29 and cf. Allen, op. cit., p. 132.
[66] Astor and Murray, p. 11.
[67] A Salter, p. IX of Introduction to Astor and Murray.
[68] *World Agricultural Report* of 1935.
[69] League of Nations *Survey of Economic Conditions* 1934–5, p. 86.
[70] Midland Bank Monthly Review, Aug.–Sept., 1934.

[71] J. H. Richardson, op. cit., p. 188.
[72] ibid., p. 197.
[73] ibid., p. 197.
[74] Gertrude Williams : *State and the Standard of Living*, p. 47.
[75] ibid.
[76] ibid.
[77] ibid., p. 334.
[78] ibid., p. 317.
[79] ibid.
[80] ibid., pp. 319-20.
[81] ibid., pp. 319-20.
[82] ibid., p. 238.
[83] Robson : *Development of Local Government*, pp. 65-7.
[84] Cmd. 4978, pp. 95-6.
[85] *Century of Municipal Progress*, Dr. Finer at p. 284.
[86] ibid., p. 286.

CHAPTER IX

GOVERNMENT AND PARTIES SINCE 1918

The Constitution in the Post-War World—The New Franchise and the character of Post-War Elections—The nature of the Party System—The Labour Party—The Liberals—The Conservatives—The transformation of the Cabinet—The position of the Prime Minister—The Work of Parliament.

IN 1914 the English system of government, in spite of many parochial and insular peculiarities, still seemed to be a model for the world. It was not formally so complete a democracy as those of Scandinavia, Switzerland, France or the United States. Its machinery of administration and of justice was hampered by a long and tenacious past. But it had secured a harmony of order with liberty which promised much for a world on the eve of revolutions in industrial organization such as those which had made England what she was. It had gone far to solve the problem of reconciling democracy with the technique of imperial administration which the clash of cultures brought by a shrinking world would require. To those who believe in progress it was easy to imagine that the English system of government was a state of political development which other less favoured States would one day reach.

At the time of writing we may be fairly sure that whatever value for the world the English system of government may yet have it is not going to be the glass of fashion and the mould of form for the twentieth century. There may yet be a Prussian Napoleon, a

Russian Augustus, a Japanese Louis XIV, but the world will never see a Prussian Gladstone, a Russian Disraeli or a Japanese Victoria.   Nor does the American variant of the English model seem to be in favour.   Certainly the Fathers of a European Constitution have not yet been born.

It is important to consider how much of the English Constitution has survived into the post-war world and how far it has and can be adjusted to the task imposed by the changing world.

The mark of the machine is now on every human activity. Government will have to achieve something of the speed and the precision of the factory. How far this can be done and at the same time secure a way of life worth living is not yet known. But many political and social forms cherished by the nineteenth century including the minimising of bureaucracy will have to be abandoned.   It may be that a Continental or even a world order may emerge leaving to national Governments only a parochial significance.   But as a Federal world Government would be loose for many decades, the spirit and the form of national systems would still have value.   It is possible that imperialism will have its way and that the only form of Government open to England will be to become part of a British Commonwealth of Nations.   It is possible also that the English people may not find it possible to keep their imperial heritage.   Finally, it may be that with the breakdown of the economic order of the nineteenth century the Soviet or the Fascist form of Government will become common.   Even if that were so it is still to be expected that the spirit of the Constitution, the technique, the style of our political artists would survive.

The essential change in the English political system since 1914 might be described as a transition from the spirit of the amateur to the spirit of the professional.   Amateurism in the nineteenth century pervaded the whole of English life. Her industrial expansion was the expression of a vigorous amateurism, as had been the agricultural revolution which preceded it, and the scientific work which had made them possible. In the structure of her Government, in the framing of her machinery of administration, even in the provision of her courts of justice, the spirit of the amateur was everywhere to be found. Amateurism in business is disappearing. In politics the same process can be seen. We have now to do by deliberation and by plan what was once done by occasional genius or the general common sense. Our corporate life, once begot by idiosyncrasy on custom, has now to be sustained by complex planning. J. S. Mill's plea for liberty has been denied.

It was some time after the war before it was realized that it was not a brave but a new world passing strange to which our political life would have to be conformed. No longer as in the early nineteenth century was it simply a question of releasing the natural man from the spell of privilege which bound him. It was the far more arduous task of extending into the sphere of politics the system and the thought which science had already imposed upon business and the home. In Poor Law, public health, education, great administrative machines had had to be created. During the war the machinery of Government had been transformed. After the war it was clear that this reorganization would have to be extended into every detail of the State—to the Cabinet, to Parliament, and to the Crown itself. Whether or not there was a formal written Constitution, a Constitution there had to be. The rule of the wise men of the tribe would not be enough. Tradition had to be codified. There was an enormous field of technical administrative work to be developed. We had passed from the brilliant vision of the *Republic* to the tough technicalities of the *Laws*. Now that religion had decayed, the simple rationalism of Bentham had to be developed for a world less stable and more violent.

In anticipation of the problems of peace a Speaker's conference had been appointed in 1917 to revise the electoral system. The war-time unity of parties made it impossible for the House of Lords to prevent a settlement of controversies which had embittered politics for generations. By the Representation of the Peoples Act, 1918, the franchise was extended to all adult males and to women who were at least thirty years old. A provision that no person might vote at an election for more than two constituences on different qualifications ended the major abuses of plural voting. The procedure of registration was greatly simplified by making the ordinary qualification six months' residence. So simple and automatic was the procedure of registration that fraud or the expenditure of party funds for the manipulation of the register was useless. All elections were to take place on one day. Returning Officers' expenses were to be paid by the Exchequer. Candidates were to be required to make a deposit of £150, to be forfeited if they did not poll more than one-eighth of the votes cast. The country was divided into single-member constituencies of approximately 50,000 voters each.

What has been the effect of this simplification and extension of the suffrage? In discussing any representative system two faults must be avoided. We must be careful not to underestimate the stability and the underlying rationality of the existing order. We must be careful also not to ignore the underlying forces of which the cumulative effects will suddenly produce a startling change. It is not the vagaries and occasional hysteria of the public mind on particular occasions that is important, but the basic changes in its habits and belief due, not merely to the experience of particular individuals, but also to changes in the actual composition of the community. Births and deaths may have more effect

on the strength of the parties than anything else. The
following table gives the outstanding facts of the post-war
Elections: —

	Percentage of votes.			Number of seats.		
	Cons.	Lab.	Lib.	Cons.	Lab.	Lib.
1922 ...	38	30	30	347	142	114
1923 ...	38	30	30	258	191	159
1924 ...	48	33	18	420	151	40
1929 ...	38	36	25	260	287	59
1931 ...	50	33	15	471	52	33
1935 ...	50	40	7	387	154	17

The table shows the astonishing uncertainty of the relation of votes cast and seats won. This is due to the English
system of single members of constituencies. The existence of
three parties contesting nearly every constituency means the
return of many members by only a minority of their electorates. There have been as many as 313 such minority
candidates in a single Parliament. At one time the dis-
appearance of the Liberal Party would have affected half the
membership of the House of Commons. There has been
a surprising incapacity on the part of the experts to foretell
the result of any particular election. It is possible for a
major party almost to be destroyed by a comparatively small
shift of votes. The elector tends to vote against the leaders
of the party which is out of favour in a particular crisis and
for any puppet of the popular cause. In 1918 it rejected
Asquith and Simon and returned Bottomley and Pemberton
Billing. In 1931 it rejected every leader of the Labour
Opposition.

What was the effect of this new distribution of power?
While it is impossible to interpret a single election, as the
elements of contingency are so many, it is possible over nearly
two decades to analyse certain tendencies. Before the war
the Liberal Party was strongest in the great industrial areas;
in poor agricultural areas; and in those agricultural areas

where there were smallholders with memories of the en-
closure movement, e.g., in the Fenlands and in Norfolk and
Suffolk.   Discrimination in the past against Nonconformity
had given Wales and Scotland to Liberalism.   Conservatism
was strongest in the rich agricultural counties: Surrey,
Sussex, Hereford and the agricultural parts of Kent.   The
system of plural voting by which a man had only to maintain a legal lodging or pay £10 for lodgings to secure a vote,
which the leisurely elections enabled him to exercise, secured
to the Conservatives the business and warehouse districts of
the boroughs.   The Labour Party was of course strongest
in the great industrial areas.

Since the war the Labour Party has naturally captured
the great industrial areas; established an overwhelming
superiority in the mining areas of Wales, Scotland and
England; shaken the Conservative hold in dockyard constituencies such as Southampton, Plymouth, Portsmouth and
Sunderland.   In 1929, of 330 seats of an industrial character
only fifty were not Labour, while the spread of industry
into suburbia had caused the fall of Acton and Romford.
But it could not shake the Conservative hold in the rich
agricultural areas.   For in agricultural areas it cannot use
its technique of door-to-door propaganda, nor has it the prestige of the great Unions.   More fundamentally, while agriculturalists may be Liberal as opposed to parson and squire,
the collectivist sort of Trade Unionism is incomprehensible
to them, and the beam of privilege more obvious in the eye
of industry than the spark of justice.

In 1929 the Liberals still held Bedford, Cornwall, Devon
and East Anglia, areas with a strong Nonconformist tradition,
but only a fraction of Scotland and the Highlands.   In the
election of 1929 the figures suggest that in the boroughs the
bulk of the new women electors had supported Labour and
in the counties the Liberals.   In 1935 Labour did well in
the mining districts and in London, which between them

provided one-third of the Labour representation. But it did badly in the Midlands (especially in Birmingham), Lancashire and in the distressed areas (except mining). While it advanced in the counties even more than in the towns, running in the West Country second to Liberalism, it made no serious impression on the Home Counties, coastal towns or University seats.

In the nineteenth century a political campaign was leisurely conducted by an army of professional voters and a cloud of amateur witnesses. The function of the statesmen was to hold the balance between the forces of opinion and the result of the election. Elections were in the nature of an ordeal by battle to determine issues derived from public opinion interpreted by political leaders. The turnover was very small. Luck gave an edge to the pleasure of contending skill. A party was a federation of diverse local interests held in some political unity by a leader who embodied principles. However the ideal might be smirched by bribery the representative was considered to express the interests of his locality. So long as the different interests were geographically distinct a system of single-member constituencies would produce a workable House of Commons providing that there was a will to agree to differ among them. With increasing unification of the country it was inevitable that it should come to be considered almost as a single constituency. Instead of a struggle in different localities to secure their support, elections became a struggle to secure the support of the whole country. Horizontal cleavages were substituted for geographical diversities. A small shift of votes could destroy a party. Paradoxically, whereas a diversity of interests had compelled attention to principles, out of a conflict of principles expressed by national parties violence is threatened.

The bargaining of groups depends upon an underlying unity, but when that unity itself is thought to be threatened it is for it, and not for their difference, that people vote.

The two-party system in a democracy is an expression of diversity in unity; but when that unity is itself threatened the party system may break down.   There is at the present time an increasing tendency for men of good will to draw up programmes upon which all members of the community may be supposed to agree.   There is intellectually and psychologically a centre party.   The old party system embodied a diversity of interests unified by a belief in argument.   Parliament was the village pub or meeting house writ large.   But argument was then important for the issues to be considered. Now the questions to be decided require the laboratory and the bureau of research.   The life of States lies not merely in debate but also in research.

In democracy politics is one profession among many.   Because of the peculiar conditions which determine admission, and the oddities of fortune which decide success, those who succeed may have no quality of leadership.   And the world is so unstable a place that the leader suitable in one decade is hopeless for another.   We must be prepared for a greater variety in our leaders.   It might be better to give more power to our rulers and to change them more often.   It is possible that the American Presidential system with its definite periodicity and concentration of power is better than the European Cabinet based on party groups.   In England a heavy responsibility lies upon the Cabinet when it determines the date and the occasion of the election.   For not only may it cause the destruction of itself, but it may do even more damage by destroying the Opposition.

A professional organizer[1] has described the new developments.   There must be no question of regarding political opponents as persons to be pacified or even to be met halfway.   The spirit sought by a good committee is fatal to electoral success.   " To regard the Opposition as merely mistaken in its ideas and not as deliberately dangerous, is wholly subversive of the will to win."[2]

There is a definite political strategy, observance of which will give a chance of success. The party should not rely on its record but endeavour to create a new situation in which it can overwhelm the Opposition. The failure of Disraeli in 1878 to go to the country after the Congress of Berlin led to his defeat in 1880. In 1900 Chamberlain secured for the Conservative Party a new tenure of power by forcing the Khaki Election. The most successful campaigns have been destructive offences, such as Mr. Lloyd George's campaign against the Peers in 1910 and the blasting by Mr. Snowden's broadcasting of his former colleagues in 1931. If possible a party should secure the initiative, present a programme of little detail, and repeat often a clear and plain tale or lie. The constructive offensive is possible but difficult. It requires careful preparation and constant watchfulness. The least hopeful is the defensive retrospective such as that of the Conservative Government in 1929.

The power of propaganda is the result of a specialization in our lives which has made those things which are our immediate interest no clue to those which indirectly will determine our future fate. The energies of man are involved in immediate tasks of thought or action, which give no clue to the nature of the whole of which they are a part. It is not merely that the propagandist produces a pseudo environment to secure action to his advantage, but it is the more radical question that if the propagandist did not make one for us we should have no environment at all. It is extremely unlikely that anyone could make himself a citizen of the twentieth-century world as he might have made himself a citizen of the eighteenth. General education for most people must stop at adolescence and it is replaced by a technique of persuasion organized for profit. The advertisers are the sophists of the modern world. But the alternative to them is that people should educate themselves or that they should accept guidance from those competent to guide. But in the present world those most competent to guide are required for the discovery of still wider worlds. Philosophers cannot be kings, because they are pre-occupied with that search for truth which is disintegrating every habit and custom of political societies. It becomes therefore possible for the sophist advertiser or dictator to give the uniformity necessary to life because the powers of mind are committed to the service of science.

In England the political resources of the parties were many. They possessed in common: (1) the advantage of the political education of war: this had the disadvantage that it had been regarded as a preface to a pre-war peace, when it should have been considered as the prologue to a strange new world; (2) that the youth of this country had been less educated than those of any other first-class power and that their education could now be commenced without the burden of a pernicious tradition; (3) there was an absence of virulent internal problems which might cause fear to cast out thought; (4) in an inarticulate way there was a deep understanding of the nature of industrial society. How else could the problem of Unemployment Insurance have been dealt with without disaster? Admit that the community was drugged that it might suffer its wounds in silence; at least it knew that it was drugged and that the drugs might hasten the recovery. In other States, where the problem was not so clearly understood, not drugging but stunning would have been the remedy chosen. Here the worker was wise in his industrial environment as the peasant elsewhere is in his. But the parties also differed widely. Here it must be noticed that there is a peculiar paradox about the two-party system. Each party feels that it could convert the whole community. Each party claims to represent the whole community. This is the essential advantage of the two-party system as compared with a system of groups. For though in theory where there is a group system unity will be secured by the arbitrament of reason between them, in practice reason will give place to

w

barter.   In a two-party system it is possible for a community to adapt itself by trial and error to a changing world.   In so far as industrialism was incompatible with individualism; in so far as planning was implicit in industrialism; in so far as the application of science to industry suggested that it was worth while to call for an attack on the problem of scarcity which would require the sacrifice of freedom for longer than was required in war, the Labour Party was raising issues which would involve all the intellectual and moral resources of the nation.   On the other side the Conservative Party was concerned to emphasize that whatever adjustment might be devised would have to take place in diverse national centres.   Labour was for planning.   Both Labour and Conservative, as against the Liberal, said that reason was not enough.   While the Conservative as against Labour was concerned to show that the plan must be national.

Until 1918 the Labour Party was a federation of Trade Union, Socialist Societies (like the Independent Labour Party and the Fabians), Local Trades Councils and Co-operative Society.   In 1918 its basis of membership was widened to include individual men and women who subscribed to its constitution and programme.   At the same time its basis became definitely Socialist.   The Trade Unions that were its main strength had been converted by the war to a belief in the possibility of a Socialist society, while the ordinary man and woman was prepared to attempt the remaking of society.   The party became a great political organization with Local Labour Parties in most constituencies and with a constitution and machinery carefully adapted to the new conditions of universal suffrage.   The Labour Party Conference of 1918 adopted a comprehensive programme drawn up in 1917, mainly by Mr. Sidney Webb, called *Labour and the New Social Order*.   In it the war was described as " the culmination and collapse of a distinctive industrial civilization, which the workers will not seek to reconstruct ".   It hoped that the individual system of private enterprise had received a deathblow. It would be the duty of Government now to secure to every member of the community all the requisites of healthy life and worthy citizenship. Unemployment was to be systematically and deliberately prevented. Economic wars, secret diplomacy, the formation of alliances, and the exploitation of subject people were to end. This programme served as a rallying-ground for all the idealism of the post-war world and secured the support necessary for some far-reaching reforms in the social services. But the party was divided between those who thought that Trade Union pressure would hasten the reform, and those who felt that constitutionalism must at all costs be preserved. In 1924 the Labour Party Conference excluded Communists from the party. In 1925 while the Trade Union Congress paid hearty attention to Pollitt and gave scant attention to Clynes and Thomas, the Labour Party Conference was dominated by the right. After the General Strike of 1926 the Labour Party Conference of 1927 showed a clear division between its executive's concern for the election and the left wing concern for the millennium. The former won all along the line. In 1928 a fresh programme *Labour and The Nation* was adopted at Birmingham. This was clearly the Socialism of MacDonald and not the Socialism of Marx. The Labour Party was described as, not " the agent of this class or that, but as the political organ created to express the need and voice the aspiration of all who share the Labour of mankind ". Its policy was one of peaceful transition " without disorder or confusion with the consent of the majority of the electors and by the use of the ordinary machinery of democratic government ". The Labour Party had in fact become a party appealing to the whole nation and not to a particular class. The I.L.P. which in the past had supplied the intellectual yeast that had leavened the Trade Union mass with Socialism, began to meet with opposition from the Trade Unions and the Parliamentary Party. In 1930 MacDonald severed his connection with the I.L.P. because of their policy of revolt. Mr. Snowden gave as his reason for resigning that " The I.L.P. as a separate body had served its purpose. . . . The Labour Party since it admitted individual membership and adopted a definite Socialist basis, adequately fulfilled all the purposes for which the I.L.P. originally existed ".

The leaders of the Labour Party held that being pledged to introduce the Socialist State within the framework of democracy it must adjust itself to the conditions of democracy as it finds them. It must do all that it could to secure a control of that superb instrument of Government, the Cabinet. After the collapse of 1931 the left wing of the Labour Party developed a movement to commit the Labour Party on assuming office, with or without power, to the promulgation of definite Socialist legislation. In 1934 the Socialist League, a newly-formed militant organization within the Labour Party, declared that their objectives were the same as the Labour Party, but differed widely from the Trade Union movement as to the methods to be adopted. Neither history nor common sense, said Sir Stafford Cripps, gave any support to the theory of gradualism. They were anxious as far as they could to create the temper for action in office. At the Labour Party Conference in 1934 their opposition to both Communism and dictatorship effected a reconciliation between Sir Stafford Cripps and the executive of the Labour Party. In 1933 the Trade Union Council had issued a manifesto that if the British working class hesitates now between majority and minority rule, and toy with the idea of dictatorship, Fascist or Communist, they will go to servitude such as they have never suffered.

The organization of the Labour Party is tripartite. There is first the Annual Conference of the Party of some 900 delegates from the Trade Unions, affiliated Socialist Societies and Local Labour Parties. This Conference elects the national party executive, which is the controlling body. No member of the General Council of the Trade Union Congress is eligible for membership of this executive council, but twelve of the twenty-three members of the executive council represent Trade Unions. The Trade Union Congress is the second part of the organization. The third is a Parliamentary Party, consisting of all Labour Members of Parliament. There is a National Joint Council representing the General Council of the Trade Union Congress, the National Executive of the Labour Party, and the Executive of the Parliamentary Labour Party. This organization is intricate but effective. The Parliamentary Labour Party decides all questions of immediate tactics in the House. When out of office they elect an executive committee to deal with party business, when in office they elect a consultative committee to confer with the Ministers. A Labour Cabinet in consultation with this committee will decide all Parliamentary issues, but on questions effecting basic principles of the party the National Joint Council would have a decisive force. Any bargain of the Labour Party with another in the constituencies would require the sanction of the National Executive.

The control of the Annual Conference and the National Committee over the party organization is very close. It determines the party basis and organization. In 1929 at the Annual Conference the proposal that there should be a class of National Associates enrolled directly by headquarters was rejected, because it was feared that persons might join the party whose only interest was in its political prospect. To secure better discipline it was laid down that affiliated organizations must accept the programme, principles and policy of the party, agree to conform to the constitution and standing orders and submit its political rules to the National Executive. Headquarters were to control the selection of candidates and to see that they conducted their campaign in accordance with the declared policy of the executive.

According to Mr. Asquith, the disintegration of the Liberal Party began with the Coupon Election of 1918. The bulk of the old Liberal parliamentary machine deserted to the Coalition and in the new House there were little more than thirty members. The Liberal re-union of 1923-26 did not heal its wounds. For the control of the party was divided between the Liberal Central Office, scantily endowed, and the Lloyd George machine, richly endowed. In 1924 the Liberal group in the House elected Lloyd George as Chairman, and a Radical group who opposed him elected Runciman. In January, 1925, there was a Liberal convention to discuss a declaration of principles made by a committee appointed by Mr. Asquith. The convention approved a proposal to raise £1,000,000 for 600 candidates at the next election. In 1926 Lord Oxford's resignation left the Liberal Party derelict. The Shadow Cabinet which had been held in readiness to form a Liberal Government ceased to exist. The Liberal Party had inherited a faith in liberty of conscience, a tradition of resistance to arbitrary power, and the theory that economic relations required only a framework of political control. The Liberal Party could never identify itself with the Socialists for two reasons: first, many Liberals were rich men and captains of industry; secondly, the Liberals feared not only the extension of the powers of Government, but also of the power of any organized section of the community. A party whose tradition had been the protection of weak minorities and resistance to strong ones could not co-operate with the policy of the Trade Union Congress. Their more fundamental difficulty was that the principle of freedom in matters of intellectual opinion could not survive the organization of economic life.

After Conservatism had been rescued from the suspected blandishments of Mr. Lloyd George in 1923, the average

Conservative regarded himself, with Mr. Churchill, as part of a " solid central body of strong common sense and moderation for the maintenance of peace and tranquillity ". After the General Strike of 1926 the situation of the Conservative Party was entirely altered. On the one hand, the Labour Party abandoned its flirtation with direct action and sought the hand of constitutional power. On the other, the possibility of a pre-war Fabianism in a post-war world was gone. Both the Conservative and the Labour Party had now to discover the political institutions necessary to preserve English institutions in a world of violence and instability. Even under the uninspiring banner of " Safety First " the Conservative Party in 1929 secured the support of 8,000,000 voters. The Labour Party was returned mainly because the threat of the strike weapon had been removed. With the economic depression which began in 1929 and the renaissance of despotism which ensued, the principles of both parties had to be reconsidered. In the case of the Labour Party it was clear that only the might and isolation of Russia could afford to wrestle with the capitalist system. An individual, but not a community, might be expected to die for the Liberal faith. For the Conservatives, our relative weakness favoured now their policy. The difficulty of all parties was increased by the fact that as all Continental countries had been taught to admire the unity of English life, the more urgent the profession of differences of principle made by the parties the more were they likely to be regarded as Machiavellian dodges to keep the nineteenth-century swag. So from 1926 onwards informed opinion in America and on the Continent was observing how the country with the highest standard of living, the largest possessions and the least rationalized system of Government or industrial organization would comport itself in a disturbed world. Granted that the Marxian theses were correct, and it was the duty of all proletarians in all lands to unite, would the British working class be so Christian as they profess and loose their standard of living that others might live? If Marxism were not true, would the British electorate be prepared to redraw that map of Europe which had been drawn at Versailles in the belief that it would be framed and hung with the assistance of American power? To all these questions no effective answer could be made by a country as vulnerable as England now was. It was a dim sense that the shape of things to come would be other than a progressive realization of nineteenth-century dreams which committed Mr. Baldwin to his programme of " Safety First ". Doubtless there were subtle reasons why the Communist Revolution should have occurred in Russia—the last place which Marx would have anticipated—but this discrepancy should have been sufficient to make a good political detective hesitate before he arrested the capitalist system on the Marxian charge. There was something else abroad in the world other than the accumulation of surplus value. The economic order had broken through its political bounds and threatened to disrupt the framework of order on which society depends. Even a world Communist State might have to operate with the technique of American gangsters to settle its administrative problems. In these circumstances it was not surprising that it was to the emotional unity offered by nationalism that rulers turned.

Even before the war of 1914-18 the Cabinet which Gladstone thought to have found " its final shape, attributes, function and permanent ordering " was changing under the pressure of business and the development of party organization. From the passing of the Reform Bill of 1832 the Cabinet had steadily absorbed the powers of the Crown and as steadily achieved a mastery of the legislature. The essential functions of the Cabinet system which Gladstone admired was that constitutionally it reconciled the legal claims of the Crown with the actual power of the parties, that politically it provided a technique for adjusting the character of the Government to the various changes in public opinion, and that administratively it secured the clear formulation of public policy and its development by legislative act and administrative devices. The Cabinet exercised the prerogative powers of the Crown, controlled the legislature, and ran the administrative machine in such relation to public opinion that neither revolution nor repression were invoked. It provided at one and the same time a centre of initiative, a target of criticism, and a method by which government could be changed without shaking the fabric of the State. The complex and subtle understandings between those by whom it was run secured that towards any possible claims to important powers by the Crown it would present a united opposition which could prevent and development of personal power; that towards the House of Commons and the House of Lords it would present the need for, and the way to, an effective policy even in a representative system; while it provided the electorate not only with a guide to be followed but, when necessary, with a scapegoat. It provided for the expression at one and the same time of the continuity of national policy, the diversity of party principles, and the flexibility of adminis-tration an age of change required.

But the Cabinet system was inevitably unstable. It had been born of revolution and by revolution it might die. It had developed as an administrative and political device by which, after the revolution of 1689, the claims of the Crown and the claims of Parliament were never pressed to the arbitrament of war. Whatever the Kings or Queens of England might do there would be someone responsible to Parliament for their act. The possibility that the Kings or Queens themselves might secure control over Parliament itself to which their Ministers were responsible was prevented by the development of parties and the extension of the suff-rage. But though the essential struggle between the Crown and Parliament was settled by the Reform Bill of 1832 and the Constitutional struggles of Victoria and her Ministers were only the dying echoes of a battle long ago fought and won, the extension of the suffrage and the growing functions of the State were to raise far more difficult questions. How was the Cabinet system to provide the adjustment between public opinion, that amalgam of passing fancies and diverse and conflicting interests, and the need for planning and continuity which the new functions of the State required? The Cabinet was an excellent eighteenth-century device to reconcile the pretension of monarchy with the diverse interests of oligarchy; it transmuted the former into a symbol of national unity and the latter into the organs by which the diverse philosophies of that unity might be urged. But with the extension of the suffrage the Cabinet had to be developed to reconcile the technique of research and the arts and science of administrative planning with the diverse interests and the many frenzies of a complex industrial society.

Even before 1914 the Prime Minister might find that his duty to the nation as First Minister of the Crown might conflict with his duty to his party. There was a latent conflict between party loyalty and national duty. The assumption that a Prime Minister in disagreement with his party had only to resign that another might succeed ignored the difficulty that the party system was only an imperfect means to the government of the State. The real problem arose when it seemed to the Minister, who at the time knew all the facts, that the party system did not provide the necessities of State. The relation of the Cabinet to the party depended upon a complexity of traditions which were different in the different parties. The differences between the Conservatives and the Liberals were not very great, being both derived from the same oligarchic tradition. But there was implicit in the rising Labour Party a new conception of the relation of party to the Government which might require a change in the Cabinet system.

The pre-war Cabinet system was an effective device for securing the advantage of committee discussion with something of the precision and rapidity of an individual decision. It was the attempt of an oligarchy to secure the unity of purpose supposed to belong to monarchy with the diversity of experience which democracy claims. Its success depended upon the complex social and political traditions which provided that for every Cabinet in power there should be a Shadow Cabinet prepared to take power. When one Phillip should become drunk with power another Phillip would have been sobered by opposition.

We have seen that the old Cabinet had to be transformed for the conduct of the war. For in the war it was no longer a question of teams in friendly rivalry standing up to one another's bowling, but of selecting champions to meet the attack of a team professionally trained. After the war the politician, like the soldier, was eager to return to Blighty. Once more might the friendly game of ins and outs be played upon the party green. But there were two reasons, one transitory, the other permanent, to prevent this. First, the problems of peacemaking were as strenuous, though less bloody, than the problems of the war; second, the brave new world of peace was to prove stranger than any had supposed. Peace was to demand victories no less renowned than war. Revolutions in science and in industry were to transform the scope and nature of the problems of the State. There have been three periods since 1918: the first from 1918 to 1922, when the Lloyd George Coalition responsible for the liquidation of the war developed all " the improvisations of an intermittent and incalculable dictatorship ";[3] the second from 1922 to 1929, when the pre-war parties attempted to control the post-war world; the third from 1929, when some idea of the new political order was brought home to all the parties by the destructive violence of the great depression and the resurrection of forms of Government which all good Liberals and sober Labourites had believed to be but " portions and parcels of the dreadful past ".

No attempt was made to reform the Cabinet on the pre-war model until the late autumn of 1919.   For a year after the Armistice the Constitution was almost suspended.   Could there be a Cabinet in England at all when the Prime Minister, Bonar Law, and the Foreign Secretary would be delegates to peace conference in Paris?   As the King was anxious that there should be someone in England to take decisions, Lloyd George toyed with the idea that there might be two Cabinets, one for Home and the other for Imperial affairs.   Bonar Law proposed that England might be ruled temporarily by a duumvirate.   Finally it was decided to continue the War Cabinet with Chamberlain as a member, though not as Chancellor of the Exchequer.   At this Cabinet the principal Ministers attended, whether they were nominally members of the War Cabinet or not.[4]

When in the late autumn of 1919 the Cabinet was re-formed on the pre-war model it consisted of eleven Unionists, eight Liberals and one Labour member (Mr. Barnes, the Member for the Gorbals Division of Glasgow), and it included the Lord-Lieutenant of Ireland.   But a rapid disintegration of this Coalition set in.   The Prime Minister found that his magician's robes of war became in peace a shirt of Nessus.   In September, 1919, Curzon was complaining that the position of Secretary of State for Foreign Affairs, acting only as a substitute for the Prime Minister, was unsatisfactory and almost humiliating.[5]   By 1921 the India Office was at war with the Foreign Office and Foreign Office with the Prime Minister.[6]   Lloyd George attacked the Turks while Curzon, his Foreign Secretary, was charged with the duty of making the best peace with them he could.   The Prime Minister's private secretariat was negotiating independently of the Foreign Office.[7]   Austen Chamberlain defended the necessity of co-operation between Unionist and

Coalition Liberals and Lloyd George in order that the Constitutional and Conservative elements of the country might be rallied in defence of the social and economic order. But it seemed to the Conservatives that Lloyd George, who had destroyed the Liberal Party, was preparing to destroy them.

On October 6th Lord Salisbury, leader of the new Conservative and Unionist movement, said that a " new method of Cabinet Government had been introduced which was disastrous . . . an exaltation of one-man rule in Government which had produced deplorable results ". On October 19th a Conservative Party meeting held at the Carlton Club decided to fight the next election as an independent party. Within three hours of this decision the Coalition Government of Lloyd George had resigned. Bonar Law was elected leader of the Unionist Party by a special meeting composed of 152 members of the House of Lords, 220 members of the House of Commons and 67 parliamentary candidates. He was asked by the King to form a Government.

He resigned on May 20th, 1923, on grounds of ill-health, the King sending for Baldwin, as he was advised that Lord Curzon was unsuitable as being member of the House of Lords, while the Conservative Party would not have Chamberlain because of his support of Lloyd George.

The liquidation of the Georgian dictatorship did not mean a return to the pre-war party world. In 1923 Baldwin decided that he was precluded from introducing Protection, which he felt was the real remedy for unemployment, until he had secured the specific mandate of the electorate. This proposal served to unite the Liberal Party. At a special conference of November 13th, Asquith, Lloyd George and Sir Alfred Mond arranged to co-ordinate their forces. The Unionists had their special difficulties. Sir Allan Smith, chairman of the Industrial Group in the House of Commons, refused to support the Government. Lord Derby, as a Lancashire magnate, was given the delicate task of retaining for the Government the allegiance of the Unionist Free Traders. At the election the Conservatives were reduced from 347 to 255, Labour secured 191 and the Liberals 158.

In these circumstances a great responsibility rested upon Baldwin and Asquith. There was strong pressure on the former from within his own party to resign immediately, so that the King might send for a Unionist prepared, as Baldwin was not, to do a deal with the Liberals. Asquith was approached by a leading banker with a message from the city Conservatives that all the solid people in the country would support an Asquith-Grey Cabinet if it were formed. Baldwin, after visiting the King on December 10th and conferring with his Cabinet the next day, decided not to resign but to meet Parliament. It was then for Asquith to decide whether he would support the Conservative Government or not. On January 21st an Amendment to the Address was carried against the Government by 328 to 256 and the Labour Party, as the next largest party, took office for the first time. Asquith's sense of constitutional propriety had secured a peaceful revolution.

The Prime Minister, MacDonald, made it clear that as a minority Government he would resign only on a direct vote of no confidence, and not any snap division on a matter of minor importance. His Cabinet contained the pick of the Trade Union officials and the teaching intellectuals of the Labour Party. Parliament adjourned for three months to give the Ministers an opportunity to get used to their departments and to draft legislation.

On the surface there followed an era of good will. The Conservative Party, having failed to prevent a Labour Government by strategy, now tried killing it by kindness. The public were perhaps ready to hope that the new Government might by simple faith succeed where Conservavtive cunning and Liberal skill had failed. The new Prime Minister, MacDonald's appeal to public sentiment secured for him something of the position previously occupied by Lloyd George. The Press gave to the new presbyter the headlines of the old priest.

But the new Government had two serious weaknesses: there was no real agreement among its members as to the nature of the task they had to do; and it did not control a majority in the House of Commons. It was in office but not in power. It rapidly fell into arrears with public business, because it could only make a sparing use of the closure and the suspension of the 11 o'clock rule for these required the support of the Liberals. It was not prepared to give the Liberals the electoral reform they were demanding in the hope that a Central Party might be developed. In April a Government Bill to prevent evictions where non-payment of rent was due to unemployment was opposed both by Chamberlain and Asquith and allowed by the Government to be talked out. The House decided by 325 to 160 that a Capital Levy would be disastrous to employment. In May the Liberal proposal for Proportional Representation was left by the Government to a free vote of the House and defeated by 238 to 144. After that the Liberals were only biding their time to turn the Government out. But they were hampered in their own manoeuvres by the division of authority and influence between Asquith and Lloyd George and the deep distrust which the latter then inspired. In July the Government suffered its eighth defeat when it opposed a Liberal amendment to the Unemployment Insurance Bill. It was compelled to accept 65 of the 76 amendments tabled by the Liberals to the Housing Bill. Finally, when the Liberals decided to require the Government to delete the provision for a loan from the proposed Russian Treaty they were compelling it to dissolve. The Government deliberately rode for a fall on a side issue. In October the Unionists moved a vote of censure on the Government's intervention in the Campbell case. The Liberals tabled an amendment for a Select Committee. Baldwin, seeing that the tactics of the Government were to defeat the vote of censure by Liberal votes and the amendment by Conservative votes, led his party to support the amendment and the Government dissolved.

The Conservative Government formed after the Conservative victory in the election of 1924 enjoyed the advantage of a natural reaction after the high hopes raised by the Labour Party had cooled. But it was itself lulled into a false sense of security by the ease with which it defeated the General Strike of 1926 and the apparent recuperation of the world from the economic losses inflicted by the war. Between 1926 and 1929 the Government made cautious advances towards Protection by introducing a few insignificant safeguarding duties. It gratified Conservative opinion by a rupture with Russia, the introduction of the eight-hour day in mines and by curtailing the power of the Trade Unions in 1927. It dare not strengthen the House of Lords nor dare it refuse the extension of the suffrage in 1928 to women on equal terms with men. Its main success, the defeat of the General Strike of 1926, was the cause of its own undoing. The defeat of the strike clearly revealed the supremacy of power enjoyed by a modern Government. The myth of the General Strike as an instrument of policy was destroyed. With the removal of the suspicion that the Labour Party was playing with conceptions of direct action their programme of social and industrial reform made rapid progress at the expense of the Liberal Party, which was committed to the barren task in politics of securing a following by the point of argument without a shaft of interest. Fundamentally, the country was moving in the direction of a planned State.

In 1929 the electorate decided that if there was little to be hoped from a Conservative Government there was even less to be feared from the Labour Party. But though the largest party, the Labour Government had not a clear

majority over all parties in the House.   MacDonald, the
Prime Minister, asked that the House should as far as possible
constitute itself into a Council of State.   Sir Herbert Samuel,
for the Liberals, welcomed the appeal and suggested that
members should be free to vote on the merits of all questions
which were not such major issues that they must decide the
fate of the Government.[8]

But on everything essential little progress was made.
Thomas, as Lord Privy Seal, with Mosley (Chancellor of the
Duchy) and Lansbury (Commissioner of Works) were made
responsible for the development of an unemployment policy.
Their efforts may have been mountainous but the results were
minute.   A conference on election reform came to nothing.
Though Lloyd George said that with a three-party system
it was no longer the first duty of an Opposition to oppose and
expressed the willingness of the Liberals to co-operate with
the Government in fair conditions,[9] he could not carry his
party through the manœuvres he had in mind.   The Government's majority was often as low as fifteen or nine.   For the
Budget of 1930 early and frequent resorts to the closure were
met by repeated motions to report progress.   No less than
twenty parliamentary days were consumed in committee
alone—three times as many as had been required for any of
Churchill's Budgets.[10]

But the party manœuvres of 1930 were overshadowed by
the financial crisis of 1931.   In January, 1931, a Treasury
memorandum declared that continued State borrowing on the
present vast scale without adequate provision for repayment
by the Unemployment Insurance Fund would quickly call in
question the stability of the British financial system.   On
February 11th a debate led to the appointment of the May
Committee.   Its report demanded drastic economies in the
public services if the Budget were to be balanced.   An Economy
Committee of the Cabinet consisting of five members with
Snowden as chairman was appointed to study its report.   On

x

August 20th the Prime Minister laid their plan before the executive committee of the Parliamentary Labour Party, the General Council of the Trade Union Congress and the leaders of the Opposition then in London.[11]   The attitude of the Trade Unions brought the difference in the Cabinet to a head. MacDonald, Snowden and Thomas were of the opinion that there should be the closest co-operation with the Bank of England.   The latter declared that they could not secure the necessary loans unless there were cuts in unemployment benefit.   The majority of the Cabinet were unable to agree.   On August 23rd the King returned to London to interview the party leaders.   It is said that late on Sunday evening, August 23rd, the Cabinet, in order not to render public business impossible, empowered the Prime Minister to tender to the King his own resignation, which they believed would automatically include the termination of their own.[12]   It is also stated that the Cabinet believed that the King would send for Mr. Baldwin.   But in the background another policy had prevailed.   MacDonald had agreed to accept the Premiership of an emergency National Government.   The dissentient members of his Cabinet professed astonishment that they were out and MacDonald Prime Minister.   They said that by betraying his party he had broken the spirit of the constitution.

The Prime Minister of the new Government said that it was not a Coalition Government in the usual sense of the term but a Government of co-operation for one purpose only —to deal with the national emergency which then existed— and that that achieved the political parties would resume their separate lives.   For the moment it was composed of four Labour members: MacDonald (Prime Minister), Snowden (Chancellor of the Exchequer), Thomas (Dominions) and Sankey (Lord Chancellor); four Conservatives: Baldwin (Lord President of Council), Neville Chamberlain (Health), Hoare (India) and Cunliffe-Lister (Board of Trade); two Liberals: Reading (Foreign Office) and Samuel (Home

Secretary). The readiness of this Ministry of all the talents to accept office placed the Labour Party in an impossible position. To deny the crisis deceived no one. To assert that the crisis could have been met by rigorous measures to prevent the effect of an international financial panic on bourgeois *morale* at home might carry conviction with those who had mastered the dogmas of the class war. But this assertion was tactically open to the fatal retort that the most powerful members of the Cabinet were not convinced of the expediency of the proposed measures. The crisis was too severe for the Opposition to take office alone. No one believed that among the members of the Labour Cabinet who did not follow the Prime Minister there was the material for an alternative Government. On August 26th a joint conference of the Trade Union Congress, the National Executive Committee of the Labour Party and the Consultative Committee of the Parliamentary Labour Party passed a resolution that the new Government should be vigorously opposed. It accused the Government of determining to " attack the standard of living of the members in order to meet a situation caused by a policy pursued by private banking interests, in the control of which the public had no part ". The Labour Party was turned towards a policy of Socialism in our time to avoid the occurrences of crises with which it had been incompetent to deal in its own.

Meanwhile on September 21st the new Government departed from that gold standard, which it had been its professed intention to defend. By the end of September it had decided that it should not, as originally intended, resign so soon as its economic schemes had been accepted by Parliament, but that it should seek from the electorate a mandate for whatever measures the future might in its wisdom require. It was returned at the election with the astonishing majority of nearly ten to one (554 to 61).

This brief and imperfect outline of as yet imperfectly

known events has been necessary to place in some perspective the changes in the nature of the Cabinet system which are taking place.   The mere change in the scope of functions which all governments have been compelled by science and by industry to undertake has imposed upon the Cabinet the necessity of providing itself with an organization fitted to the duties which it tries to perform.   The scale and pace of modern society have compelled the Cabinet as they compelled many a private firm to adopt some simple measures of effective office routine.   The old family partnership has had to develop some of the methods suitable to a complex company structure.   To these problems of scale and speed belong the development of the Cabinet Secretariat and the complex committee organization of the modern Cabinet.

The essence of the old system before the war was, Asquith explained in 1922, " corporate responsibility maintained not as a despot or even as a master by the Prime Minister, though individually he was the central and controlling figure.   The essence of the whole thing was deep mutual confidence, and not only that, but of absolute secrecy ".   It was an inflexible though unwritten rule that no member should take any note or record of the proceedings except the Prime Minister for his letter to the King.   " A Cabinet discussion " was considered by Lord Salisbury " not the occasion for the deliverance of a considered judgment, but an opportunity for the pursuit of practical conclusions."   The freedom of private conversation would inspire a flow of suggestions.   The whole spirit of the system was spoilt if one member were to *hansardise* another even in memory.

But this old Cabinet was destroyed by the war.   Even before the war it had become more of a public than a committee meeting, and the orator already had undue attention. In 1917 Lloyd George appointed a small secretariat that the Cabinet might know what it was going to discuss, and after the discussion what had been decided.   The war-time

secretariat was continued after the peace. Its early development was hindered by the fact that in addition to the reasonable and proper Cabinet secretariat under the impeccable
control of Sir Maurice Hankey, there was in fact a secretariat
attached to the person of Lloyd George, whose affiliations
and powers no man quite understood. In 1922 the indispensable Cabinet secretariat was criticized severely in the
House as tending to exalt the Prime Minister, encroaching
on the province of the Foreign Office, destroying the informality of Cabinet discussion, and indirectly impeding
Parliamentary control of the executive. Bonar Law stated
in his election programme that it would be abolished.

In fact the Cabinet secretariat has become a vital part of
the machinery of Government. The all-round pressure of
work has compelled the Cabinet to attend to the order of its
doings. The function of the secretariat are in essence the
very simplest. It has to prepare an agenda. It has to see
that those concerned with the matters to be discussed are
informed that a discussion is pending and supplied with the
relevant material. It has to secure that those affected by
Cabinet decisions are made aware that they have been come
to. It has to co-ordinate the working of the Cabinet as a
whole with the committees through which it may work. It
has to co-ordinate the work of the Cabinet with the activities
of the particular departments. But this simple expedient
of business machinery for the easing of the political arts gives
rise to problems of constitutional import. The essential
change from the pre-war system is that each Minister now
knows what matters are coming up for discussion and will
have read the documents concerned. Most important questions will have been discussed by a committee of the Cabinet
itself. There is only one Standing Committee: that on
Home Affairs. This consists of the Lord Chancellor (in
the chair), two Cabinet Ministers, the Foreign Secretary, the
Attorney-General and the Solicitor-General. It considers

the proposed course of Government business for the session and the legal aspects of Bills in draft. It does not deal with policy and its work is advisory only. But there are many *ad hoc* committees which are in fact kept continually in existence such as those on Defence, the reform of the House of Lords, and the problem of Ireland. The effect of this committee system is that the Cabinet as a body is not overworked. On any matter on which there is difference of opinion or need for inquiry an *ad hoc* committee will be appointed and its report will be accepted or rejected by the Cabinet as a whole. The long-drawn-out discussion once common on problems of Defence now take place in the Committee of Imperial Defence, whose recommendation will be considered by the Defence Committee of the Cabinet and only then brought before the Cabinet as a whole. But while this committee organization reduces the work of the Cabinet as a whole it has not made any gift of leisure to important Ministers. For it is found impossible to use the heads of minor offices for work on important committees. The important Ministers have to man the important committees.

For any question to be discussed in Cabinet the Minister must ask the secretariat to put it on the agenda. Before they will do so the department concerned must have had the problem examined by the Treasury, the Law Officers and any other departments directly concerned. The secretariat has the power to refuse to circulate any memorandum until the Chancellor of the Exchequer is agreed. If he does not agree he will produce a counter memoranda. No item will appear on the agenda unless the notice of it and the papers concerned have been in circulation for five days. The agenda is compiled on Monday, circulated the same day, and the Prime Minister has, of course, the power to strike any item off or to add any item he desires.

The minutes of the Cabinet, while they do not refer to the opinions expressed by individual Ministers, do refer to the documents upon which they may be based. They may be seen by any member of the Cabinet. But no Government may see the minutes of a previous Government without the consent of the present and the previous Prime Minister. There is a natural tendency for the existing secretariat to deprecate reference to past minutes, as such a policy would lead an outgoing Government to order its own minutes to be destroyed.

These changes in the Cabinet as an administrative machine are not so important as those which seem to be taking place in the Cabinet as a political institution. For the Cabinet as it was developed in the nineteenth century was dependent upon the Monarchy, the legislature, and a party system, the result of the efforts made by diverse interests and conflicting powers to resolve their differences by argument. Party programme had been a tribute paid by diverse interests to the reason which might unite them. But the development of industry and the extension of the franchise have entirely changed the problems with which they have to deal. Monarchy, legislature and parties have been transformed. The Monarchy has become a device by which the emotional needs of the public mind can be met. We know so little of the psychological forces involved in ceremonial, and we have so much reason to fear the power of symbols, that if we value our liberty—almost one might say if we value our sanity—we will not allow the ceremonial and the effective powers of the State to be combined. The monarchical idea must be isolated in the ceremonial and not allowed to infect the organs of administration. The Monarchy must express and not create the unity which it serves. Queen Victoria's personal power exacted an incredible expenditure of time and temper by her Ministers. It is a tribute to the decency of the nineteenth-century politics that by only one Minister was it systematically abused. During the reign of Edward VII most of the prerogatives in which he claimed a personal discretion—mercy, dissolution, dismissal and selection of Ministers, declaration of war and peace—were challenged and surrendered. But there remained one critical issue through which the monarchical idea might once again infect the body politic. The legislature, while it is concerned to mediate between organized interests and opinions and the central planning and executive machinery of the State, can no longer be the arbitrator between conflicting Governments and policies. The central problem of Government lies in determining the relation between the organized community—not to be expressed in any legislature even by the device of parties —and the central organ which is its guide and servant. It is not now a question of determining the relation between the legislature and the executive as it was when the legislature was the organ of an aristocracy and the executive a tool of a powerful Crown. It lies in the relations between the parties as an organ of the community and the Government. Should a crisis break the normal harmony between parties and Governments there is a possibility that monarchical power would be revived. It is significant that at the present time many politicians should consider it desirable that a Conservative Government should be called National. It is significant too that the Labour Party should be seeking a form of organization in which the Cabinet would be a mere Executive Committee of the Party. Among the merits of the old Cabinet system was its ability to combine the interests and energy of party with the play of reason and the sentiment of Nationality. It provided a smooth and simple technique for the change of Government. It was the virtue of the old Cabinet system that it secured Government by the few with the precision of one and the tolerance of many. It is a paradox of popular Government that the more embracing the interests to be consulted the narrower must be the final organ of decision. The heptarchy could be governed by a Witagemote; a federal State by the Senate of the United States; but the United Kingdom requires a despotic Cabinet. We might say that democracy moves by an inner necessity towards the monarchical form. The justification for the party system is that it expressed both a unity and an admission that that unity is never quite complete. A party Government is like a king who has his fool in council. It is the Opposition which must see that power does not make the Government mad. The party system is suitable for a community which desires unity, which is capable of unity, but has still an open mind as to how that unity may be secured. It is an institutional expression of the experimental method in politics.

We have seen that the responsibility of the Government for policy which requires complex legislation for its application compelled the executive to transform the procedure of the House of Commons. But even now the time devoted to Government legislation does not exceed half the sitting time of the House. In 1930 the House sat for 160 days. Of these 32 were occupied by Supply, 21 by Ways and Means and all stages of the Finance Bill, 67 by Second Readings and Motions, and 40 by all stages of other Bills beyond their second stage. It is the tradition of Parliament, and a good one, that the Opposition should get a larger proportion of the time of the House than their opponents. But a Government which is in office does not want its own supporters to raise difficulties. There is in fact a conflict between the demands on Parliament as legislative and executive machine and the demand that it should be an effective organ of publicity. The House of Commons has in fact failed to focus public attention on important issues. The use of questions has not been properly developed. They are used to make debating point rather than to secure information. It is well known that to get a thing done it is best to write to the Minister. But to develop a row a question is put down. To use the question as an effective weapon of party warfare the Minister must be driven by successive questions to divulge more and more.   Exciting as this cross-examination may be, its value is largely lost because there is no opportunity for summing up.   If possible it might be better to abolish questions and use the time for short debates.   The character of the debates themselves has changed.   Before 1914 there were three-day debates on these subjects, the leaders closed the debate by two speeches of one hour each, and a Government worsted in debate suffered serious injuries.   Now the leaders speak early, that their views may get into the Press.   The character of the questions to be discussed allows for no clash of temperaments.   Most Members when they stand up make no attempt to answer those who have sat down.   There is a growing disposition on the part of Members to make their contribution and a growing indisposition of others to listen to them.   The opponents of the Government have no machinery for pursuing the subjects discussed in practical detail.   Save for debates on a vote of censure not 10 per cent. have attended those on employment and trade.   Noncontentious legislation is obstructed in order that there should be less time for the passage of contentious measures.   There is not time for the reorganization of executive departments, even though it would raise no party issues.   Finally, while there is no reason the rules of Parliament should not be as clear as those of a popular and well-played game, to have mastered the rules of the House is now in itself a claim to political distinction.

[1] P. Cambray : *The Great Game of Politics.*
[2] ibid.
[3] Asquith, cited Ronaldshay : *Curzon,* Vol. 3, p. 318.
[4] A. Chamberlain : *Down the Years,* pp. 139–43.
[5] Ronaldshay : *Curzon,* Vol. 3, p. 204.
[6] Spender and Asquith : *Life of Asquith,* Vol. 2, p. 337.
[7] Ronaldshay : *Curzon,* Vol. 3, p. 314.
[8] *Annual Register,* 1929, p. 58.
[9] ibid., 1930, p. 2.
[10] Mallet : *British Budgets,* p. 301.
[11] *Annual Register,* 1931, p. 64.
[12] *Political Quarterly,* 1932, p. 8–9.

CHAPTER X

Some causes of Administrative Confusion—The Haldane Report
on Machinery of Government—Its Principles examined—Their development traced : In Health with special reference to Local Government—
At the Treasury in the development of Treasury Control—In the Economic
functions of the State—In research and the problems thrust by Science on
Government—The Ministry of Defence—The special case of Justice—The
Structure and technique of the Civil Service—In general—In some
selected departments—The judicial functions of Administrators—The
Expert and Government.

BEFORE 1914 the administrative machinery of this country
was becoming too tangled to provide the service our national
and social problems required. The distribution of available
funds was made more difficult than necessary by the efforts
of each department to defeat the parsimonious Treasury view.
Instead of a reasonable debate as to the best use that could
be made of the available funds the discussion of the Estimates
by the Chancellor of the Exchequer with the departments
concerned was a scuffle of dogs for the largest bite. A series
of departmental disputes was a symptom of the faulty distribution of powers and responsibilities. There was for
example great confusion as to the responsibility of the
Local Government Board, the Home Office and the Board of
Trade in relation to local government in general and for the
care of children in particular. There were prolonged disputes as to whether the Local Government Board should
allow the Home Office to inspect laundries in workhouses
or the Insurance Commissions to inspect the sanatoria provided by the local authorities; or whether the Local Government Board, as the authority responsible for local finance,

might veto the educational institutions required by the Board of Education. Administration cannot be entirely freed from those problems of the demarcating of functions which require for their settlement both toleration and skill, but the English system before the war had more than was compatible with its efficiency.

This confusion was worse confounded by the exigencies of war. Ten new Ministries and over 160 boards and commissions had been created. Border-line questions of responsibility were settled in an arbitrary fashion and definite departmental responsibility to Treasury supervision relegated to the background. But with the return of peace the financial responsibility of each department had once more to be clearly defined. But on what principles were the duties of departments to be allocated? When the Great War Ministries of Munitions, Food, and Shipping should have withered in peace, what departments were to deal with the inevitable conflicts between industrial leaders anxious to beat swords into ploughshares at the maximum speed, and for the maximum profit, and the new labour from the battlefields seeking homes for heroes? The enormous development of State control over the whole field of national industry had destroyed the pre-war concentration of the economic functions of the State in the Board of Trade. How were those functions to be performed in the future? Were there to be Government departments concerned each with some problem common to all industries—research, the conditions of labour, and the stimulus of production—or were there to be departments each concerned with all the problems of separate industries—shipping, mines, textiles, engineering? What were to be the relations between the rising Air Ministry and its earthbound and waterlogged seniors, the War Office and Admiralty? Who was to be the Prospero to this Ariel, this Stephano and this Caliban? And there were minor problems without number. Who was to be responsible for the training of disabled men—a Ministry of Labour, the Board of Education, or the Ministry of Agriculture? Was there to be a separate Ministry of Pensions to which the War Office and the Admiralty were opposed? In these circumstances the Haldane Report on Machinery of Government, 1918[1] made the most thorough examination since Bentham of the problem of the proper distribution of the functions of the executive. It attempted to formulate the principles that should govern the distribution of the work of the departments of State whatever might be the policy of the party in power. It was concerned to solve a problem in administrative science and not to determine a political programme. The fundamental question which its researches led it to face had been raised by Aristotle when he asked " should officers be divided according to the subjects with which they deal or according to the persons with whom they deal . . . should one person see to good order in general or one look after the boys and another after the women, and so on?"[2] The Haldane Commission was of the opinion that there should be a department or departments for good order in general and not separate departments for the boys and women and so on. Of the two principles on which the functions of the State could be allocated to departments: (1) " distribution according to the persons or classes to be dealt with " or (2) " distribution according to the services to be performed " the Haldane Report preferred the latter. The first would involve having separate departments to look after the interests of particular classes of persons—paupers, children, insured persons, the unemployed, and in the case of industry perhaps separate departments to deal with each particular industry in every aspect of its relation to the State—labour conditions, safety and health regulations, vocational or technical education, bounties or taxation. By the second principle there would be separate Ministries dealing with Finance, Defence, External Affairs, Research, Production,

Employment, Supplies, Education, Health and Justice. This, the report held, was less likely to lead to confusion and overlapping and most likely to secure the widest knowledge and its most useful application.

In avoiding the Lilliputian organization which would result from having separate departments of State to deal with every class of persons who could claim a separate interest in its work, the report did not wish to create the pedantries of Laputa. Classification according to services might be better than classification according to the persons concerned, but there must be provision for co-operation in all marginal cases. The work which would be the primary concern of one department would be the secondary concern of others. Every department would have to study its own problems of staffing, though the general problem of staffing would be the business of the Treasury. Every department would have a responsibility for its own financial order, though finance, too, is the main concern of the Treasury. For legal problems and the development of scientific research the same principle would apply. Specialization is sterile until mated with co-operation. The health and safety of industrial workers might be the primary concern of a Ministry of Employment, but it would require the co-operation of the Ministry of Health. The administration of the law relating to vagrancy would require concerted action between the Ministries of Employment, Justice, Health and Education. Any attempt to deal with industrial fluctuations would involve the co-operation of every department of the State. A Ministry of Supply might provide every desk, distribute the white or brown wash that every office required, and the buttons of every military or constabularic tunic, but the experimental stages of the preparation of the material of war would have to be the duty of a Ministry of Research. Subtle and complex engines of destruction would sometimes be supplied by the Ministry of Defence, while the Ministry of

Supply would produce those to which methods of mass production could be applied—poison gas from the Department of Research, bombing planes from the Ministry of Defence, and gas masks for the population from the Ministry of Supply.

The Haldane Report was simply a claim that the chaotic distribution of the work of departments which had resulted from the compromises involved in Government by discussion should be replaced by the rational order technical efficiency requires. But of course the real difficulty lies in weighing the need for compromising with political forces against the claims of technical efficiency. An important condition of the economy and efficiency of the functions of Government departments will be the fact that they have secured political acceptance. Seeming inefficiencies in planning may really be due to the skill of a statesman who has seized the only opportunity offered to extend the functions of the State in a desirable direction. It is almost inevitable in a system of Representative Government that the development of its services should be in response to casual emergencies. If the State is to advance its range of action single spies must precede the departmental battalions.

The principles advocated by the Haldane Report have since 1918 been followed to the extent of the creation of the Ministry of Health, an improvement in the organization of the Treasury and its method of co-operating with other departments, and a great advance in the provision made for investigation and thought as a preliminary to action. But the rapid changes in the economic and social structure of the country have imposed on successive Governments the necessity of meeting casual emergencies by unco-ordinated expedients. We have yet to see a Ministry of Supply, a Ministry of Production, a Ministry of Justice or a Ministry of Research. The general principle of the report, that the work of Government departments should be distributed according to the nature of the service with which they are concerned, has not been unchallenged by departmental experts.

In 1926 a committee on the amalgamation of services common to the Army and Navy[3] reported that there was " a noticeable tendency of administrative theory of the present day . . . to suppose that a reorganization of the departments of Government, by which one department shall undertake all work of a particular nature for the whole Government service, will make for economy. The view we have taken on this point is that each case must be considered on its merits and not merely on *a priori* theory ". The committee was of the opinion that the establishment of a general pool of common stores to meet the needs of the three fighting services was impracticable owing to the differences in the needs of the three services and in their organization and geographical distribution. A partial amalgamation of the work branches with the Office of Works would lead to complications which would tend to increase the administrative difficulties of the fighting services; while the whole could not be handed over because part of it was so highly technical in character. The proposal to amalgamate the work of the Stationery Office, the largest printing establishment of the Government, with the Office of Works, the largest building establishment, has received no official approval. The Treasury indeed profess " fully to recognize the importance of avoiding duplication in administration between departments " and constantly to seek " with the co-operation of the departments to avoid such duplication ". But in 1920, when they examined with the departments concerned the question of re-allocating the functions of the Home Office, the Ministry of Health, the Board of Trade, and the Ministry of Labour, they decided on practical grounds that the situation should remain unchanged.[4]

The nature of the problems involved can only here be briefly considered. It will be convenient to take the special cases of (1) the Ministry of Health; (2) the Treasury; (3) the economic functions of the State; (4) the organization of research; (5) the Ministry of Defence; (6) the Foreign Office; and (7) the Ministry of Justice. Of these the Ministry of Health is of special importance, because it involves the question of the proper relation between the central and local authorities; the Treasury shows the fruitful application of the principles the Haldane Report had analysed; the economic function of the post-war departments show the dependence of administrative logic on political persuasion; the organization of research is the most vital problem of the post-war world; the Foreign Office shows that privilege will soon have nowhere to lay its head; the Ministry of Defence raises problems new in English history; and the hope of a Ministry of Justice will be always with us.

Ministry of Health. The complex history of this department has already been described. It was the working of the Poor Law and the medical services in this country which the Haldane Report had particularly in mind when it pressed for a rationalization of our administrative machinery. The provision by the State of one set of essential services for paupers and of another set for those who were not, had led not only to an inefficient duplication in the health and education administration of the State, but was in principle not defensible. There should not be one administrative law for the rich and another for the poor. If certain health services are essential to the community they should not be provided by different authorities and in different qualities to different income groups. While it would be cruel to deprive people with moderate or large means of the superficial comforts to which they are used, it would be monstrous to give the poor an inferior scientific treatment. The wards for rich and poor may be differently furnished, but the surgeons' knives should be the same.

Actually the creation of the Ministry of Health only

Y

secured that the responsibility for the scattered health services should be concentrated in one department.   The work of the department has remained extremely complicated, because it is still responsible for the supervision of the administration by local authorities of their administration of the Poor Law. Until 1929 that Poor Law was administered by the specially-elected Guardians of the Poor.   And though the Act of 1929 provided for the abolition of the Guardians of the Poor and the transfer of their functions to the Councils of Counties and of County Boroughs, it did not provide for the replacement of a deterrent Poor Law by the development of preventative services impartially administered to rich and poor alike. Further, the Ministry of Health is the department primarily responsible both for the structure and for the finance of local government.   It is a Ministry of the Interior with a sanitary bias.   Its work bears out the popular belief that the English would rather be clean than beautiful or clever.

Changes in the location and structure of industry, in methods of transport and in the distribution of population have had profound effects upon the organization of local government.   In 1926 the Local Government (County Boroughs and Adjustments) Act provided a temporary solution to that conflict between the Counties and the County Boroughs which was inevitable when the compromise of 1888 came to be tested by the improved transport provided by the bicycle, the motor and electric trains.   The creation of new county boroughs and the extension of others had taken from the counties some 100,000 acres and 1,300,000 population. As the counties were responsible for the provision of health, education, and road services to a diverse combination of urban and rural areas this loss of population and its attendant rateable value seriously threatened their work.   The problem was made more awkward by the fact that the incidence of the effect of the growth of the large towns was more severe in some areas (e.g. Lancashire and South Wales) than it was in others.   In some counties it seemed that if the expansion of the county boroughs were to continue the heart would be taken out of the county in which they were situated.   The Act of 1926 provided that no municipal borough could be constituted a county borough by Provisional Order and that no Private Bill could be promoted for such a purpose unless the population of the borough was at least 75,000.   In the case of the extension of county boroughs a Private Bill would also be required unless the proposal were unopposed by all those concerned.   This placed the onus of proof upon the growing authority, and the increase in the population required provided a temporary lull in the conflict.

The Act of 1888 had left within the counties a complex problem of relating the different urban and rural authorities, responsible mainly for sanitary services, to the county authority responsible mainly for those services which required for their administration a wider area.   The tendency, as we have seen, before the war had been to increase the powers of the county, but no effective reorganization of the areas of the urban and rural districts into which it was divided was secured.   In 1929 a far-reaching reorganization was begun.   It was provided by the Local Government Act of that year not only that the Boards of Guardians, whose abolition had been recommended by the Poor Law Commission of 1905-9, should cease to be and their powers be exercised by the councils of county boroughs and the councils of counties, but also that there should be transferred to the county all the highway functions of rural areas and the responsibility for all important roads except those of the larger urban districts (about 20,000 population).   Further, the county was made responsible for a periodical review of the areas of urban and rural districts and for the adjustment of their areas into a reasonable relation to the duties which they had to perform.

The same Act carried a step further the revolution in the

finance of local government which had been going on since 1888. The essence of that revolution was that the dependence of local authorities for their financial resources upon the proceeds of that very peculiar Elizabethan tax, the rate levied on the occupier of immovable property, produced a fantastic disproportion between the necessities and the resources of different areas. The derating of agricultural land before 1914 had made it necessary that the State should contribute to local authorities out of money raised from central taxation some part of the revenue lost by derating. In 1929 this principle was radically developed and the basis laid of a new balance of power between the Central Government and the local authorities. The Local Government Act of 1929, like so many important administrative reforms in English history, arose out of a particular emergency. The opportunity was taken to deal with the various problems which had accumulated in relation to local government since the last great reform of 1888. The exposed position of our exporting industries in world markets and the burden of poor relief in hard-hit industrial areas created a demand for the derating of immovable property used entirely in industry. The rate had previously been criticized as a tax on a commodity called a house; it was now criticized as a tax on the equipment of our vital industries. Into the extremely complex issues involved we cannot here enter. The rating system is a no-man's-land between the frontiers of administration and economic theory where only experts dare venture and from which few return unscathed. The Act provided that agricultural land and houses should be entirely derated, and that industrial hereditaments and freight transport should be derated by three-fourths. This had a far-reaching effect upon the relations between the Central Government (particularly the Ministry of Health) and the local authorities. For some part of the revenue lost to local authorities by derating had to be made good. It was decided at the same time that the complex system of grants in aid already existing should be tidied up. In general terms the result was that local authorities were to receive in lieu of an estimated loss of £24,000,000 from derating (the estimate was based on the revenue which local authorities would have had in a standard year had the provisions of the Act not been in force) and in lieu of £16,000,000 of discontinued grants, a sum of £45,000,000, known as the General Exchequer Contribution, which was to be distributed to local authorities in accordance with a formula which took account of their special needs. But because the Central Government was to make this substantial contribution the Ministry of Health was given the power to vary the grant to any local authority if it were dissatisfied with its efficiency and progress in public health, or if it were satisfied that the expenditure of the council had been unreasonable, or if the Minister of Transport had certified that he was satisfied that the council had failed to maintain their main roads.   It is to be remembered that the new scheme left untouched the Police Grants, the Education Grants, the Housing Grants, and a part of the Road Grants. But it did provide that the Central Government should be responsible for an increased proportion of the cost of local services, and therefore gave to the Ministry of Health an increased power of control. The Central Government operating one large grant, which is to be fixed for a term of five years, and able to vary that grant as in its discretion it shall think fit (subject to the approval of Parliament), is in a much more powerful position than when it was merely making specific grants to the cost of particular services or parts of services.[5]

The Treasury. The Government of any highly-organized community must have a department or departments responsible for: (1) the control of banking and currency and the public debt; (2) the imposition of taxation and the collection of revenue and the provision of the day-to-day expenses of the Government; (3) in addition to these purely financial duties it will have to make provision for the determination of the amount which the various departments of State may spend. In theory it is possible to separate the three functions of securing financial order, collecting revenue and the determination of expenditure. In an economic Utopia, where production and distribution moved to their appointed ends guided by the foresight of a milliard *entrepreneurs*, the function of the State in securing financial order might be reduced to the observation of astronomical phenomena important for the determination of the trade cycle and the broadcasting of financial statistics. The expenditure of the State would be balanced by its receipts for services rendered or the income from State property, and the collection of revenue by compulsion would be unnecessary; or perhaps where the expenditure of departments exceeded their receipts for services rendered the deficit would be so slight that they had merely to indicate their needs and the revenue department would meet them without question from the proceeds of a special broadcast appeal.

This financial fantasy reveals by contrast the essential problem of Treasury administration in England. That lies in the concentration of the responsibility for determining expenditure and the raising of revenue in the same department. It has been felt essential that the Minister responsible for raising revenue should have a predominant voice in deciding on the amount and in some degree on the character of expenditure. As the expenditure of the State becomes an increasing proportion of the total national income the interdependence of the determination of financial policy, the scale of expenditure and the raising of revenue increases. In a completely Communist State they would be diverse aspects of a single problem. The financial order would be the resources of the State and its resources would be its expenditure. In a very rich *laissez-faire* community, such as the United States before the war, the collection of revenue would be a mere executive stage in the carrying out of a policy determined independently of financial control.   While the *laissez-faire* State has merely to send a bucket to the well which man and Providence have filled, the interventionist State is concerned with the maintenance of reservoirs and the control of irrigation.

The Haldane Committee found that there was a tradition that all departments have a natural disposition to be extravagant and that the Treasury was irreconcilably opposed to all increases of expenditure whether meritorious or not.   To improve their relations it proposed: (1) that the obligation of the department to state a reasoned case for increased expenditure should place upon the Treasury a corresponding obligation not to assume an attitude merely negative; (2) that more frequent inquiries should be made by the Treasury into the general administration of departments; (3) that in each department there should be an establishments officer concerned with problems of staff, and in the Treasury itself an Establishment Branch.

In 1919 to meet the problems of staffing and reorganization in the Civil Service created by the war, a separate Establishments Branch was created in the Treasury and separate establishment officers in each department.   These establishment officers are appointed by the head of the department in consultation with the Treasury, and they are the eyes and ears of the head of their department in all problems of staffing.[6] They are expected to know the practice of other departments in staffing problems and to know the general trend of staffing policy throughout the Service.   There is a committee of establishment officers and frequent informal discussions by the permanent heads of all departments.   Before the war the Treasury only knew of increases of staff through proposed increases in the Estimates; decreases of staff or possible reorganization they only heard of if the departments voluntarily disclosed them. Now " the officers of the Establishment Department of the Treasury are in and out of the departments the whole time. They are not at arm's length but they are in intimate touch. . . . If a department is shortening work . . . there will no endeavour on the part of the department to conceal it. . . . The Treasury has powers under Order in Council to order an examination of the staffing of departments, but it does not need to use them ".[7] The Treasury has taken the departments into council. It tells them the amount that is in the till and persuades them to the necessary sacrifices.[8] It is the Treasury and the departments in commission which determine the allocation of available revenue. The Treasury is continuously engaged in co-ordinating and supplementing the efforts of departments to do their work in the most economical way. There is, for example, a particular section of the Treasury which consists of people skilled in the use of every conceivable kind of labour-saving device, and these are continually going round the departments to see if they can equal and if possible surpass the most advanced business organizations.[9] " The process ", wrote the May Committee, " is not spectacular, but it is continuous and effective . . . such economies as are from time to time possible will be secured as opportunities arise and will not be accelerated by any recommendations which we could make."[10]

The Committee on National Expenditure, 1918, recommended that the Public Accounts should be cast in the form of Income and Expenditure Accounts in place of the mere cash accounts which gave no clear account of the real position. The new system was introduced experimentally into the War Office, but was rejected by the Public Accounts Committee of 1925 because it required an administrative decentralization to which the Army Council were unable to agree. But the Trading Accounts of departments whose work is of the nature of a commercial undertaking are kept on an Income and

Expenditure basis, while in others the practice of making special financial studies provides the administrative officer with as much information as possible about the financial implications of his work.[11]

(3) *Economic functions of the State.* The Haldane Report envisaged the economic functions of the State organized around three Ministries—one concerned with conditions of employment, another engaged in the stimulation of private enterprise, and a third operating such enterprises as time had ripened or politicians taken for nationalization. But since 1918 the machinery of the State in its dealings with our economic life has been transformed by temporary expediences to meet a series of emergencies. There have developed an astonishing variety of unco-ordinated devices of investigation, advise and control. Politicians in travail have produced a litter of commissions; and boards have come not single spies but in battalions. The pre-war tendency to concentrate the economic functions of the State in the Board of Trade was broken by the war itself. In the confusion of an economic retreat distressed industries have each sought and found their own nurse and shelter in the ample bosom of the State. The Board of Trade deals with coal; the Ministry of Agriculture attempts whatever miracles may be performed with loaves and fishes; Transport has its own Ministry; and the reconstruction of our basic industries is indirectly attempted by a Tariff Commission. For the determination of general economic policy an Economic General Staff has remained a Utopian dream.

The underlying causes of this confusion lie partly in the weaknesses of our parliamentary procedure, which are such that a majority, however determined, cannot pass with the ordinary procedure half the measures necessary to bring the law up to date,[12] but mainly in the fact that there is a fundamental uncertainty in all parties shared by all honest minds as to the policy to be pursued. The Labour Party does not really believe that the evils that men do are due to the existence of private property; the Liberal Party does not really think that Cobden has new worlds to conquer; and the Conservative Party does not know what order it should patriotically defend. The Cobdens of the nineteenth century could assume their society though it might be merely Manchester; the Cobdens of the twentieth century have seen Manchukos created by Japan. They cannot be so sure that the loom is mightier than the sword. The parties to the left are not quite sure that the battle is to the poor; nor are the parties to the right certain that property is not sometimes theft.

In such conditions administrative empiricism was inevitable. And wisely was empiricism adhered to when far-reaching reorganization was suggested again and again. The problem of unemployment was compared to the problem of war. " I do suggest ", said Sir Oswald Mosley, " that to grapple with this problem it is necessary to have a revolution in the machinery of government. After all it was done in the war; there were revolutions in the machinery of government one after another, until the machine was devised and created by which the job could be done."[13] But appeals to the experience of war are often a symptom of the weakness which follows that disease. " The job to be done " in war was the organization of the nation for victory in the field at whatever cost to the living or those yet to be born. It was a limited objective to be gained or lost within a few years. The cure of unemployment is entirely different. It is not a question of finding the means at whatever cost to secure a definite end but of discovering the conditions necessary to the co-operation of men in society. As well expect to organize a League of Nations by the same means as in war a general staff is created as to solve the problem of unemployment by " revolutions in the machinery of government one after another ". It will probably be found that it was some remnant of political wisdom that survived the wreck of war which saved us from revolutions in the machinery of government to deal with the symptoms of a disease whose nature we do not understand. That is not to say that governments and industry did not fail to do many of the things they might have done or that they did not rush to do many things which only the intoxication of peace following the hysteria of war could excuse. For a time everyone was under the delusion that the efforts of war could be sustained in peace though directed to ends which were rational and general instead of to one end which was instinctive and passionate—self-preservation and victory.

As the full complexity of the post-war problem was revealed old departments were reorganized, new departments created, and innumerable experiments made in the public control of economic activities.

The Ministry of Labour was created in 1916 and has been responsible for the organization of the labour market through its administration of the Labour Exchanges, the promotion of conciliation and arbitration under the Conciliation Act of 1906 and the Industrial Courts Act, 1919, and since 1917 the administration of the Trade Boards system. But the special problems of agriculture and coal-mining required that their wage problems should be controlled by special departments. In 1924 the Ministry of Agriculture and Fisheries was made responsible for a system of agricultural wages committees in each county or group of counties analagous to Trade Boards. In 1912 the Coal Mines (Minimum Wage) Act provided that minimum rates should be fixed in each district by similar boards.

In 1919 the Ministry of Transport provided for the concentration in a single department of the scattered powers of the State relating to inland transport. But the control of civil aviation remained with the Air Ministry and coastwise shipping, navigation and pilotage with the Board of Trade.

It is obvious that the proper functions of a Ministry of Transport, concerned as it is with a vital instrument of trade and commerce, are most difficult to determine.   Its powers conceivably could be distributed: roads going to the Home Office; rail transport and bridges to the Board of Trade; or alternatively, it might control every aspect of communication by sea, air, road and rail, and perhaps even the Post Office.   It is a good example of the technical, economic and political forces which determine the distribution of the work of Government Departments.   During the war the railways were run under the Board of Trade by a committee consisting of the General Managers of the dozen leading companies.[14] After the war they were not nationalized, partly because to do so would have meant the hindering of the development of other forms of transport.   The Railway Act of 1921 laid down the outlines of the amalgamations desirable and established an Amalgations Tribunal to control their formation. The rapid development of road transport led in 1920 to the Road Act and then to the Road Traffic Act of 1930.   By the latter twelve bodies of regional commissioners (three in each area) were established, with wide discretionary powers to determine the conditions of competition in the road transport industry, empowered by the Minister of Transport to expend money in " disseminating knowledge and otherwise informing the minds of the people ", and marked an important stage in the development of State action from force to persuasion by empowering the Minister of Transport to publish a code which not only was to be a language which all could understand, but was not to have statutory force in the sense that breaking it would not in itself constitute an offence. But the vital problems remain.   The Ministry of Transport must inevitably become responsible for the main roads for whose maintenance the revenue of local authorities cannot be fairly charged, as the cost would bear no obvious relation either to their ability to pay or to the benefit which they received from the highways within their jurisdiction. A *thoroughfare* cannot be a local charge. But in becoming responsible for roads the Ministry of Transport will be forced into close co-operation with the Ministry of Health as the main town-planning authority. Finally, the Ministry of Transport has raised the general question of the nature of the public authority which should be responsible for economic services which political forces determine must be publicly regulated.

It is generally agreed that, whatever the need for State regulation of particular industries, direct Ministerial responsibility for their management by a State department would be unwise. For it would mean a plague of Ministers on an already overcrowded front bench and their pre-occupation with executive detail rather than with principles of statesmanship.[15] Either the inherent flexibility of industrial organization would provide problems too numerous for political control or political exigencies would destroy the vitality of the industrial order. They would make a plan and call it wealth. There have therefore been many experiments in the forms of public concerns able competently to conduct particular services in the public interest.[16] In 1919 the powers and duties of the Board of Agriculture and Fisheries, the Board of Agriculture for Scotland and the Department of Agriculture and Technical Instruction for Ireland were transferred to the Forestry Commissioners. In 1919 also five Electricity Commissioners appointed by the Board of Trade (after 1920 by the Ministry of Transport) were made responsible for the conduct of the whole of the policy dealing with the electrical industry in the country. Their duties were those of co-ordination rather than of the complete executive control of the industry. In 1927 the Central Electricity Board was established consisting of a chairman and seven members. The Board was composed of men of wide experience in finance and business organization rather than representatives of particular interests, and was appointed by the Ministry of Transport after consultation with a large number of associations and individuals representing local government, electricity companies, industry, transport, agriculture and labour. Their commercial discretion was to be unfettered; they were not to be a Government Department in any sense of the word. They were to prepare a scheme to be submitted to the Electricity Commissioners who, acting in a semi-judicial capacity, would give the interested parties an opportunity of being heard and would then confirm the scheme with or without modifications.[17]   In 1926 it was decided by a committee of inquiry[18] that for the control of the unknown powers of radio the most appropriate organization would be a public corporation.   " Such an authority would enjoy a freedom and flexibility which a Minister of State himself would scarcely exercise in arranging for performances and programmes and in studying the variable demands of public taste and necessity."[19] The actual commissioners were not to be persons representative of various interests, such as music, science, drama, education and industry, but " persons of judgment and independence, free of commitments " and able to " inspire confidence by having no other interests to promote than that of the public service ".[20] While the State, through Parliament, was to retain the ultimate control, the Postmaster-General being the spokesman on broad questions of policy, the commission was not to be the subject of " the continuing Ministerial guidance and direction which apply to Government offices ".[21]

Because it seemed that the long era of expansion of the British coal industry was at an end, and that its 1,500 independent concerns producing coal caused a widespread and continuous dissipation of effort at a time when there was need for concentration of effort against a common peril, the Coal Mines Act of 1930 established the Coal Mines Reorganization Commission.   It was intended to secure the concentra-

tion of production in selected pits and to assist the majority
in particular areas who were hampered by a minority from
carrying out a reorganization scheme.   The chairman was Sir
Ernest Gowers, appointed for seven years, and formerly
Chairman of the Board of Inland Revenue.[22]

In 1931 the abandonment of Free Trade led to the appointment of the Import Duties Advisory Committee of three
members: Sir George May, the chairman (£5,000 a year);
Sir S. J. Chapman (late Economic Adviser to His Majesty's
Government) and Sir George Allen Powell.

Finally it should be noted that the special problems of the
agricultural industry have been responsible for a variety of
administrative experiment. The State has attempted entirely
to reconstruct the industry in some of its most important
functions and completely to revise our economic relations with
foreign countries.[23]   In 1931 the Agricultural Marketing Act
was passed as an enabling measure to facilitate the organization and distribution of any given commodity by a majority
of its producers, a dissentient minority notwithstanding. The
Act of 1933 was designed to raise the prices of agricultural
products by the quantitative limitation of imports and by the
control of domestic agricultural production.   It established
a twin dictatorship by the President of the Board of Trade
and the Minister of Agriculture, which went far to introduce
a rigid system of State control over one of the largest of our
basic industries.[24]   The first part of the Act enabled the
Board of Trade to restrict the imports of any agricultural
products subject to a marketing scheme if the Board, after
consultation with the Minister of Agriculture, was satisfied
that such a scheme could not be brought into effective operation without the limitations of imports.   The second part of
the Act provided for development schemes to be administered
by boards composed of three members appointed by the
Minister and a number of other persons elected by the con-
stituent boards.

(4) *The organization of research.* The Haldane Report expressed the opinion " that in the sphere of central government the duty of investigation and thought as a preliminary to action might be more definitely recognized ". Such thinking, it said, could not be carried out in the spare time of an efficient administrator. It urged (1) that in all departments better provision should be made for enquiry, research and reflection before policy was defined and put into operation; (2) that for some purposes a special department was necessary to supervise and carry out the necessary enquiry and research; (3) that special attention should be paid to the methods of recruiting the staff to be employed in such work and (4) that in all departments the higher officials in charge of administration should have more time to devote to this portion of their duties.

Most Government departments have developed an intelligence branch concerned partly with the investigation of specific problems related to current policy and partly with inquiries that have established a claim to disinterested research. They will be able to collect information inaccessible to the private individual through the exercise of powers given to them by Parliament. But these powers will have been determined by the exigencies of the particular political or administrative crisis in which they were required. Their powers of investigation are secreted in the interstices of political and constitutional procedures. The Government's " very knowledge of the nation it rules is only the by-product of its specialized administrative activities ".[25] The attempts made so far to cure the sickness of an acquisitive society have involved all Government departments in a confusion of publicity and measurement. The strange principle " that Government is to seek only such information and is only to record such statistics as are incidental to its current information " has made our research organizations a myopic and squinting Argus. Outside the research work of particular departments the development of special departments for investigation and research " has taken place in almost every instance in response to the pressure of a practical need and not in pursuance of a reasoned policy ".[26]

Until recently the British system of statistics was in a state of chaos.   There were four Government departments responsible for industrial statistics—the Registrar-General, the Board of Trade, the Inland Revenue Department and the Ministry of Labour;[27] five separate departments separately undertook the work of classifying employers of labour according to their trade: the Board of Trade, Ministry of Labour, Census Office, Inland Revenue, Home Office.[28]   The Board of Trade and the Inland Revenue Department compiled and published estimates of the value of income from overseas investments, each disavowing the work of the other.[29]   The statistical and research work of the Ministry of Agriculture was divided among seven departments, with the result that in the mind of the farming community " the Ministry was associated with the idea of nagging inspection, not with the idea of disinterested advice ".   The need for co-ordination has been recognized.   An inter-departmental committee has co-ordinated the classification of industries and occupations used in the population census and in industrial and labour statistics.   Information as to earning has been related to the census of production.   There is now a permanent committee on official statistics,[30] which, to a certain extent, keeps the whole field under review.   A new cost of living index has replaced the one founded on a special survey undertaken more than twenty-five years ago of less than 2,000 budgets.[31]   But the creation of a central statistical department is still considered impossible on the grounds that statistics are collected by departments for use in their work.[32]

It has been wisely said that " before the modern world can feel confidence in trusting its fortunes either to planning or to *laissez-faire*, or to some mixture of both, the apparatus and

z

technique of investigation into social and economic problems will need to be vastly improved and strengthened ".[33] But the provision of such improved technique raises problems which go to the root of government. It is easy to say that responsibility for policy must be separated from responsibility for routine administration.[34] A policy involves the co-ordination of the work of many departments. The research and planning for the former may involve serious modifications of the work of particular departments. How is an adjustment to be made between the time given in particular departments to specific investigations on matters of immediate administrative and political urgency and the time given to the investigations appropriate to general policy? When there are conflicting policies within a Cabinet the research facilities of each department will be used by each Minister for his own ends. Serious co-ordination can only come from a Minister or a Committee of Ministers in a position to override the obstruction of particular departments. The comparative failure of the Economic Advisory Council was partly due to this very difficulty.

The Economic Advisory Council was established in 1930. It was intended to provide a continuous study of economic problems over a wide field. It was placed directly under the Cabinet with the deputy secretary to the Cabinet as its secretary. Its inquiries were to be with the sanction of the Prime Minister and the results were to be communicated to the Cabinet. It was composed of three elements: an advisory council of business men, Trade Unionists, economists and technical experts and others; the Prime Minister as chairman and such other Ministers whose departments might be particularly concerned; and a small full-time staff of expert economists. It has not been a success because neither the problems it was to study nor the resources of investigation which it might use were defined.[35] It could not co-ordinate the economic activities of other departments without itself exercising executive powers which would have made it practically a department of the Prime Minister.[36]   It has remained " an appendage hooked on rather than an integral digestive organ ".[37]   If its powers were ill-defined its membership was ill-assorted.   A miscellaneous collection of economists, Trade Union leaders and business men, invited to speculate at large on problems of policy, will only succeed in darkening each other's light.   In matters calling for immediate action the practical men will seek support in theories they do not understand; while the speculative thinkers will rely on experience they are ill-fitted to judge when their own theoretical insight begins to fall.   A combination of the theory of practical men and the policy of academic men produces pontifical obscurity.   There will be a confusion between the necessities of purely theoretical discussion and the necessities of action.   In practice the Advisory Council has only been effective when it has functioned through small committees which have considered measures submitted to them by the Prime Minister and have received from him and the Chancellor of the Exchequer power to override departmental obstruction.

But economics is not the only science with which Governments are now anxiously concerned.   Increasingly in the present century they have had to devise a policy and administrative machinery for the relation of the physical and biological sciences to the problems of government.   We have only time to outline the bare bones of the problems of policy that have arisen.   The first principle is that it is dangerous to organize pure research.   " The less the scientific worker is concerned to produce some specific result and the more he is animated by the spirit of disinterested scientific curiosity the more likely he is to hit upon fruitful discoveries."[38]   Pure scientists, like great poets, are the gifts of nature.   The wind of the spirit bloweth where it listeth and no meteorological office can forecast or control its vagaries.   But if we cannot raise the wind we can supply the windmills. A Government must decide how far the material embodiment of the spirit of science is to be encouraged. It must decide how far the machinery of the State needs to be adjusted to these spirits from the vasty deep. Scientists may be the unacknowledged legislators of the world, but the strength of law is in its administration.

In the first place experience has shown that there are certain types of research essential to the progress of pure science itself and of direct importance to industry which cannot be left to private initiative: e.g. the determination of physical constants and the standardizing of instruments. In 1901 the National Physical Laboratory was founded as a public institution for standardizing and verifying instruments and for testing materials and for determining physical constants. Until 1918, except for a small State grant, the Royal Society bore the whole financial responsibility. The Laboratory was then taken over by the Department of Scientific and Industrial Research and a policy determined. The Laboratory can pursue fundamental research work on its own initiative and its own discretion. It can do work for outside persons and firms as well as for the Government on payment of a fee. But such special investigations are only undertaken if they cannot be done elsewhere and when the results are likely to be of general interest and on condition that they are available for the confidential information of the Government.[39]

Secondly, there are certain services so fundamental that the State must concern itself with their efficiency. The Department of Scientific and Industrial Research assumes direct responsibility for industrial research in food, fuel, building and clean water supply. Sometimes the solution of a specific problem—such as the best way of detecting the presence of a submarine—may be of urgent interest to the State. Sometimes a group of industries may be induced to co-operate in the solution of some common problem, e.g., the stress of bridges, or the best locomotive design. Sometimes a new industrial process may be established by well-planned research, e.g., the economical extraction of oil from fuel. The State has here to attempt the delicate task of guiding and supplementing the demand of private industry and the provision made by private endowment for particular forms of research. It has to secure such a union between pure research and business acumen as shall be fruitful of material advantages to the community. It has to overcome the suspicion and hostility that many industrialists show to the potentialities of scientific investigation. The ordinary citizen of the nineteenth century could not see that education paid, and a twentieth-century industrialist cannot see that research pays. How can they make convincing calculations for their shareholders for the development of a province on the edge of the unknown. " Research being a venture into the unknown success is not certain . . . except in such a case as the cure of disease it is rarely possible to estimate the economic return even if success is attained."[40]   The time-lag between a new discovery in the laboratory and its commercial development is too long for the technique of business forecasting or the investors' courage to span. It was two generations before Faraday's electro-magnetic experiments were of interest to a Chancellor of the Exchequer. Many of the most valuable conclusions to be drawn from the Rothampstead experiments did not emerge until the trial plants had been continued under the same treatment for twenty or thirty years. It took a million pounds and twenty years to place artificial indigo on the market after it had been synthetized in the laboratory.[41]

In what cases Government intervention is justified is as subtle a problem to decide as the analogous problem of the duty of the State to provide the necessary conditions of freedom, e.g., in making education compulsory. Unless there is a certain framework of scientific knowledge and research in existence it is impossible for the industrialists or consumers concerned to know the significance of what is happening around them.

The third and most delicate problem of all is to encourage and assist the movement for industrial research without encroaching on activities best carried out by industry itself.[42] Industrial research is often as integral a part of production and distribution as advertisement or insurance, and its progress is best promoted by measures which enlist the active co-operation of industrialists themselves.   Before the war the Development Commission pointed out in their fourth report that there were two methods by which the State could assist research: by a series of grants to specific objects; by the provision of a permanent revenue to certain institutions.   The first had the advantage that the commitments of the State could be limited.   But it was not always possible to determine the expenditure and indicate the nature of the research proposed in advance.   In the case of agriculture there was no organized body to whom the grant might be made.   The study of animal diseases had not received the philanthropic support which had been given to human sickness and there were in existence no organized body of veterinary surgeons or research workers.   The essential nature of the problems of agricultural research precluded intermittent grants for distinct and clearly defined ends.   " The distinguishing character of agricultural research is that a continuous policy is essential; the investigator is often in possession of a method rather than a particular scheme of work which will succeed or fail within a given time."   After the war the Department of Scientific and Industrial Research, instead of forming a central institution to which industries could turn for the purpose of having their research problems carried out, adopted a scheme of research associations.   These—which are without parallel in any other country—are organizations set up by the industry for the industry.   They appoint their own staffs and decide their own policy but they receive a grant in aid if they satisfy the department that they are duly prosecuting research. The department keeps in touch with the work of all research associations. A clearing-house has been established, so that if a discovery emerges in one association of no direct interest to itself it is passed on to where its importance may be vital.

Underlying all schemes of Government co-operation with industry are vital questions of economic policy. " Accuracy and caution are part of the essence of scientific research and nothing is more destructive to its true spirit than the immediate demand for something definite to win applause or satisfy impatience."[43] It is necessary to take due precautions " against transferring to the State the burden of ordinary industrial research which have become one of the essential costs of production ".[44] But it is when we come to the so-called development schemes where a policy of doles may be covered by a veneer of research that the danger is found. Doubtless private enterprise has done those things which it ought not to have done and left undone those things which it should have done. But a blind State may lead those with short sight down a steep place. Before the war the Development Commission had to explain that decaying harbours and local industries had no claim to support against the competition of efficient rivals. After the war they were saying that in the absence of credit facilities which would give to village artisans power and machine aids " it would hardly be contrary to economic science . . . to make the attempt to supply them ".[45] In 1930-31 they were saying that " the spread of well-designed and well-constructed machinery has at the present time discounted the qualities of the old-fashioned craftsmen; but as competition increases our world markets may depend upon our using their skill ".[46] How far should this preservation of what once was useful but now is valueless, but may have value in the future, be carried? Should the State garrison economic deserts because they may one day blossom like the rose?

The development of the administrative machinery for the supervision of research has been slow and cautious. The Development Commission was appointed first in 1911. It was at once involved in administrative toils. It had only powers to recommend; it had no executive powers and no knowledge of proposals made for grants except through the Treasury, with whom the final decision rested. While no scheme could be financed without its approval, no scheme could be carried out without the co-operation of the Government Department concerned. The Commission was hampered by the complications of the administrative machinery of the United Kingdom. Where a problem required a plan for the whole United Kingdom negotiations might be necessary with two authorities in England and Wales, one in Scotland and one or two in Ireland. There were acute difficulties when any plan involved the co-operation of central and local authorities. In the case of canal development, fishing harbours and the prevention of coast erosion there might be no executive body to whom a grant might be made. In the case of agriculture and rural industries, forests and afforestation, the number of men really qualified to conduct research was very small. Before the war the organization of a research top to our educational system was considered by the Board of Education. At that time only 1,500 research workers were employed in British industry. In 1915 a special committee of the Privy Council and in 1916 a special department under it was provided for enlarging and organizing the work of scientific research. The political and financial responsibility lies with the committee of the council, presided over by the Lord President, but the actual work is done by an advisory council of persons appointed for their scientific, or scientific and industrial, qualifications by the Lord President after consultation with the President of the Royal Society. The secretary of the advisory council is the permanent head of the department—

the Department of Scientific and Industrial Research.   The
advisory council or scientific experts working harmoniously
under a lay chairman plan a policy of scientific research within
the financial limits laid down by the department and suggest
to the department the best means of carrying out the accepted
policy.[47]   Following the recommendation of a Cabinet committee on the co-ordination of research work, an inter-
departmental conference was set up in May,1922, to consider
border-line cases between the Development Commission, the
Department of Scientific and Industrial Research, and
Medical Research Council.   The discussions of the conference drove home the lesson that a national policy in
research, complex as it must be and directed by diverse and
suitably-designed organs, must be conceived and implemented
as a unity.[48]   In 1911 the National Health Insurance Act
established a committee to administer a fund for medical
research.   The amount was about £53,000, the equivalent
of a penny for every insured person.   In 1913 a Medical
Research Committee began to frame a policy and plan a
programme of work.   By the Ministry of Health Act, 1919,
administrative control was transferred to a committee of the
Privy Council.   In 1920 a Medical Research Council
succeeded to the Medical Research Committee and took its
place by the side of the Department of Scientific and Industrial Research.[49]   In 1931 a committee of the Privy Council
for the organization and development of agricultural research
was also established.   Its relations on the one side with the
Medical Research Council and the Department of Scientific
and Industrial Research and on the other with Ministry of
Agriculture and the Development Commission make its
administrative work both complicated and difficult.[50]
    It might appear at first sight as difficult to make
philosophers kings as to combine activities so distinct as
administration and scientific research.   The methods of
research are " anarchical and ought to be continuously

destructive of accepted opinion ", while it is the function of government everywhere to prevent anarchy. But their seeming antipathy veils a deeper harmony. The anarchy of science is rooted in a profound order, and the order of government must rest ultimately not on force but upon persuasion. " The method of science seeks to conquer doubt by cultivating it and encouraging it to grow until it finds its natural limits and can go no further."[51] It must be ready always to abandon a conclusion, but when such abandonment is based on evidence the logical consistency of the whole system is thereby strengthened,[52] if the certainties of science are based upon the scepticism of research the order which governments seek depend upon the skill with which they can adjust their organs to a changing world. The development of science now imposes a rate of change faster than the most skilful and autocratic rulers have ever achieved. It is breaking the crust of custom on which rulers have hitherto relied. Only as allies can science and government secure the knowledge and the peace which are their complementary aims.

Governments must take account of all those changes in scientific knowledge which might threaten its superiority in physical force: policemen must have motor cars; Scotland Yard its poison experts; Customs officials their X-ray apparatus. The State, as our detective fiction should remind us, holds its own only by paying that tribute which force must always pay to knowledge. But the advance of science has compelled Governments also to consider far more closely their duty to provide those goods and services which, necessary as they are, have not been and maybe cannot be produced by private enterprise alone. That some pure research should be endowed would seem to be as obvious as that some teachers should be endowed. But it is difficult to determine how far the State should subsidize technical experiments and research. Perhaps the economic system is self-regulating; perhaps we are led by an invisible hand; perhaps it is unwise to flee the goods we have for others that we know not of except under the spur of profit and guided by the reins of effective demand. But the evidence would seem to be overwhelming that there are more things on earth that men could have and would desire than are to be won without the assistance of the State. What would be to the benefit of all may not be to the profit of any one. It does not, for example, pay anyone to make a concerted attack on dirt,[53] or to discover the essential principles of dietetics. The interdependence of the methods and results of scientific research make it impossible for private enterprise to estimate the cost of every service it might desire to provide. Bovril may put beef into men, for the cost of breeding beef is known. Vitamins may put life into men, but the cost of their discovery is not. For any application of science to human needs depends upon a combination of basic research such as animal breeding or the science of the soil or mineralogy, with *ad hoc* research on urgent problems such as the life history of a destructive insect, and the development and application of their results, and all this in a scientific background provided by the fundamental scientific concepts of the age.[54] The community should support laboratories as it once supported Cathedrals. The State could remove hindrances to freedom by guaranteeing in peace some of the experiments it directly makes under the stimulus of war. Were war abolished the State would have funds for audacious experimental research which would have the further advantage of providing a psychological equivalent for war. Even this side of Utopia some provision for research could be made by diverting some of the funds now spent on self-evident quackery. A special tax on worthless medicines would help the Cancer Fund.

Defence. The Haldane Report assumed that the three great departments of defence—War, Admiralty and Air—would in the future, as in the past, be independent Ministries.

General supervision would be normally effected by the Committee of Imperial Defence under the Prime Minister. This Committee of Imperial Defence was a purely advisory and consultative body which inquired into and made recommendations on problems brought before it by the separate department concerned. The Prime Minister was alone responsible for anything in the nature of a consistent policy. In 1923 it was proposed that responsibility for the initiation of policy should rest with the Chairman of the Committee of Imperial Defence, with the assistance of the three Chiefs of Staff of the War Office, Admiralty and Air Ministry. The Committee of Imperial Defence was to consist of the Prime Minister as president, a chairman, the Secretary of State for War, the Secretary of State for Air, the First Lord of the Admiralty, the Chancellor of the Exchequer, the Secretaries of State for Foreign Affairs, for the Colonies and for India, the three Chiefs of Staff and the Permanent Secretary to the Treasury. In the absence of the Prime Minister the chairman was to preside, to report recommendations to the Cabinet and to interpret in matters of detail the decision of the Cabinet to the departments. Assisted by the three Chiefs of Staff, he was to keep the defence situation as a whole constantly under review. The three Chiefs of Staff were to be individually and collectively responsible for advising on defence policy as a whole and to constitute a " super chief of war staff in committee ".[55] Since 1927 these recommendations have been followed. Instead of the initiative resting entirely with the Prime Minister, the three Chiefs of Staff have as a " super chief of war staff in committee " had a direct responsibility for advising the chairman (invariably the Prime Minister) of the Committee of Imperial Defence on the initiation of policy. They furnish the Committee of Imperial Defence every year with a survey of the whole problem of defence which is itself founded on a separate survey of the international situation provided by the Foreign Office. They constitute a sub-committee of the Committee of Imperial Defence over which the Prime Minister presides; their report sweeps the whole field of imperial defence in its minor as well as its major aspects.   Their report is discussed by the Committee of Imperial Defence and then it is sent to the Cabinet.   The Secretary to the Committee of Imperial Defence is also the secretary to the Cabinet.   There are four assistant secretaries, one each for the Air, Navy, Army and Indian Army.   Separate Ministerial committees are concerned with special problems such as the defence of India or of the Middle East.   Over fifty sub-committees deal with such problems as disarmament, censorship, imperial communication, oil, fuel, insurance in time of war, air raid prevention, etc., etc., and a co-ordinating committee keeps the war book up to date.   It is claimed that co-ordination between the services has improved out of all knowledge;[56] that the existing system preserves the responsibility of the Cabinet, provides for the continuous investigation of every kind of problem of defence whether of policy or of detail, and that it could pass by easy transition from a state of peace to a state of war.

But this system has been frequently criticized.   It has been said that the Chiefs of Staffs sub-committee " has done very little to explore and still less to settle " the " larger problems of defence policy ".   " Unanimity has been too often reached by tacit agreement to exclude vital differences of opinion "; and that there is no provision for the examination of defence requirements untrammelled by departmental compromises.[57] It is felt by some that the advance of science is tending to make the three services into three branches of one defence force and that it is an anachronism that they should scramble for their estimates; that with the rapid changes in the forces of the Great Powers without careful co-ordination the three services might find themselves preparing each to meet a different danger: the Navy a threat in the Pacific; the Army a threat to the Indian frontier; the Air Force a threat in Europe, without any decision being come to as to which of the possibilities was probable. For these reasons and because it is impossible for the Prime Minister with all his other duties really to supervise both the Committee of Imperial Defence and the Chiefs of Staffs sub-committee, or to state their problems to the Cabinet, or to hold the balance between the conflicting financial claims of the three services, there are advocates of a Ministry of Defence. This proposal has so far been doubly damned. " No substantial reduction of cost would follow from its creation ";[58] " there would be serious risk that the efficiency of the service might be impaired by the alteration of the system involved ".[59] For as Lord Haldane once said, " the Ministry of Defence, if established with anything like adequate power of control . . . would be bound to interfere in administration . . . by reason of (his) direct responsibility to Parliament ". He would be looked to as responsible not only for efficiency but for economy. " He would therefore require a considerable staff, whose duties would overlap and duplicate those of existing departmental staffs." A Minister of Defence " would . . . be in considerable danger of proving himself to be either too great or too little. If he were effective for the job he would be the rival of the Prime Minister. But in fact the problems of organization for modern defence require powers of influence only to be exercised by the Prime Minister.[60] The conduct of a war is only to be carried out by a small body of Ministers having no other duties to perform. As this organization is not feasible in peace its place is best taken not by a Minister of Defence, but by a Council of Imperial Defence, which might form a nucleus for war.[61]

With the transformation of the European scene by the rise of the Nazi dictatorship the organization of defence was examined by a sub-committee of the Committee of Imperial Defence composed of Secretary to the Committee of Imperial

Defence, the Permanent Secretary to the Treasury, the Permanent Under-Secretary of State for Foreign Affairs and the Chiefs of Staffs.   Their conclusions were submitted to a Defence Policy and Requirements Committee presided over by the Prime Minister, who invited Lord Weir to become a member.   This Defence Policy and Requirements Committee served both as a general purposes committee of the Committee of Imperial Defence and as a committee of liaison between the Committee of Imperial Defence and the Cabinet.[62]   In 1936 a Minister for Co-ordination of Defence was appointed with the duty of generally supervising the Committee of Imperial Defence and the co-ordination of whatever executive action its defence plans might require and in particular the education of the reconditioning plans already determined upon.   The new Minister is the deputy-chairman of the Committee of Imperial Defence and of the Defence Policy and Requirements Committee, and will be, in the Prime Minister's absence, chairman of the Committee of Imperial Defence.   He has the right personally to consult with the Chiefs of Staffs together, including the right to convene under his chairmanship the Chiefs of Staffs Committee whenever he or they think it desirable.[63]

Of the effectiveness of this new office it is not possible to speak.   Possible defects are indicated by the emphatic criticism of Mr. Churchill, who said that the new Minister " had an office so absurdly constructed that the very conditions of his commission revealed a confusion of mind in those who had defined it ".   His responsibilities were so " strangely, so inharmoniously and so perversely grouped " he was endowed with powers " so cribbed and restricted that no one, not even Napoleon himself, would be able to discharge them with satisfaction ".   They included " the co-ordination of high strategic thought on land, sea and air including food supply in time of war; the securing of the punctual execution of the existing very large programme; the planning and organization of British industry so that it would be ready for war expansion ".[64]

The root of these difficulties over so fundamental a problem lies in the fact that the Committee of Imperial Defence was adapted to meet a situation where sea power came first and where the two other services were in some measure merely its adjuncts and to meet the necessities of the self-governing dominions which are united to us only by unwritten and elastic obligations. The Committee of Imperial Defence is an organization that has nothing quite resembling it in any other country. But the development of the air forces of European powers means that while sea power remains a necessary condition for survival, it is no longer a sufficient condition either for safety or for victory.

The Foreign Office. Investigation has shown that of the 249 men who served in the higher ranks of the foreign or the diplomatic services between 1851 and 1929 only nine had been to schools other than public schools or one of the recognized naval and military colleges. There was therefore a wan hope after the war that if many battles won on the playing fields of Eton had been unnecessarily provoked by the esoteric doctrines taught in her schoolrooms the democratization of the service might in future strengthen the forces making for peace. In short in 1919 the requirements that a candidate for the Foreign Office or the diplomatic service must, before he could sit for the examination, have received a nomination from the Secretary of State and be possessed of some £400 a year were abolished. The two services were at the same time amalgamated. The delicate operation had begun of removing the last decaying fragments of eighteenth-century privilege from the twentieth-century constitution.

The peculiarity about the nineteenth-century Foreign Office had been the absence of any rational division of labour. Its old men had little time for vision and its young men more than enough time to dream dreams. In 1905 a committee of investigation was appointed to discover the way business might be done. In consequence a General Registry was created and Foreign Office clerks began to produce their own detailed suggestions on problems which would come to be decided by their superiors. The Office became a body with a highly influential opinion of its own to be reckoned with by the Secretary of State.

With the growth of the complexity of international affairs the Foreign Office provided a complex example of the distribution of departmental business. Obviously most of its work would have to be divided geographically. But there would be some departments—Treaty, News, Consular and Library—which must deal with blocks of subjects in all countries. A few need not only universal handling but require to be controlled by the department most nearly concerned with a given area. So the American Department deals with Disarmament; the Department concerned with Central Europe with the execution of the Peace Treaties; the Eastern Department with the Foreign Relation of Palestine; the Far Eastern Department with the traffic in dangerous drugs; the Northern Department with Bolshevism; the Western Department with the League of Nations.[65]

Ministry of Justice. In 1918 the Committee on Machinery of Government, inspired by Lord Haldane, were of the opinion that there was a strong case for the appointment of a Minister of Justice. It was impressed " by the representations made by men of great experience, such as the President of the Incorporated Law Society, as to the difficulty of getting the attention of the Government to legal reform, and as to the want of contact between those who are responsible for the administration of the work of the Commercial Courts and the mercantile community, and by the evidence adduced that the latter are in consequence and progressively withdrawing their disputes from the jurisdiction of these

AA

courts ". They were no less impressed " with the total inadequacy of the organization which controls the general administration of the very large staffs, with the voluminous business, required to give effect to the decrees of the Courts of Justice throughout the country ". They were of the opinion that " one of the chief reasons for this inadequacy " was " the magnitude and variety of the duties with which the Lord Chancellor is charged, without really being allowed either the time or the machinery requisite for their performance ".[66] We cannot here explore the dusty chambers of " old father antique, the law ". The exigencies of war had brought many of our legal experts into consultation and collaboration with those of Allied powers, with some wholesome shocks to their insular pride. A Ministry of Justice was wanted primarily because there was no general machinery to improve the law of England. It was also wanted that there might be some authoritative body, other than those professional organizations in which the best minds were given to the labours of heavy and lucrative practice, for the development of research and training in the law. It is a paradox that among the people who are the most law-abiding in the world there should be the least general knowledge of the nature and principles of law. It is about the only subject of which an Englishman thinks it folly to be wise. " For the most part the public take but little interest in the machinery of the law, which is in itself difficult to understand and makes but small appeal to the popular imagination." It is as true now as it was in 1872, when Fawcett said that " there is no country in the world whose legal system is so complicated as ours and where the process of obtaining justice is so dear and so slow ".[67] It is said that " every practising lawyer is aware that the public are rapidly losing faith in the present judicial system as a means of settling disputes ".[68]

What then are the objections to a Ministry of Justice in this country? The need for such a Ministry is deemed to be self-evident in every Continental country.[69]   " Nor has Great Britain ever ventured to argue otherwise in taking over responsibility for a country which has previously had one, in however imperfect a form."[70]   It is feared perhaps that the pressure upon a Minister of Justice in the House of Commons for patronage would be unbearable.[71]   " What keeps the English lack of system going, apart from vested interests, is a Whig feeling (still powerful in our mental make-up) about the danger of efficient public controls."[72] It is argued that the position of the Lord Chancellor as a member of the executive government and head of the judiciary provides a link between two sets of institutions which should not be severed.   " It is difficult to believe that there is no necessity for the existence of such a personality, imbued on the one hand with legal ideas and habits of thought and aware on the other of the problems which engage the attention of the executive Government."[73]   Only a man equipped with the prestige or the authority or the personality of the ambitious and successful barrister can be a successful head of the profession and competent to push forward legal reform.[74]   But it may be replied that the danger of patronage may be avoided by continuing our present system of keeping promotions as rare as possible.[75]   At present the amount of promotion from one grade of judge to another is so small as to be negligible.[76]   The Bench could be recruited by a com- mittee of the judges themselves from men of some age at the bar.[77]   Under our present system the Lord Chancellor or the Lord Chief Justice and the Master of the Rolls are appointed by the Prime Minister usually from his political followers—the Law Officers (or ex-Law Officers) of his party's present (or last) Government.   The seven Law Lords similarly are appointed by the Prime Minister usually from among barristers who have rendered political services in politics, but held no previous judicial post; and the President of the Probate, Divorce and Admiralty Division and the five

Lord Justices are also appointments in the hands of the Prime Minister.[78] So that the possibility of political mis-appointments remains. To those who fear efficient public controls it may be pointed out that the creation of the departments responsible for education and for health alone overcame the deficiencies of those services, and did so without impairing the self-guidance of the professions concerned.[79] Finally there is no reason why the peculiar merits of the Lord Chancellor's combination of experience of the world with the learning of the law should not be retained by making him the Minister of Justice.

The Civil Service, like the Constitutional Monarchy, Parliament or the Cabinet is *sui generis*. We cannot say that the politician is concerned with principles while the Civil Service is concerned with details. Nor can we say that the politician is concerned with opinion and the civil servant with research. Nor that the civil servant is concerned with the permanent aspects of policy and the politician with innovation. We can only say that the civil servant is concerned with that part of the work of Government which is not done by Parliament and the Ministry. And the civil servant does not have to consider while the politician does the necessity of securing the support of the electorate. The civil servant is the kind of expert which the party system requires.

The Civil Service has to work under the special conditions of representative government. It is this which distinguishes it from bodies engaged in scientific research or the staffs of private businesses. The most important problems of the modern Civil Service arise from the fact that many of the problems formerly dealt with by private enterprise or academic research it has now to deal with under the very special conditions of parliamentary control. What then are those conditions?

In the first place everything that the civil servant does is an exercise of the power of the State. As an agent of the

Government entitled in the last resort to use force for the enforcement of its commands, he has a duty of fairness greater than that of one engaged in private enterprise. For the civil servant business is not merely business but an act of State. It is his duty to attempt an equality in the application of the law to all whom it may concern, for to do otherwise is to undermine the very principle upon which his power is based— that the State is the organ of the common will.

In private enterprise it may not pay to discriminate between customers—charging one price to a man in furs and another to a man in rags—but there is no duty to give equality of treatment. It may be unwise but it is not wrong to make the good customer pay indirectly for the debts of the bad. The competitive system assumes that there is a trial of wits between all buyers and all sellers into which justice does not enter except in the form of the prevention by the State of certain frauds, and the enforcement of agreements made in a certain way. If the buyer or seller does more than the law commands it is to please his conscience or because he feels that honesty pays. In business no omission or commission is a sin except those to which a legal penalty or possible loss of business is attached. But the State must collect the last local licence even though it would cost less to let them go unpaid not merely because to do so would encourage non-payment but because the State as such has a duty to apply the law equally to all. It would not be right for any individual to be discriminated against or to derive an advantage from the administration of a code which had not been envisaged by the code itself.

Even without a representative system this duty of fairness might be regarded as binding upon the officials of the State. But where there is a representative system the performance of this duty is safeguarded in certain very special ways. Criticism of the administration becomes a part of the tactics of party warfare, and any individual case may be made the test of a principle and determine the fate of a Government. In private enterprise the rising curve of sales is the approved sign of efficiency; in the public service it is the fairness of any individual case. This means that the civil servant has to do his work in a particular way. He must be " able at short notice to put the Minister in a position of justifying anything that he has done down to quite small details ".[80]   It means that public departments have to be organized so that there is a consilience between their decisions made for different places and at different times. Not only must there be such consilience but its existence must be capable of demonstration to unfriendly critics. This necessitates an administrative machine of a complexity unknown to private enterprise. In private enterprise a policy can and must depend to a large extent upon the men at the head of a particular department; but in a Government office there has to be a complex organization in which each grade of officials has a defined authority delegated to them and which even in the lowest grades will be quite extensive. This complexity which is the safeguard for justice popular Government demands, affects every detail of the civil servant's work. He must show with the most meticulous detail that the money he has spent has been spent only for the purpose for which it was intended. In the absence of the automatic test of profit every proposal for fresh expenditure and nearly every proposal for an alteration in the direction and scale of Government activity has to be made convincing in advance on paper. The civil servant has to work by written memoranda and in accordance with general regulations decided at the appropriate level in the hierarchy. Thus red tape correctly used is the symbol of the citizens' equality before the law.

A Government department has to determine policy and to apply policy already decided. It has to assist the Minister to determine what legislation shall be passed and to see that

legislation which has been passed is applied. It is its function to make the best use of permitted means to ends commanded or allowed. In applying whatever powers they
possess they must be gathering the experience necessary for
the future adjustment of their powers to new conditions.
" It is not only necessary that the legislature should make
provision in the laws for their due execution; it is also
desirable that the executive agency should work towards new
legislation on the same topics. For the execution of laws
deals with those particulars by an induction of which the
results to be aimed at in legislation are to be ascertained;
and the generalization from those particulars can only be
well effected when the lowest in the chain of functionaries is
made subsidiary to the operations of the highest in a sugges-
tive as well as in an executive capacity—that is, when the
experience of the functionary who puts his last hand to the
execution of any particular class of enactments, is made available for the guidance of the legislature ".[81]

It is under these very special conditions that the politician
and the civil servant have to work together. Their relations
have been determined by long experience and countless subtle
precedents which have become part of the spirit of the constitution. But while their relations have become a vital
part of the conventions of the constitution, continuity with
the past is defensible only so long as it produces a tradition
capable of being adapted to whatever changes the future
may hold. No hard and fast rules can be laid down for
the guidance of the two parties to this vital partnership.

Any attempt to describe this most important part of our
working constitution is limited by certain obvious difficulties.
The civil servant it has been said must take the triple vow
of poverty, anonymity and obedience.[82] Their biographies are
scanty, anecdotal and discrete. Those who possess too much
or too little character to remain in the service are restrained
in their revelations by the Official Secrets Acts. In the

biographies of statesmen the few references to their permanent and silent collaborators are as complimentary but
uninformative as tombstones. Even in evidence before
Royal Commissions and departmental inquiries the greatest
reserve is shown by politicians and civil servants on the subject of their official relations. The work of a department
like the Foreign Office can only be understood by studying the
marginalia on dispatches, private correspondence of Cabinet
Ministers and M.P.'s and ambassadors in London.[83]   And
doubtless it is in the public interest that the relations between
politicians and civil servants should be a marriage of true
minds with no impediment of publicity to its consummation.

The war conditions of 1914-18 broke down some of the
traditional reticence of statesmen. We have Dr. Addison's
opinion that the Admiralty has a habit of " going its own way
regardless of other people, and that some of the officials at
the Local Government Board were just a little slippy.[84]
We know that Mr. Lloyd George was more than thankful
when the Admiralty could not see their way to lend him any
of their staff for his new Ministry of Munitions.[85]   He has
also described " the amazing and incomprehensible difficulties
encountered in inducing the Admiralty even to try the convoy
system ".[86]   But in all these cases we must be careful to
distinguish between the limitations of individual civil
servants, the limitations of the organization and traditions
of particular departments, the general limitations of the
expert and his special limitations in an emergency.

With the change in the scale and nature of government
the civil servant has come to play a part so intrinsically
important that the glamour of political office may have no
superior attraction. Macaulay's schoolboy might well hesitate between the office of Mr. Eden and the office of Mr.
Vansittart. The peculiar eminence of Victorian statesmen
belongs now to no one in the world of politics. It is true
that the technique of boosting has been so developed that a

single mannikin can sway regions vaster than Cæsar ever knew; but that kind of power can be enjoyed by so many other public persons besides politicians, and its character is known by so many to be a fake that it has lost more than half its charm. So numerous are the gods which propaganda serves that mere mortality is preferable to apotheosis. In a world of Hitlers, Mussolinis and Charlie Chaplins the sweets of hidden power are more attractive than ever. Better to have one's ear to the ground than one's mouth always at the loudspeaker.

It has been said that the civil servant has the duty " to set the wider and more enduring considerations against the exigencies of the moment which may be the concern of his perhaps fleeting political partner ".[87] Or more bluntly: " In this democratic age it is absolutely essential that you should have at the head of a department a man who will express his opinion absolutely fearlessly . . . whether or not the Minister accepts his advice. It is vital to the interests of the country that successive waves of political opinion in a department should be confronted by this wall of experienced opinion."[88] It was once the duty of the Minister to tell the civil servant what the public would not stand; it is now the duty of the civil servant to tell the Minister what the facts will not allow.

But the distinctions between the sphere of the civil servant concerned with enduring and the sphere of the Minister concerned with ephemeral things is both superficial and misleading. It may be true that some politician after the orgy of lying into which the technique of a modern election may have seduced him will require the sobering influence of departmental detail to restore his sense of reality. But the number of politicians of ministerial quality who are deceived by their own election speeches must be very small. If it is the function of the civil servant to sober the Minister it is equally the function of the Minister to inspire the expert. However brief may be his term of office he must try to reveal to his technical experts the wider and enduring problems underlying their specialized knowledge.   Constitutional conventions and a strong tradition of mutual respect has produced a working system of co-operation.   But any sudden change in the nature and scope of political activity might show that the principles of their co-operations are only imperfectly understood.   The factors are many and various.

First, the bulk of official activity is concerned with the application of principles and the running of machinery previously established.   In normal times no government attempts to establish a new machinery of government.   Most of the activities therefore of departments will be routine and non-political.   Unless some change in social conditions or opinion produces unexpected difficulties the Minister must necessarily be guided by his experts on any detail of this traditional policy.   But the relation between the application of policy already approved by Parliament and the determination of fresh policy is complex and subtle.   " The application to particular cases of general principles laid down in statutes or the administration of financial provisions made by Parliament will involve also the preparation or study of proposals for the alteration of existing law in the light of changed circumstances or new policies or experience."[89]   Morant at the Board of Education, by skilfully revealing the weaknesses of the system he had to administer, secured the passing of the Education Act, 1902.

The work of Morant at the Board of Education and of Llewellyn Smith at the Board of Trade shows that with the new responsibilities which the State is undertaking the permanent head of a Government department must himself be a statesman in everything except the ability to lead a party or inspire an electorate, or sway the House of Commons.   " My own conception of the permanent head of a large Government department is that he is not (except by accident) a specialist in anything, but rather the general adviser of the Minister, the general manager and controller under the Minister, with the ultimate responsibility to the Minister for all the activities of the department . . . including those directed to secure economy in policy and management. The Permanent Secretary is a general manager rather than an expert. His duty is to shopwalk the department and to see that the Minister gets the best technical advice."[90]

The permanent head and his immediate assistants have three complex tasks: they must see that the department, in the exercise of the powers given by Parliament conflicts neither with the law nor provokes public or parliamentary criticism which the government of the day cannot successfully answer in Parliament; they must be able to interpret to the Minister the policy which the experience of the department suggests. There is in fact in every department a tradition which only the strongest Minister can override. Even the Permanent Secretary himself can do little more than assist the Minister to the discovery of whatever knowledge corporate or individual there is. Thirdly, they must be able to organize the resources of the department for the assistance of the Minister in whatever policy he may decide to adopt. " The popular fiction that the civil servants are anxious to foist their own policy upon Ministers is not true. . . . The Civil Service like their Minister to do well; they feel personally humiliated if he makes blunders; they take enormous pains to give him all the facts and to warn him against pitfalls. If they think the policy he contemplates is wrong they will tell him why, but always on the basis that it is for him to settle the matter. And if the Minister, as is sometimes the case, has neither the courage nor the brains to evolve a policy of his own, they will do their best to find him one; for after all it is better that a department should be run by its civil servants than that it should not be run at all."[91] The part played by the civil servant in the determination of policy varies with the nature of the problem to be decided. Proposals for legislation, for example, fall into three main classes: the more important Bills which the Government have announced that it is their policy to carry into law and on which they stake their political existence; the principal departmental Bills which reflect Government policy which are not concerned with major issues; Bills of a non-controversial type which reflect departmental policy on particular points and which it is thought will prove useful additions to the statute book. In the case of the first class the broad outlines of the Bill are usually settled by the Ministers themselves with such assistance as they may require from the various departments; the other two are mainly the work of the individual departments.[92]

A Minister at the head of a large department will find that not only is there a departmental tradition but that within that tradition there are conflicting schools and policies. His real problem is to lay bare the unconscious presuppositions upon which his civil servants are working. This will be particularly difficult when in a large department the Permanent Secretary himself has to interpret the various technical policies which exist within the department. For the Permanent Secretary may be in relation to the technical experts in the same position as the Minister is to himself. Both he and the Minister are amateurs in relations to the various technical advisers on whom they both depend. But in some cases the permanent head of a department will be himself an expert on policy. Were, for example, Lord Hugh Cecil, as Minister for Foreign Affairs, to propose a certain policy of disarmament it would be possible for the Permanent Secretary of the Foreign Office to present him with a memorandum stating the common-sense objections to the policy proposed. In such a discussion the civil servant will have only that advantage over the Minister normally possessed by a mind trained to consider problems over a mind skilled to sway opinion.   But in most cases the policy which is to be adopted will depend upon the interpretation of a variety of expert opinions.   The Ministry of Agriculture no doubt possesses certain economic and statistical experts.   It is possible that neither the Permanent Secretary nor the Minister can secure from their crowd of experts guidance to a consistent policy.

Where the department realizes that the Minister is committed to a policy for which there is nothing to be said, their duty is simple—those who cannot lead the blind must in mercy soften their fall.   But the real difficulty occurs when a difference between the leading civil servants in a department and the Minister is thought by the latter to be due to the former misunderstanding their own technical experts. Strong Ministers hold that they are not " forbidden by any rule of honour or etiquette from sending for any person either inside or outside his office, whatever his rank, to seek enlightenment on any subject affecting his administration. If a Minister learns that any subordinate in his department possesses exceptional knowledge or special aptitude on any question he should establish direct contact with him.   The political head of a department has not merely the right, but the duty to send for anyone who will help him to discharge his trust to the public ".[93]

When an entirely new policy is being started, e.g., Old Age Pensions, National Health Insurance or Unemployment Insurance, all the outstanding men in the Civil Service will be brought in.[94]   And not only should a Minister responsible for a difficult Bill call upon the whole resources of the Civil Service; a Cabinet faced with a vital problem of policy is entitled to hear the opinion of civil servants even if it be contrary to the political head of the department from which they come.   " If an official disagrees with the head of his department it is usually his duty not to resign, but to state fully to the head of his department and, should any proper occasion arise, to other members of the Ministry, what are the nature of his views."[95]   A first Lord of the Admiralty cannot expect his Admiralty civil servants to support him against other Ministers when the position is so serious that a joint consultation has been called. How far a consilience of expert opinion scattered in a variety of departments will be revealed depends upon the steps which the Cabinet takes for investigation and thought.   It would be interesting to know how far a few economic experts isolated in a lonely protest within the Ministry of Agriculture could join forces with their more powerful colleagues in the Board of Trade or the Treasury.

The simplest form of the problems involved in the relation between the permanent or administrative head of a Government department and its technical experts is the question whether or not such experts—medical, engineering, economic, biological, etc.—should have the right of direct access to the Minister. Has the Medical Officer of Health the right directly to challenge the presentation of departmental opinion made by the Permanent Secretary to the Minister? Sir Warren Fisher has stated that no Permanent Secretary would refuse to permit his technical experts to communicate with the Minister should they wish.   But it is also desirable that there should be systematic co-operation between experts in different fields employed in separate departments. In the case of finance it has been made obligatory upon Establishment Officers to keep in the closest relation one with another and for accounting officers to communicate directly with the Treasury.   The influence of the Whitley system and the urgent need for economy since the war has imposed on the heads of departments a practice of consultation since the war which was unusual before.   On all questions of staffing and administrative organization they hold frequent consultations. In the nineteenth century permanent heads of departments did not pool their ideas on such matters.   The purchase of a typewriter or the employment of a typist was then a domestic detail of the department immediately concerned. What has been found desirable in finance and administrative organizations should be applied to other matters of common concern.   Before the establishment of the Cabinet Secretariat there was no method by which departments were informed as a matter of course of all Cabinet decisions which concerned them.   Only recently has the responsibility for advising the Cabinet on matters of Defence been made the joint and several responsibility for the three Chiefs of Staff to the War Office, Admiralty and Air Ministry. If the Treasury can have its eyes and ears in every department so could the statistical and research departments.   It is the older departments which cling to a tradition of non-co-operation.   The Admiralty has been perhaps the greatest offender.   But the legal departments, save in the technical matter of drafting, fail to use the experience of those trained in jurisprudence.

The conditions which we have described as common to all Civil Service work—the duty of fairness and the need of producing a detailed defence of any action which may be challenged—has to be satisfied under a great variety of conditions in the different departments.   But in the organization of all Government departments there are certain common features.

Most departments will have a registry—a section in which are noted all letters and documents that enter or leave the department or pass from one division of a department to another.   It is the function of a registry to record all movements of documents in and out of a department and to be a storehouse of precedents.   In 1930 the Board of Education dealt with 1,350,000 letters, the Ministry of Agriculture with 1,300,000, the Ministry of Labour with 825,000 and the Ministry of Health with 750,000.[96]   It is from the standpoint of the registry that the efficiency of a department can most easily be judged.   One department " selected a high official, placed him in personal charge of the registry, instructed him to observe from that point of vantage what was going on and armed him with power to interfere and get things put right. He was not concerned with what the decision might be, but he was concerned to see that there was a decision taken at the proper time and properly arrived at ".[97]

This registration of all correspondence at a single point enables the official before coming to any decision to study the life history of any question impaled on a large file. This file is both an instrument of co-ordination and a record of official action. It has certain obvious drawbacks. Only one section can use a file at a time and one of the minor arts of the civil servant is the retention for his own use of files which may be sought by others.

In every department there will be an Establishments Branch concerned, in consultation with Establishments Branch of the Treasury, with all problems of staffing. It is the duty of all Establishments Officers to know not only the detailed conditions in their own department but to be familiar with the general conditions throughout the Service. On them depends the making of the proper use of the available staff and the contentment and efficiency which come from an understanding of its merits. In all departments there will be an Accounting Branch concerned with whatever financial control the Treasury consider to be necessary for the particular work which the department has to perform. In the larger departments like the War Office and the Admiralty, the Accounting Branch will amount almost to a Treasury within a department. The essential function of an Accounting Branch is to see that the letter and the spirit of the authority to spend given by Parliament is observed. All departments require legal assistance to advise them on the scope of their powers and duties and to conduct any business requiring legal training, e.g., the conduct of cases before the courts and the drafting of bills and rules and orders. Some departments have their own solicitors' department; others have their own legal advisers but the Treasury Solicitor does their litigious work, while in others all their legal business is transacted by the Treasury Solicitor.   Departments draft their own rules and orders but the final instructions for a Bill go from the department concerned to the Parliamentary Counsel.   Finally large departments will have a special branch concerned with publicity and the provision of answers to parliamentary questions.

These sections are necessary because all State business must be on record, must be as economical as possible, and all departments be staffed without the power of hire and fire possessed by a private employer, and their actions must be within the scope of power given by Parliament.

The earlier classification of the work of the civil servant into routine and policy has developed into administrative, executive and clerical, with complex variations of " other executive," " other clerical " and a growing number of professional and technical workers.   Administrative work has been defined as that which is concerned with policy or the formation of policy; executive, that which is concerned with giving effect to policy that has been determined—the application of a code of law or administration to obtain results.   While clerical work deals with particular cases in accordance with well-defined regulations, instructions or general practice.

The work of the adminstrator varies widely from department to department.   In each department a different form of ability of a high order will be required.   The Treasury requires the intellectual equipment capable of mastering a complex problem in currency or finance.   The Foreign Office requires a social, if not a spiritual, gift of tongues.   The Colonial Office has always been a governing department with for most of its decisions no further check beyond what there is within the walls of its own office.   For while it performs the functions which are common to other departments

BB

in this country it is also charged in regard to all Crown Colonies with many of the duties which would in other cases be dealt with by separate departments, e.g., the construction of a public building, police, education and the raising of loans. Its decisions include in respect to some fifty communities all the questions which can arise in any country. It has to appoint an overseas staff competent to establish a régime which shall preserve what is best in the traditional native culture. Its staff must be capable of producing reports which can be published as State Papers in distant communities; and most important of all they are concerned with the impact of science on the structure of backward communities. The Admiralty is not only the architect of the house in which Jack floats, but his butcher, baker and candle-stick-maker as well. The Home Office is not only primarily responsible for internal order but for all business not assigned to some other department. It secures through its inspectors the efficiency of the local police, supervises reformatory and industrial schools and sends representatives to international conferences on industrial relations, opium, and the traffic in women and children. The Board of Trade studies the course of trade but also is responsible for the administration of a variety of statutes relating to patents, industrial and commercial standards and the mercantile marine. The Ministry of Health is concerned, not only with the supervision of the medical profession in its relation to the general public where health insurance is concerned, but is responsible for the structure and efficiency of local government as a whole. Both at the Ministry of Health and the Board of Education it is an important part of the duties of an administrator to maintain good relations with the representatives of a variety of local authorities while securing the application by them of the standards of local administration Parliament has prescribed. In the Ministry of Agriculture and Fisheries the administrator has the almost impossible task of harmonizing the science of animal and plant breeding with the intuitions of economists and the conflicting prejudices and experience of landlord, tenant and consumer.[98]

Administrators may be classified into three groups: (1) the Permanent Under-Secretary of State with a Deputy Secretary, found in the larger departments and the Principal Assistant Secretary; (2) the Assistant Secretaries; (3) the Principals and Assistant Principals.

The first groups form a kind of Civil Service general head-quarters. It is mainly concerned with consideration of general policy, with administrative decisions in which Parliament is likely to be directly interested or with specialized functions which cover the whole range of a department's work. The Permanent Secretary is a general manager rather than an expert. Of some twenty posts of this status (that is carrying over £3,000 a year) fourteen were held in 1930 by men promoted from other departments. Since 1918 the increased complexity of the Government problems and the influence of Whitleyism has secured a habit of continuous and informal co-operation between the Permanent Head of the Depart-ments under the Permanent Secretary to the Treasury, now the official head of the Civil Service.

The division of duties between the Permanent Secretary and the Deputy Secretary, where one exists, is determined by the nature of the work which the department does. In some cases policy will be the concern of the Permanent Secretary while the general control and direction of the running of the department is assigned to the deputy; in others both policy and general supervision will be divided between them on a functional basis. The Principal Assistant Secretaries either directly supervise finance or establishments or they take final responsibility for such part of the administrative work as can be disposed of without the personal consideration of the Permanent Head or the Minister. The Assistant Secretaries are usually at the head of a unit known as a Branch, which can be organized on either a functional or a territorial basis. In the Home Office, Assistant Secretaries are at the head of seven branches—industrial, aliens, criminal, children, miscellaneous (the Kings' pleasure, vivisection and dangerous explosives), police, Ireland (Northern Ireland and the Channel Islands and the Isle of Man).[99]   In the Colonial Office the division of the work is territorial.   In the Board of Education there is both a functional and a territorial organization, so that there are men in the department aware of the general situation in any part of the country with whom a particular local Director of Education can confer.   Where conditions require that the work of a branch should be divided into sections a Principal will direct the work of each.   In the Board of Trade a Principal has charge of the administration of the Merchant Shipping Acts.   In the Board of Education the Principal is the opposite number of the Director of Education.   The Assistant Principals are the understudies and assistants to the Principals.   They are regarded as a cadet corps from which a selection should be made for higher administrative posts.

The tendency is to do more and more of the work in the higher ranges by discussion and less and less by writing letters or putting minutes on official files.   In the nineteenth century there was a fantastic accumulation of detailed work for which the Minister was responsible.   The mass of unimportant work was considered to have helped the death of Lord Clarendon, who had to initial a heap of trash.[100]   The clerks in the Foreign Office were mere copyists.   Waddington of the Home Office thought that minuting was the exclusive function of the Under-Secretary.[101]   In the Colonial Office clerks were early encouraged to make their own memoranda. By 1872 minuting and drafting were not restricted to any class of clerks.[102]   In the Board of Trade by 1888 even a junior clerk was encouraged to put his ideas on paper.   The system was established in all departments that the juniors should settle what they could and what they could not they should send up to their superiors.

An executive officer is required to give effect to a pre-determined policy as distinct from the Administrator, who has to decide the policy to be followed.[103]   His work involves the interpretation and application of law and regulations in cases which require decision.   He has often to apply a very difficult and complex code of law to the circumstances of individual cases.   The Executive class developed when a body of men was required to be responsible for the application of the complex codes of law which developed after 1870.   The difficulty of their position is that they exist as a class only in those departments where there is sufficient work for a special class of officers to carry out policy rather than to advise and devise. There are, for example, no executives in the Home Office, though it would be fantastic to say that there was no executive work for them to do.[104]   Executive officers are used mainly for the Accounts, Finance and Supply branches of Government departments.   There are a few large and important classes known for want of a better name as Other Executives. Such are the outdoor staff of the Customs and Excise Department, the tax inspectorate, the staff of the Estate Duty Office of the Inland Revenue and the Employment Officers of the Ministry of Labour.

It has been said that a clerical officer is required to know but that he is not required to exercise discretion.[105]   He prepares the material on which the administrative or executive officers will form a judgment.   He drafts simple letters and keeps records.   The best example of their work is provided by the various registries.   In the Board of Education a clerical officer is responsible for collecting and keeping the various precedents on secondary education; a higher clerical officer drafts and replies to petitions and congratulatory messages received by the King; another sanctions the disposals of human remains.   In fact the average citizen will meet the

State in the personality and phrasing of a clerical or junior executive officer.

There are two other classes of officers which play a vital part in the work of Government departments—the Inspectors and the professional and scientific staff. There are more than 2,000 inspectors employed in twenty-eight different departments. They are charged with duties of inspection and report, but not with responsibility, for the execution of any decision. And it is this which mainly distinguished them from other civil servants. Their duties obviously cover a wide field, e.g., the inspection of schools, reformatories, factories and workshops, mines, quarries and Poor Law Institutions. The great majority of them possess technical and professional qualifications which relate them to the professional and technical staff. But the essential duty of these latter is to participate in the formation of policy and its execution. Of the problems raised by the importance of science for the work of the State a little has been said. Here it is only necessary to indicate how complex and varied are the professional and scientific groups now employed. They all possess some professional qualification granted by an outside body, e.g., the qualification possessed by a barrister, doctor, solicitor, architect, valuer, surveyor, etc. Half the legal officers (about 550) are employed in the legal branches or solicitors' departments of Government departments; the others in legal or quasi legal departments such as the Supreme Court of Judicature, the County Courts departments and the Land Registry. The medical officers are employed in the Ministry of Pensions (200), the Ministry of Health (114) and the Prison Commission (52). The Office of Works employs over 400 architects and surveyors and over 200 others are shared between the Defence Departments, the Ministry of Agriculture and Fisheries and the Department of Agriculture for Scotland. Over 1,200 engineers, civil, mechanical and electrical, are employed by the Defence Departments, the

Office of Works, the Post Office, the Ministry of Transport and the Mercantile Marine Department of the Board of Trade. The Department of Scientific and Industrial Research employs over 350 chemists, scientific and industrial research workers; the Department of the Government Chemist another 79, and over 300 are employed in the research departments of the Defence Departments.

The complex structure of some of our departments is shown by the Ministry of Agriculture and Fisheries—though that, like the miracle of the loaves and fishes, is a special case. Altogether there are, or were in 1930, twelve divisions: (1) Education and Research under a permanent assistant secretary; (2) land drainage and rural life under an assistant secretary; (3) markets division under an assistant secretary; (4) economics division under a principal assistant secretary; (5) livestock division under an assistant secretary. It is appropriate that this officer is also the principal establishment officer; (6) a land division under an assistant secretary; (7) diseases of animals under the Chief Veterinary Surgeon; (8) Fish department under a principal assistant secretary; (9) Wales has of course a Welsh secretary; (10) Establishments; (11) Finance; (12) Legal; and the Royal Botanical Gardens. The Ministry is also partly responsible for the Ordnance Survey.

Where there is this complex combination of administrators, technicians, scientists and professional men it is sometimes said that the professional men do not have the access to the political head that is enjoyed by the non-technical staff. Experts, it is alleged, have had sometimes to choose between their salary and their conscience. Sir Warren Fisher, the Permanent Head of the Treasury, has specifically denied this.[106] The senior technical officer has the right of direct access to the Minister. He has the status but does not act as a Secretary. He does not, for example, sign letters.[107] It is the duty of the technical officer to inform the administrator of the possible consequences of his action in so far as his special knowledge enables him to do so. He must indicate the technical consequences of an administrative act. He cannot decide the wisdom of that act in all its bearings. But he is entitled to know who is responsible for a decision. Before a recommendation of his is reversed he is entitled to be consulted.[108] But these principles are difficult to apply. In the first place a matter which requires the opinion of the highest technical expert may on the administrative side be rejected on good grounds by someone low in the administrative hierarchy. Or secondly, a matter of the greatest importance on the administrative side may be referred to a scientist or economist who has no professional superior to whom he can refer for support in his rejection of the scheme which comes with all the weight of the department. What is the position of a research worker in statistics or economics attached to a division of a department engaged in the formation of a detailed policy for the consideration of the Ministry? How far should he be able to refer his difficulties officially to the general statistical and economic wisdom of the service? It is said that no administrative department will overrule the advice of its legal expert on matters of *ultra vires* without reference to the law officers of the Crown. How far is it desirable that the statistician or economist should be able to appeal to his technical and professional superiors perhaps in other departments? In the Ministry of Agriculture and Fisheries there is a system of conferences on monthly reports from each division: the Minister, the heads of the professional branches and the inspectors are all present.[109] But unless the expert view is brought in at an early stage in the formation of a decision it is difficult to get the technical view properly considered.[110] Also it is possible that in discussions of policy questions may be raised which are in fact technical though the non-technician may not realise that they are. On the one hand questions of policy cannot be formulated without expert knowledge; but at the same time it is difficult to secure that the judgment of experts will not themselves be shot through by considerations of policy. For there is " a very common infirmity of human nature, inclining us to be more curious and conceited in matters where we have least concern, and for which we are least adapted either by study or nature ".

The growth of the technical services of the State will make it desirable for the administrator to receive some definite training in the art of co-operating with his scientific colleagues. The Colonial Office already provides that its district officers should receive some training in the art of co-operating with the various scientists with whom they work. But in few departments in England is there any real provision for the proper use of expert knowledge and scientific thought. When it was suggested that the efficiency of departments which are concerned with a large proportion of technical and scientific matters was lowered by the practice of not appointing a technical expert as the permanent head, the Anderson Committee[111] reported that they did not agree " that an officer appointed for his technical knowledge is necessarily the best man to control a department. The duties and outlook of an administrator differ from those of the technical man. Although men with high technical qualifications occasionally prove themselves to be first-rate administrators the head of a department should . . . be so detached from technical bias that he can weigh the advice of his various officers and judge correctly between competing claims each of which may to its technical advocate seem to be paramount.[112] The relation between the analytical and speculative thinker and men wise in action, between those who understand the causes of things and those who could with mastery administer the unforeseen is at the heart of the problem of government. To secure a proper relation between the expert and the man of affairs is one of the tasks of education. Scientific method has a very complex relation to action which has yet to be understood. " In matters of conduct we are frequently compelled to decide at once between exclusive alternatives. In theoretic issues we may avoid either alternative by suspending judgment." Delay will not destroy what the thinker seeks, but in action we must at once succeed or perhaps for ever fail.

The administrator and the technical and scientific staff of a department have a delicate task if they are properly to co-operate. It will be difficult for them to know when they are considering the same problem. The administrator may not grasp the abstract character of the scientific analysis. The scientist may not have realized the full complexity of the concrete case. It has been said that any expert is better for twenty minutes' cross-examination by a layman. Equally, most laymen would be better for twenty months' discipline in an expert field. At present the administrator may find the greatest difficulty in defining for the scientist the problem with which he is concerned. He may be crushed by irrelevant pedantries when he attempts to formulate his problem. He will have the greatest difficulty in recognizing where, in the case in question, expert knowledge ends and uncertainty begins. This will be worst where the administrator has to deal not with pure scientists who may be forced to formulate their case for the criticisms of their fellow experts, but with professional men like doctors, lawyers, economists, whose knowledge and art have their own unresolved problems of policy which wait on action as much as the affairs of State themselves. A proposed policy may involve risks both of an administrative and of a technical character which it is impossible to reduce to a common measure, between which a choice must be made, e.g., will a particular policy increase or decrease unemployment; whether it does so or not, will it or will it not cause a riot. In an emergency the technician's judgment may be coloured by an intuition or prejudice as to the whole situation the greater because the precision of his vision in one direction has made him more blind than usual in others. The uncertainty which he does feel he can only communicate in the technical language which he knows and its significance may therefore be lost upon the administrator. The administrator himself may not be able to communicate his difficulties in any language which his technician understands. To meet these difficulties the relation between the administrative and the scientific staff of Government departments is being carefully watched. The expert is as far as possible associated with the process of modification which experience may impose on his original suggestion and he is kept informed of the verifications or otherwise which events give to his judgment. As far as possible he is given the opportunity to accept responsibility for the application of his own advice.

It must be obvious that the increase in the rules that the State has to enforce will mean that there will also be an increase in the number of cases where decisions will have to be made on disputed points in their application to particular circumstances. The greater the number of organized games the more referees will be required. It is not therefore surprising that there should have been a great increase in the number of authorities which have been given power to decide disputed points in the application of the law. But it has caused some perturbation in technically judicial minds that special ministerial tribunals should have been given this responsibility in place of the ordinary courts of law. Sometimes the determination of disputes in the application of a statute will require speed, an expert knowledge for the determination of a special class of facts, and cheapness for the litigants concerned. Specialized courts have been appointed for the determination of such disputes. In some cases the Minister himself has been given the power to determine disputed points in the application of the law that would normally have been left to the ordinary courts. There are large numbers of cases where the department has to determine disputes between itself and private individuals or between itself and statutory authorities or between different statutory authorities themselves because the issues involved are not of the kind that could be left to a court of law. Bureaucracy's infinite variety can be suggested by a few examples. The Admiralty may, where it appears to them that a sailor has deserted his wife and children compulsorily, deduct from his pay for their maintenance. The Commissioners of Customs and Excise are entitled to require proof to be given to their satisfaction that a business has been permanently discontinued. The Board of Inland Revenue must determine whether a transfer *inter vivos* has been for valuable consideration and whether a transaction has been carried out by a dealer in the ordinary course of his business. The decision by the Post-master-General as to the description of a postal package is final, as it is also as to the length of a telephone talk. For the exemption of death duties the Treasury may determine what objects are of national or scientific or historic interest or in what occupations the risk of death is the same as that of active service. The Minister of Health can remove a doctor from the medical list after inquiry if he is satisfied that the doctor's continuance on the list would be prejudicial to the efficiency of the insurance scheme. The Board of Trade may suspend or cancel the certificate of a master.

These cases suggest that there is no essential difference between the function of administration and that of adjudication. The administrator who is determining the application of a rule to particular circumstances has to investigate the facts, see the relation of the rule to the facts, and decide whether to act or not. But the Report on Ministers' Powers[118] drew a distinction between judicial, quasi judicial and administrative decisions. In a true *judicial* decision there is a dispute between two or more parties, the presentation of their case by the parties involved, the ascertainment of facts by means of evidence adduced by the parties, followed by a decision which disposes of the whole matter by a finding upon the facts in dispute and an application of the law of the land to the facts so found, including where required a ruling upon any disputed question of law. In a *quasi judicial* decision, while there must be a hearing of the parties to a dispute, there is no mere application of the law of the land to the facts found, but an administrative action determined by the Minister's free choice. In an *administrative* decision there is no legal obligation upon the person charged with the duty of reaching a decision to consider and weigh submissions and arguments or to collate evidence or to solve any issue. The ground upon which he acts and the means which he takes to inform himself before acting are left entirely in his discretion. It is the existence of a dispute and parties to the dispute which separates the judicial and quasi judicial function from the administrative. A quasi judicial decision is an administrative decision some stage or some element of which possessed judicial characteristics. From these distinctions the report drew the conclusion that judicial functions should normally be entrusted to the ordinary courts of law; that where Parliament considered it necessary to depart from the normal course it should entrust the judicial functions involved to a ministerial tribunal rather than to the Minister personally. Quasi judicial decisions should be left to the Ministers themselves and not given to courts of law or ministerial tribunals. The jurisdiction of the High Court of Justice to compel Ministers and ministerial tribunals to keep within their powers and to exercise their power in good faith uninfluenced by extraneous and irrelevant considerations ought to be viligantly maintained.

Does this analysis meet the heart of the problem involved? Surely it does not. Every tribunal administers something. " The only pertinent question is what does it administer."[114]

But while a judicial tribunal's business is well defined—it administers justice, the business of an administrative tribunal has remained unclassified.[115] Judicial tribunals profess to be bound by the law—a fixed and settled objective standard. Administrative tribunals are only bound by their own sense of what within their powers in fitting. The ordinary courts of justice have a procedure and traditions which go back to before the development of the modern State—before the community had accepted the idea of an innovating legislature. The courts were mainly concerned to determine the application of customary law or laws which could be discerned by the insight of the good and wise as fitting for the solution of the particular cases brought before them. They were experts on local custom whose opinion could be got for a fee. Needless to say, such courts were in the habit of creating the law they professed to discover. But as they did not claim to legislate, but merely to apply an already existing law, the question of their responsibility was not raised. They were experts in the determination of special kinds of problems: property contracts, thefts, murder, treason, etc. They had a special skill in the interpretating of documents and could exercise a useful control over the pretension of the Crown or the Parliament to control the community. But as the duties of Government become more complex and the matters with which they deal enter less and less within the special knowledge of our traditional courts there is no reason why the investigation of facts, the interpretation and application of rules made by Parliament or implied in the situation to be dealt with should not be a function of many kinds of tribunals.

One of the obvious problems of the immediate future will be the fact that both politicians and civil servants will be drawn from a more violent and less stable world. For the politician the technique of the manipulation of opinion is becoming every day more important. The mass stamping of the gutter Press replaced the oratorical duel and has itself been superseded by the hypnosis of the stage-managed plebiscite. The maintenance of political power requires abilities and means which are in startling conflict with the abilities and means required to solve the real problems of the State. One is reminded of the concurrent processes of the deification of the emperor and the spread of Eastern mythology with the development of the bureaucracy and the subtleties of Roman law in the later Roman Empire.

What can be said of the future co-operation between the expert and the politician? In the first place both the civil servant and the politician have a problem of weighing evidence every day more complex than the day before. But this need not be exaggerated. For with the advance of scientific knowledge the nature of the evidence which they have to consider may be greater in bulk but more manageable in form. Quantitatively there may be an increase, but qualitatively there may be greater simplicity. In the formative days of our political and administrative traditions the worlds of the professions and the sciences were even more chaotic than those of Government itself. The only order anywhere to be found was in the routine of custom, the inexplicable order of trade and commerce, and the general unseen order providence was supposed to maintain. Now many of our problems, though yet unsolved, are in matters of a measurable and demonstrable kind. To deal with them need not rouse the black passions of a threatened creed. The nature of the trade cycle may occasion heated argument and lead some to take up intellectual arms against their spiritual fathers, but it has not the dividing power of a disputed theory of eternal salvation. Even an economist may call his economic brother a fool without feeling in danger of hell fire. But agreement to discuss and the toleration of differences in theory does not remove the fact that the material consequences of the application of the wrong theory may be more serious than before.

Economic experts at the Treaty of Versailles may not have felt in danger of hell fire, but their errors have played the devil with our affairs.   If the penalty for spiritual error was once supposed to be physically painful, intellectual error may now be materially devastating.   And the real problem of government lies in the fact that such disasters are felt by those who suffer to be due to men like themselves who can be held accountable.   It is not a question of offering propitiatory sacrifices to unknown gods, but of deposing and even punishing household gods of insufficient skill.   The time and the technique required by those who could really help may not correspond with the pace and action of those who can secure to them the power to act.   There is a widening gap between the arts of persuasion and the technique of research, between the power of leaders and their vision.   In Plato's language, reason, courage and the instincts were never more widely divorced.   The danger is that unless those who are really capable of dealing with the problems that arise can secure the co-operation they require others may rule who can secure co-operation by fear.   If philosophers cannot be kings, despots will come in.

---

[1] Cd. 9230, 1918.
[2] Aristotle :   *Politics*, Book IV, p. 15.
[3] Cmd. 2649, VIII, 1926 Report of Committee on Amalgamation of Services Common to the Navy, Army, and Air Force.
[4] 1926, VI, Qu. 297, Select Committee on Estimates.
[5] For details see W. I. Jennings :   *The Law Relating to Local Authorities*, Part III.
[6] Sir John Anderson before the *Royal Commission on the Civil Service*, 1929–31, Qu. 2591.
[7] Sir Warren Fisher before *Royal Commission on the Civil Service*, 1929–31 Qu. 18960.
[8] ibid., 18733.
[9] *Public Accounts Committee*, 1932, Sir R. Hopkins, Qu. 5377.
[10] *Economy Committee* (Chairman, Sir George May), July, 1931.
[11] Waldegrave :   article in *Journal of Public Administration*, July, 1935.
[12] Lord Eustace Percy :   *J.P.A.*, XI, p. 3.
[13] *Hansard*, 5th Series, Vol. 239, 1350, May 28th, 1930.
[14] Cmd. 3751, pr. 62.
[15] H. S. Morrison :   *Socialization and Transport*, pp. 139–41.
[16] ibid., p. 156.

[17] *Hansard*, 5th Series, Vol. 193, 1698.
[18] Cmd. 2599.
[19] ibid., pr. 5.
[20] ibid., pr. 8.
[21] ibid., pr. 16.
[22] Cmd. 4468, 1933 Report of Coal Mines Reorganization Commission.
[23] *Agricultural Register*, 1933–4, p. 2.
[24] Article in the *Economist*, March 25th, 1933.
[25] Lord Eustace Percy : *Democracy on Trial*, p. 30.
[26] *Haldane Report*, Cd. 9230.
[27] Colin Clark : *J.P.A.*, 1932, X, p. 261.
[28 and 29] ibid.
[30] Lloyd : *J.P.A.*, July 7th, 1935.
[31] Lord Eustace Percy : *Democracy in Transition*, p. 35.
[32] Lloyd : *J.P.A.*, July 7th, 1935.
[33] ibid.
[34] Lord Eustace Percy, op. cit., pp. 37–8.
[35] Colin Clark, J. P. A. Vol. X, 265–6.
[36 and 37] Lord Eustace Percy : op. cit : 45–6
[38] Cmd. 320, 1919, pp. 12–14, Report of Committee of Privy Council in Scientific and Industrial Research, 1918–19.
[39] Cmd. 2491, ibid. for 1924–5.
[40, 41 and 42] based on reports of *Department of Scientific and Industrial Research*.
[43, 45 and 46] Reports of the *Development Commission*.
[44] May : *Economy Committee*, 1931, pr. 280.
[47] Cmd. 1937, Scientific and Industrial Research, 1922–3.
[48] Cmd. 1937, 1922–3.
[49] Cmd. 4503, Report of C. of P. C. for Medical Research, 1932–3.
[50] Cmd. 4718, Report of Agricultural Research Committee for 1931–3.
[51] Morris R. Cohen : *Reason and Nature*, p. 85.
[52] ibid., p. 87.
[53] Julian Huxley : *Scientific Research and Social Needs*, Chapter XIII, for the general problems involved.
[54] ibid., p. 253.
[55] Cmd. 1938, XV, 1923, Recommendation of the National and Imperial Defence Committee.
[56] *Hansard*, Vol. 287, pr. 1325, March 21st, 1934.
[57] Trenchard : Letter to the *Times*, December 16th, 1935.
[58] May : *Economy Committee Report*, 1931, pr. 200–1.
[59] ibid.
[60] Cmd. 2029, X, 1924, pr. 25.
[61] ibid., pr. 28.
[62] Statement on Defence, March 3rd, 1936.
[63] Mr. Baldwin, February 22nd, 1936.
[64] Winston Churchill, House of Commons, July 20th, 1936.
[65] R. T. Nightingale : *The Personnel of the British Foreign Office and Diplomatic Service*, 1851–1929. Greaves : *Reactionary Britain*. Tilley and Gaselee : *The Foreign Office*.
[66] Cd. 9230, p. 64.
[67] Fawcett : *Speeches*, 1872, p. 242.
[68] James Dickinson : Letter to *Times*, March 18th, 1933, and cf. Article *Quarterly Review*, Vol. 262, p. 190.
[69] R. C. K. Ensor : *Courts and Judges*, p. 97.
[70] ibid., p. 97.
[71] Birkenhead : *Points of View*, Vol. I, p. 119.
[72] R. C. K. Ensor, op. cit., p. 100.
[73] Birkenhead : *Points of View*, Vol. I, pp. 112–3.
[74] ibid., p. 115.
[75] R. C. K. Ensor : *Courts and Judges*, p. 101.

CC

[76] R. C. K. Ensor : *Courts and Judges*, p. 1
[77] ibid., p. 102.
[78] ibid., pp. 3–6.
[79] ibid., pp. 98–9.
[80] Anderson before *Royal Commission on Civil Service*, 1929–31, Qu. 2451.
[81] Henry Taylor : *The Statesman* (1836), pp. 206–7.
[82] Sir William Beveridge : *The Public Service in War and Peace* (1920).
[83] C. K. Webster : *Lord Palmerston at Work*, 1831–41 : *Politica*, 1934.
[84] Christopher Addison : *Four and a Half Years*, Vol. 1, Chap. 1 ; a good account of departmental activity.
[85 and 86] Lloyd George, *Memoirs*.
[87] *Appendix VIII* to *Minutes of Evidence of Royal Commission on the Civil Service*, 1929–31, is a statement by the Association of First Division Civil Servants of their duties as they understand them.
[88] *Minutes of Evidence* to *Royal Commission on the Civil Service*, 1929–31, Qu. 22, 451.
[89] Appendix VIII, op. cit.
[90] Sir Warren Fisher in evidence to *Royal Commission, op. cit.*
[91] Morrison : *Socialization and Transport*, pp. 106–7.
[92] Gwyer evidence submitted to *Royal Commission on Civil Service, op. cit.*
[93] Lloyd George : *Memoirs*, pp. 1172–2.
[94] Addison : *Politics from Within.*
[95] Cd. 8409.
[96] Minutes of Evidence *Royal Commission on the Civil Service*, 1929–31, see Index under *Registry.*
[97] *Journal of Public Administration*, Vol. VIII.
[98] See *passim*, the *Whitehall Series*, edited by Sir James Marchant.
[99] Sir Edward Troup : *The Home Office*, pp. 255–6.
[100] 1871, VII, Select Committee on Diplomatic and Consular Services, Qu. 1146.
[101] 1888, XXVII, Qu. 10,994, Evidence to C. 5545, 2nd Report of Royal Commission on Civil Establishments.
[102] Dr. H. L. Hall : MSS. on *Colonial Office.*
[103] *Royal Commission on the Civil Service*, 1929–31, Appendix VIII, pr. 27.
[104] ibid., Qu. 9396.
[105] ibid., Qu. 2185, and cf. *Statement of Case by Civil Service Clerical Association to Royal Commission on Civil Service*, 1929–31.
[106] ibid., Qu. 16,698.
[107] ibid., Qu. 12,645.
[108] ibid., Qu. 2,736.
[109] ibid., Qu. 15,849.
[110] ibid., Qu. 16,036.
[111] *Committee on Pay, etc., of State Servants*, 1923.
[112] ibid., pr. 28.
[113] Cmd. 4060.
[114 and 115] D. M. Gordon : *Law Quarterly Review*, Vol. 49, 1933, pp. 106–8.

APPENDIX I

THE PARLIAMENT ACT

1 and 2 Geo. V, Cap. 13, 1911

An Act to make provision with respect to the powers of the House of Lords in relation to those of the House of Commons, and to limit the duration of Parliament (18th August, 1911).

Whereas it is expedient that provision should be made for regulating the relations between the two Houses of Parliament :

And whereas it is intended to substitute for the House of Lords as it at present exists a Second Chamber constituted on a popular instead of hereditary basis, but such substitution cannot be immediately brought into operation :

And whereas provision will require hereafter to be made by Parliament in a measure effecting such substitution for limiting and defining the powers of the new Second Chamber, but it is expedient to make such provision as in this Act appears for restricting the existing powers of the House of Lords :

Be it therefore enacted by the King's Most Excellent Majesty, by and with the advice and consent of the Lords Spiritual and Temporal, and, Commons, in this present Parliament assembled, and by the authority of the same, as follows :

1.—(1) If a Money Bill, having been passed by the House of Commons and sent up to the House of Lords at least one month before the end of the session, is not passed by the House of Lords without amendment within one month after it is so sent up to that House, the Bill shall, unless the House of Commons direct to the contrary, be presented to His Majesty and become an Act of Parliament on the Royal Assent being signified, notwithstanding that the House of Lords have not consented to the Bill.

(2) A Money Bill means a Public Bill which in the opinion of the Speaker of the House of Commons contains only provisions dealing with all or any of the following subjects, namely, the imposition, repeal, remission, alteration, or regulation of taxation ; the imposition for the payment of debt or other financial purposes of charges on the Consolidated Fund, or on money provided by Parliament, or the variation or repeal of any such charges ; supply ; the appropriation, receipt, custody, issue or audit of accounts of public money ; the raising or guarantee of any loan or the repayment thereof ; or subordinate matters incidental to those subjects or any of them. In this subsection the expressions " taxation," " public money," and " loan " respectively do not include any taxation, money, or loan raised by local authorities or bodies for local purposes.

(3) There shall be endorsed on every Money Bill when it is sent up to the House of Lords and when it is presented to His Majesty for assent the certificate of the Speaker of the House of Commons signed by him that it is a Money Bill. Before giving his certificate, the Speaker shall consult, if practicable, two members to be appointed from the Chairmen's Panel at the beginning of each Session by the Committee of Selection.

2.—(1) If any Public Bill (other than a Money Bill or a Bill containing any provision to extend the maximum duration of Parliament beyond five years) is passed by the House of Commons in three successive sessions (whether of the same Parliament or not), and, having been sent up to the

House of Lords at least one month before the end of the session, is rejected by the House of Lords in each of those sessions, that Bill shall, on its rejection for the third time by the House of Lords, unless the House of Commons direct to the contrary, be presented to His Majesty and become an Act of Parliament on the Royal Assent being signified thereto, notwithstanding that the House of Lords have not consented to the Bill : Provided that this provision shall not take effect unless two years have elapsed between the date of the second reading in the first of those sessions of the Bill in the House of Commons and the date on which it passes the House of Commons in the third of those sessions.

(2) When a Bill is presented to His Majesty for assent in pursuance of the provisions of this section, there shall be endorsed on the Bill the certificate of the Speaker of the House of Commons signed by him that the provisions of this section have been duly complied with.

(3) A Bill shall be deemed to be rejected by the House of Lords if it is not passed by the House of Lords either without amendment or with such amendments only as may be agreed to by both Houses.

(4) A Bill shall be deemed to be the same Bill as a former Bill sent up to the House of Lords in the preceding session if, when it is sent up to the House of Lords, it is identical with the former Bill or contains only such alterations as are certified by the Speaker of the House of Commons to be necessary owing to the time which has elapsed since the date of the former Bill, or to represent any amendments which have been made by the House of Lords in the former Bill in the preceding session, and any amendments which are certified by the Speaker to have been made by the House of Lords in the third session and agreed to by the House of Commons shall be inserted in the Bill as presented for Royal Assent in pursuance of this section :

Provided that the House of Commons may, if they think fit, on the passage of such a Bill through the House in the second or third session, suggest any further amendments without inserting the amendments in the Bill, and any such suggested amendments shall be considered by the House of Lords, and, if agreed to by that House, shall be treated as amendments made by the House of Lords and agreed to by the House of Commons ; but the exercise of this power by the House of Commons shall not affect the operation of this section in the event of the Bill being rejected by the House of Lords.

3. Any certificate of the Speaker of the House of Commons given under this Act shall be conclusive for all purposes, and shall not be questioned in any court of law.

4.—(1) In every Bill presented to His Majesty under the preceding provisions of this Act, the words of enactment shall be as follows, that is to say :—

" Be it enacted by the King's most Excellent Majesty, by and with the advice and consent of the Commons in this present Parliament assembled, in accordance with the provisions of the Parliament Act, 1911, and by authority of the same, as follows."

(2) Any alteration of a Bill necessary to give effect to this section shall not be deemed to be an amendment of the Bill.

5. In this Act the expression " Public Bill " does not include any Bill for confirming a Provisional Order.

6. Nothing in this Act shall diminish or qualify the existing rights and privileges of the House of Commons.

7. Five years shall be substituted for seven years as the time fixed for the maximum duration of Parliament under the Septennial Act, 1715.

8. This Act may be cited as the Parliament Act, 1911.

APPENDIX II

MINISTRIES AND PARTIES

1835–41. Second Melbourne.

1841–6. Second Peel.

1846–52. First Russell.

1852. First Derby.

1852–5. Aberdeen.

1855–8. First Palmerston.

1858–9. Second Derby.

1859–66. Second Palmerston.

1866–8. Third Derby and First Disraeli.

1868–74. First Gladstone.

1874–80. Second Disraeli.

1880–5. Second Gladstone.

1885–6. First Salisbury.

1886. Third Gladstone.

1886–92. Second Salisbury.

1892–5. Fourth Gladstone and Rosebery.

1895–1905. Third Salisbury and Balfour.

1905–15. Campbell-Bannerman and Asquith.

1915–6. Asquith Coalition.

1916–22. Lloyd George Coalition.

1922–4. Bonar Law and First Baldwin.

1924. First MacDonald.

1924–29. Second Baldwin.

1929–31. Second MacDonald.

1931. MacDonald-Baldwin Coalition or National.

APPENDIX III
THE ELECTORATE AND THE HOUSE OF COMMONS

ELECTORATE

1831 .. .. 435,391 }	..	.. increase 217,386	..	.. 49%
1833 .. .. 652,777 }				
1866 .. .. 1,056,659 }	..	.. increase 938,427	..	.. 88%
1869 .. .. 1,995,086 }				
1883 .. .. 2,618,453 }	..	.. increase 1,762,087	..	.. 67%
1885 .. .. 4,380,540 }				

1918 added 13,000,000 new voters making total of 21,000,000.
1928 added 5,000,000 new voters making total of 28,500,000.

HOUSE OF COMMONS

	Before 1832	1832	1867–8	1885	1918
England and Wales	513 ..	500 ..	495 ..	495 ..	528
Scotland	45 ..	53 ..	60 ..	72 ..	74
Ireland	100 ..	105 ..	103 ..	103 ..	105
Totals	658	658	658	670	707

After creation of Irish Free State, Northern Ireland 13 and Total, 615.

APPROXIMATE STRENGTH OF PARTIES IN THE HOUSE OF COMMONS
Elections.

Dec., 1832. Reformers 487, Tories 171.

Jan., 1835. ,, 365, ,, 293.

July, 1837. ,, 339, ,, 319.

July, 1841. ,, 289, ,, 369.

July, 1847. Liberals 337, Peelites 116, Protectionists 202.

1852. Liberals 323, Conservatives 331.

1857. ,, 373, ,, 281.

1859. ,, 347, ,, 307.

1865. ,, 360, ,, 298.

1868. ,, 382, ,, 278.

1874. ,, 249, ,, 352, Home Rulers 51.

1880. ,, 350, ,, 238, ,, 64.

1885. ,, 335, ,, 249, Nationalists 86.

1886. Conservatives 316, Liberal Unionists 78, Gladstone 191, Parnell 85.

1892. ,, 268 ,, 47, ,, 274, Irish 81.

1895. ,, 340, ,, 71, Rosebery 177, ,, 82.

1900. ,, 334, ,, 68, Liberals 186, Nationalist 82,

1906. Unionists 167, Liberals 377, Labour 43, Irish 83.

Jan., 1910. Unionists 273, Liberals 275, Labour 40, Nationalist 82.

Dec., 1910. ,, 272, ,, 272, ,, 42, ,, 84.

1918 Coupon election. Coalitionist 526, Labour 63, Independent Liberals 33, Irish 80, and Independents 5.

For other elections, see page 348 of text.

APPENDIX IV
GROWTH OF THE CIVIL SERVICE

1832. 21,305.

1841. 16,750, exclusive of many clerks, messengers, and many engaged also in trade.

1851. 39,147.

1861. 31,943.

1871. 53,874, including some workmen.

1881. 50,859. Telephone and telegraph not included.

1891. 79,241.

1901. 116,413. G.P.O. included.

1914. 280,000. Scotland and Ireland included.[1]

1929. 434,000, including 122,000 Industrial workers; 178,500 Manipulative staff employed mainly in the Post Office; 16,500 messengers and porters, etc.; *all other grades*, 117,000.[2]

The 117,000 all other grades included:

Administrative	1,140
(General) Executive	4,357
" Other " Executive	11,050
(General) Clerical	23,265
Departmental Clerical	16,577
Inspectorates	2,154
Professional, Scientific and Technical Staffs[2] ..	6,504

1932. 316,229, including 179,435 minor and manipulative; 16,693 messengers, porters and charwomen; all other grades, 120,101.

Another analysis is given by the May Committee.

	1914		1923		1930	
	No.	Cost £	No.	Cost £	No.	Cost £
Administrative ..	1,077	713,000	1,596	1,474,500	1,708	1,755,900
Prof., Sc., Tech. and Insp.	20,356	4,708,700	24,943	10,746,700	21,764	8,650,200
Executive and Clerical	33,329	4,416,000	78,504	17,770,100	82,900	25,100,500
Writing Assistants and Typists ..	3,034	198,300	11,198	1,443,600	14,046	1,917,600
Totals ..	57,706	10,036,000	116,241	31,434,900	120,418	37,433,200

In 1931 the average administrator cost £985 per annum; the average Professional £372.5; the average Executive and clerical officer £281.4; and the average writing assistant and typist £124.5.

In 1932 the estimated number of non-industrial whole-time civil servants receiving £3 and under was 135,000. (Hansard, Vol. 273, para. 204–5).

There were 2,184 in receipt of £1,000 or over. Only 48 were in receipt of £2,000 or over. (Hansard, Vol. 274, para. 655).

[1] From Dr. Finer: *The Theory and Practice of Modern Government*, pp. 1294–5.
[2] Treasury Memoranda for Royal Commission on Civil Service 1929–31, pp. 3–8.

APPENDIX V

TAXATION DIRECT AND INDIRECT

	Indirect Taxation	Direct Taxation	Per Head
1874–5	£42.5 millions, 67.2%	£20.7 millions, 32.8%	£1 18s. 11d.
1894–5	£46.8 millions, 54.6%	£38.9 millions, 45.4%	£2 4s. 1d.
1914–5	£75.8 millions, 39.9%	£114.2 millions, 60.1%	Not known
1919–20	£280.3 millions, 28%	£720.6 millions, 72%	£21 14s. 4d.[1]

In 1903 on £100 earned income nothing was payable in direct taxes and 5.6% in Indirect.

In 1903 on £500 earned income 3.5% was payable in direct taxes and 1.8% in Indirect.

In 1903 on £10,000 earned income 4.7% was payable in direct taxes and .3% in Indirect.

In 1913–4 on £100 earned, direct taxation was nil ; Indirect 5.4%.

In 1913–4 on £500 earned, direct taxation was 2.6% ; Indirect 1.8%.

In 1913–4 on £10,000 earned, direct taxation was 7.7% ; Indirect .3%.

In 1923–4 on £100 earned, direct taxation was nil ; Indirect 14.1%.

In 1923–4 on £500 earned, direct taxation was 3.2% ; Indirect 4.8%.

In 1923–4 on £10,000 earned, direct taxation was 35.9% ; Indirect 1.2%.[2]

[1] Adapted from B. Mallet and C. O. George, *British Budgets,* second series, Table XX.
[2] *Ibid.,* Table XXI.

SELECT BIBLIOGRAPHY

The purpose of the following selection is twofold. First: to indicate the sources from which the facts and ideas of the preceding essay have been derived. Only a small part of so wide a field can have been covered by research in original authorities. Second: An exhaustive bibliography might run to over fifty pages and even then mislead because it was comprehensive but uncritical, while a select bibliography may put the general reader and the student in the way of finding what he wants to know. I have therefore included two kinds of works: (1) standard authorities which will usually contain exhaustive and critical bibliographies in their own field; and (2) essays and books on special themes which have come my way and which may serve to supplement the former and to direct attention to underlying problems.

General Social Conditions Relevant to the Development of Government

The general history of the nineteenth century and the twentieth century to the war of 1914–18 is being gradually covered by a series of comprehensive studies. I have used Halévy: *History of the English People*, Vols. 1, 2, 3, from 1815 to 1841; Vol. 4, 1894–1905; Vol. 5, 1905–1915. J. H. Clapham: *An Economic History of Modern Britain;* Vols. 1 and 2 so far published cover 1848–1886. G. M. Young: *Early Victorian England;* 2 vols. 1934, provides a diversity of essays on many topics and includes a brilliant survey of the character of the period by G. M. Young. R. C. K. Ensor: *England, 1870–1914,* in the Oxford History of England, is the latest and best general book on the period.

Foreign Policy is covered by the *Cambridge History of British Foreign Policy*, Vol. 3, but there is a vast literature on the foreign policy of the pre-war world of which Fay: *Origins of the World War;* A. F. Pribram: *England and the European Powers;* and Gooch: *Before the War*, Vol. 1, may serve as an introduction.

The war period is dealt with in the many monographs published by the Carnegie Endowment, e.g.:—E. M. H. Lloyd: *Experiments in State Control;* Sir William Beveridge: *British Food Control;* Humbert Wolfe: *Labour Supply and Regulation;* T. H. M. Middleton: *Food Production in War;* Francis Hirst: *The Consequences of the War to Great Britain;* and many others.

The post-war world is covered in various ways by D. C. Somervell: *The Reign of George V;* J. A. Spender: *Great Britain, 1886–1935.* Economic conditions are best summarized in Bowley: *Economic Consequences of the War* (Home University Library); Sir W. T. Layton: *The Economic Situation of Great Britain;* Pigou: *Economic Position of Great Britain, 1927;* and Pigou and Colin Clarke: *The Economic Position of Great Britain, 1936* (the two latter both published by the London and Cambridge Economic Service). G. C. Allen: *British Industries* (1935); *Britain's Industrial Future*, the Liberal Industrial Report of 1928; the report and minutes of evidence of the *Macmillan Report on Finance and Industry*, Cmd. 3897, 1931; and J. H. Richardson: *British Economic Foreign Policy*, provide an introduction to contemporary economic history.

For the general reader of politics who requires the essential economic and social background : H. L. Beales : *The Industrial Revolution, 1750–1850* (W.E.A. Series) ; J. F. Rees : *A Survey of Industrial Development* (valuable because it links the pre- and the post-war world) ; Bowley's *England's Foreign Trade* (1922 edition) ; Layton's *Introduction to the Study of Prices ;* Loveday : *Britain and World Trade* would give the essentials.

POLITICAL AND SOCIAL THEORY RELEVANT TO THE DEVELOPMENT OF GOVERNMENT

Dicey's *Law and Opinion in England* is the best introduction to the interplay between thought and political action in this period, but Halévy : *Philosophical Radicalism ;* Leslie Stephen : *The English Utilitarians ;* Beers : *History of British Socialism ;* Brinton : *English Political Thought in the Nineteenth Century ;* J. Bonar : *Philosophy and Political Economy ;* and A. N. Whitehead : *Science and the Modern World* are all vital. In the post-war world the essential conflicts of theory will be found in H. J. Laski : *The State in Theory and Practice ;* L. Robbins : *The Nature and Significance of Economic Science ;* A. Salter : *Recovery ; Tariffs : The Case Examined* by Sir William Beveridge and others ; The Liberal Industrial Report on *Britain's Industrial Future in* 1928.

Special studies.—The student or general reader who wishes to come most swiftly to the underlying ideas should read :—Jacob Viner : *Adam Smith and Laissez-Faire* (Chapter 5 of *Adam Smith,* 1776–1926, University of Chicago Press, 1926) ; J. M. Keynes : *The End of Laissez-Faire ;* B. and S. Webb : *The Decay of Capitalist Civilization ;* Bagehot's *Economic Studies ;* W. S. Jevons : *The State in Relation to Labour ;* W. Y. Edgeworth's *Mathematical Psychics,* 1881 ; J. A. Hobson : *Imperialism.* He may then embark with some security on the contemporary flood of pro- and anti-communist literature.

THE NATURE OF THE CONSTITUTION

Three key books are Bagehot : *The English Constitution ;* Dicey : *The Law of the Constitution ;* W. I. Jennings : *The Law and the Constitution.* These are the best introductions to the constitution before 1867, the constitution before the Parliament Act, 1911, and the constitution at the present day respectively. W. I. Jennings has in the press a book on the *Cabinet* which will be authoritative. For reference on legal minutæ Halsbury's *Laws of England* (the Volumes on Constitution Law) and the many editions of Anson's *Law and Custom of the Constitution* are indispensable. A. L. Lowell : *The Government of England,* 2 vols., provides an excellent survey of the pre-war constitution.

Special studies.—*Cabinet Government to the Accession of Queen Victoria,* by W. I. Jennings, *Economica,* November, 1931, and February, 1932 ; H. J. Laski : *The British Cabinet : A Study of its Personnel,* 1801–1924 (Fabian Tract 223) ; *The Constitution Under Strain,* by W. I. Jennings, *Political Quarterly,* 1932, p. 194 ; Sidney Webb : *What Happened in* 1931 (Fabian Tract 237). R. L. Schulyer : *Parliament and the British Empire* (New York, 1929), Chapter 5, is the best introduction to the constitutional development of the Empire. A. B. Keith's collection of *Speeches and Documents on the British Dominions,* 1918–1931 (World's Classics) is essential for post-war conditions.

PARTIES AND POLITICS

The essential documents are scattered among innumerable biographies and autobiographies. No one of the political parties has yet inspired a good and comprehensive history of itself. A few of the more important biographies, autobiographies and letters are :—*The Letters of Queen Victoria,* edited by A. C. Benson, Viscount Esher and G. E. Buckle, in 9 vols. ; Sir Sidney Lee :

Edward VII ; C. S. Parker : *Sir Robert Peel from his private papers,* 3 vols., and *Life and Letters of Sir James Graham ;* Morley's *Lives* of Gladstone and Cobden ; the *Life* of Disraeli, by Moneypenny and Buckle ; Gwynn and Tuckwell : *Life of Sir C. W. Dilke ;* G. M. Trevelyan : *Life of John Bright ;* Bernard Holland : *Life of the Duke of Devonshire ;* Lady Victoria Hicks-Beach : *Life of Michael Hicks-Beach ;* Lady Gwendolen Cecil : *Life of Robert, Marquis of Salisbury* (in progress) ; The Marquis of Crewe : *Lord Rosebery ;* A. G. Gardiner : *Life of Sir William Harcourt ;* Lord Edmond Fitzmaurice : *Life of Lord Granville ;* J. A. Spender's *Life* of Campbell-Bannerman ; J. L. Garvin : *Life of Joseph Chamberlain* (in progress) ; The Earl of Ronaldshay : *Life of Lord Curzon ;* J. A. Spender and Cyril Asquith : *Life of Lord Oxford and Asquith ;* Lord Balfour's *Chapters of Autobiography* and Blanche E. C. Dugdale : *Arthur James Balfour, First Earl of Balfour ;* Sir Austen Chamberlain : *Down the Years* and *Politics from the Inside ;* D. Lloyd George : *War Memoirs ;* Lord Snowden's *Autobiography.*

For the early nineteenth century the *Greville Journal* and for the later the *Journals and Letters of Reginald Viscount Esher* have a special value.

Special studies.—J. R. M. Butler : *The Passing of the Great Reform Bill ;* H. W. C. Davis : *The Age of Grey and Peel* (1929) ; S. Maccoby : *English Radicalism ;* Charles Seymour : *Electoral Reform in England and Wales, 1832–1885 ;* C. S. Emden : *The People and the Constitution* (Oxford, 1933) ; W. E. Williams : *The Rise of Gladstone to the Leadership of the Liberal Party* (1934) ; Frank Hardie : *The Political Influence of Queen Victoria ;* Graham Wallas : *Human Nature in Politics* (1908) ; E. Wertheimer : *Portrait of the Labour Party ;* G. T. Garratt : *Mugwumps and the Labour Party* (1932).

PARLIAMENT

G. F. M. Campion : *Introduction to the Procedure of the House of Commons* (1929) provides a useful introduction to the standard and voluminous works of Anson : *Law and Custom of the Constitution ;* May : *Parliamentary Practice ;* and Redlich : *Procedure of the House of Commons* (3 vols., tr. by A. E. Steinthal, 1908).

For the House of Lords, Lees-Smith : *Second Chambers in Theory and Practice ;* J. A. R. Marriott : *Second Chambers ;* G. B. Roberts : *Functions of an English Second Chamber* (1926) ; two Fabian Pamphlets : 183, *The Reform of the House of Lords ;* and 213, *The Problem of a Second Chamber* should also be consulted.

Special studies.—J. A. Thomas : *The House of Commons, 1832–67 ; A Functional Analysis* in *Economica,* March, 1925 ; and a longer work by the same author on the same subject in MSS. at the University of London Library ; H. R. G. Greaves : *Personal Origins and Inter-relations of the Houses of Parliament* (since 1832), *Economica,* June, 1929 ; W. I. Jennings : *Parliamentary Reform,* 1934, the best critical survey of the present position of parliamentary procedure.

ADMINISTRATION

There is no good general history of the development of government departments since 1832 though there are excellent studies of some departments. A. R. Lowell : *The Government of England* provides a good general survey. The *Whitehall* series, edited by Sir James Marchant, is a series of studies of individual departments. Among them are Sir Thomas L. Heath : *The Treasury ;* Sir Edward Troup : *The Home Office ;* Sir Evelyn Murray : *The Post Office ;* Sir H. Llewellyn Smith : *The Board of Trade.* H. Finer : *Theory and Practice of Modern Government* contains a study of the nature and necessity of administrative machinery.

Special studies of departments.—A. J. V. Durell : *Parliamentary Grants* (Gieves, 1917) is the best authority on all aspects of Treasury control. It contains an exhaustive bibliography of the relevant parliamentary reports.

It should be supplemented by the *Minutes of Evidence to the Royal Commission on the Civil Service*, 1929–31, particularly the evidence of Sir Warren Fisher. The *Report on Machinery of Government*, Cmd. 9230, of 1918, is the key to many post-war developments. There is a collection of MSS. material in the library of the London School of Economics on which the report of this commission was based. The problem of a Ministry of Justice is discussed in R. C. K. Ensor : *Courts and Judges*.

The organization of the Civil Service.—The best introduction to the modern Civil Service is to be found in three government publications : *Report of the Royal Commission on the Civil Service*, 1929–31, Cmd. 3909, 1931 ; Introductory Memoranda relating to the Civil Service submitted by the Treasury, 1930 ; Appendix VIII to the *Minutes of Evidence of the Royal Commission on the Civil Service.*

Special studies.—Sir William Beveridge : *The Public Service in Peace and War ;* Prof. H. J. Laski's Introduction to Sir Henry Taylor's *The Statesman* (reprint by Heffer) ; Flynn : *Problems of the Civil Service*, 1928. Also *The Development of the Civil Service* (P. S. King, 1922) ; Leonard D. White : *Whitley Councils in the British Civil Service.* There are many important articles in the *Journal of Public Administration* on general and technical problems of Civil Service organization.

Delegated Legislation and Administrative Law.—On Delegated Legislation, Carr : *Delegated Legislation*, 1921 ; Willis : *Parliamentary Powers of English Government Departments* (Harvard) should be consulted. On Administrative Law, W. A. Robson : *Justice and Administrative Law* (1928) ; F. J. Port : *Administrative Law*, 1929 ; and the *Report on Ministers' Powers*, Cmd. 4060.

Local Government.—W. I. Jennings : *Principles of Local Government Law*, 1931 ; W. A. Robson : *The Development of Local Government ;* Maud : *Local Government* (Home University Library) ; H. Finer : *English Local Government ;* and the *Monumental History of Local Government*, by S. and B. Webb.

INDEX OF PERSONS

INDEX OF SUBJECTS

NATIONALIZATION, 327–8
Nationalism, 170–1
Nationalist Party, 191, 195
National Government, 370–2
National Health Insurance, 250, 337
National Physical Laboratory, 404
National Liberal Federation, 197
National Service, Ministry of, 291, 292
Nature, idea of natural harmony, 15–8
Naval Air Force, 300
Navy, two-power standard, 178
Navy Board, 96. See Admiralty
New Model, 197
New Zealand, 172, 175
Niger Company, 177
Nonconformity, 185, 226, 349

OFFICIALS. See Civil Service
Opposition, leader of, 193, 213 ; function of, 227 ; King and, 232 ; war and, 281 ; three parties and, 369 ; procedure and, 377
Ordnance, Board of, 94
Origin of Species, 168–70
Ottawa Agreement, 322
Oxford Movement, 322

PARLIAMENT, representation in, 1832–70, 19, 55–6 ; bribery parliament, 1841, 50. See House of Commons ; House of Lords ; Procedure
Parties, character of, 51–9, 353–4, 362, 377 ; in war, 305–6
Party funds, 198–9
Party government, 377
Party leader, 204, 225
Party Machinery, 49–51, 196–9, 234 ; registration and, 49
Patronage, Church and, 31
Political campaigns, 350–4

Politician and experts, 247
Politics as affected by economic and scientific changes, 182–3 ; post-war, 345–7 ; as profession, 351–2
Postmaster-General and Radio, 398
Preventative medicine, 163
Prerogative, influence on departments, 90 ; Edward VII and, 375–6 ; Peers and, 230–1 ; in war, 304
Press, 201, 217
Prices, 316–7
Prime Minister : In general, 80–1, 193, 198, 215 ; Crown and, 207, 222 ; Defence and, 412–6 ; formation of Cabinet and, 217–8, 283–4 ; Party loyalty and National duty, 362 ; power to require Cabinet Minister to resign, 209, 223–4 ; selection of, 365 ; war and, 284
Prime Minister's Private Secretariat, 364, 373
Prince of Wales, 219
Privilege, of Established Church, 30–1. See Aristocracy
Privy Council, Committee of, 90, 100, 105, 118, 250, 253 ; research and, 408–10
Procedure. See House of Commons
Propaganda, 193, 352–3
Proportional Representation, 367
Protection, 143, 158, 182, 320–2, 365, 368
Public Accounts Committee, 107
Public Concerns, 329
Public Houses, 195, 196. See ConservativeParty
Public Mind, 347–8

QUEEN VICTORIA. See Crown, Victoria
Question, 377–8

RADICALS ; Church and, 32, 49, 51, party in 1832, 54–5, 183, 185, 195, 209, 217
Radical Imperialism, 221
Radical Programme, 212
Railroad Commission, 255
Railways, problems of, 27–8 ; Railway Department of Board of Trade, 28
Rates and derating, 388–90. See Local Government
Rationalization, 327, 331
Redistribution, 190, 192. See Reform Bills
Reform Bills : 1832—93 ; 1867—166, 189–96, 194–9 ; 1884—191–6, 196–9, 215, 234–6, 273–4 ; 1918—347–8 ; effect of Reform Bills on local government, 126–9 ; on delegated legislation, 269–70
Registry, 431–2
Religion in English politics, 29–32
Representative Government, theory of, in nineteenth century, 11–3 ; influence of, 1832–70, 36 ; in war, 278–9 ; post-war, 347–8
Research, problems of, 400–11
Responsible Government, effect on administration, 90, 91 ; in Empire, 172–3 ; in war, 279–80
Revenue, 322–3
Roman Catholics, 29
Rothampstead, 405
Russia, 178, 180, 181, 236

SAFETY FIRST, 359, 360
Safeguarding, 320
School of Tropical Medicine, 155
Science and government, 142–3
Science and Art Department, 258. See Education